THE PRESUMPTION OF INNOCENCE

The presumption of innocence is universally recognised as a fundamental human right and a core principle in the administration of criminal justice. Nonetheless, statutes creating criminal offences regularly depart from the presumption of innocence by requiring defendants to prove specific matters in order to avoid conviction. Legislatures and courts seek to justify this departure by asserting that the reversal of the burden of proof is necessary to meet the community interest in prosecuting serious crime and maintaining workable criminal sanctions. This book investigates the supposed justifications for limitation of the presumption of innocence. It does so through a comprehensive analysis of the history, rationale and scope of the presumption of innocence. It is argued that the values underlying the presumption of innocence are of such fundamental importance to individual liberty that they cannot be sacrificed on the altar of community interest. In particular, it is argued that a test of 'proportionality', which seeks to weigh individual rights against the community interest, is inappropriate in the context of the presumption of innocence and that courts ought instead to focus on whether an impugned measure threatens the values which the presumption is designed to protect. The book undertakes a complete and systematic review of the United Kingdom and Strasbourg authority on the presumption of innocence. It also draws upon extensive references to comparative material, both judicial and academic, from the United States, Canada and South Africa.

Volume 8 in the Criminal Law Library series

Criminal Law Library

Volume 1: Self-Defence in Criminal Law
Boaz Sangero

Volume 2: Evidence of Bad Character
John Spencer

Volume 3: The Management and Enforcement of Community-Based Sentences: A Practitioner's Guide
Clare Fazal

Volume 4: Fair Trials: The European Criminal Procedural Tradition and the European Court of Human Rights
Sarah Summers

Volume 6: Homicide Law in Comparative Perspective
Edited by Jeremy Horder

Volume 7: Case Management in the Crown Court
HH Judge Roderick Denyer QC

Volume 8: The Presumption of Innocence: Evidential and Human Rights Perspectives
Andrew Stumer

The Presumption of Innocence

Evidential and Human Rights Perspectives

Andrew Stumer

•HART•
PUBLISHING

OXFORD AND PORTLAND, OREGON
2010

Published in the United Kingdom by Hart Publishing Ltd
16C Worcester Place, Oxford, OX1 2JW
Telephone: +44 (0)1865 517530
Fax: +44 (0)1865 510710
E-mail: mail@hartpub.co.uk
Website: http://www.hartpub.co.uk

Published in North America (US and Canada) by
Hart Publishing
c/o International Specialized Book Services
920 NE 58th Avenue, Suite 300
Portland, OR 97213-3786
USA
Tel: +1 503 287 3093 or toll-free: (1) 800 944 6190
Fax: +1 503 280 8832
E-mail: orders@isbs.com
Website: http://www.isbs.com

British Library Cataloguing in Publication Data
Data Available

ISBN: 978-1-84946-036-1

Typeset by Hope Services, Abingdon
Printed and bound in Great Britain by
Lightning Source UK Ltd

For Carly

FOREWORD

It is a particular pleasure to have been invited to contribute a foreword to this book, since its subject-matter was touched upon in Dr Stumer's very first BCL tutorial, on the burden and standard of proof, with me in Oxford. Since then I have enjoyed seeing its evolution and expansion through an MPhil dissertation, and a DPhil thesis into this full monograph.

Its subject matter lies at the intersection of legal theory and practice, public and private law, and substance and procedure. It is at the very heart of the discipline of law. Partly for this reason, it is no surprise that it should be under constant scrutiny and subject to innumerable suggestions for change in a myriad different ways. It is crucial for the whole topic of human rights, and helps to provide one of the essential components in the spine that provides both structure and control to the enterprise of law. As such it deserves serious analysis, rather than the sometimes glib justifications, and no less glib criticisms, of its elements, customarily provided elsewhere, especially in political circles, but regrettably sometimes in judicial pronouncements.

The hallmark and success of Dr Stumer's work is the careful and conscientious dissection and discussion of the sometimes high-flown rhetoric in which not only the fundamental provisions, but even their judicial applications, are so often cast. Everyone can pay lip-service to some conception of the presumption of innocence, perhaps expressed in numerical calculation of the number of guilty persons acquitted rather than that of innocent convicted. But what are the implications of the nature of the relevant crimes of the guilty or of the severity of the sentences passed upon the innocent?

This book examines from a strict legal perspective the way in which the relevant provisions of the European Convention, especially article 6(2), have been construed both by the European Court of Human Rights, and in the national courts of the member states, especially those of the United Kingdom. The aim of the analysis is to guide both the direction of further development within Europe, but every bit as importantly to examine and promote the use of that analysis in the interpretation and construction of similar provisions elsewhere, especially in other common law jurisdictions.

The main theme that emerges is strong affirmation of the use of the presumption so as to prevent the conviction of the innocent, and strict interpretation of any derogation on the basis of vague community values. The merit of this work is that it shows in clear detail just how this line can be held against inroads inspired by blurred and imprecise conventional slogans and sound-bites.

It is only by work of this character and quality that the institutions of human rights can be made to operate as effective and acceptable tools to direct legal decisions, rather than as affirmations of loose aspirations. This book sets the tone, and opens the door, for a fresh approach to this whole area.

Professor Colin Tapper
Magdalen College, Oxford
September 2009

TABLE OF CONTENTS

LIST OF ABBREVIATIONS

Abbreviation	**Full Title**
CLJ	*Cambridge Law Journal*
Crim LR	*Criminal Law Review*
Cross & Tapper	Colin Tapper *Cross and Tapper on Evidence* 11th edn (OUP, Oxford 2007)
Dennis	IH Dennis *The Law of Evidence* 3rd edn (Sweet & Maxwell, London 2007)
E & P	*International Journal of Evidence and Proof*
LQR	*Law Quarterly Review*
MLR	*Modern Law Review*
Munday	Roderick Munday *Evidence* 4th edn (OUP, Oxford 2007)
OJLS	*Oxford Journal of Legal Studies*
PL	*Public Law*
Roberts & Zuckerman	Paul Roberts & Adrian Zuckerman *Criminal Evidence* (OUP, Oxford 2004)

TABLE OF CASES

Australia

Canada

European Commission and Court of Human Rights

European Court of Justice

Alphabetical

Chronological

Germany

Ireland

New Zealand

South Africa

United Kingdom

United States of America

Zimbabwe

TABLE OF LEGISLATION

Australia

Austria

Belize

Canada

France

Germany

Granada

Hong Kong

India

New Zealand

Singapore

South Africa

Trinidad and Tobago

United Kingdom

United States of America

TABLE OF CONVENTIONS, TREATIES ETC

INTRODUCTION

The presumption of innocence is universally recognised as a core principle in the administration of criminal justice.[1] Any system that regarded a person as guilty merely by virtue of accusation would fall short of commonly accepted standards of fairness. The presumption of innocence tilts the scales of justice in favour of a defendant by requiring the prosecution to establish guilt to a high standard of certainty. As a result, convictions are made more difficult and there is an increased likelihood that the guilty will escape punishment. Every system of criminal law therefore faces a constant tension between protecting the rights of defendants and the community interest in convicting the guilty. On many occasions, this tension is resolved by measures that undermine the presumption of innocence. In all parts of the world, those who define the rules of criminal justice must have some means of deciding whether, and if so when, limitations on the presumption of innocence may be justified.

In the past decade, English lawyers have confronted these issues in a direct fashion, due to the introduction of the Human Rights Act 1998 (HRA). The HRA gives quasi-constitutional status to the Convention for the Protection of Human Rights and Fundamental Freedoms, commonly known as the European Convention on Human Rights (ECHR). Article 6(2) of the ECHR states: 'Everyone charged with a criminal offence shall be presumed innocent until proved guilty according to law.' While Article 6(2) is expressed in unqualified terms, the Strasbourg Court has declared that the right protected therein is subject to 'reasonable limits'.[2] On six occasions since 1999, the House of Lords has endorsed the notion that the presumption of innocence is subject to 'reasonable limits' and has applied a proportionality test to determine the scope of those limits.[3] This book considers

[1] See Universal Declaration on Human Rights (adopted 10 December 1948) Article 11(1); International Covenant on Civil and Political Rights (adopted 16 December 1966, entered into force 23 March 1976) Article 14(2); Convention for the Protection of Human Rights and Fundamental Freedoms (adopted 4 November 1950, entered into force 3 September 1953) Article 6(2); American Convention on Human Rights (adopted 22 November 1969, entered into force 18 July 1978) Article 8(2); African Charter on Human and Peoples' Rights (adopted 27 June 1981, entered into force 21 October 1986); Declaration of the Rights of Man and of the Citizen (France, August 1789) Article 9; Canadian Charter of Rights and Freedoms 1982, s 11(d); Constitution of the Republic of South Africa 1996, s 35(3)(h); Charter of Human Rights and Responsibilities Act 2006 (Vic), s 25(1); New Zealand Bill of Rights Act 1990, s 25(c). In the United States, the presumption of innocence has been held to be implicit in the "due process" guarantee of the Fifth and Fourteenth Amendments: see *Coffin v US*, 156 US 432, 453–461 (1895) (White J); *Estelle v Williams*, 425 US 501, 503 (1976) (Burger CJ, for the Court); *Taylor v Kentucky*, 436 US 478, 484 (1978) (Powell J, for the majority).

[2] *Salabiaku v France* (App No 10589/83) (1991) 13 EHRR 379 [28].

[3] *R v DPP; ex p Kebilene* [2000] 2 AC 326 (HL) 384 (Lord Hope); *R v Lambert* [2002] 2 AC 545 (HL) [34] (Lord Steyn), [87] (Lord Hope), [150] (Lord Clyde); *R v Benjafield* [2003] 1 AC 1099 (HL) 1153 [15] (Lord Steyn); *R v Johnstone* [2003] 1 WLR 1736 (HL) [48] (Lord Nicholls); *Sheldrake v DPP;*

whether, and if so to what extent, the presumption of innocence ought to be subject to restriction. It will be argued that limits on the right to be presumed innocent cannot ordinarily be justified. They should be permitted only in a narrow set of circumstances when the values underpinning the presumption of innocence are not truly threatened.

Academics have identified two facets to the presumption of innocence.[4] The first is a rule applicable at trial that the burden of proof is on the prosecution to prove the guilt of the defendant beyond reasonable doubt. This facet was described in *Woolmington v DPP* as the 'golden thread' of English criminal law.[5] It is the more familiar aspect of the presumption of innocence, at least to common law lawyers, and it is sometimes treated as exhaustive of its content.[6] The second facet is a more general principle that the treatment of the defendant throughout the criminal process should be consistent, as far as possible, with his or her innocence. Used in this broader sense, the presumption of innocence underpins the whole range of rules intended to ensure fairness to defendants.[7] Specifically, the Strasbourg Court has stated that it would be a breach of the presumption of innocence for a decision concerning the defendant to reflect his or her guilt prior to conviction.[8] Hence, the refusal of bail pending trial,[9] an order for confiscation of property without proof of an illegal source,[10] and even the publication of the name of the defendant prior to conviction[11] could be said to breach the presumption of innocence. In the same vein, the Strasbourg Court has stated that the right to

AG's Reference (No 4 of 2002) [2005] 1 AC 264 (HL) [12] (Lord Bingham); *R v Chargot Limited* [2009] 1 WLR 1 (HL) [27] (Lord Hope). See also *McIntosh v Lord Advocate* [2003] 1 AC 1078 (PC) [30] (Lord Bingham); *AG of Hong Kong v Lee Kwong-kut* [1993] AC 951 (PC) 969 (Lord Woolf).

4 P Healy 'Proof and Policy: No Golden Threads' [1987] Crim LR 355, 364; PJ Schwikkard 'The Presumption of Innocence: What is it?' (1998) 11 *South African Journal of Criminal Justice* 396, 403; S Summers 'Presumption of Innocence' (2001) 1 *The Juridical Review* 37, 57; L Laudan 'The Presumption of Innocence: Material or Probatory' (2005) 11 *Legal Theory* 333, 333–334; A Ashworth 'Four Threats to the Presumption of Innocence' (2006) 10 E & P 241, 243; M Redmayne 'Rethinking the Privilege Against Self-Incrimination' (2007) 27 *Oxford Journal of Legal Studies* 209, 218–219.

5 *Woolmington v DPP* [1935] AC 462 (HL) 481–482 (Viscount Sankey LC).

6 See N Bridge 'Presumptions and Burdens' (1949) 12 MLR 273, 282; G Williams *The Proof of Guilt: A Study of the English Criminal Trial* 3rd edn (Stevens, London 1963) 184; Cross & Tapper 144.

7 See WS Laufer 'The Rhetoric of Innocence' (1995) 70 *Washinton Law Review* 329, 333–334.

8 *Minelli v Switzerland* (App No 8660/79) (1983) 5 EHRR 554 [37].

9 *Caballero v UK* (App No 32819/96) (2000) 30 EHRR 643 [43]. *Cf Bell v Wolfish*, 441 US 520, 533 (1979) (Rehnquist J, for the majority): 'Without question, the presumption of innocence plays an important role in our criminal justice system . . . But it has no application to a determination of the rights of a pretrial detainee during confinement before his trial has even begun.'

10 Such orders have been held to fall outside the scope of Art 6(2) since they do not involve the determination of a 'criminal charge': *McIntosh v Lord Advocate* [2003] 1 AC 1078 (PC) [25] (Lord Bingham), [43] (Lord Hope); *R v Benjafield* [2003] 1 AC 1099 (HL) 1152 (Lord Steyn); *R v Briggs-Price* [2009] UKHL 19 [40] (Lord Phillips), [64] (Lord Rodger), [13] (Lord Mance), *cf* [94] (Lord Brown); *Phillips v UK* (App No 41087/98) ECHR 5 July 2001; *Van Offeren v The Netherlands* (App No 19581/04) ECHR 5 July 2005. However, the House of Lords has held that the presumption of innocence is implicit in Art 6(1), which applies to the sentencing stage of a criminal proceeding: *R v Briggs-Price* [2009] UKHL 19 [41] (Lord Phillips), [65] (Lord Rodger).

11 R Munday 'Name Suppression: An Adjunct to the Presumption of Innocence and to Mitigation of Sentence' [1991] *Criminal Law Review* 680 and 753.

silence and privilege against self-incrimination are closely associated with the presumption of innocence.[12]

This book is concerned exclusively with the burden and standard of proof and does not directly address the second, broader facet of the presumption of innocence. One reason for this is that the first facet of the presumption has a more clearly definable legal content: the burden of proof must be on the prosecution, and guilt must be proved beyond reasonable doubt. It has been suggested that the presumption of innocence should be understood exclusively in this more restricted sense, since otherwise it would become a 'vaporous euphemism for fairness'.[13] A second reason for focusing on the burden and standard of proof is that English cases so far decided under Article 6(2) have been primarily concerned with this aspect. In the English cases, Article 6(2) has been used to challenge the practice of imposing burdens of proof on defendants. A burden of proof on the defendant is referred to as a 'reverse burden' since it is a departure from the ordinary rule requiring the prosecution to prove guilt.

In understanding the conflict between reverse burdens and the presumption of innocence, there is much to be learned from other jurisdictions that have addressed the problem. Useful comparative material is found in the United States, Canada, South Africa and, to a lesser extent, New Zealand. The courts in these jurisdictions have grappled with questions very similar to those faced under Article 6(2). Both Strasbourg[14] and the House of Lords[15] have warned against the use of comparative law in interpreting and applying Article 6(2). This is because differences in the language and structure of national constitutions may affect the interpretation of the presumption of innocence in other jurisdictions. Nevertheless, the comparative law is useful in shedding light on concepts and problem that are faced by the English courts. Accordingly, the comparative law on the presumption of innocence is worked throughout each of the chapters in this book, wherever it assists in illuminating the discussion of a key concept.

Chapter one is foundational and introduces key concepts such as the burden and standard of proof. The central theme of this book is outlined in Chapter two. Chapter two argues that there is a dual rationale for the presumption of innocence: protecting the innocent from wrongful conviction and promoting the rule of law. The first of these rationales is of such importance that it cannot, in general, be subjugated to other interests. Only when this rationale is not called into play or is called into play in an attenuated sense should the courts consider approving limits on the presumption of innocence through the use of reverse burdens. The rationale of protecting the innocent may be attenuated either because there is a

[12] *Saunders v UK* (App No 19187/91) (1997) 23 EHRR 313 [68]; *Heaney and McGuinness v Ireland* (App No 34720/97) (2001) 33 EHRR 12 [40], [59]; *Weh v Austria* (App No 38544/97) (2005) 40 EHRR 37 [39]. The connection has also been noted in Canada and South Africa: *R v Noble* [1997] 1 SCR 874, 921 (Sopinka J); *Dubois v The Queen* [1985] 2 SCR 350, 357 (Lamer J); *S v Zuma* 1995 (2) SA 642 (CC) [27] (Kentridge AJ).

[13] Healy (see n 4 above) 365. See also Schwikkard (see n 4 above) 404; Summers (see n 4 above) 56.

[14] *Bates v UK* (App No 26280/95) EComHR 16 January 1996.

[15] *Sheldrake v DPP; AG's Reference (No 4 of 2002)* [2005] 1 AC 264 (HL) [33] (Lord Bingham).

low risk of wrongful conviction, or because the consequences of conviction are minimal. In cases where the rationale of protecting the innocent is attenuated, the courts can take account of the community interest in obtaining convictions by applying a proportionality analysis. In this analysis, the courts must give weight to the continually applicable rationale of promoting the rule of law.

The remaining chapters work through the consequences of this understanding of the presumption. Chapter three argues that the presumption of innocence is an entirely procedural protection and therefore does not have consequences for the substance of the criminal law. It also argues that the presumption of innocence requires, as a *prima facie* matter, that the prosecution bear the burden of proof with respect to every matter necessary for conviction. Chapter four analyses the decisions of the Strasbourg Court concerning Article 6(2). It will be shown that the Strasbourg Court has routinely permitted reversal of the burden of proof. Since this practice is inconsistent with the best understanding of the presumption of innocence, the English courts ought to depart from it. Chapter five discusses the proper approach to the proportionality inquiry when it is relevant to the presumption of innocence. It will be argued that the proportionality inquiry should focus upon the 'necessity' of a reverse burden, and not upon its 'reasonableness' or 'balance'. Chapter six ties together each of the points made in the earlier chapters by considering the relative weight to be given to each of the factors relevant to the allocation of the burden of proof.

The presumption of innocence is one of the most fundamental human rights. Underlying it is the principle that the state must not take coercive action against any individual unless it has been proved that the person is guilty of a criminal offence and is properly subject to punishment. The guarantee that the state will not interfere with its citizens except when it has demonstrated the justification for the interference is essential for any state with aspirations of conforming to the liberal ideal. This ideal requires that each individual be treated as an end, not as a means, and that the pursuit of life's goals be left to the best endeavours of the individual, without unnecessary intervention. The coercive powers of the state in the field of criminal law, in particular the power of imprisonment, have the potential to deprive individuals of the right pursue their own objectives and to fashion the path of their own lives.

The liberal ideal frequently comes up against the harsh realities of criminal justice, in which perfect procedures which result in no wrongful convictions are impossible. The pressure to ensure public safety leads governments into curtailing the rights of criminal defendants who, as a class, are viewed unsympathetically by many in the community. Yet, if the liberal ideal is to be put into practice, criminal procedure must continue to protect the rights of defendants and limit the abuse of the coercive powers of the state. In forging a way through the conflict between the aspiration to fulfill the liberal ideal and the needs of criminal justice, a proper understanding of the role of the presumption of innocence is essential. This book seeks to provide that understanding, in a manner that will guide both the legislature, in the passage of criminal legislation, and the courts, who are charged with protecting the presumption of innocence in the context of the Human Rights Act.

1

The Presumption Before the HRA

THE PURPOSE OF this chapter is to describe the role of the presumption of innocence in English law before the introduction of the HRA. This is necessary so that the potential impact of Article 6(2) on English criminal procedure can be fully understood. Part A of this chapter discusses the history of the rule that the prosecution must prove the guilt of the defendant. Part B introduces the concept of the burden of proof. It discusses two types of burdens, persuasive and evidential, that are placed on defendants under English law. Part C explains the meaning of proof beyond reasonable doubt, contrasting it with the standard of proof on the balance of probabilities. Part D discusses the introduction of Article 6(2) into English law. The general principles laid down in the HRA for implementation of Convention rights are considered. Further, Part D analyses and explains the use of section 3 of the HRA to 'read down' burdens of proof placed on a defendant by statute. The concepts discussed in this chapter are foundational and thc definitions adopted herein will be relied upon in each of the following chapters.

A. History of the Presumption of Innocence

The idea that the prosecution must prove its case is an ancient concept going back to Roman times.[1] The *Code of Justinian* stated: 'Let all accusers understand that they are not to prefer charges unless they can be proven by proper witnesses or by conclusive documents, or by circumstantial evidence which amounts to indubitable proof and is clearer than day.'[2] It can be seen from this statement both that the prosecutor was required to prove the charges and that evidence had to be 'conclusive' or 'indubitable'. An anecdote included in the *Res Gestae* by the Roman

[1] The idea may have originated even earlier with the Babylonians: see J Sassoon *Ancient Laws and Modern Problems: The Balance between Justice and a Legal System* (Third Millenium, London 2001) 42; AH Godbey 'The Place of the Code of Hammurabi' (1905) 15 *The Monist* 199, 210: 'It is a fundamental principle of the Code of Hammurabi that the presumption is always in favour of the innocence of the accused: the burden of proof is thrown upon the accuser.'

[2] *Code of Justinian*, Book IV, Title 19, Clause 25. Translation from *Coffin v US*, 156 US 432, 454 (1895) (White J). This judgment mistakenly cites Book IV, Title 20 as the source of the quote. The error has unfortunately been replicated in many other sources.

historian Ammianus Marcellinus (c 330–391 AD) illuminates the Roman attitude to the need for proof. In a trial before the Emperor Julian, the defendant limited his case to a bare denial of guilt, as the prosecutor had not presented sufficient proof against him. The prosecutor complained: 'Can anyone, most mighty Caesar, ever be found guilty, if it be enough to deny the charge?' To this, the Emperor Julian responded: 'Can anyone be proved innocent, if it be enough to have accused him?'[3] The danger of convicting the innocent was acknowledged in the *Digest of Justinian* which stated that it was 'preferable that the crime of a guilty man should go unpunished than an innocent man be condemned'.[4]

By contrast, early medieval law had little use for the definitive proof of guilt since the procedure of trial by ordeal left the final declaration of the defendant's guilt to the infallible decision of God.[5] However, with the abolition of trial by ordeal pursuant to an order of the Lateran Council in 1215, lawyers needed to develop principles and procedures to ensure the accuracy of fact-finding.[6] Canon lawyers looked to the Roman law as a valuable source for the principles of proof and concluded that guilt must be proved and not presumed.[7] For example, in around 1250, Henry de Bracton, who was heavily influenced by canon law, wrote in *Laws and Customs of England* that 'it is presumed that every man is good until the contrary is proved'.[8] In the continental systems, an accepted method for supplying proof of guilt was a confession obtained by torture, so that the presumption of innocence was probably recognised more in theory than in practice.[9] In England, juries were used to make the final decision concerning the guilt of the

[3] Ammianus Marcellinus, *Res Gestae*, Book XVIII, 1.4. Translation from JC Rolfe *Ammianus Marcellinus, vol 1* (Harvard University Press, Cambridge 1935) 405. While this incident may be apocryphal, its inclusion in the *Res Gestae* nevertheless reveals the importance that Roman law attributed to the need for proof.

[4] *Digest of Justinian*, Book 48, Title 19, Clause 5. See also Book 50, Title 17, Clauses 56, 155.2, 192.1. Translation from T Mommsen, P Krueger & A Watson (eds) *The Digest of Justinian, Vol IV* (University of Pennsylvania Press, Philadelphia 1985) 846, 960, 966, 968.

[5] JB Thayer, *A Preliminary Treatise on Evidence at the Common Law* (Sweet & Maxwell, London 1898) 34–39; JH Langbein *Torture and the Law of Proof: Europe and England in the Ancien Regime* (University of Chicago Press, Chicago 1977) 6–7.

[6] RM Fraher 'Conviction According to Conscience: The Medieval Jurists' Debate Concerning Judicial Discretion and the Law of Proof' (1989) 7 *Law and History Review (L & Hist Rev)* 23. See also WS Laufer 'The Rhetoric of Innocence' (1995) 70 *Washington Law Review* 329, 332.

[7] Kenneth Pennington records that the first person expressly to refer to a 'presumption of innocence' was a canon lawyer, Johannes Monachus, who died in 1313: K Pennington 'Innocent Until Proven Guilty: The Origins of Legal Maxim' (2003) 63 *Jurist* 106, 115. Pennington quotes a gloss by Monachus, *Rem non novam*, in which it is stated: 'item quilbet presumitur innocens nisi probetur nocens'. See also Johannes de Pogiali (c1398) and Frederick von Spee (1591–1635): ibid 118, 122.

[8] Henry de Bracton (d 1268) *De Legibus et Consuetudinibus Angliae* 193: 'de quolibet homine praesumitur quod sit bonus donec probetur in contrarium'. Translation from SE Thorne (ed) *Bracton on the Laws and Customs of England, Vol III* (Harvard University Press, Cambridge 1977) 91. This statement was not made in the context of criminal procedure, and it is not clear whether it had any impact in criminal trials: Thayer (see n 5 above) 553.

[9] RM Fraher 'The Theoretical Justification for the New Criminal Law of the High Middle Ages: "Rei Publicae Interest ne Crimina Remaneant Impunita"' (1984) *University of Illinois Law Review* 577. *Cf* Pennington (see n 7 above) 118 fn 31.

defendant.[10] It is doubtful whether the defendant was presumed innocent in early jury trials and it may even have been possible to obtain a conviction in the absence of any evidence other than the grand jury indictment.[11]

The Roman law ideas of proof, however, laid the foundation for the recognition in principle that a person should not be convicted in the absence of clear evidence. From as early as the fifteenth century, English legal writers echoed the *Digest of Justinian* by stating that it was better to acquit the guilty than to convict the innocent.[12] This principle became a maxim of English law, as immortalised by Blackstone who stated: '[I]t is better that ten guilty persons escape than that one innocent suffer.'[13] Blackstone's maxim acknowledged that the conviction of the innocent was a grave injustice and was a powerful expression of the need for certainty in the proof of guilt.[14]

By the middle of the eighteenth century, as legal representation became more common in criminal trials,[15] defence counsel began to use the notion of presumed innocence to articulate the need for proof of guilt.[16] For example, in *Murphy's Case* in 1753, counsel for the defendant stated: '[E]very man, my Lord, is by law

[10] Trial by wager of law and trial by combat continued after the abolition of trial by ordeal. These two forms of judgment relied upon divine approval for the winning side: see JH Baker *An Introduction to English Legal History* 4th edn (Butterworths, London 2002) ch 29. Trial by combat was not formally abolished in England until 1818, following its surprising re-emergence in *Ashford v Thornton* (1818) 1 B & Ald 405.

[11] JH Baker 'Criminal Courts and Procedure at Common Law 1550–1800' in JS Cockburn (ed) *Crime in England 1550–1800* (Methuen, London 1977) 15, 39. As late as 1794, a prosecutor suggested, without objection from defence counsel or the trial judge, that the defendant had the right to be presumed innocent 'except so far as that presumption is met by the single, simple fact that he has been indicted by a grand jury of his country': *Hardy's Case* (1794) 24 St Tr 199, 243 (Sir John Scott AG, for the prosecution).

[12] Sir John Fortescue (1385–1479) *De Laudibus Legum Anglie*, ch xxvii: 'I should, indeed, prefer twenty guilty men to escape death through mercy, than one innocent to be condemned unjustly.' Translation from SB Chrimes (ed) *De Laudibus Legum Anglie* (CUP, Cambridge 1942) 65. See also Sir Matthew Hale, 2 Hale P.C. 290: '[I]t is better five guilty persons should escape unpunished than one innocent person should die.'

[13] W Blackstone *Commentaries on the Laws of England: Book the Fourth* (Clarendon Press, Oxford 1769) 352. See also *Hobson's Case* (1823) 1 Lew CC 261, 261 (Holroyd J): 'It is a maxim of English law, that it is better that ten guilty men should escape than that one innocent man should suffer.' *Cf* S Romilly *Observations on the Criminal Law of England* (T Cadell and W Davies, London 1810) 72–76.

[14] For a detailed history of this maxim see A Volokh '*n* Guilty Men' (1997) 146 *University of Pennsylvania Law Review* 173.

[15] See JH Langbein 'Criminal Trial Before the Lawyers' (1978) 45 *University of Chicago Law Review* 263, 707–14; JH Langbein *The Origins of Adversary Criminal Trial* (OUP, Oxford 2003) chs 1–2; AN May *The Bar and the Old Bailey, 1750–1850* (University of North Carolina Press, Chapel Hill 2003) 233–35. See also *Coleman's Case* (1678) 7 St Tr 1, 14 (Scroggs CJ).

[16] References to the presumption of innocence can be found before this time, although often in unexpected contexts. In one case, it was held that an indictment for conspiracy to falsely charge a man with fathering an illegitimate child need not assert that the man was not the father. The reason for this was that 'every man is presumed innocent until the contrary appears': *R v Best* (1705) 6 Mod 185, 186–87 (Holt CJ). In another case, there was said to be a 'strong presumption of innocence' following an acquittal: *Castell Vid v Bambridge et Corbet* (1730) 2 Str 854, 855. Other early references to the presumption of innocence are collected in F Quintard-Morénas 'The Presumption of Innocence in the French and Anglo-American Legal Traditions' (2010) 58 *American Journal of Comparative Law* 107.

presumed to be innocent, till he is proved to be guilty.'[17] Judges were slower to adopt this principle, or even to acknowledge that the defendant should receive the benefit of any doubt concerning his or her guilt. Some juries were directed simply that 'if you are satisfied, you will find him guilty, if not you will find him not guilty.'[18] By contrast, in a trial at the Old Bailey for burglary in 1784, the trial judge directed the jury 'if it be a matter indifferent as to the whole of the charge whether the prisoner is guilty or innocent, the presumption is ever in favour of innocence.'[19] The direction that any doubt as to guilt should result in an acquittal was repeatedly delivered by judges during the Dublin Treason Trials of 1803.[20] In 1856, at the trial of William Palmer for poisoning, Lord Campbell directed the jury in the following terms:[21]

> [T]he law of England is different [from other countries], and, presuming every man to be innocent until his guilt is established, it allows his guilt to be established only by evidence directly connected with the charge brought against him . . . [T]here must be the strongest conviction in your minds that he was guilty of this offence; and if there be any reasonable doubt remaining in your mind, you will give him the benefit of that doubt . . .

As can be seen from this direction, the presumption of innocence was closely linked to the need for proof of guilt in a criminal trial.[22] The following decade, the

[17] *Murphy's Case* (1753) 19 St Tr 693, 702 (Mr Nares, for the defendant). See also *Despard's Case* (1803) 28 St Tr 345, 437, 458 (Sergeant Best, for the defendant); *Ryland's Case* (26 July 1783) *The Proceedings of the Old Bailey 1674–1834*, 624, 637 (Defendant's Speech) available at www.oldbaileyonline.org; *Dingler's Case* (14 September 1791) *The Proceedings of the Old Bailey 1674–1834*, 312, 482 (Mr Garrow, for the defendant) available at www.oldbaileyonline.org. In Scotland, see *Stewart's Case* (1752) 19 St Tr 1, 214 (Mr Brown, for the defendant).

[18] *Miller's Case* (1770) 20 St Tr 869, 895 (Lord Mansfield). See also *Heath's Case* (1744) 18 St Tr 1, 194 (Blennerhassett J); *Barbot's Case* (1753) 18 St Tr 1230, 1316–17 (President Burt); *Canning's Case* (1754) 19 St Tr 283, 670 (Recorder Moreton); *Blandy's Case* (1752) 18 St Tr 1117, 1187 (Baron Legge) *Cf Maha Rajah Nundocomar's Case* (1776) 20 St Tr 923, 1078 (Lord Impey CJ); *Hill's Case* (1777) 20 St Tr 1317, 1363 (Baron Hotham).

[19] *Norburg's Case* (14 January 1784) *The Proceedings of the Old Bailey 1674–1834*, 150, 170 (Jury Direction) available at www.oldbaileyonline.org. See also, in Scotland, *Gerrald's Case* (1794) 23 St Tr 803, 811 (Lord Eskgrove); *HM Advocate v McKinley* (1817) 33 St Tr 275, 518 (Lord Pitmilly), 538 (Clerk LJ), 506 (Lord Gillies, dissenting).

[20] *Shields' Case* (1803) 28 St Tr 620, 682 (Day J); *Kearney's Case* (1803) 28 St Tr 684, 774 (Finucance J); *Kirwan's Case* (1803) 28 St Tr 776, 849 (Baron Daly); *Begg's Case* (1803) 28 St Tr 850, 886 (Lord Norbury); *Clare's Case* (1803) 28 St Tr 888, 925 (Finucane J); *Rourke's Case* (1803) 28 St Tr 926, 991 (Baron George); *Killen and McCann's Case* (1803) 28 St Tr 996, 1040 (Baron Daly); *Donnelly's Case* (1803) 28 St Tr 1070, 1096–97 (Finucane J); *Emmet's Case* (1803) 28 St Tr 1098, 1171 (Lord Nurbury); *Howley's Case* (1803) 28 St Tr 1184, 1213 (Baron George); *Keenan's Case* (1803) 28 St Tr 1240, 1268 (Lord Norbury); *Redmond's Case* (1803) 28 St Tr 1272, 1310 (Baron George).

[21] A Bennett *The Queen v Palmer: Verbatim Report of the Trial of William Palmer at the Central Criminal Court, Old Bailey, London, May 14, and following days, 1856* (J Allen, London 1856) 307, 324.

[22] *Cf Coffin v US*, 156 US 432 (1895) where the US Supreme Court held that the presumption of innocence was not co-extensive with proof beyond reasonable doubt but rather a distinct piece of evidence in itself upon which the jury needed to be directed. Thayer convincingly criticised this conception of the presumption of innocence: Thayer (see n 5 above) 551–76. See more recently *Taylor v Kentucky*, 436 US 478, 484 (1978) (Powell J, for the majority): 'While the legal scholar may understand that the presumption of innocence and the prosecution's burden of proof are logically similar, the ordinary citizen may well draw significant additional guidance from an instruction on the presumption of innocence.'

direction that the jury should not convict unless satisfied 'beyond reasonable doubt' gained widespread approval following the decision in *R v White.*[23] Throughout the nineteenth century, the presumption of innocence was routinely affirmed both judicially[24] and in academic writing.[25]

Despite these references to the presumption of innocence, it did not follow that the burden of proof in English criminal trials was always upon the prosecution.[26] Blackstone recorded that in homicide cases, 'all . . . circumstances of justification, excuse, or alleviation, it is incumbent upon the prisoner to make out, to the satisfaction of the court and jury.'[27] On this formulation, once the prosecution had proved the facts constituting the crime, the defendant was lumbered with the burden of proving any exculpatory facts. In relation to statutory offences, this principle hardened into a rule of evidence placing the burden of proof on the defendant with respect to any 'exception, exemption, proviso, excuse or qualification'.[28] As a result, a defendant could be convicted even if the fact-finder entertained a reasonable doubt concerning his or her guilt.

The imposition of a burden of proof on the defendant was justified in the cases on the basis that evidence presented by the prosecution raised a 'presumption' against the defendant. For example, in *R v Turner*,[29] Bayley J stated that the presence of illegal game in the defendant's wagon 'raises a presumption . . . that it was there with his knowledge.'[30] Accordingly, evidence of possession was sufficient to

[23] *R v White* (1865) 4 F & F 383 (Martin B). See the extensive Reporter's Note of T Atkinson esq.

[24] Most frequently, the presumption of innocence, or sometimes a presumption of compliance with law, was relied upon in civil cases: *Williams v The East India Company* (1802) 3 East 192, 199 (Lord Ellenborough CJ); *R v Twyning* (1819) 2 B & Ald 386, 388 (Bayley J); *Sissons v Dixon* (1826) 5 B & C 758, 759 (Bayley J); *Wargent v Hollings* (1832) 4 Hag Ecc 245, 259 (Sir John Nicholl); *Spill v Maule* (1869) LR 4 Exch 232, 237 (Cockburn CJ); *Laughton v The Bishop of Sodor and Man* (1872) LR 4 PC 495, 509 (Sir Robert Collier); *N v N* (1852) 3 Sw & Tr 234, 238. *Cf R v Harborne* (1835) 2 Ad & E 540, 545 (Lord Denman CJ); *Lapsley v Grierson* (1848) 1 HLC 498. See also *Bird v Bird* (1753) 1 Lee 209, 212. In one late 18th century civil case, there was said to be a 'presumption of innocence' once some evidence of innocence had been led: *Anderson v Marshall* (1799) 7 Bro PC 612, 621.

[25] L MacNally, *The Rules of Evidence on Pleas of the Crown Illustrated from Printed and Manuscript Trials and Cases* (J Butterworth, London 1802) 19; T Starkie, *A Practical Treatise of the Law of Evidence and Digest of Proofs in Civil and Criminal Proceedings Vol III* (J & WT Clarke, London, 1824) 1248–50; W Best, *A Treatise on Presumptions of Law and Fact: With the Theory and Rules of Presumptive or Circumstantial Proof in Criminal Cases* (SSweet, London, 1844) 18, 29, 64; W Best, *A Treatise on the Principles of Evidence and Practice as to Proofs in Courts of Common Law: With Elementary Rules for Conducting the Examination and Cross-Examination of Witnesses* (S Sweet, London, 1849) 331, 334; S Greenleaf *A Treatise on the Law of Evidence* 3rd edn (Stevens & Norton, London 1846) 97–102; JP Taylor, *A Treatise on the Law of Evidence as Administered in England and Ireland with Illustrations from the American and Other Foreign Laws* (A Maxwell & Son, London 1848) 94–99; JF Stephen, *A Digest of the Law of Evidence* (MacMillan & Co, London 1876) 97 (Art 94); SL Phipson, *The Law of Evidence* (Stevens & Haynes, London 1892) 423.

[26] See BP Smith 'The Presumption of Guilt and the English Law of Theft, 1750–1850' (2005) 23 *L & Hist Rev* 133; N Landau 'Summary Conviction and the Development of the Penal Law' (2005) 23 *L & Hist Rev* 173; BP Smith 'Did the Presumption of Innocence Exist in Summary Proceedings?' (2005) 23 *L & Hist Rev* 191.

[27] Blackstone (see n 13 above) 201.

[28] The history and continuing effect of this rule are discussed in more detail below: see text accompanying nn 85–106.

[29] (1816) 5 M & S 206.

[30] Ibid 212.

warrant conviction unless the defendant presented 'evidence satisfactory to the justices' that he was unaware of the presence of the game.[31] Similarly, in *R v Burdett*,[32] the use of presumptions in the criminal law was approved and encouraged. All the judges rejected the submission of counsel that no presumption ought to be made in a criminal case.[33] Best J stated that there could be no presumptions without evidence, but that there was 'scarcely a criminal case, from the highest down to the lowest' in which the courts did not act upon presumptions.[34] Hence, as Best J explained, on a charge of treason, intent to kill the King could be presumed upon rebellion or excitement to rebellion. On a homicide charge, malice was to be presumed upon proof of the fact of killing. In burglary and highway robbery, a person found in possession of recently stolen goods was presumed guilty unless he could account for their possession.[35]

In *Burdett*, the King's Bench approved reliance upon presumptions in criminal cases by analogy with the practice in civil cases. Best J stated: 'It has been solemnly decided, that there is no difference between the rules of evidence in civil and criminal cases. If the rules of evidence prescribe the best course to get at truth, they must be and are the same in all cases, and in all civilized countries.'[36] Glanville Williams has observed that the tendency to reason from civil rules of evidence to criminal rules was a major source of confusion in the early cases.[37] In civil cases, the courts adopted a general rule that the proponent of any fact would bear the burden of proving that fact.[38] Applying this logic to criminal cases, the defendant would bear the burden of proving any fact he or she raised as a defence. As a result, if the defendant admitted the facts alleged by the prosecution but raised a defence, the burden of proof and the risk of non-persuasion fell almost entirely upon the defendant.

This harsh consequence of the analogy to civil cases was not corrected until the watershed decision of the House of Lords in *Woolmington v DPP*.[39] In that case, the defendant, Reginald Woolmington, was charged with the murder of his estranged wife, Violet. Woolmington testified that he had gone to his mother-in-law's house, where Violet was staying, to convince Violet to return home with him. He had concealed a sawn-off gun under his overcoat. He testified that when his wife refused to return he threatened to shoot himself, unbuttoned his overcoat and drew the gun across his waist. As he did this, the gun went off by accident and

[31] Ibid.

[32] (1820) 4 B & Ald 95.

[33] Ibid 140 (Holroyd J), 161–62 (Abbott CJ), 149 (Bayley J, dissenting). Counsel for the defendant had argued that the presumptions relied upon by the prosecution were 'contrary to the principle of English law, by which the presumption is always in favour of innocence, until guilt is proved': (1820) 3 B & Ald 717, 745.

[34] (1820) 4 B & Ald 95, 122 (Best J).

[35] Ibid.

[36] Ibid. The same reasoning appears in Phillipps (see n 25 above) 124.

[37] G Williams 'The Logic of "Exceptions"' (1988) 47 *Cambridge Law Journal* (*CLJ*)261, 271.

[38] *Amos v Hughes* (1835) 1 Mood & R 464 (Alderson B); *Soward v Leggatt* (1836) 7 C & P 613, 615 (Lord Abinger CB).

[39] [1935] AC 462 (HL).

Violet was shot through the heart. The trial judge, Swift J, directed the jury that there was a presumption of malice once it was shown that the victim had died through the act of the defendant. The presumption would stand unless the defendant could prove circumstances of alleviation, justification or excuse. Woolmington consequently carried the burden of proving that the killing was an accident. He was convicted of murder and appealed on the ground of a material misdirection.

Swift J's direction regarding the presumption of malice was drawn from a passage in the highly respected *Foster's Crown Law* (1762)[40] and supported by a long line of cases.[41] Nevertheless, the House of Lords held that the jury had been misdirected and quashed the conviction. Viscount Sankey made the following memorable remarks on behalf of the House:[42]

> Throughout the web of the English Criminal Law one golden thread is always to be seen, that it is the duty of the prosecution to prove the prisoner's guilt subject to what I have already said as to the defence of insanity and subject also to any statutory exception . . . No matter what the charge or where the trial, the principle that the prosecution must prove the guilt of the prisoner is part of the common law of England and no attempt to whittle it down can be entertained.

The decision of the House of Lords in *Woolmington* reflected the principle that, in criminal cases, the guilt of the defendant is always the ultimate fact in issue and the prosecution is the proponent of guilt. Hence, whether a fact is part of the prosecution case or an issue raised by the defendant, the prosecution should bear the burden of proving guilt. In a criminal trial, unlike in a civil trial, the court is not attempting to reach a fair settlement of a dispute between two parties. Rather, the court is determining whether the conviction of an individual, and the exercise of the state's coercive powers against him or her, is warranted.[43]

By his reference to the 'golden thread', Viscount Sankey implied he was merely implementing a long-established rule in English criminal law. However, as Lord Devlin held in *Jayasena v The Queen*,[44] 'by far the greater strength of previous authority supported the view which the House rejected.'[45] Consequently, Woolmington heralded a change in the law and opened the door for increasing recognition of the principle that the prosecution should bear the burden of proof. Over the next 30 years, the English courts set about applying this principle to the

[40] M Foster *Crown Law* (Clarendon Press, Oxford 1762) 255. See also Taylor (see n 25 above) 98; Greenleaf (see n 25 above) 97–98; Starkie (see n 25 above) 1250; Phillipps (see n 25 above) 124.

[41] *Mackalley's Case* (1611) 9 Co Rep 65b, 67b; *R v Legg* (1674) Kelyng 27; *R v Mawgridge* (1706) Kelyng 119; *R v Oneby* (1727) 2 Ld Raym 1485, 1493; *R v Greenacre* (1837) 8 C&P 35, 42 (Tindal CJ).

[42] [1935] AC 462 (HL) 481–82.

[43] GP Fletcher, 'Two Kinds of Legal Rules: A Comparative Study of Burden-of-Persuasion Practices in Criminal Cases' (1968) 77 *Yale Law Journal (YLJ)* 880, 888.

[44] *Jayasena v The Queen* [1970] AC 618 (PC).

[45] Ibid 625. See also R Cooke *Turning Points of the Common Law* (Sweet & Maxwell, London, 1997) 32–33; JC Smith 'The Presumption of Innocence' (1987) 38 *Northern Ireland Legal Quarterly* 223, 225. *Cf* A Stein 'From Blackstone to Woolmington: On the Development of a Legal Doctrine' (1993) 14 *Legal History* 14, 17.

whole range of criminal defences, including provocation,[46] self-defence,[47] duress[48] and automatism.[49] Hence, even if the 'golden thread' had not always been part of English law, it came to be recognised as central to criminal procedure following Woolmington.

The 'golden thread' rule has two mutually reinforcing aspects. First, the burden of proof is on the prosecution. Second, a high standard of proof is required, traditionally conveyed by the words 'beyond reasonable doubt' and more recently by the instruction that the jury must be 'sure' of guilt.[50] These two aspects have been described as the 'twin evidentiary pillars of the presumption of innocence in action'.[51] Both aspects must be present to ensure the full application of the presumption of innocence. The following two parts explore the burden of proof and the standard of proof in greater detail.

B. Burden of Proof

Evidence lawyers distinguish between two different types of burdens which may rest upon a party at trial: the persuasive (or legal) burden and the evidential burden. The persuasive burden is satisfied by convincing the fact finder of the truth of a proposition to the relevant standard. The evidential burden is satisfied by ensuring that there is sufficient evidence before the court to require the fact-finder to decide an issue.[52] Despite the presumption of innocence, English law imposes both persuasive burdens and evidential burdens on defendants. In brief, when a persuasive burden is imposed upon the defendant the issue is taken to be proved

[46] *Mancini v DPP* [1942] AC 1 (HL) 12–13 (Viscount Simon LC).

[47] *Chan Kau v R* [1955] AC 206 (PC) 211 (Lord Tucker); *R v Lobell* [1957] 1 QB 547 (CCA) 550–51 (Lord Goddard CJ). This overruled the dicta to the contrary in *R v Smith* (1837) 8 C & P 160, 162 (Bosanquet J).

[48] *R v Gill* [1963] 1 WLR 841 (CCA) 846 (Edmund-Davies J). See also *R v Bone* [1968] 1 WLR 983 (CA) 985 (Lord Parker CJ). *Gill* overruled the decision to the contrary in *R v Steane* [1947] KB 997 (CCA) 1005–06 (Lord Goddard CJ).

[49] *Bratty v AG for Northern Ireland* [1963] AC 386 (HL) 407 (Lord Kilmuir), 413–14 (Lord Denning), 416–17 (Lord Morris).

[50] Judicial Studies Board, *Specimen Directions* (2008) available at www.jsboard.co.uk/criminal_law/cbb, last visited 28 September 2009.

[51] Roberts & Zuckerman 348. See also *R v Lifchus* [1997] 3 SCR 320, 332 (Cory J): 'If the presumption of innocence is the golden thread of criminal justice then proof beyond a reasonable doubt is the silver and these two threads are forever intertwined in the fabric of criminal law.' *Lego v Twomey*, 404 US 477, 487 (1972) (White J): 'a high standard of proof is necessary . . . to ensure against unjust convictions by giving substance to the presumption of innocence.'

[52] The distinction between the two types of burdens was first articulated in 1890 in a groundbreaking article by James Thayer: JB Thayer 'The Burden of Proof' (1890) 4 *Harvard Law Review* 45. See also Thayer (see n 5 above) 355. By the late 1940s, a succession of academic articles brought greater prominence to the distinction in English law: J Stone, 'Burden of Proof and the Judicial Process: A Commentary on *Joseph Constantine Steamship, Ltd v Imperial Smelting Corporation, Ltd*' (1944) 60 *Law Quarterly Review* (*LQR*) 262; AT Denning 'Presumptions and Burdens' (1945) 61 *LQR* 379; GC Rankin 'Presumptions and Burdens' (1946) 62 *LQR* 135; N Bridge 'Presumptions and Burdens' (1949) 12 *Modern Law Review(MLR)* 273.

against the defendant unless he or she satisfies the fact-finding tribunal on the balance of probabilities to the contrary. By contrast, when a defendant is subject only to an evidential burden, the matter is taken to be proved against the defendant unless there is sufficient evidence before the court to raise an issue on that matter. If there is sufficient evidence, the prosecution bears the burden of proving the issue beyond reasonable doubt.[53] The remainder of this section expands on the meaning of the two types of burdens and shows how each may be imposed on a defendant.

1. Persuasive Burdens

The allocation of the persuasive burden determines which party is responsible for convincing the court of a fact in issue. There may be more than one fact in issue in a case, and the persuasive burden may be allocated differently with respect to each issue.[54] If the persuasive burden is not discharged, the party to whom the burden was allocated will fail on that issue. If the issue is determinative of the outcome in the case, the party who bears the persuasive burden with respect to that issue will fail in the case if unable to discharge the burden.[55] Consequently, the persuasive burden can be seen as a method of allocating the risk of failure to prove a certain matter.[56]

When the persuasive burden is allocated to the defendant, he or she bears the risk of non-persuasion and may be convicted even when the jury is not certain of guilt. Indeed, when the defendant bears the persuasive burden, he or she may be convicted when the jury is simply unable to decide, on the relevant issue, whether the defendant has discharged the burden.[57] Hence, when the defendant carries the persuasive burden, there is an enhanced risk that an innocent person may be convicted. The risk of convicting an innocent person helps to explain the general principle that the persuasive burden ought to be carried by the prosecution.[58] Even in *Woolmington*, however, Viscount Sankey stated that the general principle was subject to two exceptions: the burden of proof with respect to insanity, and any statutory exceptions.[59]

[53] This summary is derived from *R v S* [2003] 1 Cr App R 35 (CA) [6] (Rose LJ). Lord Woolf CJ has suggested that there might be 'practical benefits' to a variation of the evidential burden 'not only requiring the defendant to raise an issue but to raise a doubt': *R v Lambert, Ali and Jordan* [2002] QB 1112 (CA) [9]. It is hard to see a practical distinction between raising an issue and raising a doubt, since evidence sufficient to raise an issue must be capable of causing a jury to have a reasonable doubt about the matter in question. The point has not been taken up in any later cases.

[54] Cross & Tapper 130; Dennis 438.

[55] See *R v Schwartz* [1988] 2 SCR 443, 466–67 (Dickson CJ, dissenting).

[56] Roberts & Zuckerman 330. See also A Stein *Foundations of Evidence Law* (OUP, Oxford 2005) ch 6.

[57] *R v Lambert* [2002] 2 AC 545 (HL) [38] (Lord Steyn). In civil cases, the option of deciding the case purely on the failure to discharge the burden of proof, even when the fact-finder is simply uncertain, has been accepted by the House of Lords and the Australian High Court: *Rhesa Shipping Co SA v Edmunds* [1985] 1 WLR 948 (HL) 955–56 (Lord Brandon); *Briginshaw v Briginshaw* (1938) 60 CLR 336 (HCA) 349 (Latham CJ), 361 (Dixon J).

[58] As will be shown in Ch2, it is not the complete explanation. The promotion of the rule of law is a further reason for placing the burden of proof on the prosecution.

[59] [1935] AC 462 (HL) 481.

At common law, insanity is the only exception to the rule that the persuasive burden in a criminal trial rests on the prosecution.[60] However, the defendant bears the burden of proving certain pre-trial pleas in bar such as autrefois acquit or convict[61] and fitness to plead.[62] The allocation of the burden of proof with respect to these pre-trial matters is an exception to the general rule that the prosecution ought to bear the risk of non-persuasion in criminal cases. This exception has been supported on the ground that these matters do not relate to the guilt of the defendant, but rather to the jurisdiction of the court.[63] If an error is made in the determination of a jurisdictional issue, it does not result in a risk that an innocent person may be convicted.[64] However, pleas of autrefois convict or acquit or unfitness to plead do not relate only to the jurisdiction of the court, but also to the fairness of trying the defendant. There may be unfairness to the defendant if the court permits a conviction despite a previous acquittal, permits conviction for an offence in respect of which the defendant has already been punished, or allows the defendant to be tried when he or she is unfit. At the level of principle, there is no reason why the prosecution should not bear the burden of proving these matters since it is the prosecution that seeks to justify the imposition of criminal sanctions against the defendant.

While only limited exceptions to the 'golden thread' rule are recognised in the common law, it has always been open to Parliament to alter the allocation of the burden of proof by statute. English courts have recognised that reverse persuasive burdens may be imposed either by the express language of a statute or by necessary implication. The following sub-sections discuss the express and implied allocation by statute of the persuasive burden.

(a) Express Allocations by Statute

Statutory drafters do not use the terms 'persuasive burden' and 'evidential burden'.[65] Nevertheless, certain forms of words are interpreted by the courts as expressly imposing the persuasive burden on the defendant. A phrase such as 'it shall be a defence for the accused to prove'[66] is a typical example. The House of

[60] *M'Naghten's Case* (1843) 10 C & F 200, 210 (Lord Tindal CJ). This exception was expressly recognised and preserved in *Woolmington*: [1935] AC 462 (HL) 475–76, 481 (Viscount Sankey LC).

[61] *R v Coughlan and Young* (1976) 63 Cr App R 33 (CA).

[62] *R v Podola* [1960] 1 QB 325 (CA). Fitness to plead may also be raised during the trial: Criminal Procedure (Insanity and Unfitness to Plead) Act 1991, s 4. In *R v H* [2003] UKHL 1; [2003] 1 WLR 411, the House of Lords held the procedure laid down in this Act was not inconsistent with Art 6 of the ECHR.

[63] BD Underwood 'The Thumb on the Scales of Justice: Burdens of Persuasion in Criminal Cases' (1977) 86 *YLJ* 1299, 1342.

[64] See *R v Burdett* (1820) 4 B & Ald 95, 123 (Best J); *Thompson v The Queen* (1989) 169 CLR 1 (HCA) 141–42 (Brennan and Deane JJ); *Balcombe v The Queen* [1954] SCR 303, 305–06 (Fateux J). *Cf Graham v R* (1983) 11 Aust Crim R 21 (VCCA). These cases all related to territorial jurisdiction. In such cases, it is more true to say that there is no unfairness to the defendant in requiring him or her to disprove the jurisdiction of the court. Further, placing the risk of non-persuasion on the prosecution, even if the required standard was proof on the balance of probabilities, would raise the risk that no court could be shown to have jurisdiction, with the effect that a crime would go unpunished.

[65] Cross & Tapper 148.

[66] Misuse of Drugs Act 1971, s 28(2). See also Health and Safety at Work Act 1974, s 40; Insolvency Act 1986, s 352; Environmental Protection Act 1990, s 33(7); Criminal Justice Act 1988, s 139(4),

Lords has held that the 'ordinary meaning' of this phrase is to impose a persuasive burden on the defendant.[67] A variation on this formula is the phrase 'it is a defence for a person . . . to show'.[68] The Court of Appeal has held that this is 'classic language' for imposing a persuasive burden on the defendant and that 'show' was to be taken as synonymous with 'prove'.[69] By contrast, language such as 'in the absence of contrary evidence' is likely to impose an evidential burden.[70] Some recent statutes have been more explicit in indicating that the defendant must point to some evidence to raise an issue, but that the persuasive burden with respect to that issue will then rest on the prosecution.[71]

The express allocation of a persuasive burden to the defendant is often made in conjunction with a presumption. The use of the word 'presumption' can cause confusion since there are different types of presumptions and different ways of categorising them.[72] In one sense, a fact is 'presumed' whenever that fact need not be the subject of evidence. However, the central case of a presumption is when proof of one fact, the basic fact, is substituted for proof of another fact, the presumed fact.[73] For example, if proof of possession may be taken as evidence that the defendant had knowledge of the thing possessed there is a presumption of the requisite knowledge. To understand this further, a distinction must be drawn between discretionary and mandatory presumptions.[74]

(5); Terrorism Act 2000, s 57(2) and sch 13, para 4(2); Merchant Shipping Act 1995, ss 132–33; Trade Marks Act 1994, s 92(5); Water Resources Act 1991, s 48; Human Fertilisation and Embryology Act 1990, s 41(10) and (11); Road Traffic Act 1988, s 5(2); Medicines Act 1968, s 46; Gangmasters (Licensing) Act 2004, s 13(2).

67 *R v Lambert* [2002] 2 AC 545 (HL) [72] (Lord Hope), [132] (Lord Clyde), [17] (Lord Slynn), [41] (Lord Steyn), [182] (Lord Hutton). See also *R v Carr-Briant* [1943] KB 607 (CCA) 612 (Humphreys J). *Cf R v Ward* [1915] 3 KB 696 (CCA) 698 (interpreting Larceny Act 1861, s 58); *Talbot v Van Boris* [1911] 1 KB 854 (CA) 866 (interpreting Bills of Exchange Act 1882, s 30(2)). Both of these decisions held that the word 'prove' meant only that the defendant should introduce evidence upon which a jury could base a verdict.

68 Trade Marks Act 1994, s 92(5). See also Protection of Badgers Act 1992, s 7(1); Water Resources Act 1991, s 80(3); Private Security Industry Act 2001, s 5; Hunting Act 2004, s 4.

69 *R v S* [2003] 1 Cr App R 35 (CA) [20] (Rose LJ).

70 *R v Downey* [1992] 2 SCR 10, 39 (Cory J) interpreting those words in a Canadian statute. In South Africa, the Constitutional Court has held that if the basic fact is described as 'prima facie evidence' of the presumed fact, the defendant bears only an evidential burden: *Scagell v AG of the Western Cape* 1997 (2) SA 368 (CC) [11]–[12] (O'Regan J).

71 Terrorism Act 2000, s118(2); Regulation of Investigatory Powers Act 2000, s 53(3); Sexual Offences Act 2003, s 75(1).

72 The categorisation of presumptions was a preoccupation in early textbooks on the law of evidence: see eg WA Best *A Treatise on Presumptions of Law and Fact: With the Theory and Rules of Presumptive or Circumstantial Proof in Criminal Cases* (S Sweet, London 1844). See also EM Morgan 'Presumptions' (1937) 12 *Washington Law Review* 255; E Ullmann-Margalit 'On Presumption' (1983) 80 *Journal of Philosophy* 143.

73 Cross & Tapper 146. On this definition, the presumption of innocence is not a 'true' presumption. Rather it is a rhetorical device for expressing the rule that the prosecution must prove guilt beyond reasonable doubt.

74 Discretionary presumptions are sometimes referred to as 'presumptions of fact' while mandatory presumptions are referred to as 'presumptions of law': PJ Schwikkard & SE Van der Merwe *Principles of Evidence* 2nd edn (Juta Law, Cape Town 2002) 469–71.

Discretionary presumptions operate to assist the fact-finder in drawing inferences between facts. The fact-finder is invited to infer the existence of the presumed fact from proof of the basic fact. However, the fact-finder is not compelled to draw that inference. All the relevant evidence is to be taken into account in deciding whether the presumed fact is true. In a jury trial, the judge may instruct the jury that it is possible to infer one fact from another. For example, in a trial for handling stolen goods, the judge may direct the jury that, once it is proved that the defendant was in possession of recently stolen goods, they may, but not must, in the absence of any reasonable explanation, find that the defendant had knowledge the goods were recently stolen.[75] Presumptions in this category are a method of organising the fact-finding process and lending some formal endorsement to conclusions that ought to follow from logic or common sense. If the purported link between the basic and presumed fact is irrational, a discretionary presumption could result in unfairness to the defendant. A jury direction that incorporated an irrational presumption might therefore deprive the defendant of a fair trial.[76] However, discretionary presumptions do not alter the burden of proof and consequently are not at odds with the presumption of innocence.[77]

By contrast, in the case of mandatory presumptions, the fact-finder has no discretion in drawing the link between the basic and presumed fact. The classic formula for a mandatory presumption is a phrase such as 'upon proof of x, it shall be presumed that y unless the contrary of y is proved'. In this formula, x is the basic fact and y is the presumed fact. The presumption is mandatory since the fact-finder is obliged to find the existence of the presumed fact following proof of the basic fact. Under this formula, the presumption is rebuttable since the defendant has the opportunity to disprove the presumed fact. Mandatory rebuttable presumptions are a common method of statutory drafting used to impose persuasive burdens on defendants.[78] As such, they are a prime example of interference with the right to be presumed innocent.

[75] *R v Abramovitch* (1916) 11 Cr App R 45 (CCA) 49. See also *R v Falconer* (1990) 171 CLR 30 (HCA) 61, 83 (presumption that an act by an apparently conscious person was done voluntarily); *Pickup v Thames and Mersey Marine Insurance Co* (1878) 3 QBD 594 (CA) (presumption of unseaworthiness for a vessel that founders shortly after leaving port). Contrast the so-called 'presumption of intention' discussed in *Vallance v R* (1961) 108 CLR 56 (HCA) 82: 'What a man does is often the best evidence of the purpose he had in mind. The probability that harm will result from a man's acts may be so great, and so apparent, that it compels an inference that he actually intended to do that harm. Nevertheless, intention is a state of mind. The circumstances and probable consequences of a man's act are no more than evidence of his intention. For this reason this court has often said that it is misleading to speak of a man being presumed always to intend the natural and probable consequences of his acts.'

[76] *Cf* RJ Allen 'Structuring Jury Decision-Making in Criminal Cases: A Unified Constitutional Approach to Evidentiary Devices' (1980) 94 *Harvard Law Review* 321, 331–32. In the US, a discretionary presumption will be in contravention of 'due process' if there is no rational connection between the basic fact and the presumed fact: *Leary v US*, 395 US 623 (1969); *County Court of Ulster County v Allen*, 442 US 140 (1979).

[77] *R v DPP; ex p Kebilene* [2000] 2 AC 326 (HL) 384 (Lord Hope). See also *R v Kowlyk* [1988] 2 SCR 59, 74–75 (McLachlin J, for the majority). *Cf* B Emmerson, A Ashworth & A Macdonald *Human Rights and Criminal Justice* 2nd edn (Sweet & Maxwell, London 2007) 346 fn 8.

[78] See eg Prevention of Corruption Act 1916, s 2; Road Traffic Offenders Act 1988, s 15(2); Terrorism Act 2000, s 57(3); Trade Marks Act 1994, s 95(2).

Finally, some mandatory presumptions are irrebuttable. Upon proof of the basic fact, there is no opportunity to prove the contrary of the presumed fact.[79] Presumptions in this category may best be regarded as constituting rules of substantive law. They are not a procedural device for allocating the burden of proof but rather a means of clarifying the effect of the law.[80] A good example of this is seen in the South African decision of *Scagell v AG of the Western Cape*.[81] In that case, the Constitutional Court considered the compatibility of section 6 of the Gambling Act 1965 with the presumption of innocence protected by section 25(3)(c) of the Interim Constitution. Section 6(1) of the Act made it an offence to permit the playing of a gambling game on premises under the control of the defendant. Section 6(6) stated that bankers, dealers, croupiers, porters, doorkeepers or servants at a place where gambling was taking place would be 'deemed' to be in control of that place. The Constitutional Court found that section 6(6) operated to define the persons who were 'in control' of premises for the purposes of the offence; it did not impose a reverse burden on the defendant. In this way, the irrebuttable presumption in section 6(6) was a 'rule of substantive law', not a 'rule of evidence'.[82] Bankers, dealers, croupiers etc, at a gambling house fell within the substantive prohibition created by the Act and were guilty of the offence, provided the prosecution proved all the other necessary elements.

Irrebuttable presumptions often result in mixed messages regarding the scope of a criminal prohibition.[83] For example, while the offence considered in *Scagell* was described as an offence of being 'in control' of a place where gambling took place, the scope of the prohibition in fact extended beyond people who were 'in control'. Doorkeepers and others were guilty of the offence regardless of whether they had control over the premises. By mislabeling the offence with which the defendant is charged, irrebuttable presumptions pose a special threat to the clarity of criminal law. In this sense, irrebuttable presumptions are not fully equivalent to other methods for creating rules of substantive law.[84] However, in their effect on the scope of a criminal prohibition, as opposed to their effect in communicating to the public and officials, irrebuttable presumptions are identical to substantive rules of law. Consequently, they ought to be treated as rules of substantive law when considering compatibility with the presumption of innocence. There is controversy over whether rules of substantive law may breach the presumption of innocence. This question is fully addressed in Chapter Three.

[79] See eg Sexual Offences Act 2003, s 76(2)(a), interpreted in *R v Jheeta* [2007] EWCA Crim 1699. See also Road Traffic Offenders Act 1988, s 15(2) interpreted in *Parker v DPP* (2000) 165 JP 213.

[80] Roberts & Zuckerman, 341; Morgan (see n 72 above) 255–56.

[81] *Scagell v AG of the Western Cape* 1997 (2) SA 368 (CC).

[82] Ibid [30] (O'Regan J).

[83] SP Green 'Six Senses of Strict Liability: A Plea for Formalism' in AP Simester (ed) *Appraising Strict Liability* (OUP, Oxford 2005) 1, 14–16.

[84] *Cf* P Roberts, 'Strict Liability and the Presumption of Innocence: An Exposé of Functionalist Assumptions' in AP Simester (ed) *Appraising Strict Liability* (OUP, Oxford 2005) 151, 175–85.

(b) Implied allocation by statute

In English law, reverse burdens may be implied into statutes in accordance with a rule of statutory interpretation that the defendant bears the persuasive burden of proving any 'exception, exemption, proviso, excuse or qualification'. This rule is currently enacted, for the purpose of summary trials, in section 101 of the Magistrates' Courts Act 1980.[85] In *R v Edwards*,[86] the Court of Appeal held that the rule expressed in section 101 reflected a principle of the common law, so that it also applied in trials on indictment. The applicability of this principle to trials on indictment was affirmed by the House of Lords in *R v Hunt*.[87]

As the Court of Appeal stated in *Edwards*, the rule relating to proof of exceptions was 'hammered out on the anvil of pleading'.[88] In its earliest form it was a command that an exception incorporated in the body of a clause ought to be pleaded by the person who pleaded the clause, whereas an exception in a subsequent clause was to be pleaded by the person who relied upon it.[89] As the rule was originally a matter of pleading, it did not necessarily determine who bore the burden of proof.[90] In *R v Stone*,[91] the King's Bench split on the question of whether the prosecutor needed to prove the absence of a qualification as well as pleading the absence.[92] However, in *R v Turner*,[93] it was accepted that the defendant bore the burden of proof with respect to exceptions, even when the prosecutor had to plead the negative of the exception. The decision in *Turner* hinged upon practical considerations such as ease of proof and not upon the technical pleading distinction.[94] Throughout the nineteenth century, it became established both in case law[95] and by statute[96] that the defendant would bear the burden of proving any exceptions.

[85] Previously Magistrates' Courts Act 1952, s 81, Summary Jurisdiction Act 1879, s 39(2) and Summary Jurisdiction Act 1848, s 14. The rule was enacted for the purpose of some specific offences by Game Act 1831, s 42 and Petty Sessions Act 1851, s 20(1).

[86] [1975] QB 27 (CA).

[87] [1987] AC 352 (HL).

[88] [1975] QB 27 (CA) 40 (Lawton LJ).

[89] *Jones v Axen* (1696) 1 Ld Raym 119, 120 (Treby CJ); *R v Ford* (1723) 1 Stra 555; *R v Jarvis* (1756) 1 East 463n, 646n (Lord Mansfield); *Spieres v Parker* (1786) 1 TR 141, 144 (Lord Mansfield CJ); *R v Hall* (1786) 1 TR 320, 322; *R v Pratten* (1796) 6 TR 559, 559–60; *Gill v Scrivens* (1796) 7 TR 27, 31 (Lawrence J).

[90] See *Spieres v Parker* (1786) 1 TR 141, 144 (Lord Mansfield CJ); *Jelfs v Ballard* (1799) 1 B&P 467, 468 (Buller J). See also the illuminating discussion of this point in A Zuckerman 'The Third Exception to the Woolmington Rule' (1976) 92 *LQR* 402, 405.

[91] (1801) 1 East 639.

[92] Lord Kenyon CJ and Grose J held the prosecution bore the burden of proof with respect to qualifications: ibid 650–51 (Lord Kenyon CJ), 651–52 (Grose J). Lawrence J and Le Blanc J held the defendant bore the burden: ibid 253–54 (Lawrence J), 254 (Le Blanc J).

[93] (1816) 5 M & S 206.

[94] Ibid 209–10 (Lord Ellenborough CJ), 211–12 (Bayley J).

[95] *The Apothecaries' Company v Bentley* (1824) 1 C & P 538, 540 (Abbott CJ); *Taylor v Humphries* (1864) 17 CB NS 539 (Erle CJ); *Davis v Scrace* (1869) LR 4 CP 172.

[96] Summary Jurisdiction Act 1848, s 14. A re-enactment in the Summary Jurisdiction Act 1879, s 39(2) confirmed that the defendant bore the burden of proving exceptions, whether the exception appeared in the clause that created the offence, or in a subsequent clause.

For some time, it was arguable that the burden imposed under this principle was an evidential burden, not a persuasive burden.[97] On this argument, the principle was intended only to relieve the prosecution of the need to negate numerous exceptions when there was no evidence in support of them. An evidential burden on the defendant with respect to each exception would have been sufficient to narrow the issues. However, the Court of Appeal in *Edwards*[98] and subsequently the House of Lords in *Hunt*[99] rejected the idea that the burden on the defendant was merely evidential. Rather, if the relevant statute could properly be construed as imposing a burden, the burden would be persuasive.

In *Edwards*, the Court of Appeal held that the rule imposing the persuasive burden was limited to offences arising under enactments which prohibited an act save in specified circumstances, or by persons of specified classes, or with special qualifications, or with the licence or permission of specified authorities.[100] The Court of Appeal stated: 'If the true construction is that the enactment prohibits the doing of acts, subject to provisos, exemptions and the like, then the prosecution can rely upon the exception.'[101] The Court of Appeal thus made the application of the rule dependent in the first instance upon the construction of the statute. In *Hunt*, the House of Lords also held that the allocation of the burden was a matter of statutory construction.[102] However, when the construction of the statute was unclear, as it often would be, the House of Lords considered it appropriate to look to other considerations. According to Lord Griffiths, these 'practical considerations' included the mischief at which the Act was aimed and, in particular, 'the ease or difficulty that the respective parties would encounter in discharging the burden'.[103]

In *Lambert*,[104] Lord Steyn appeared to suggest that reverse burdens within the 'narrow exception' recognised in *Edwards* and *Hunt* would not interfere with the right protected by Article 6(2).[105] A subsequent decision of the Court of Appeal, interpreting Lord Steyn's comments, held that implied persuasive burdens were capable of interfering with Article 6(2).[106] Whether a persuasive burden is imposed by necessary implication or by express words, the interference with the presumption of innocence is the same. The risk of failure to prove a matter is allocated to the defendant and he or she may be convicted despite the absence of proof beyond

[97] R Cross *Evidence* (Butterworth & Co, London 1958) 81; M Dean 'Negative Averments and the Burden of Proof' [1966] *Crim LR* 594; Fletcher (see n 43 above) 908.

[98] [1975] QB 27 (CA) 40 (Lawton LJ, for the Court).

[99] [1987] AC 352 (HL) 385 (Lord Ackner).

[100] [1975] QB 27 (CA) 40 (Lawton LJ, for the Court).

[101] Ibid.

[102] [1987] AC 352 (HL) 374 (Lord Griffiths), 380 (Lord Ackner).

[103] Ibid 374. The principles relating to implied allocation of reverse burdens were more recently discussed in *Hogan v DPP* [2007] EWHC 978 (Admin) in the context of s 329(1) and (2) of the Proceeds of Crime Act 2002.

[104] *Lambert* [2002] 2 AC 545 (HL).

[105] Ibid [35].

[106] *R (Grundy & Co Excavations Ltd) v Halton Division Magistrates Court* (2003) 167 JP 387 (QBD) [60]–[61] (Clarke LJ). See also *Hogan v DPP* [2007] EWHC 978 (Admin) [32] (Irwin J).

reasonable doubt. Consequently, an implied reverse burden may be examined for compatibility with Article 6(2) in the same way as an express reverse burden.

2. Evidential Burdens

The mechanism of an evidential burden is a convenient and efficient method of narrowing the matters in issue in a criminal trial. The party carrying the evidential burden with respect to any issue is required to ensure that sufficient evidence is before the court to raise that issue. If the evidential burden is not discharged, the fact finder need not consider that issue. A jury, for example, need concern itself with a question of fact only if the judge has determined that it is 'a live issue fit and proper to be left to the jury'.[107] This has the effect of focusing the attention of the fact-finder on the matters that are shown to be relevant on the evidence. Since it is the judge who decides whether the evidential burden has been satisfied, the burden has been described as the duty of 'passing the judge'.[108]

In *Jayasena v The Queen*,[109] Lord Devlin noted that it is misleading to describe an evidential burden as a burden of proof since it can be discharged by evidence that falls short of proof.[110] The party carrying the evidential burden is not required to convince the fact-finder of the truth of any proposition. The evidential burden may be described as involving 'proof' only in the limited sense that the introduction of facts in a trial could be described as offering 'proof' of those facts.[111] Accordingly, the evidential burden is sometimes described as a 'burden of adducing evidence'.[112] Even this phrase is not quite accurate since the defendant need not testify or even tender evidence to satisfy the evidential burden. Evidence sufficient to satisfy the evidential burden may be found in the case presented by the prosecution.[113] It might take the form of a partially exculpatory statement to the police at the scene of the crime or in interview or something said to the defendant by another witness. Evidence sufficient to raise an issue might also be elicited by the defendant in cross-examination.

This does not mean, as some judges have supposed, that the evidential burden on the defendant is not a burden at all.[114] The burden consists in the consequence that, unless sufficient evidence is placed before the court, the trial judge will not

[107] *R v Gill* [1963] 1 WLR 841 (CCA) 846 (Edmund-Davies J).

[108] Roberts & Zuckerman 349; Cross & Tapper 133.

[109] [1970] AC 618 (PC).

[110] Ibid 624. See also *R v Schwartz* [1988] 2 SCR 443, 466–67 (Dickson CJC, dissenting).

[111] Roberts & Zuckerman 333; F Adams 'Onus of Proof in Criminal Cases' in RS Clark (ed) *Essays on Criminal Law in New Zealand* (Sweet & Maxwell, Wellington, 1971) 67, 69–70.

[112] H Malek et al (eds) *Phipson on Evidence* 16th edn(Sweet & Maxwell, London, 2005) 6–02.

[113] *R v Lambert* [2002] 2 AC 545 (HL) [91] (Lord Hope) (quoting *Salmon v HM Advocate* 1999 JC 67, 75); *L v DPP* [2003] QB 137 (QBD) [23] (Pill LJ); *Sheldrake v DPP* [2004] QB 487 (QBD) [52] (Clarke LJ).

[114] *AG's Reference (No 1 of 2004)* [2004] 1 WLR 2111 (CA) [9] (Lord Woolf CJ); *L v DPP* [2003] QB 137 (QBD) [23] (Pill LJ).

consider the issue, or direct the jury in relation to it.[115] Crucially, to satisfy the evidential burden, it is necessary to point to evidence admitted in the case and probative of the issue. The House of Lords has stated that 'it is not every facile mouthing of some easy phrase of excuse that can amount to an explanation'[116] nor is it enough to 'mouth the words of the section'.[117] Hence, the mere allegation of some fact, such as putting the fact to a witness in cross-examination, would not be sufficient to satisfy the evidential burden. One High Court decision has held that an entirely self-serving, out of court statement would not discharge the evidential burden.[118]

There is no universally accepted formula to describe how much evidence must be placed before the court to satisfy the evidential burden. The evidence will of course differ depending on the nature of the issue to which the burden relates. The evidence will also vary based on who bears the evidential burden, and whether that party also bears the persuasive burden. When the prosecution bears the evidential burden, it must show that sufficient evidence is before the court for a properly directed jury to be able to find the defendant guilty beyond reasonable doubt.[119] When the defendant bears the evidential burden, and also the persuasive burden, he or she must show that sufficient evidence is before the court for a properly directed jury to be able to find for the defendant on that issue on the balance of probabilities.

It is more typical for the defendant to bear the evidential burden but not the persuasive burden. Various phrases have been adopted to describe the type of evidence that would suffice to discharge this burden, such as evidence that could not be 'dismissed as wholly and obviously without foundation'[120] or, in one case, just a 'scintilla of evidence'.[121] In the context of the defence of provocation, it has been held that the evidence must do more than raise a 'speculative possibility that there has been an act of provocation'.[122] The ultimate test, in a jury trial, is whether the evidence is such that, if believed, it would be capable of causing the jury to have a reasonable doubt as to the guilt of the defendant.[123] If evidence of this nature is

[115] *R(P) v Liverpool City Magistrates* [2006] EWHC 887 (Admin) [22]-[23] (Collins J) stating in relation to the offence of failing without reasonable justification to ensure a child attends school: 'It is not sufficient for the accused to say: "Yes, I knew that he was failing to attend, but you have not proved that the failure was without reasonable excuse." If there is a failure to attend, the Justices, if no material was put before them which could support a case that there was a reasonable justification, would be bound in the circumstances to convict . . .". See also *DPP v Wright* [2009] EWHC 105 (Admin) [59].

[116] *Bratty v AG for Northern Ireland* [1963] AC 386 (HL) 417 (Lord Morris).

[117] *R v Lambert* [2002] 2 AC 545 (HL) [17] (Lord Slynn). See also [37] (Lord Steyn).

[118] *R v Newcastle-upon-Tyne Justices, ex p Hindle* [1984] 1 All ER 770 (QBD) 777 (Robert Goff LJ). See also G Dingwall 'Statutory Exceptions, Burdens of Proof and the Human Rights Act 1998' (2002) 65 *MLR* 450, 459.

[119] While the satisfaction by the prosecution of its evidential burden is not identical to surviving a submission of no case to answer, the function of the two is similar: Munday 85. As to a submission of no case to answer see *R v Galbraith* [1981] 1 WLR 1039 (CA) 1042 (Lord Lane CJ).

[120] *R v S* [2003] 1 Cr App R 35 (CA) [7] (Rose LJ).

[121] *DPP v Walker* [1974] 1 WLR 1090 (PC) 1094 (Lord Salmon).

[122] *R v Acott* [1997] 1 WLR 306 (HL) 313 (Lord Steyn).

[123] *R v Lambert* [2002] 2 AC 545 (HL) [90] (Lord Hope). See also *Bratty v AG for Northern Ireland* [1963] AC 386 (HL) 419 (Lord Morris); *Jayasena v R* [1970] AC 618 (PC) 623 (Lord Devlin).

before the court, the judge has a duty to leave the matter to the jury. This is so even if the matter is not raised by counsel for the defendant and even if the matter is inconsistent with the defence upon which the defendant relies.[124]

The English cases have held that an evidential burden on the defendant does not conflict with the presumption of innocence.[125] The reason for this is that the evidential burden, unlike a persuasive burden, does not present the risk that the defendant will be convicted despite a reasonable doubt in the mind of the jury.[126] It has been argued, however, that the evidential burden is inconsistent with the right to silence because it may require the defendant to testify in cases where this is the only way to discharge the burden.[127] Despite the concerns related to the right to silence, the evidential burden is an essential device for narrowing the issues in a criminal trial. Another method of limiting defences, adopted in section 5 of the Criminal Procedure and Investigations Act 1996, is to require the defendant to give notice of any defences upon which he or she intends to rely. As a means of narrowing issues, this method is open to abuse by defendants who could raise large numbers of spurious issues. If the mere giving of notice were sufficient to require the prosecution to discharge the persuasive burden in relation to every conceivable issue, the cost and length of trials would greatly expand.

In some limited situations, the imposition of an evidential burden on the defendant may constitute an interference with the presumption of innocence. If a statute were, hypothetically, to impose an evidential burden on the defendant in relation to every aspect of an offence, when the prosecution had done nothing but present an indictment, this would undoubtedly breach the presumption of innocence.[128] The prosecution must, at a minimum, present a positive case supported by evidence and capable, in the absence of evidence to the contrary, of justifying the imposition of a criminal sanction. This minimum requirement is inherent in the proper relationship between the state and its citizens. The state cannot require

[124] *R v Hopper* [1915] 2 KB 431 (CCA) 435 (Lord Reading CJ); *Mancini v DPP* [1942] AC 1 (HL) 7 (Viscount Simon LC); *Bullard v The Queen* [1957] AC 635 (PC) 642 (Lord Tucker); *R v Porritt* [1961] 1 WLR 1372 (CCA) 1376–77 (Ashworth J); *R v Kachikwu* (1968) 52 Cr App R 538 (CA) 543 (Winn LJ); *Palmer v R* [1971] AC 814 (PC) 823 (Lord Morris); *R v Von Starck* [2000] 1 WLR 1270 (HL) 1275 (Lord Clyde); *Shaw v R* [2001] 1 WLR 1519 (PC) [28] (Lord Bingham); *R v Banton* [2007] EWCA Crim 1847 [16] (Toulson LJ). See also S Doran 'Alternative Defences: the Invisible Burden on the Trial Judge' [1991] *Crim LR* 878.

[125] *R v Lambert* [2002] 2 AC 545 (HL) [37] (Lord Steyn); *R v DPP; ex p Kebilene* [2000] 2 AC 326 (HL) 379 (Lord Hope); *R v Bianco* [2001] EWCA Crim 2516 (Laws LJ); *AG's Reference (No 1 of 2004)* [2004] 1 WLR 2111 (CA) [52] (Lord Woolf CJ). In Canada, see *R v Osolin* [1993] 4 SCR 595, 688, 690–91 (Cory J). *Cf R v Laba* [1994] 3 SCR 965, 1011 (Sopinka J, for the Court). In South Africa, see *Scagell v AG of the Western Cape* 1997 (2) SA 368 (CC) [12], [16]-[18] (O'Regan J). *Cf S v Mbatha; S v Prinsloo* 1996 (2) SA 464 (CC) [26] (Langa J, for the Court). In Ireland, see *Hardy v Ireland* [1994] IR 550 (SC(I)) 566 (Egan J); 568 (Murphy J); *O'Leary v AG* [1995] ILRM 259 (SC(I)). The Strasbourg appeal from *Hardy* may also be taken as supporting the compatibility of evidential burdens with Art6(2): *Hardy v Ireland* (App No 23456/94) EComHR 29 June 1994.

[126] Cross & Tapper 142.

[127] I Weiser 'The Presumption of Innocence in Section 11(d) of the Charter and Persuasive and Evidential Burdens' (1989) 31 *Criminal Law Quarterly* 318, 341.

[128] See *Tot v US*, 319 US 463, 469 (1943) (Harlan J).

citizens to defend themselves against a criminal charge unless the state has first presented evidence supporting the charge.

Less dramatically, the presumption of innocence may be threatened if the evidential burden is placed on the defendant when the prosecution has not proved facts capable of raising a *prima facie* case against the defendant.[129] For example, there may be an interference with the presumption of innocence if the evidential burden is placed on the defendant with respect to a presumed fact, after the prosecution has proved a basic fact with no rational connection to the presumed fact.[130] Whether the evidential burden would be deemed compatible with the presumption of innocence would depend on whether the burden is likely to be difficult to discharge.[131] This may be the case if the defendant has no realistic means of obtaining and presenting evidence. For the most part, however, an evidential burden is not difficult to discharge and the risk that a defendant will be convicted solely on the basis of an inability to meet an evidential burden is minimal.[132] In the English cases, the solution when a persuasive burden is found to breach Article 6(2) is to convert the persuasive burden to an evidential burden.[133] Far from being inconsistent with Article 6(2), the evidential burden usually represents a solution to the problem posed by a reverse persuasive burden.

C. Standard of Proof

English law recognises two standards of proof.[134] The first is proof on the 'balance of probabilities' or the 'preponderance of the evidence'. This is the standard applicable in civil trials and also the standard of proof expected from a defendant who bears the persuasive burden with respect to any matter in a criminal trial.[135] The second standard is proof beyond reasonable doubt. This is the required standard in criminal cases when the prosecution bears the burden of proof. This

[129] See *Telfner v Austria* (App No 33501/96) (2002) 34 EHRR 7.

[130] PJ Schwikkard *Presumption of Innocence* (Juta & Co, Kenwyn, 1999) 117. See also *R v Downey* [1992] 2 SCR 10, 44–45 (McLachlin J, dissenting).

[131] HA Ashford & DM Risinger 'Presumptions, Assumptions and Due Process in Criminal Cases: A Theoretical Overview' (1969) 79 *YLJ* 165, 184–86.

[132] See *R v Wholesale Travel Group Inc* [1991] 3 SCR 154, 202 (Lamer CJ, dissenting).

[133] See below nn 158–81.

[134] English courts have rejected an intermediate standard of proof, between the balance of probabilities and reasonable doubt: *Re B (Children) (Care Proceedings: Standard of Proof)* [2009] 1 AC 11 (HL) [5] (Lord Hoffmann); *Re D* [2008] 1 WLR 1499 (HL). See also P Mirfield 'How Many Standards of Proof are There?' (2009) 125 *LQR* 31. Ho argues there is only one standard of proof, which varies depending on the context of the case, in particular the consequences that follow from the decision of the court: HL Ho *A Philosophy of Evidence Law: Justice in the Search for Truth* (OUP, Oxford 2008) 213–28. This view takes some support from House of Lords decisions which have suggested there is little to distinguish a heightened civil standard from the criminal standard: eg *Re H (Minors) (Sexual Abuse: Standard of Proof)* [1996] AC 563 (HL) 586 (Lord Nicholls); *R (McCann) v Crown Court at Manchester* [2003] 1 AC 787 (HL) [37] (Lord Steyn).

[135] *R v Carr-Briant* [1943] KB 607 (CCA) 612 (Humphreys J).

section is primarily concerned with the meaning of proof beyond reasonable doubt. The phrase 'beyond reasonable doubt' is heavily laden with historical and rhetorical baggage and its meaning is notoriously difficult to pin down.[136]

On one interpretation of the phrase, the word 'reasonable' modifies the word 'doubt', so that it is permissible for the jury to convict while they have a doubt about guilt, provided the doubt is not reasonable. A reasonable doubt is a doubt based upon reason and therefore capable of articulation.[137] On this view, the standard of 'beyond reasonable doubt' is a concession to the difficulty of eliminating all doubt, since so high a standard would either require the allocation of massive resources to prosecutors, or else result in a drastic reduction in the number of convictions.[138] Anthony Morano has sought to give this view some historical pedigree by arguing that the qualifier 'reasonable' was first introduced by a prosecutor during the Boston Massacre trials in order to reduce the standard of proof required of him.[139] However, this interpretation of the phrase 'beyond reasonable doubt' is inconsistent both with its history and with the current application of the standard in English courts.

Legal historians investigating the origins of the reasonable doubt standard have demonstrated that the term 'reasonable doubt' is connected to the concept of 'moral certainty'.[140] These historians have drawn attention to the distinction drawn by theologians in the seventeenth century between different standards of certainty. Moral certainty was the standard of certainty that could be reached regarding matters established upon the testimony of others. It was to be contrasted with physical certainty, concerning matters directly perceived, and mathematical certainty, concerning matters provable by abstract investigation.[141] In the parlance of the theologians, facts were established with moral certainty if the evidence was such 'as not to admit of any reasonable doubt concerning them.'[142] This conception of certainty was subsequently adopted by lawyers. For example, in

[136] See L Laudan *Truth, Error and Criminal Law: An Essay in Legal Epistemology* (CUP, Cambridge 2006) ch 2.

[137] *Smith v Balkcom*, 660 F 2d 573, 580 (5th Cir1981); *R v Brydon* [1995] 95 CCC (3d) 509, 511.

[138] See CRM Dlamini 'Proof Beyond a Reasonable Doubt: An Analysis of Its Meaning and Ideological and Philosophical Underpinnings' (1998) 11 *South African Journal of Criminal Justice* 423, 461; A Ashworth, *Human Rights, Serious Crime and Criminal Procedure* (Sweet & Maxwell, London, 2002) 16.

[139] A Morano 'A Reexamination of the Development of the Reasonable Doubt Rule' (1975) 55 *Boston University Law Review* 507, 515–19.

[140] T Waldman 'Origins of the Legal Doctrine of Reasonable Doubt' (1959) 20 *Journal of the History of Ideas* 299; B Shapiro *Beyond Reasonable Doubt and Probable Cause: Historical Perspectives on the Anglo-American Law of Evidence* (University of California Press, Berkeley, 1991); B Shapiro '"To a Moral Certainty": Theories of Knowledge and Anglo-American Juries 1600–1850' (1986) *Hastings Law Journal* 153; T Mulrine, 'Reasonable Doubt: How in the World is it Defined?' (1997) 12 *American University Journal of International Law and Policy* 195, 199–202; S Sheppard 'The Metamorphoses of Reasonable Doubt: How Changes in the Burden of Proof have Weakened the Presumption of Innocence' (2003) 78 *Notre Dame Law Review* 1165.

[141] See eg J Wilkins *Of the Principles and Duties of Natural Religion* 8th edn (J Knapton, London, 1722) (original 1678) 4–7; J Locke *An Essay Concerning Human Understanding* (OUP, Oxford 1979) (original 1690) 661–62 (bk 4, ch 16, ss 6–7).

[142] Wilkins, ibid, 8.

A Practical Treatise of the Law of Evidence (1824), Thomas Starkie stated that 'absolute, metaphysical, and demonstrative certainty' was not essential and that evidence for guilt was sufficient if it produced 'moral certainty to the exclusion of every reasonable doubt'.[143] Hence, on the historical evidence, the 'reasonable doubt' standard implies the highest degree of certainty that is possible concerning past events in the absence of first-hand knowledge.

The application of the standard of proof in English criminal cases also suggests that 'reasonable doubt' denotes the highest degree of certainty that can be reached concerning past events. Over the years, judges have adopted different methods for explaining the meaning of 'reasonable doubt' to juries. In 1865, Pollock CB directed a jury that they could convict upon the same degree of certainty 'with which you should transact your own most important concerns in life.'[144] Very shortly afterwards, this direction was criticised for being contrary to precedent and diluting the standard of proof.[145] More recently, courts have discouraged any elaboration upon the meaning of reasonable doubt as it is likely to cause confusion.[146] In 1955, the Court of Criminal Appeal stated that the form of words used was not vital; it would be sufficient to say 'you must be satisfied beyond reasonable doubt', 'you the jury, must be completely satisfied' or 'you must feel sure of the prisoner's guilt'.[147] The specimen direction of the Judicial Studies Board currently recommends the direction that the jury must be 'sure' of the guilt of the defendant. If any reference is made during the trial to proof 'beyond reasonable doubt' the jury should be told that it is the same as being 'sure'.[148] This formulation of the standard of proof suggests that any doubts held by the jury would be sufficient to require a verdict of acquittal.

The standard of proof beyond reasonable doubt has also been described as requiring 'a high degree of probability', specifically, a higher degree of probability than is required in civil cases.[149] There are dangers in associating standards of proof with notions of probability. Studies suggest that people differ widely when asked to convert the reasonable doubt standard into an expression of probability.[150]

143 Starkie (see n 25 above) 514.

144 *R v Muller*, January 1865 (quoted in *R v White* (1865) 4 F & F 383 (Reporter's Note)).

145 *R v White* (1865) 4 F & F 383 (Reporter's Note). See more recent criticism in *Walters v R* [1969] 2 AC 26 (PC) 30 (Lord Diplock); *R v Gray* (1973) 58 Cr App R 177 (CA) 183 (Megaw LJ); *R v Ching* (1976) 63 Cr App R 7 (CA) 10 (Lawton LJ).

146 *R v Kritz* [1950] 1 KB 82 (CCA) 90 (Lord Goddard CJ).

147 *R v Hepworth and Fearnley* [1955] 2 QB 600 (CCA) 603. See also *R v Allan* [1969] 1 WLR 33 (CA) 36 (Fenton-Atkinson LJ); *Walters v R* [1969] 2 AC 26 (PC) 30 (Lord Diplock); *Ferguson v R* [1979] 1 WLR 94 (PC) 99 (Lord Scarman); *R v Bracewell* (1979) 68 Cr App R 44 (CA) 49 (Ormrod LJ).

148 Judicial Studies Board *Specimen Directions* (2008) available at www.jsboard.co.uk/criminal_law/cbb, last visited 28 September 2009. More detailed guidance on the meaning of 'reasonable doubt' is given in Canada and the US: *R v Lifchus* [1997] 3 SCR 320, 336–37 (Cory J); *Victor v Nebraska*, 511 US 1 (1994). In Australia, judges are not permitted to elaborate on the meaning of 'reasonable doubt': *Thomas v R* (1960) 102 CLR 584 (HCA) 595 (Kitto J), 605 (Windeyer J); *Dawson v R* (1961) 106 CLR 1 (HCA) 18 (Dixon CJ); *Green v R* (1971) 126 CLR 28 (HCA) 32–33.

149 *Miller v Minister of Pensions* [1947] 2 All ER 372 (QBD) 373 (Denning J).

150 See M Zander 'The Criminal Standard of Proof—How Sure is Sure? (2000) 150 *New Law Journal* 1517; RJ Simon 'Judges' Translations of Burdens of Proof into Statements of Probability' [1969] *Trial Law Guide* 103; RJ Simon & T Mahan 'Quantifying Burdens of Proof: A View from the Bench, the Jury and the Classroom' (1971) 5 *Law & Society Review* 319; RJ Simon, '"Beyond a Reasonable Doubt": An

Further, the direction that guilt must be highly probable could be interpreted as an easier standard to satisfy than a direction that the jury be 'sure' of guilt. A juror could estimate the probability of an event at 98 or 99 per cent and yet still not be 'sure' that the event occurred. A defendant should only be convicted when it is known that the person is guilty. This is not to suggest that the standard of proof is capable of eliminating any risk of erroneous conviction. A jury may be 'sure' of the guilt of the defendant even though the defendant is innocent, perhaps because the evidence presented was tainted or because one of the witnesses was able to lie in a convincing way, or simply because the jury has made an error of judgment in assessing the evidence. While a high standard of proof does not eliminate all risk of wrongful convictions, there is no doubt that dilution of the standard of proof can result in convictions in cases that would otherwise have resulted in acquittals.[151] Hence, the standard of proof beyond reasonable doubt is an important protection for defendants.

D. Impact of the HRA

The protection given to the presumption of innocence in English law was subject to a train of criticism over a forty year period preceding the HRA. Glanville Williams, for example, accused Parliament of treating the presumption of innocence with 'indifference' and 'contempt' and noted that statutory drafting often imposed the persuasive burden on a defendant 'through carelessness or lack of subtlety'.[152] In fairness to statutory drafters, it should be noted that the imposition of reverse burdens was sometimes urged by the courts as an alternative to strict liability.[153] In 1972, the Criminal Law Revision Committee (CLRC) advised that burdens on the defendant should be evidential only.[154] One reason for this was that otherwise a defendant could be convicted in the absence of proof beyond a reasonable doubt. Another was that an evidential burden would suffice to solve the problem of defendants raising spurious claims of no case to answer without having presented any evidence. In *Hunt*,[155] Lord Griffiths stated that such a

Experimental Attempt at Quantification (1970) 6 *Journal of Applied Behavioral Science* 203; LM Solan 'Refocusing the Burden of Proof in Criminal Cases: Some Doubt About Reasonable Doubt' (1999) 78 *Texas Law Review* 105, Pt III.

[151] See *Re Winship* 397 US 358, 369–70 (1970); *Mizzi v The Queen* (1960) 105 CLR 659 (HCA) 664; *Sodeman v The King* (1936) 55 CLR 192 (HCA) 220 (Dixon J). *Cf Khawaja v Secretary of State for the Home Office* [1984] AC 74 (HL) 112 (Lord Scarman); *R v Hepworth v Fearnley* [1955] 2 QB 600 (CCA) 603 (Lord Goddard CJ). Empirical research demonstrating the importance of the standard of proof is found in LSE Jury Project 'Juries and the Rules of Evidence' [1973] *Crim LR* 208.

[152] G Williams *The Proof of Guilt* 3rd edn (London, Stevens, 1963) 184–85.

[153] *Warner v MPC* [1969] 2 AC 256 (HL) 280 (Lord Reid), 307 (Lord Pearce); *Sweet v Parsley* [1970] AC 132 (HL) 150 (Lord Reid), 157 (Lord Pearce).

[154] Criminal Law Revision Committee, *Eleventh Report, Evidence (General)* (Cmnd 4991) (HMSO London 1972) [140].

[155] [1987] AC 352 (HL).

'fundamental change' could be brought about only by an Act of Parliament.[156] The recommendation of the CLRC on this point was never implemented. By the mid-1990s, the protection given to the presumption of innocence could only be described as patchy. In 1996, Ashworth and Blake reported that 219 out of 540 offences triable in the Crown Court imposed some form of persuasive burden on the defendant.[157]

The passage of the HRA in 1998 presented an opportunity to rejuvenate the presumption of innocence. Schedule 1 to the HRA incorporated selected articles from the European Convention on Human Rights and gave them direct effect in English law. By this means, Article 6(2) of the ECHR, which protects the right to be presumed innocent, was incorporated into English law. The HRA elevates Convention rights to quasi-constitutional status by subjecting all legislation to a test of compatibility with the Convention. This is achieved through the network of rules in sections 3, 4 and 6 of the HRA.

Under section 6 of the HRA, it is unlawful for public authorities, including courts, to act in a way which is incompatible with a Convention right, unless the authority could not act differently as the result of the provisions of primary legislation. This has the effect that a court is prohibited from treating a defendant in a manner inconsistent with a Convention right, unless that result is demanded by statute. Section 3 of the HRA gives the courts the ability to look beyond the ordinary meaning of statutory language in cases involving infringement of Convention rights. Section 3 states: 'So far as it is possible to do so, primary legislation and subordinate legislation must be read and given effect in a way which is compatible with the Convention rights.' If a statute cannot be read in a manner compatible with the Convention, the higher courts are given power by section 4 of the HRA to make a declaration of incompatibility. The offending statute will continue in operation despite the declaration until the government amends the legislation in accordance with section 10 of the HRA.

Following the commencement of the HRA, it became necessary to ask whether it was 'possible' under section 3 to read a statute imposing a persuasive burden on the defendant as imposing only an evidential burden. In particular, it was asked whether the requirement for the defendant to 'prove' a matter could be read to impose an evidential burden. A stumbling block to such an interpretation was the strong statement of Lord Devlin in *Jayasena* that an evidential burden did not require a defendant to prove any matter.[158] Even before the enactment of the HRA, however, Williams had suggested that such a reading was available to courts in order to avoid imposing unfair persuasive burdens on defendants.[159] He argued

[156] Ibid 376. See also *Sheldrake v DPP; AG's Reference (No 4 of 2002)* [2005] 1 AC 264 (HL) [42] (Lord Bingham).

[157] A Ashworth & M Blake 'The Presumption of Innocence in English Criminal Law' [1996] *Crim LR* 306, 309.

[158] [1970] AC 618 (PC) 624.

[159] G Williams 'The Logic of Exceptions' (1988) 47 *CLJ* 261.

that the word 'proof' is 'open to different shades of meaning'[160] and could reasonably be taken to impose an evidential burden only. He stated:[161]

> If, where an evidential burden lies on the defendant, the jury acquit, this is because they feel at least a reasonable doubt whether the defendant is guilty. It does not appear to be wholly discordant with ordinary language to say that, in such a case, at least a reasonable doubt as to guilt has been established; and if 'established' why not 'proved'? It may not be the best use of words, but if there is a reasonable possibility that this is how the words 'prove' and 'proves' have been intended, and if this interpretation diminishes the likelihood of miscarriages of justice, we should accept it.[162]

The flaw in this analysis is that, when the prosecution bears the burden of proof, the defendant is not required to 'establish' any matter. It is for the prosecution to eliminate the presence of reasonable doubt in the mind of the jury. Nevertheless, the interpretation put forward by Williams was described as a 'respectable argument' by Lord Steyn in *Kebilene*[163] and used as justification for the conclusion that a persuasive burden imposed upon a defendant could be read down so as to impose an evidential burden only. Lord Steyn referred to Williams' argument again in *Lambert*,[164] reaching the conclusion that a statute requiring the defendant to 'prove' a matter could be interpreted under section 3 of the HRA as imposing an evidential burden.[165] The remaining members of the majority also accepted that a persuasive burden that undermined the presumption of innocence to an impermissible extent could be read down under section 3 to impose only an evidential burden. Lord Slynn, for example, stated: 'Even if the most obvious way to read section 28(2) is that it imposes a legal burden of proof I have no doubt that it is 'possible', without doing violence to the language or to the objective of that section, to read the words as imposing only the evidential burden of proof.'[166] The statements to this effect in both *Kebilene* and *Lambert* were *obiter* as both cases were decided on the basis that the HRA did not apply retrospectively.

The proposal of 'reading down'[167] a persuasive burden to an evidential burden was not without its detractors, both in the courts[168] and in academic writing.[169] In

160 Ibid 264.

161 Ibid 265–66, n 10.

162 See also *R v Appleby* [1972] SCR 303, 307 (Ritchie J) stating it was hard to distinguish between 'establishes' in s 224A(1)(a) of the Canadian Criminal Code and the word 'proves' used in other sections of the Criminal Code.

163 [2000] 2 AC 326 (HL) 370 (Lord Steyn). See also 373 (Lord Cooke). *Cf* 398 (Lord Hobhouse).

164 [2002] 2 AC 545 (HL).

165 Ibid [42].

166 Ibid [17]. See also [84], [91], [94] (Lord Hope); [131], [157] (Lord Clyde).

167 See R Edwards 'Reading Down Legislation under the Human Rights Act' (2000) 20 *Legal Studies* 353.

168 *L v DPP* [2003] QB 137 (QBD) [23] (Pill LJ), [29] (Poole J); *R v Daniel* [2003] 1 Cr App R 6 (CA) [26]–[28] (Auld LJ). See also *R v Phillips* [1991] 3 NZLR 175, 177 (Cooke P): Williams' approach was described as 'a strained and unnatural interpretation which, even with the aid of the New Zealand Bill of Rights Act, this Court would not be justified in adopting'. (Considering s 6 of the New Zealand Bill of Rights Act 1990.) On this point, *Phillips* was followed in *R v Hanson* [2007] NZSC 7 [39] (Elias CJ).

169 D Birch, 'Burden of Proof: *R v Lambert*' [2001] *Crim LR* 806, 809; P Mirfield, 'Silence, Innocence and Human Rights' in P Mirfield & R Smith (eds), *Essays for Colin Tapper* (LexisNexis, London, 2003) 126, 132; Dingwall (see n 118 above) 461.

R v S,[170] the Court of Appeal made reference to these misgivings but held, following *Kebilene* and *Lambert*, that 'it must be taken as settled at this judicial level' that section 3 of the HRA is 'in principle' capable of being invoked so as to read down a reverse persuasive burden to impose an evidential burden.[171] The controversy is for all practical purposes resolved by the House of Lords decision in *AG's Reference (No 4 of 2002)*.[172] That case followed *Lambert* in confirming that it is possible to read down a persuasive burden to an evidential burden under the interpretative obligation in section 3 of the HRA.[173] As this finding about the capacity for reading down constituted part of the ratio of the decision, it is binding on all lower courts. This may result in a strained reading of some statutes but it is probably consistent with the general approach taken by the House of Lords to interpretation under section 3.[174] Under this approach, the limit to what is a 'possible' interpretation under section 3 is that the meaning ascribed must not be inconsistent with 'a fundamental feature of the legislation'[175], must not go against the grain or remove the 'pith and substance' of the legislation[176] and must not violate a cardinal principle of the legislation.[177]

In *AG's Reference (No 4 of 2002)*,[178] the Act under review contained a list of sections that were to be read as imposing an evidential burden. The section which created the offence in question was not included in this list, but the House of Lords held that the section ought to be read as though it were so included.[179] The structure adopted by the statute for allocating burdens was not treated as a 'fundamental feature' so as to be a barrier to reading down. Following this liberal approach to interpretation, there should normally be no difficulty in reading statutes that require a defendant to 'prove' or 'show' a matter, as imposing an evidential and not a persuasive burden.[180] Ian Dennis puts the point strongly: 'It will not matter

[170] *R v S* [2003] 1 Cr App R 35 (CA).

[171] Ibid [42] (Rose LJ). See also *R v Johnstone* [2003] ETMR 1 (CA) [82] (Tuckey LJ). Lord Woolf CJ has stated that it is possible, using s 3 of the HRA, to interpret a reverse burden created by s 352 of the Insolvency Act 1986 as evidential in relation to one offence, but persuasive in relation to another: *AG's Reference (No 1 of 2004)* [2004] 1 WLR 2111 (CA) [45].

[172] [2005] 1 AC 264 (HL).

[173] Ibid [53] (Lord Bingham) with whom Lord Steyn and Lord Phillips agreed: ibid [55], [56].

[174] *Ghaidan v Godin-Mendoza* [2004] 2 AC 557 (HL).

[175] Ibid [33] (Lord Nicholls).

[176] Ibid [110]-[113] (Lord Rodger).

[177] Ibid [116] (Lord Rodger). See also [49] (Lord Steyn).

[178] [2005] 1 AC 264 (HL) [53].

[179] Ibid [53] (Lord Bingham).

[180] The Privy Council, interpreting the Constitutions of other jurisdictions has held that legal burdens should be read down to evidential burdens: *Vasquez v The Queen* [1994] 1 WLR 1304 (PC) 1314 (Lord Jauncey) (interpreting s 6(3)(a) of the Constitution of Belize); *Yearwood v The Queen* [2001] UKPC 31 (interpreting s 8(2)(a) of the Constitution of Grenada). In Canada, the Supreme Court has held that the words 'unless he establishes' could be severed from a statute so that an evidential burden was imposed rather than a persuasive burden: *R v Laba* [1994] 3 SCR 965, 1011–16 (Sopinka J). The Constitutional Court of South Africa has held it has the power to 'read in' words so as to convert a persuasive burden to an evidential burden: *S v Manamela* 2000 (3) SA 1 (CC) [27] (Madala, Sachs and Yacoob JJ); *S v Singo* 2002 (4) SA 858 (CC). See also in Ireland: *Hardy v Ireland* [1994] IR 550 (SC(I)) 566 (Egan J); 568 (Murphy J); *O'Leary v AG* [1995] ILRM 259 (SC(I)).

what Parliament says in the statute creating the reverse onus; it can always be contradicted by the contrary intention which the courts derive from s 3 of the HRA.'[181] This very broad interpretation of section 3 gives the courts the capacity to insist that defendants not be inflicted with persuasive burdens in virtually any case where the burden is incompatible with Article 6(2).

F. Conclusion

This Chapter has demonstrated that, although the principle that the prosecution must prove the guilt of the defendant has a lengthy history in English law, there have always been exceptions, either at common law or by statute. The incorporation of Article 6(2) into English law provided judges with a means of reviewing these exceptions in light of the general principle of the presumption of innocence. The use of 'reading down' to turn persuasive burdens into evidential burdens is an accepted method for altering previous interpretations of statutes. English judges, however, have not treated Article 6(2) as requiring the elimination of all exceptions to the rule that the prosecution should prove guilt. Rather, the courts have held that interference with the presumption of innocence by reversal of the burden of proof will be acceptable whenever this measure is proportionate to a legitimate objective. In order to determine whether this is the correct approach to Article 6(2), it is necessary to develop a more detailed understanding of why the presumption of innocence is important. The following chapter undertakes this task.

[181] IH Dennis 'Reverse Onuses and the Presumption of Innocence: In Search of Principle' [2005] Crim LR 901, 926.

2

Rationale for the Presumption

THE KEY CONCERN of this book is whether limits on the presumption of innocence can be justified, and if so to what extent. In order to answer this question it is necessary to understand why the presumption of innocence is important. The values served by the presumption of innocence must clearly be set out before we can begin to consider whether the right ought to be limited through the use of reverse burdens. Part A of this chapter will argue that the presumption of innocence serves two mutually-reinforcing values: first it is instrumental in preventing the conviction and punishment of the innocent; and second it promotes the rule of law by insisting that criminal sanctions not be imposed unless guilt has been publicly demonstrated to a sufficient standard of certainty.

Having clarified these values, it will be possible to consider whether the values promoted by the presumption of innocence ought ever to be subjugated to other values, such as protection of the community or efficiency in the justice system. Part B of this chapter will argue that the right of the innocent to be protected from the risk of wrongful conviction should not be balanced against the interest of the community in pursuing other objectives. Only when the rights of the innocent are not endangered or are called into play in an attenuated sense should reversal of the burden of proof be contemplated. This may be the case when the risk of wrongful conviction is low or when there is a minimal penalty upon conviction. However, even when the rationale of protecting the innocent is attenuated, the rationale of promoting the rule of law continues to operate. The remainder of the book will work through the implications of the conclusions reached in this chapter.

A. Two Rationales for the Presumption

In *Sheldrake v DPP*,[1] Lord Bingham presented what he took to be the underlying rationale for the presumption of innocence:[2]

> There can be no doubt that the underlying rationale of the presumption in domestic law and in the Convention is an essentially simple one: that it is repugnant to ordinary

[1] *Sheldrake v DPP* [2005] 1 AC 264 (HL).
[2] Ibid [9].

> notions of fairness for a prosecutor to accuse a defendant of crime and for the defendant to be then required to disprove the accusation on pain of conviction and punishment if he fails to do so.

This statement by Lord Bingham obliquely captures two important truths concerning the rationale for the presumption of innocence. To begin with, conviction and punishment ought only to be imposed on people who have contravened the criminal law. Further, if the state makes an accusation of criminality it ought to be required to prove the truth of the accusation before conviction and punishment may be visited on the defendant. This part aims to build upon the intuitive appeal of Lord Bingham's statement to explain in greater detail why requiring a defendant to prove his or her innocence is 'repugnant to ordinary notions of fairness'.

1. Protecting the Innocent

The most obvious reason for insisting upon the presumption of innocence is that it is instrumental in protecting the innocent from wrongful conviction.[3] It may seem self-evident that the innocent should not be convicted but to understand the significance of this principle some further explanation is required. This section makes two important points. First, it explains why it is wrong to convict the innocent and why a state committed to fairness must operate a criminal justice system in a way that minimises the risks of convicting the innocent. Second, it shows how allocating the burden of proof to the prosecution and insisting on proof beyond reasonable doubt assist in protecting the innocent.

Conviction for a criminal offence carries a variety of negative consequences in the form of punishment, censure and stigma. Most prominent is the imposition of punishment or 'hard treatment', in the form of fines, community sentences or imprisonment.[4] Also important is the censure that is expressed by the community through the medium of its judicial agents when a person is convicted.[5] The conviction and the act of punishment send the message that the person is an offender against the standards of conduct expected by the community of its members. Associated with censure is the stigma that attaches to those who have been convicted of a criminal offence.[6] Stigmatisation can have consequences for the way in which a person is treated in the community, either informally or formally through measures such as registration as an offender, disqualification from some forms of employment and compulsory disclosure regimes.[7] Before these consequences can be imposed on an individual there must be a sound justification.

[3] *R v Oakes* [1986] 1 SCR 103, 119–20 (Dickson CJC).
[4] See A Von Hirsch & A Ashworth *Proportionate Sentencing: Exploring the Principles* (OUP, Oxford 2005) 21–27.
[5] See A von Hirsch *Censure and Sanctions* (OUP, Oxford 1993).
[6] See N Walker *Punishment Danger and Stigma* (Blackwell, Oxford 1980) ch 7.
[7] A Ashworth 'Four Threats to the Presumption of Innocence' (2006) 10 *E & P* 241, 247.

The justification for the imposition of criminal sanctions, particularly the aspect of punishment, is one of the classic questions of legal philosophy.[8] Opinion is divided between consequentialists, who find the justification for punishment in the benefits it produces, and retributivists, who argue that punishment is the just and correct response to the offender's breach of expected standards. Within the consequentialist camp, incapacitation of the offender is one justification for punishment that has been said to enjoy 'dominance by default'.[9] Critics object to this justification for punishment because it relies upon questionable predictions as to the offender's likelihood of committing other crimes,[10] and also because it obscures the connection between the penalty imposed and the offender's past conduct.[11] Until the 1970s, rehabilitation was often posited as a justification for punishment on the ground that sanctions such as imprisonment or community service orders provide opportunities for the offender to be reformed and then re-integrated into the community as a law abiding member.[12] This justification was criticised on the ground that there was no evidence that rehabilitation was effective,[13] and also that rehabilitative goals could justify intervention in the offender's life that was disproportionate to the original offence.[14]

The most prominent consequentialist argument in favour of punishment is that it has a deterrent effect. In the simplest sense, the threat of punishment provides a reason, in addition to any relevant moral reasons, for people to comply with legal rules.[15] In a broader sense, by expressing social disapproval of the offender's behaviour, punishment helps 'reaffirm, reinforce or stabilise the moral norms

[8] Some useful summaries of the opposing views are: T Honderich *Punishment: The Supposed Justifications Revisited* (Pluto Press, London 2006); L Zedner *Criminal Justice* (OUP, Oxford 2004) 84–111; RA Duff *Punishment, Communication and Community* (OUP, Oxford 2001) ch 1; N Walker *Why Punish?* (OUP, Oxford 1991); CL Ten *Crime, Guilt and Punishment: A Philosophical Introduction* (Clarendon Press, Oxford 1987); H Packer *The Limits of the Criminal Sanction* (Stanford University Press, Stanford 1969) chs 3–4.

[9] FE Zimring & G Hawkins Incapacitation: Penal Confinement and the Restraint of Crime (OUP, New York 1995) ch 1.

[10] Zedner (see n 8 above) 100.

[11] T Honderich 'On Justifying Protective Punishment' (1982) 22 *British Journal of Criminology (BJ Crim)* 268; A von Hirsch 'Selective Incapacitation: Some Doubts' in A von Hirsch & A Ashworth (eds) *Principled Sentencing: Readings on Theory and Policy* (Hart Publishing, Oxford 1998) 119; D Wood 'Dangerous Offenders, and the Morality of Protective Sentencing' [1988] *Crim LR* 424, 432–33.

[12] B Wootton *Crime and the Criminal Law* (Stevens, London 1963); K Menninger *The Crime of Punishment* (Viking Press, New York 1968). On the reintegrative aspect of punishment, see also: J Braithwaite *Crime, Shame and Reintegration* (CUP, Cambridge 1989); J Braithwaite and P Pettit *Not Just Deserts: A Republican Theory of Criminal Justice* (Clarendon Press, Oxford 1990).

[13] R Martinson 'What Works? Questions and Answers About Prison Reform' (1974) *Public Interest* 22.

[14] Zedner (see n 8 above) 97–98. See also CS Lewis 'The Humanitarian Theory of Punishment' (1949) in L Walmsley (ed) *CS Lewis Essay Collection: Literature, Philosophy and Short Stories* (Harper Collins, London 2000) 290, 294: 'To be "cured" against one's will and cured of states which we may not regard as disease is to be put on level with those who have not yet reached the age of reason or those who never will; to be classed with infants, imbeciles, and domestic animals. But to be punished, however severely, because we have deserved it, because we "ought to have known better", is to be treated as a human person made in God's image.'

[15] J Bentham, *An Introduction to the Principles of Morals and Legislation* (Methuen, London 1982) (original 1789) chs 13–14.

among citizens that restrain criminal behaviour'.[16] Under this broader banner, punishment upholds the value of criminal prohibitions by emphasising that harsh treatment will be visited upon those who breach them.[17] When deterrence is posited as the sole justification for criminal punishment, two objections arise. First, it is notoriously difficult to quantify the extent to which punishment is effective in deterring crime.[18] Second, it is objected that the goal of deterrence places no limits on punishment—even deliberate punishment of the innocent would be justified if it could be shown to operate as an effective deterrent.[19] Further, like all the consequentialist justifications for punishment, deterrence theory is susceptible to the criticism that it fails to treat offenders as autonomous moral agents: that is, that it treats offenders as a means to the fulfilment of some other end, rather than as an end in themselves.[20]

Responding to this weakness in the consequentialist justifications for punishment, retributivists argue instead that punishment is the proper response to an offender's breach of the criminal law. The retributivist argument does not depend on the benefits that flow from punishment, but rather insists that punishment is the normative response to the breaking of legal rules. Hence, Kant famously opined that even if society were on the point of dissolution 'the last murderer remaining in prison would . . . have to be executed, so that each has done to him what his deeds deserve.'[21] Retributivism avoids the allegation of treating the offender as a means, since the criminal justice system speaks directly to the offender as an agent capable of making decisions and understanding the censure or condemnation implied by the punishment.[22] Retributivism also imposes limits on punishment. If the justification for punishment is to 'pay back' the offender for the wrong he or she has committed, punishment can only be visited upon those who are guilty. Further, punishment must not be disproportionate to the severity of the offence.[23]

[16] Von Hirsch & Ashworth (see n 4 above) 16 (citing two German authors C Roxin and M Baurmann).

[17] Packer (see n 8 above) 39–45.

[18] A von Hirsch et al *Criminal Deterrence and Sentence Severity: An Analysis of Recent Research* (Hart, Oxford 1999); D Beyleveld 'Identifying, Exploring and Predicting Deterrence' (1979) 19 *BJ Crim* 205; P Robinson & J Darley 'Does Criminal Law Deter? A Behavioural Science Investigation' (2004) 24 *OJLS* 173.

[19] The utilitarian response to this is that deliberately punishing the innocent would undermine the authority of and support for the system, and so would be counterproductive: J Rawls 'Two Concepts of Rules' (1955) 64 *Philosophical Review* 3.

[20] *Cf* I Kant, H Paton (trans) *Groundwork of the Metaphysic of Morals* (Hutchinson, London 1948) 90–93 (original 1785); I Kant, J Ladd (trans) *The Metaphysical Elements of Justice* (Bobbs-Merrill, Indianapolis 1965) 99–100 (original 1797).

[21] Quoted in Zedner (see n 8 above) 86.

[22] The communicative aspect of punishment is emphasised in A von Hirsch *Censure and Sanctions* (Clarendon Press, Oxford 1993); RA Duff *Punishment, Communication and Community* (OUP, Oxford 2001).

[23] Von Hirsch & Ashworth (see n 4 above). On theoretical and practical problems concerning the proportionality of punishment see PH Robinson 'Competing Conceptions of Modern Desert: Vengeful, Deontological and Empirical' (2008) 67 *CLJ* 145.

The retributivist justification for punishment 'seems to accord with our deepest intuitions concerning justice.'[24] However, it is difficult to rationalise why retribution in the form of punishment is the normative response to criminal behaviour. Various explanations have been advanced, none of which is fully satisfactory.[25] One explanation is that retributive punishment rectifies the 'unfair advantage' which the offender has obtained by acting outside the rules.[26] By imposing hardship on the offender, the advantages that he has gained by offending are cancelled out. However, we do not view punishment as an attempt to take back from the offender what he has wrongly appropriated—that is the purpose of restitution. The idea of reversing an 'unfair advantage' does not explain why, for example, we punish a thief as well as requiring him or her to return the stolen property. Another explanation for retributive punishment is that it vindicates the rights of the victim.[27] This is not the same as saying that punishment compensates the victim for his or her loss. Rather, punishment seeks to 'annul' the deprivation of the victim's rights by reasserting those rights through the imposition of some commensurate harm on the offender. However, since punishment cannot reverse the deprivation of the victim's rights, this argument seems to be merely a re-statement of the consequentialist idea that punishment reaffirms the value of the criminal prohibition.[28] It is not a normative explanation for retribution. Finally, a more recent theory is that retribution is normative because it is always right to acknowledge the wrong that has been done and to communicate this to the offender, treating him or her as a person who is capable of understanding the intended condemnation.[29] This theory may explain why it is right to censure the offender, but it does not explain why that censure must be communicated through punishment, rather than by some other means.[30]

We are left with the apparent conclusion that no justification for punishment is adequate. Retributivism cannot be explained as a normative response to wrongdoing beyond its apparent intuitive appeal. Consequentialism is ruled out because it treats the offender as a means rather than an end, and because it provides no grounds for limiting the punishment in proportion to the severity of the offence. This dilemma leads to the possibility that the justification for punishment can be

[24] J Kleinig *Punishment and Desert* (Martinus Nijhoff, The Hague 1973) 67. See also MS Moore 'The Moral Worth of Retribution' in F Schoeman (ed) *Responsibility, Character and the Emotions* (CUP, Cambridge 1987) 179.

[25] A more detailed discussion than is possible here is contained in Walker (see n 8 above) ch 9.

[26] J Finnis *Natural Law and Natural Rights* (Clarendon Press, Oxford 1980) 262–64. See also H Morris 'Persons and Punishment' (1968) 52 *Monist* 475; JG Murphy *Retribution, Justice and Therapy* (Reidel, Dordrecht 1979) 82–115. Both Morris and Murphy have subsequently criticised the 'unfair advantage' idea: H Morris 'A Paternalistic Theory of Punishment' (1981) 18 *American Philosophical Quarterly* 263; JG Murphy 'Retributivism, Moral Education and the Liberal State' (1985) 4 *Criminal Journal of Ethics* (*Crim J Ethics*) 3.

[27] DE Cooper 'Hegel's Theory of Punishment' in ZA Pelczynski (ed) *Hegel's Political Philosophy: Problems and Perspectives* (CUP, Cambridge 1971) 151.

[28] Ten (see n 8 above) 40.

[29] Duff (see n 22 above); Von Hirsch (see n 5 above).

[30] Von Hirsch (see n 5 above) 9–13. See also von Hirsch & Ashworth (see n 4 above) 21–27.

found in an explanation including both consequentialist and retributivist aspects.[31] At this point, it is important to maintain a distinction between the general justifying aim of a system of punishment, and the questions of who may be punished and to what extent.[32] When the questions are divided in this way, it is possible to argue that incapacitation, rehabilitation and deterrence, either individually or collectively, provide grounds to justify a system of punishment. In particular, the use of punishment as a means to reaffirm the values expressed through criminal law provides a sound justification. Punishment is the most appropriate way to indicate that the offender is a culpable rule-breaker, and hence to reaffirm for society the value of the broken rule.

However, on the questions of who may be punished and to what extent, retributivist principles play a necessary role. When an offender has contravened a legal rule, it is proper to censure that conduct and, for consequentialist reasons, we express that censure through the hard treatment of punishment. Within this framework, retributivist concerns operate as a limiting force on punishment by insisting that the penalty must correspond to the personal responsibility of the offender for his or her conduct. To punish a person only to reaffirm the value of the criminal law would treat that person only as a means, not as an end. The consequence of this is that punishment may be inflicted only on the guilty. An innocent person does not deserve to be censured, punished or stigmatised and can legitimately demand that the state not impose these consequences on him or her.[33] In addition, an innocent person convicted of a crime suffers the 'moral harm' of wrongful conviction.[34] This is not just the wrongful imposition of punishment, censure and stigma, but also the separate injustice of unfair treatment. As a result, it may be accepted that: 'People have a profound right not to be convicted of crimes of which they are innocent.'[35] If the imposition of criminal sanctions is to be justified the criminal justice system must take steps to ensure that only the guilty are made subject to criminal liability.

No criminal justice system is perfect. There is a risk of error in all human decision-making. The innocent can be convicted in the criminal justice system even when the prosecution is required to prove its case beyond reasonable doubt.[36] Despite the ever-present risk of error, there is ample justification for a criminal justice system designed to detect offenders, make authoritative judgments as to

[31] This has been the response of several theorists: HLA Hart *Punishment and Responsibility* (Clarendon Press, Oxford 1968) ch 1; A von Hirsch *Past or Future Crimes* (Manchester University Press, Manchester 1986) ch 5; von Hirsch (see n 5 above) ch 2; Packer (see n 8 above) ch 3.

[32] Hart Ibid 3. See also A von Hirsch 'Proportionality in the Philosophy of Punishment: From "Why Punish?" to "How Much?"' (1990) 1 *Criminal Law Forum* 259.

[33] Duff (see n 22 above) 10.

[34] RM Dworkin 'Principle, Policy and Procedure' in CFH Tapper (ed) *Crime, Proof and Punishment: Essays in Memory of Sir Rupert Cross* (Butterworths, London 1981) 193, 201–02. Republished in R Dworkin *A Matter of Principle* (Harvard University Press, Cambridge 1985) ch 3. Page numbers below from *Crime, Proof and Punishment.*

[35] Ibid 193. See also A Ashworth *The Criminal Process: An Evaluative Study* 2nd edn (OUP, Oxford 1998) 50–52; Roberts & Zuckerman 344.

[36] Roberts & Zuckerman 345–46.

their guilt, and administer punishment.[37] Modern states are so complex that the censure of wrongdoing and vindication of the rights of victims cannot remain a matter of private dispute settlement between the victim and offender.[38] A state that respects individuals is obliged to have an apparatus to vindicate the rights of those individuals when others in the community breach those rights by criminal acts.[39] Without the apparatus of police and courts, the role of enforcing shared standards of proper conduct would fall to individuals and only the strong would be able to protect themselves. It is in part for this reason that individuals in a modern state forego the right to use force in return for the promise of protection from the state.[40] Moreover, if vindication of breached rights was left to individuals there would be no institution capable of making authoritative determinations on when the standards of conduct had been breached, and so punishment for offences would result in cycles of revenge violence. Even in the most minimalist conception of the role of the state, there is recognition that the state must be responsible for criminal justice.[41]

A modern state is therefore obliged to operate a criminal justice system. At the same time, it is obliged to conduct the system in a manner that minimises the risks of wrongful conviction. The presumption of innocence is a vital feature of criminal trials that aims to protect the innocent. Of course, it is not the only principle that aims to protect the innocent.[42] All the aspects of a 'fair trial' such as the right to know the charges, the right to present evidence, and the right to cross-examine witnesses are instrumental in protecting the innocent. Specifically, there are three ways in which a rule placing the burden of proof on the prosecution and requiring proof beyond reasonable doubt helps to protect the innocent by reducing (but not eliminating) the risk of wrongful conviction: (1) it allocates the burden of proof to the party with the greater resources; (2) it acts to counter a tendency in criminal trials to assume the guilt of the defendant and to discount the defendant's evidence; and (3) it allocates the risk of non-persuasion to the prosecution.

The first contribution of the presumption of innocence is to allocate the burden of proof to the party with the greater resources. As we saw above, the state is responsible for operating a system of criminal justice designed to prevent crimes and to detect and punish offenders. As part of this apparatus, the state has access to resources that

[37] Cf W de Haan *The Politics of Redress: Crime, Punishment and Penal Abolition* (Unwin Hyman, London 1990); T Mathiesen *The Politics of Abolition: Essays in Political Action* (Martin Robertson, Oxford 1974).

[38] *Cf* N Christie 'Conflicts as Property' (1977) 17 *BJ Crim* 1. Christie argues that the criminal justice system appropriates a dispute that is properly between victim and offender.

[39] J Gardner 'Punishment—in Proportion and in Perspective' in A Ashworth & M Wasik (eds) *Fundamentals of Sentencing Theory* (OUP, Oxford 1998) 31.

[40] See generally D Boucher & P Kelly (eds) *The Social Contract from Hobbes to Rawls* (Routledge, London 1994).

[41] R Nozick *Anarchy, State and Utopia* (Basil Blackwell, Oxford 1974) esp chs 2, 4–5.

[42] Here, I refer to the legally innocent, rather than the morally innocent. Efforts to define criminal offences so that the substantive law criminalises only the morally innocent are also important. Whether these efforts should be pursued under the banner of the presumption of innocence is a topic addressed in Ch 3.

are vastly superior to those available to most defendants.[43] The state has a dedicated force of professional investigators who have both the labour-capacity and the legal powers to conduct extensive inquiries to discern facts surrounding a crime. The state has access to technological facilities such as DNA-profiling and forensics experts who are capable of deriving convincing testimony from small amounts of physical evidence. By contrast, the individual defendant typically does not have the resources to employ these types of techniques to establish his or her innocence. If the defendant bore the burden of proof, the lack of access to resources necessary to prove innocence could lead to convictions contrary to the merits. On this reasoning, the prosecution should be required to prove guilt because it has the greater resources. The disparity of resources is not a complete explanation for placing the burden of proof on the prosecution. The problem of disparity could be mitigated by other means such as placing greater facilities at the defendant's disposal, free of charge. However, in the context of a system where one side nearly always has greater resources than the other it is right to acknowledge the resources imbalance. Further, the following two contributions of the presumption of innocence would be indispensable even if the resources imbalance were corrected.

The second contribution of the presumption of innocence is to counteract a tendency to discount the evidence of the defendant and to assume his or her guilt. Defendants might be thought to have an advantage over the prosecution in that they have direct knowledge of their own actions in relation to a crime. However, this advantage tends to be neutralised because knowledge of facts does not equate to ease of proof of those facts. In particular, juries may give only a limited weight to the testimony of the defendant since the defendant has an obvious personal interest in the outcome of the trial.[44] That is, the defendant's testimony may be treated as less credible because the defendant has a motivation to lie in order to avoid imprisonment.[45] Further, a defendant may be faced with an assumption that he or she is more likely guilty than innocent because otherwise he or she would not have been placed on trial.[46] Carleton Allen observed over seventy years ago:[47]

> The magnanimous disposition of our law towards the accused is the more striking because it is perfectly well known to every intelligent person that the vast majority of accused persons are guilty of the crimes with which they are charged. Assuming general

[43] P Roberts 'Taking the Burden of Proof Seriously' [1995] *Crim LR* 783, 787.

[44] The defendant was not competent to give evidence until 1898: see Criminal Evidence Act 1898, s 1. Similarly, parties to a civil case were excluded from giving evidence prior to 1843, on the ground that they had an interest in the outcome of the case: see Evidence Act 1843.

[45] D Dripps 'The Constitutional Status of the Reasonable Doubt Rule' (1987) 75 *California Law Review* 1665, 1695.

[46] AA Putnam *Ten Years a Police Court Judge* (Funk & Wagnells, New York 1884) 207–08: 'It is greatly to be feared that the so-called presumption of innocence in favor of the prisoner at the bar is a pretence, a delusion, and empty sound. It ought not to be, but—it is . . . How can a person be presumed innocent who is presumably guilty? The fact that he is restrained of his liberty presumes guilt. There is no other construction to be placed on the restraint. Human nature is not capable of any other. Yet human nature ought to presume innocence until the contrary is proved.'

[47] CK Allen *Legal Duties and Other Essays in Jurisprudence* (Clarendon Press, Oxford 1931) 255 (original emphasis).

> confidence in the police system—and there is considerable, though perhaps increasingly critical, confidence in it in England—it is very difficult to resist the impression that if a man is in the dock, there is *probably* a very good reason for his being there.

Due to assumptions of this kind, a defendant may well face the practical need to prove his or her innocence even if the formal burden of proof is on the prosecution. The prospect that the defendant will be declared guilty merely because he or she has been accused is the nightmare scenario of criminal justice.[48] Placing the burden of proof on the prosecution, and reminding the fact-finder that the prosecution must prove guilt is a means of adjusting for the institutional bias against defendants.[49]

The third and most important contribution of a rule requiring the prosecution to prove guilt beyond reasonable doubt is that it ensures the risk of non-persuasion is borne by the prosecution and not the defendant. If the defendant bears the burden of proof on any matter that is determinative of the outcome of a trial, the fact-finder will be required to convict even if undecided about that matter. That is, the fact-finder will convict even after concluding that it is just as likely as not that the defendant is innocent. Lord Steyn articulated this danger while discussing a persuasive burden of proof placed on the defendant in *Lambert*:[50]

> It necessarily involves the risk that, if the jury are faithful to the judge's direction, they may convict where the accused has not discharged the legal burden resting on him but left them unsure on the point . . . If the jury is in doubt on this issue, they must convict him. This may occur when an accused adduces sufficient evidence to raise a doubt about his guilt but the jury is not convinced on a balance or probabilities that his account is true. Indeed it obliges the court to convict if the version of the accused is as likely to be true as not.

There is a severe moral problem when a defendant can be convicted even though there is no clear cut evidence of guilt, and an even more obvious problem when the defendant can be convicted even though it is just as likely as not that he or she is innocent.[51] Of course, the allocation of the persuasive burden will not be determinative of the outcome in every case. But since it cannot be determined in advance when the allocation of the burden will be crucial it is necessary to have a consistent rule placing the risk of non-persuasion on the prosecution. This has the practical effect of protecting the innocent by ensuring that only the highest standard of certainty concerning guilt will suffice.

Related to the allocation of the burden of proof is the requirement of proof beyond reasonable doubt. The reasonable doubt standard denotes the highest

[48] See F Kafka, W & E Muir (trs) *The Trial* (Vintage, London 1999) 139: 'But they all agree on one thing, that charges are never made frivolously, and that the Court, once it has brought a charge against someone, is firmly convinced of the guilt of the accused and can be dislodged from that conviction only with the greatest difficulty.'

[49] BD Underwood 'The Thumb on the Scales of Justice: Burdens of Persuasion in Criminal Cases' (1977) 86 *Yale Law Journal (YLJ)* 1299, 1306–07.

[50] *R v Lambert* [2002] 2 AC 545 (HL) [37]–[38] (Lord Steyn).

[51] P Roberts, 'Strict Liability and the Presumption of Innocence: An Exposé of Functionalist Assumptions' in AP Simester (ed) *Appraising Strict Liability* (OUP, Oxford 2005) 151, 188–89.

degree of certainty that can be attained in relation to past events in reliance upon the testimony of others.[52] Like the allocation of the persuasive burden to the prosecution, the reasonable doubt standard operates to reduce the likelihood of wrongful convictions. However, it does not do this by promoting the overall accuracy of trials: the reasonable doubt standard reduces the risk of wrongful convictions but also increases the risk of wrongful acquittals.[53] Hence, the reasonable doubt standard has been described as a 'steeply asymmetrical standard of proof'.[54] Adoption of the reasonable doubt standard represents a value judgment that conviction of the innocent is a greater evil than acquittal of the guilty. As Lord Clyde stated in *Lambert*: 'if any error is to be made in the weighing of the scales of justice it should be to the effect that the guilty should go free rather than that an innocent person should be wrongly convicted.'[55]

One reason for making this value judgment is that the interest of the defendant in the outcome of the case is greater than the interest of the prosecution. The defendant faces all the negative consequences of conviction including punishment, censure and stigmatisation: most seriously the defendant may face the deprivation of liberty. This distinguishes a criminal trial from a civil trial when, in general, the risk of losing the case is equal for both sides.[56] As the United States Supreme Court has stated:[57]

> There is always in litigation a margin of error, representing error in fact finding, which both parties must take into account. Where one party has at stake an interest of transcending value—as a criminal defendant his liberty—this margin of error is reduced as to him by the process of placing on the other party the burden of producing a sufficiency of proof in the first instance, and of persuading the fact finder at the conclusion of the trial of his guilt beyond a reasonable doubt.

Further, when the criminal justice system errs by convicting an innocent person, the consequences of the error fall entirely upon the wrongfully convicted person. By contrast, when the system errs in favour of acquitting the guilty, the consequences caused by the failure to register disapproval for the wrongful conduct are diffused over the whole of society.[58] The victim of the crime might suffer more acutely than others as a result of the wrongful acquittal, although this is a difficult harm to assess.[59] In any case, the consequence does not rest solely upon the

[52] See Ch 1, 19–21.

[53] D Hamer 'The Presumption of Innocence and Reverse Burdens: A Balancing Act' (2007) 66 *CLJ* 142, 148; D Hamer 'Probabilistic Standards of Proof, Their Complements, and the Errors that are Expected to Flow from Them' (2004) 1 *University of New England Law Journal* 71, 87–95.

[54] Roberts & Zuckerman 351.

[55] [2002] 2 AC 545 (HL) [156].

[56] Dworkin (see n 34 above) 210; A Ashworth & M Redmayne, *The Criminal Process* 3rd edn (OUP, Oxford 2005) 23–24.

[57] *Speiser v Randall*, 357 US 513, 525–26 (1958) (Brennan J, for the Court).

[58] Ashworth (see n 7 above) 113.

[59] M Redmayne 'Rethinking the Privilege Against Self-Incrimination' (2007) 27 *OJLS* 209, 227. See also A Ashworth 'Victim Impact Statements and Sentencing [1993] *Crim LR* 498; A Ashworth 'Victims' Rights, Defendants' Rights and Criminal Procedure' in A Crawford and J Goodey (eds) *Integrating a Victim Perspective within Criminal Justice* (Ashgate, Dartmouth 2000) 185.

victim. These reflections are ultimately what underline the ancient and oft-affirmed maxim that it is better for the guilty to go free than for the innocent to be convicted.[60] Placing the burden of proof on the prosecution and adopting the standard of proof beyond reasonable doubt give effect to the value judgment that the risk of non-persuasion should be borne by the prosecution.

2. Promoting the Rule of Law

As well as its instrumental value in protecting the innocent from wrongful conviction, the presumption of innocence promotes the rule of law by insisting that conviction and punishment be reserved for cases where the guilt of the defendant is clearly demonstrated. There is no agreed definition of all that is required by the rule of law.[61] However, any version of the rule of law requires, at a minimum, that state action against an individual conform to pre-ordained legal standards capable of interpretation and application by the courts.[62] In the context of the criminal law, this manifests itself in the proposition that a person must not be subjected to criminal sanctions unless that person has been shown to have breached a generally applicable and pre-ordained legal prohibition.[63]

By imposing the burden of proof on the prosecution and insisting on proof beyond reasonable doubt, the presumption of innocence seeks to ensure sufficient certainty that the defendant has, in fact, breached a legal prohibition. If people were to be subjected to criminal sanctions without proof that they were guilty, the rule of law would be undermined: there would be the ever-present prospect that criminal sanctions were being imposed on the innocent, and people could not conduct their affairs in the confidence that they were safe from unjustified coercive interference by the state. This section aims to explain in greater detail why the presumption of innocence is integral to the rule of law. It will be suggested that there are two explanations for this: (1) the presumption of innocence ensures that guilt is publicly demonstrated; and (2) the presumption of innocence reduces the likelihood that a conviction will communicate a false message.

[60] See ch 1, 3.

[61] In particular, there is disagreement over whether the rule of law is a formal/procedural concept or a concept encompassing substantive protections: see P Craig 'Formal and Substantive Conceptions of the Rule of Law: An Analytical Framework' [1997] *PL* 467; D Dyzenhaus 'Form and Substance in the Rule of Law: A Democratic Justification for Judicial Review?' in C Forsyth (ed) *Judicial Review and the Constitution* (Hart, Oxford 2000) 141; J Raz 'The Rule of Law and its Virtue' (1977) 93 *LQR* 195.

[62] J Locke *Two Treatises of Government* (CUP, Cambridge 1967) (original 1690) II, xi, para 136: 'the legislative or supreme authority cannot assume to itself a power to rule by extemporary arbitrary decrees, but is bound to dispense justice and decide the rights of the subject by promulgated standing laws, and known authorised judges.'

[63] By 'pre-ordained', I do not mean that retrospective prohibitions are necessarily contrary to the rule of law, but rather that the legal prohibition must be laid down in a generally applicable law prior to the imposition of conviction and punishment. The antithesis of the rule of law, on this conception, is the bill of attainder, by which the legislature declares that a particular individual is to be subject to punishment: see *Liyange v R* [1967] 1 AC 259 (PC): *Kable v DPP (NSW)* (1996) 189 CLR 51 (HCA).

In a criminal trial, the prosecution is the proponent of guilt. The purpose of the trial is to determine whether the defendant is guilty of the conduct attributed to him or her by the prosecutor and, accordingly, whether the imposition of censure and punishment is justified. Unless the prosecution demonstrates that the conduct of the defendant falls within a legal prohibition, the justification for censure and punishment has not been made out. Criminal procedures which are designed to ensure that individuals may be subjected to conviction and punishment only when it is proved that they have contravened the criminal law are necessary for the legitimacy of any state. This goes beyond ensuring that the innocent are protected and touches upon the 'the proper conception of the relationship between the State and its citizens'.[64] It is not for the citizen to prove that the state has no right to take punitive action against him or her. It is for the state to prove that conviction and punishment is justified in relation to the individual citizen.

The demonstration by the prosecutor of the guilt of the defendant ensures the continued justification of the criminal justice system.[65] As we saw above, the hard treatment, censure and stigma meted out by the courts are justified only when the defendant is, in fact, guilty. In accordance with the rule of law, guilt must be demonstrated and not simply assumed. Without that demonstration, the system arrogates to itself the power to take arbitrary and unexplained action against the individual. This is the reason why trials should occur in public, why the prosecution must present evidence and bear the burden of proof and why the guilt of the defendant must be established beyond reasonable doubt. Unless these things are done, there is an unacceptable risk that the negative consequences associated with conviction are being imposed without justification. Even if the defendant is, in fact, guilty, the absence of clear demonstration from the prosecution that the defendant is guilty undermines the justification for the conviction. Placing the burden of proof on the prosecution, so that the grounds of criminal liability are publicly demonstrated, ensures that the justification for the conviction is sufficiently clear, both to the offender and to the public.

The rationale for the presumption of innocence is sometimes couched in terms of maintaining the 'moral force' of the criminal law. For example, in *Re Winship*,[66] Brennan J of the United States Supreme Court stated:[67]

> [U]se of the reasonable-doubt standard is indispensable to command the respect and confidence of the community in applications of the criminal law. It is critical that the moral force of the criminal law not be diluted by a standard of proof that leaves people in doubt whether innocent men are being condemned.

Put in this way, the presumption of innocence is essential to ensure that people do not lose confidence in the justice system. At the most extreme, if people lost confidence in the system they might be unwilling to co-operate as witnesses or as

[64] Ashworth (see n 7 above) 249.
[65] Dennis 51.
[66] 397 US 358 (1970).
[67] Ibid 364.

jurors and the system would be unable to operate. However, this is an unstable way of stating the rationale for the presumption of innocence.[68] To begin with, there is no way of determining how much each wrongful conviction might undermine public confidence in the system of justice. Further, it must be remembered that insistence on the presumption of innocence increases the likelihood of wrongful acquittals. The acquittal of the guilty can undermine public confidence in the criminal justice system just as assuredly as the conviction of the innocent. There is grave public concern when a person perceived as guilty is set free and public disgust is further aggravated if that person goes on to commit other crimes. Reliance upon public confidence does not explain why criminal procedure should be tilted in favour of the defendant. It is not the threat that the criminal justice system will be undermined in the eyes of the public that motivates the presumption of innocence; it is the risk that the criminal justice system will, in fact, be unjustified.

In addition to the demonstration of guilt, the presumption of innocence promotes the rule of law by reducing the risk that a criminal conviction will communicate a false message concerning the defendant. A criminal conviction and the attendant punishment have an 'expressive function'.[69] First, conviction and punishment communicate to the defendant the disapprobation, censure, disapproval or blame of the community concerning his or her conduct.[70] Second, through the conviction, the court communicates to criminal justice officials that certain types of treatment are now appropriate toward the defendant. Most obviously, officials are authorised to carry out any judicially approved punishment, but there is also an effect on the way the convicted person is treated in the future, for example, in the possible use of the conviction at a later trial. Third, the conviction communicates to members of the community that the convicted person is an offender against the legally required standards of behaviour.[71] It is vital that the messages communicated by the criminal justice system are honest. To facilitate honest communication in the message sent by a conviction it is important that the conviction is preceded by the public and certain demonstration of guilt. In the absence of this, there is a risk that the criminal justice system will communicate a falsehood concerning the defendant.

The nature of the falsehood is obvious when the defendant is in fact innocent of the crime: an innocent person is declared to be guilty. In addition, when the

[68] See A Ashworth, *Human Rights, Serious Crime and Criminal Procedure* (Sweet & Maxwell, London 2002) 113–14.

[69] J Feinberg 'The Expressive Function of Punishment' in J Feinberg, *Doing and Deserving: Essays in the Theory of Responsibility* (Princeton University Press, Princeton 1970) 95. *Cf* M Adler 'Expressive Theories of Law: A Skeptical Overview' (2000) 148 *University of Pennsylvannia Law Review* 1363.

[70] Douglas Husak describes the content of what is expressed as 'condemnation': D Husak 'Limitations on Criminalization and the General Part of Criminal Law' in S Shute & AP Simester (eds) *Criminal Law Theory: Doctrines of the General Part* (OUP, Oxford 2002) 13, 26–27. Victor Tadros favours 'indignation' as the best description: V Tadros 'Recklessness and the Duty to Take Care' in S Shute & AP Simester (eds) *Criminal Law Theory: Doctrines of the General Part* (OUP, Oxford 2002) 227, 242.

[71] On communication to the defendant, officials and the community see V Tadros *Criminal Responsibility* (Oxford, OUP 2005) 71–73.

burden of proof is placed on a defendant, there is a risk that the court may communicate falsely, even if the defendant is guilty. One objective of a criminal trial is to deliver a morally authoritative determination of the guilt of the defendant and his or her fitness for punishment.[72] In accordance with this objective the criminal justice system makes claims to moral authority. The pronouncements of the court are not advisory, tentative or provisional. A criminal conviction purports to carry the authority of the court's own careful and fair examination of the merits of a charge, and the court's considered view that the defendant is guilty. The message conveyed is that the court is satisfied of the defendant's guilt. Following the court's determination, the conviction is treated in later cases as providing presumptive evidence of guilt.[73]

However, when a conviction is obtained in reliance upon a reverse burden of proof it is not necessarily the case that the court was satisfied of guilt. It may have been that the court was undecided regarding some matter the defendant was required to prove and therefore made a declaration of guilt in accordance with the risk of non-persuasion entailed by the allocation of the burden of proof. Nonetheless, the criminal conviction does not carry any of this sense of ambiguity. In this sense, a reverse burden of proof can lead the court to communicate falsely. While the conviction signals the court's satisfaction of the guilt of the defendant there may in fact be no such satisfaction. This problem is particularly acute if the conviction follows the decision of a jury, when no reasons are given for the verdict. The prospect of false communication is a threat to the rule of law because it undermines the authoritative nature of the court's pronouncement of guilt.

B. Limitation of the Presumption

Having set out the dual rationale for the presumption of innocence it is now possible to consider whether the presumption ought to be subject to limitation. The proportionality analysis, in the words of Lord Hope, requires that 'a fair balance must be struck between the demands of the general interest of the community and the protection of the fundamental rights of the individual'.[74] By adopting proportionality as the touchstone of compliance with Article 6(2), the English courts have accepted that, in principle, the presumption of innocence is subject to limitation when there is a competing community interest. This approach assumes that any limitation of an individual right can be justified if the conflicting community interest is sufficiently strong. This Part will argue that the presumption of

[72] Dennis 49–55.

[73] Hence, for example, s 74(3) of the Police and Criminal Evidence Act 1984 creates a presumption in later judicial proceedings that a person convicted of an offence committed that offence, unless the contrary is proved. In accordance with Pt 11 of the Criminal Justice Act 2003, the conviction is then admissible in certain circumstances as evidence of a defendant's bad character.

[74] *R v DPP; ex p Kebilene* [2000] 2 AC 326 (HL) 384.

innocence protects values of such fundamental importance that, in general, it cannot be limited on the basis of a competing public interest. Proportionality analysis, incorporating considerations of the community interest, should be invoked as a ground for limiting the rights of defendants only when there is a minimal threat to the values protected by the presumption of innocence. This Part will sketch this approach to limitation of the presumption of innocence in broad outline, leaving the details to be worked out elsewhere, mostly in Chapters Five and Six.

1. Limitation of Rights

In recent years, legal theorists have paid much attention to the question of the extent to which individual rights are subject to limitation in pursuit of other objectives, most commonly objectives associated with the interests of the community. At one end of the spectrum, rights are perceived as a contingent articulation of individual interests that must always be 'balanced' against other competing interests. David Beatty is a key proponent of this position.[75] Another theorist well-known for espousing a theory of 'balancing' is Robert Alexy.[76] Alexy argues that rights are 'optimisation requirements'[77] that must be recognised when pursuing other goals to the fullest extent compatible with the realization of those goals. By contrast, other theorists urge that rights are not merely optimisation requirements but that they should take priority over other interests. For instance, Jürgen Habermas treats rights as a 'firewall' between the interests of the individual and the interests of the community.[78] Similarly, Ronald Dworkin argues that: 'Rights are best understood as trumps over some background justification for political decisions that state a goal for the community as a whole.'[79]

The debate over the correct way to treat rights is a deeply complicated philosophical conundrum which cannot be resolved here.[80] This chapter will focus instead on the specific question of whether the community interest ought to be 'balanced' against the presumption of innocence. However, it is important to note that even the most ardent defenders of rights against the vagaries of 'balancing' accept that, in some situations, rights might be subject to limitation. Dworkin, for

[75] D Beatty *The Ultimate Rule of Law* (OUP, Oxford 2004) esp 171: 'Indeed, when judges rely on the principle of proportionality to structure their thinking the concept of rights disappears . . . When rights are factored into an analysis organised around the principle of proportionality, they have no special force as trumps. They are really just a rhetorical flourish.'

[76] R Alexy, J Rivers (trans) *A Theory of Constitutional Rights* (OUP, Oxford 2002) ch 3 and Postscript.

[77] R Alexy 'Constitutional Rights, Balancing and Rationality' (2003) 16 *Ratio Juris* 131, 135.

[78] J Habermas, W Regh (trans) *Between Facts and Norms* (Polity Press, Cambridge 1996) 256–59.

[79] R Dworkin 'Rights as Trumps' in J Waldron (ed) *Theories of Rights* (OUP, Oxford 1984) 153, 153.

[80] A good discussion is found in M Kumm 'Political Liberalism and the Structure of Rights: On the Place and Limits of the Proportionality Requirement' in G Pavlakos (ed) *Law, Rights and Discourse: The Legal Philosophy of Robert Alexy* (Hart, Oxford 2007) 131.

example, identifies three situations in which he considers it would be acceptable to place limits on rights.[81]

> I can think of only three sorts of grounds that can consistently be used to limit the definition of a particular right. First, the Government might show that the values protected by the original right are not really at stake in the marginal case, or are at stake only in some attenuated form. Second, it might show that if the right is defined to include the marginal case, then some competing right, in the strong sense I described earlier, would be abridged. Third, it might show that if the right were so defined, then the cost to society would not be simply incremental, but would be of a degree far beyond the cost paid to grant the original right, a degree great enough to justify whatever assault on dignity or equality might be involved.

In one form or another, each of these scenarios will be addressed below. In respect of the first category, it will be argued that the rationale for the presumption of innocence is 'attenuated' when the risk of wrongful conviction is low, or when the consequences of wrongful conviction are low because the penalty is minimal. As to the second category, involving a clash of rights, I will deal with arguments that a wrongful acquittal can be seen as impinging on the rights of the victims, or on the rights of the others in the community to be safe from crimes. In respect of the third category, I will consider whether some crimes are so dangerous to society that persons suspected of involvement in them should be subject to imprisonment even in the absence of proof beyond reasonable doubt that they are guilty.

Before examining scenarios in which it has been argued that reverse burdens are acceptable, there are some features of criminal procedure rights that ought to be emphasised. First, in the context of criminal justice, the state is the 'singular antagonist of the individual'.[82] That is, the state proposes to take direct action against the defendant in the form of criminal sanctions. This feature distinguishes criminal procedure rights from rights which involve demands for distributive justice. By this I mean what are sometimes termed social and economic rights such as a right to housing or a right to an education. In the case of these rights, a demand is made on the state to make provision, whereas in the context of criminal procedure the state is called upon to refrain from exercising its coercive powers in an unjust way. In the latter case, the obligation of the state to respect rights ought to be enforced more stringently, on the principle that it is worse to cause harm by direct action than to allow it to occur by omission.[83]

[81] R Dworkin *Taking Rights Seriously* (Duckworth, London 1977) 200.

[82] *Irwin Toy Ltd v Quebec (AG)* [1989] 1 SCR 927, 994; *R v Laba* [1994] 3 SCR 965, 1009 (Sopinka J, for the Court).

[83] This is not to say that governments and individuals are not at all responsible for omissions. On positive obligations of states under the ECHR see: K Starmer 'Positive Rights under the Convention' in J Jowell & J Cooper (eds) *Understanding Human Rights Principles* (Oxford, Hart 2001) 139. On individual criminal responsibility for omissions see V Tadros *Criminal Responsibility* (OUP, Oxford 2005) ch 7; A Ashworth 'The Scope of Criminal Liability for Omissions' (1989) 105 *LQR* 424; AP Simester 'Why Omissions are Special' (1995) 1 *Legal Theory* 311; P Smith 'Omission and Responsibility in Legal Theory' (2003) 9 *Legal Theory* 221.

Second, criminal procedure can result in the deprivation of physical liberty through imprisonment. Short of execution, this is the most extreme form of interference that the state can exercise over the individual. As Joseph Raz states, 'The coercion of criminal penalties is a global and indiscriminate invasion of autonomy.'[84] Physical liberty is a prerequisite for the ability of an individual to exercise decisions over the course of his or her life. It is essential to autonomy: a person imprisoned is deprived (for the period of imprisonment) of the ability to fashion his or her life through a successive series of decisions.[85] Hence, when a person is faced with deprivation of liberty the most stringent standards must be followed to ensure that the person is properly subject to that restriction.[86]

The special character of criminal procedure rights is reflected in the language of the ECHR. Under the ECHR, the rights of fair criminal procedure in Article 6 are not made subject to any express limitations.[87] By contrast, the ECHR in Articles 8–11 makes the right to privacy, freedom of religion and conscience, freedom of expression and freedom of association subject to general limiting provisions. The special character of criminal procedure rights must be kept in mind when considering whether the right to be presumed innocent should be 'balanced' against the interests of the community.

2. Threat of Serious Crime

There is a fundamental tension in a liberal state between the need to protect citizens through the criminal law and the need to protect the rights of defendants. The presumption of innocence accords recognition to the principle that the criminal justice system must operate in a manner that minimises wrongful convictions. This is because wrongful conviction deprives the individual of his or her right to be treated as an independent moral agent. However, the only way of avoiding all wrongful convictions would be to have no criminal justice system at all. This position is unacceptable in a liberal state because a criminal justice system is necessary so that breaches of individual rights can be censured and punished, and so that individuals are protected against further invasions of rights.[88] Maintaining a criminal justice system in the knowledge that, however carefully the system operates, some wrongful convictions are inevitable represents a decision that the right not to be wrongfully convicted is not absolute: it must give way at least to the extent of having a criminal justice system.

[84] J Raz 'Autonomy, Toleration and Harm Principle' in R Gavison (ed) *Issues in Contemporary Legal Philosophy* (Clarendon Press, Oxford 1987) 313, 331.

[85] Ibid. See also J Raz *The Morality of Freedom* (OUP, Oxford 1986) chs 14–15.

[86] R Dworkin *Is Democracy Possible Here?* (Princeton University Press, Princeton 2006) 44.

[87] Although the Strasbourg Court has found 'implied limitations' to Art 6 rights: eg *Ashingdane v UK* (App No 8225/78) (1985) 7 EHRR 528 [57]. See criticism of 'implied limitations' in R Clayton & H Tomlinson *The Law of Human Rights* (OUP, Oxford 2000) [6.114]–[6.122].

[88] Roberts & Zuckerman 347.

Once this foothold on the limitation of the right to avoid wrongful conviction is established the argument can proceed further. In the case of dangerous crimes, the 'balance' to be struck between individual liberty and the community interest shifts. If we are prepared to countenance the risk of wrongful conviction in order to have a criminal justice system, we might be prepared to accept an increased risk of wrongful conviction when the danger to society from certain crimes is greater than usual. Reverse burdens of proof are a limitation on the presumption of innocence which makes it harder for the guilty to escape conviction. Should they be permitted when there is an enhanced community interest in ensuring that the guilty are convicted? Reasoning of this kind is not new. Responding to Blackstone's 10:1 maxim, James Stephen argued that: 'Everything depends on what the guilty men have been doing, and something depends on the way in which the innocent man came to be suspected.'[89] To this, Carleton Allen added that: 'It also depends on the general social conditions in which they have been doing it.'[90] More recently, Michael Dorf has stated: 'I think that people are a little nervous about applying that maxim where the 10 guilty men who are going to go free could have biological weapons.'[91]

Before going further, we must clarify what is meant by a 'danger to society'. At the highest end of the spectrum are dangers so heinous and so far-reaching in their effects that they threaten the very existence of society. To cater for such situations, Article 15 of the ECHR permits a state to derogate from most of the rights protected by the Convention, including the Article 6 rights, '[i]n time of war or other public emergency threatening the life of the nation'.[92] Consequently, the ECHR is not a 'suicide pact' requiring states to remain impotent in the face of existential threats.[93] The UK Government has availed itself of the power to derogate from the ECHR, most notably in ordering indefinite detention,[94] and later 'control orders' for suspected terrorists.[95] When the state acts under the derogation power, there is no pretext that procedural rights under Article 6, including the presumption of innocence, are being upheld. The application of the right is simply suspended for the duration of the emergency. The conditions under which rights may be suspended due to a 'threat to the life of the nation' are controversial.[96] However, we

[89] JF Stephen *A History of the Criminal Law of England* (London, MacMillan 1883) 438.

[90] Allen (see n 47 above) 286.

[91] Quoted in J Waldron 'Security and Liberty: The Image of Balance' (2003) 11 *Journal of Political Philosophy* 191, 204.

[92] The derogation will also take effect under the HRA in accordance with ss 14–17.

[93] Cf R Posner *Not a Suicide Pact: The Constitution in a Time of National Emergency* (OUP, New York 2006).

[94] See *A v Secretary of State for the Home Department* [2005] 2 AC 68 (HL), finding that indefinite detention was not 'strictly required' in accordance with Art 15.

[95] Prevention of Terrorism Act 2005. See the interpretation of this Act in *Secretary of State for the Home Department v MB and AF* [2008] AC 440 (HL); *Secretary of State for the Home Department v AF* [2009] UKHL 28.

[96] See D Dyzenhaus *The Constitution of Law: Legality in a Time of Emergency* (CUP, Cambridge 2006); B Ackerman 'The Emergency Constitution' (2004) 113 *YLJ* 1029; O Gross 'Chaos and Rules: Should Responses to Violent Crises Always be Constitutional? (2003) 112 *YLJ* 1011; D Cole 'The Priority of Morality: The Emergency Constitution's Blind Spot' (2004) 113 *YLJ* 173; LH Tribe & P Gudridge 'The Anti-Emergency Constitution' (2004) 113 *YLJ* 1801.

are concerned here with cases where the state purports to respect the presumption of innocence while still using a reverse burden, rather than cases where the right is suspended.

Lower down the spectrum are crimes which could have extremely deleterious effects on society, but fall short of constituting an existential threat. Terrorist offences are the most obvious candidate in this category. Terrorist attacks targeted at civilians or civilian infrastructure, even if not a threat to the life of the nation, can have catastrophic consequences. Accordingly, the courts have cited the threat of terrorism as a justification for imposing reverse burdens.[97] In the context of reverse burdens, the courts have also emphasised the serious and dangerous nature of drug-trafficking due to its widespread effects and connection with other criminal activity.[98] The question arises whether it is proper to insist upon minimising the risks of wrongful convictions, even if the consequences of failure to control such offences could be serious and far-reaching.

Another manifestation of the community interest is in the case of regulatory regimes that pursue important public goals, such as road traffic safety. In these cases, it is not the danger of individual acts that is invoked to justify reduced procedural protections, but rather the wide-spread nature of the regulated activity, and the benefits to society to be derived from compliance with the regime. The courts have argued that the benefits to society from the proper regulation of certain activities outweigh the risk of wrongful convictions.[99] It is not hard to imagine that the classes of offences falling within the scope of this argument could be very large.

Finally, it is possible to envisage a point at which the criminal justice system is obtaining so few convictions that it ceases to be effective as a means of enforcing moral norms. As Carleton Allen observed, if the guilty are escaping conviction in sufficiently great numbers 'there comes a point when the whole system of justice has broken down and society is in a state of chaos.'[100] Similarly, in *Secretary of State for the Home Department v AF*,[101] Lord Hoffmann stated:[102]

> It is sometimes said that it is better for ten guilty men to be acquitted than for one innocent man to be convicted. Sometimes it is a hundred guilty men. The figures matter. A system of justice which allowed a thousand guilty men to go free for fear of convicting one innocent man might not adequately protect the public.

Following this reasoning, if the integrity of the criminal justice system, or some part of the system, is at risk, it might be argued that it is justifiable to alter the balance away from the protection of individual rights towards the interest in obtaining more convictions.

[97] *R v DPP; ex p Kebilene* [2000] 2 AC 326 (HL) 386–87 (Lord Hope).
[98] *R v Lambert* [2002] 2 AC 545 (HL) [153] (Lord Clyde), [190] (Lord Hutton).
[99] *R v S* [2003] 1 Cr App R 35 (CA) [48] (Rose LJ); *R v Johnstone* [2003] 1 WLR 1736 (HL) [52] (Lord Nicholls); *Sheldrake v DPP* [2004] QB 487 (QBD) [112] (Henriques J, dissenting).
[100] Allen (see n 47 above) 287.
[101] *Secretary of State for the Home Department v AF* [2009] UKHL 28.
[102] Ibid [74].

One obvious problem with this type of reasoning is that criminal procedure rights are designed to ensure that it is only the guilty who are subject to criminal sanctions. Limiting criminal procedure rights has the effect of increasing the likelihood that the innocent will be prosecuted and convicted. The state does not have any legitimate interest in convicting the innocent. It only has an interest in convicting the guilty. Indeed, convicting the innocent may be counterproductive from the point of view of the state as it leaves the true culprits at large and able to commit further offences. Of course, no one advocates the conviction of people whom we know to be innocent. Rather, the 'balancing' argument holds that a higher number of inadvertent wrongful convictions is a satisfactory price to pay for preventing negative consequences such catastrophic or dangerous crimes, or a general ineffectiveness in the justice system.

This form of 'balancing' is an inappropriate response to the perceived risks. To begin with, the initial calculation of the criminal procedure rights that a defendant is entitled to expect takes into account the seriousness of crime and the need to obtain convictions. In deciding that the prosecution should prove guilt beyond reasonable doubt, it has already been determined that the interest of the defendant in avoiding wrongful conviction outweighs the interest of the state in obtaining a conviction. To deliberately operate a system which countenances the conviction of people in the absence of proof beyond reasonable doubt treats those individuals as a means in the struggle against crime, rather than an end in themselves.

There are three other objections to the balancing of individual rights against the rights of the community.[103] First, the reduction of the rights of defendants has a disproportionate impact on certain individuals. The people whose rights are trammeled tend to come from a particular class, race or religion leading to the allegation that the rights of some groups count for less than the rights of others.[104] Second, when defendants' rights are restricted there is the risk that the state will use its increased power over defendants not only in cases involving catastrophic consequences but also in less serious cases. Hence, the limitation of the right that is said to be justified in order to protect people against a particularly serious crime is in fact used in relation to other less serious crimes.[105] Third, the 'balancing' argument assumes that the reduction of the defendant's rights will have the desired consequence. In fact, convicting certain defendants in the absence of proof beyond reasonable doubt only incrementally reduces the risk of catastrophic crimes and debilitating crimes. Other measures are necessary to offer more complete protection against these crimes. A greater 'feeling' of safety cannot be a reason for restricting the right of the individual to be treated as innocent.

[103] These points are each made in Waldron (see n 91 above). See also A Ashworth 'Security, Terrorism and the Value of Human Rights' in L Lazarus & B Goold *Security and Human Rights* (Hart Publishing, Oxford 2007) 203, 209–10; L Zedner 'Securing Liberty in the Face of Terror' (2005) 32 *Journal of Law and Society (J L & Soc)* 507; L Zedner 'Seeking Security by Eroding Rights: The Side-Stepping of Due Process' in L Lazarus & B Goold *Security and Human Rights* (Hart Publishing, Oxford 2007) 257.

[104] D Luban 'Eight Fallacies about Liberty and Security' in RA Wilson (ed) *Human Rights in the 'War on Terror'* (CUP, Cambridge 2005) 242, 243–44.

[105] Ashworth (see n 68 above) 107; Ashworth (see n 103 above) 209.

The argument for greater protection of the community is sometimes recast as an argument about a conflict of rights.[106] John Finnis has suggested that the community interest is, in fact, inseparable from the interests of the individuals who make up the community.[107] Hence, for example, the interest of the community in protecting houses from the danger of fire is simply the aggregate of the interest each individual has in his or her house not being burnt.[108] As we saw above, Dworkin accepts that rights may be subject to limitation when they conflict with other rights. However he qualifies this by excluding consideration of individual rights reconstituted from the community interest.[109] The reconstitution of the community interest into individual rights may take one of two forms.

First, the right of the defendant to be treated as innocent until proven guilty is contrasted with the right of a victim of crime to have his or her rights vindicated by the state through a successful prosecution. This version of the 'conflicting rights' argument appears singularly weak. The right to have the state impose retribution on behalf of the victim cannot be placed on the same level as the right of the defendant to avoid wrongful conviction. The first is the case of a demand that the state take some action to vindicate an injustice; the second is the far more important claim that the state must not itself impose an injustice. Further, the victim does not have a right to have retribution sought against people who are innocent, only against people who are guilty.[110] The safeguard of the presumption of innocence helps to ensure that only the guilty are subject to retribution.

The second form of the 'conflict of rights' argument involves a conflict between the rights of the defendant and the rights of other individuals in the community to be free from the deleterious consequences of crime. The right of an individual not to be blown up by a terrorist or killed by a drink driver is contrasted with the defendant's right to be presumed innocent. The idea that people have such a 'right to security' is gaining currency in the literature.[111] However, the argument that this right can be used to justify restriction of the right to be presumed innocent is not compelling.

To begin with, it assumes that restricting the presumption of innocence is the only means of protecting the rights of others. In fact, there are other options at the disposal of states to prevent offences.[112] If the prosecution does not have the evidence to secure a conviction for a serious offence, it may nevertheless be able to charge the defendant with a lesser offence and impose a shorter period of incarceration, effectively incapacitating the offender and preventing future crimes (apart, of course, from crimes that might be committed in prison). If the authorities are

[106] See generally Ashworth (see n 68 above) 77–80.

[107] J Finnis 'A Bill of Rights for Britain? The Moral of Contemporary Jurisprudence' (1985) *Proceedings of the British Academy* 303, 318–20.

[108] Ibid 320.

[109] Dworkin (see n 81 above) 194–95

[110] Ashworth (see n 7 above) 243: 'Victims of crime have no interest in the number of unsafe convictions.'

[111] L Lazarus & B Goold *Security and Human Rights* (Hart Publishing, Oxford 2007) Part III.

[112] Ashworth (see n 68 above) 110–11.

unable to obtain a conviction for any offence, and hence unable to impose a period of incarceration, options such as extensive surveillance are also available to keep track of suspected offenders.

In addition, the principle that a state is more responsible for its acts than for its omissions must be recognised. Waldron puts the point in this way: 'Failing to do what is necessary to save P's life (because this would actively violate Q's rights) is not a way of disrespecting P; the responsibility rests with those—the terrorists—who kill P, not with the government that refuses to violate rights in order to stop them.'[113] The inability on the part of the state to prevent a terrorist offence can lead to tragic consequences—but the primary responsibility for those consequences rests with the terrorists. By contrast, the violation of the right to be presumed innocent, with all of the attendant risks to the innocent and to the rule of law, is a serious breach of faith between the state and its citizens.

We have seen in this section that the argument for the limitation of the presumption of innocence when there is a conflicting community interest is not strong. It is unsupportable even in the cases of the most serious offences, such as terrorism. *A fortiori*, considerations of the public interest should not be invoked in the case of lesser threats such as the ineffectiveness of regulatory regimes. This need not, however, lead to the conclusion that no limits on the presumption of innocence are permissible, or that reverse burdens should never be used. It may be that reverse burdens are permissible when the threat to the rights of the innocent is minimal. The following section investigates this claim.

3. When the Rationale is Attenuated

As Dworkin concedes, rights may be subject to limitation when 'the values protected by the original right are not really at stake in the marginal case, or are at stake only in some attenuated form.'[114] Following this reasoning, it might be possible to argue for use of reverse burdens of proof when the interest of the defendant in avoiding wrongful conviction is attenuated. This section will consider two such scenarios. First, when risk of wrongful conviction is low; and second when the penalty for the offence is minimal. In such cases, the individual right to be presumed innocent is not 'balanced' against the community interest, since it has already been determined, based on a principled understanding of the value of the right, that the interest of the individual is not truly at stake. This chapter will deal with these arguments only in general terms in order to illustrate what is meant by an attenuation of the rationale for the presumption of innocence. A more detailed discussion taking into account all the factors relevant to the allocation of the burden of proof is undertaken in Chapter Six.

[113] Waldron (see n 91 above) 199. See also F Kamm 'Conflict of Rights: Typology, Methodology and Non-Consequentialism (2001) 7 *Legal Theory* 239.

[114] Dworkin (see n 81 above) 200.

(a) Low Risk of Wrongful Conviction

In some situations, the prosecution has proved facts that reduce the risk of an innocent person being convicted. In such situations, it might be said that a reverse burden is justified, especially if it will make trials cheaper, more efficient and more likely to convict the guilty. There are three classes of cases in which this situation might exist. The largest and most complex class involves cases where the prosecution has proved wrongful conduct by the defendant and a reverse burden is imposed in relation to a factor that does not bring the defendant outside the realm of wrongfulness.[115]

The contours of this class can be explored using the example of section 28 of the Misuse of Drugs Act 1971.[116] That section creates a defence to a drugs charge if a person in possession of proscribed drugs neither knew, nor suspected, nor had reason to suspect, that he or she was carrying drugs. When a person is in possession of prohibited drugs, the wrong of possession and the harm that may flow from it is fully constituted. Even if the defendant was unaware that he or she was carrying drugs, he or she can be regarded as having acted wrongfully if each person is taken to have a duty to avoid taking drugs into his or her possession.[117] A duty of this kind is not inconceivable in a moral sense since possession of drugs and the facilitation of drug trafficking can cause harm to others. Consequently, as the argument goes, proof of mere possession demonstrates some degree of guilt. If a defendant is given the opportunity to avoid conviction by proving that he or she neither knew nor had reason to suspect that the thing possessed was a controlled drug, the reverse burden does not involve a risk that a person who is completely innocent will be convicted. The prosecution has already proved facts constituting wrongfulness, although not culpability in the full sense. If the defendant is unable to satisfy the reverse burden with respect to knowledge, he or she may be treated as having committed the crime intentionally and the punishment may reflect this. It is important that a person should be punished only in proportion to the degree of culpability that properly attaches to them. However, punishing a guilty person more than he or she deserves might be thought a lesser wrong than punishing an innocent person who is entirely undeserving of punishment.

The second class of cases in which there might be a lower risk of wrongful conviction comprises those in which the prosecution has proved matters that make it almost certain that the defendant is guilty of the complete offence, and a reverse burden is imposed with respect to an inherently improbable defence. Again, the defence provided by section 28 of the Drugs Misuse Act 1974 is illustrative. The

[115] Most obviously, this class would include 'excuses' such as duress and insanity. These examples are discussed in detail in Ch 6.

[116] Since the introduction of the HRA, the House of Lords has held this section imposes an evidential burden on the defendant: *R v Lambert* [2002] 2 AC 545 (HL).

[117] This is how Lord Woolf interpreted s 28 of the Misuse of Drugs Act 1971 in [2002] QB 1112 (CA) [24]: 'What the offence does is to make the defendant responsible for ensuring that he does not take into his possession containers which in fact contain drugs.'

defendant's claim to have been unaware of the contents of a package will often come within the realm of inherently improbable defences. There is something implausible in the claim that a person would entrust a valuable package to another person who is entirely ignorant of the contents.[118] It is further implausible that a person being paid a large amount of money to deliver a small package would not at least have reason to suspect that the contents of the package might be illegal. Hence, it is likely that a person found in possession of a package containing drugs has knowledge of, or at least a reason to suspect, the true nature of the contents and is culpable for possession. As the argument goes, imposing a reverse burden in such a case does not involve a high risk of convicting an innocent person. The risk is probably very low due to the inherent implausibility of the claim. Whether this is a sufficient basis for reversing the burden of proof is a question I will deal with more fully in Chapter Six. At present, the salient point is that the risk of convicting an innocent person is lower in cases where the defence is inherently implausible than in cases where the defence is more plausible but still difficult to prove.

The third class of cases involves those in which the defendant, if innocent, could be expected to prove the circumstances giving rise to innocence. The paradigm example of this scenario is when the defendant is called upon to prove possession of a licence. If the defendant has a licence to engage in a certain type of conduct, it ought to be a simple matter to produce it. Hence, it can be argued that a reverse burden with respect to possession of a licence involves a very low risk of wrongful conviction. If the defendant has a licence, it will be produced and the defendant will be acquitted or, more likely, not prosecuted in the first place.

Even if we accept in these three categories that there is a reduced risk of convicting a person who is innocent, a reverse burden is still in conflict with the second rationale for the presumption of innocence. It is contrary to the rule of law for the state to demand the conviction of a person when it has not proven all the matters necessary for conviction. The state is the proponent of guilt and throughout the trial is attempting to justify the imposition of conviction and punishment. If the prosecution has not demonstrated the fitness of the defendant for conviction, encompassing the entirety of the matters which will be reflected in the conviction, the state has not justified the conviction. Nor has it demonstrated the justification for any proposed punishment. The rationale of promoting the rule of law continues to operate even if the risk of wrongful conviction is reduced due to factors internal to the processes of proof. Consequently, it is necessary to resist calls for the limitation of the presumption of innocence even in those cases where (arguably) the risk of wrongful conviction is low.

(b) Minimal Penalty

When there is a low penalty for an offence, it might be said that the interest of an innocent person is reduced since the consequences of conviction are not serious.

[118] *R v Lambert* [2002] 2 AC 545 (HL) [43] (Lord Steyn).

We must be careful with an argument of this kind. It is necessary to remember that the consequences of conviction include not only punishment, censure, and stigma. There is also the sense of 'moral harm' inherent in the wrongful conviction. Having said this, however, it seems undeniable that a wrongful conviction leading to a small monetary penalty is not so great an imposition on the individual as a wrongful conviction leading to a term of imprisonment. Hence, in cases of low penalties, the rationale of protecting the innocent is significantly diminished. Again, however, the second rationale for the presumption of innocence, promotion of the rule of law, continues to operate. In accordance with the rule of law, the state is not permitted to impose penalties on individuals unless those individuals, by their conduct, have made themselves properly liable to the penalty. It is for the state to prove that the defendant has fallen within the relevant criminal prohibition. The rule of law requires this as a reflection of the proper relationship between the state and the individual. Hence, even if the rationale for the presumption of innocence is attenuated because the consequences of wrongful conviction are minimised, the rationale does not disappear altogether. The rationale of promoting the rule of law continues to operate even in cases where the consequences of wrongful conviction are minimal.

C. Conclusion

This chapter has argued that there is a dual rationale for the presumption of innocence: (1) it protects the innocent from wrongful conviction; and (2) it promotes the rule of law. The rationale of protecting the innocent is strong enough to resist subjugation to other interests. When there is a high risk of convicting an innocent person, questions of community interest, such as those related to the severity of the crime, cannot be used to justify a reduction in protection of the innocent through a reversal of the burden of proof. There are some circumstances in which the risk of wrongful conviction is low or the consequences of conviction are minimal. Such cases present a more convincing case for a reversal of the burden of proof since the rationale of protecting the innocent only applies in an attenuated sense. However, the rationale of promoting the rule of law continues to operate in these cases with full force. This must be kept firmly in mind when considering the propriety of a reversal of the burden of proof. Reverse burdens should be used in cases of low risk of wrongful conviction or minimal consequences only if there is a reasonable case for their use. Otherwise, the rule of law is not being respected. The following chapter discusses the scope of the presumption of innocence, and includes discussion of the extent to which different approaches to the scope of the presumption meet the dual rationales of protecting the innocent and promoting the rule of law.

3

Scope of the Presumption

THIS BOOK TREATS the presumption of innocence as synonymous with the rule that the prosecution must prove the guilt of the defendant beyond reasonable doubt.[1] Adopting this definition does not foreclose questions about the scope of the presumption of innocence. It remains necessary to have a clear conception of what is meant by 'guilt' and 'innocence'. The scope of the presumption depends on determining *what* the prosecution is required to prove beyond reasonable doubt. This question has generated a substantial body of cases and literature in jurisdictions with a constitutionally protected presumption of innocence. Three distinct approaches to the scope of the presumption can be discerned: (1) the substantive approach; (2) the narrow procedural approach; and (3) the broad procedural approach.[2]

Part A of this chapter discusses the substantive approach.[3] Under the substantive approach, the presumption of innocence requires the prosecution to prove conduct by the defendant that corresponds to the consequences of conviction. Proponents of the substantive approach argue, for example, that strict liability offences breach the presumption of innocence because the prosecution is not required to prove culpability on the part of the defendant. Part B of this chapter discusses the narrow procedural approach.[4] The narrow procedural approach

[1] See Introduction, xiv–xv.

[2] *Cf* SE Sundby 'The Reasonable Doubt Rule and the Meaning of Innocence' (1988) 40 *Hastings Law Journal* 457, who uses the categories substantivism, restrictive proceduralism and expansive proceduralism. It should be noted that the movement from (1) to (3) does not involve a progression from more protection for defendants to less protection. While the substantive approach would place the most limits on criminal law and procedure, the narrow procedural approach would involve fewer limits than the broad procedural approach.

[3] For key articles in support of the substantive approach see: JC Jeffries & PB Stephan III 'Defences, Presumptions and the Burden of Proof in Criminal Law' (1979) 88 *Yale Law Journal (YLJ)* 1325; RJ Allen 'Structuring Jury Decision-Making in Criminal Cases: A Unified Constitutional Approach to Evidentiary Devices' (1980) 94 *Harvard Law Review (Harv L Rev)* 321; A Paizes 'A Closer Look at the Presumption of Innocence in our Constitution: What is an Accused Presumed to be Innocent *of*?' (1998) 11 *South African Journal of Criminal Justice* 409; V Tadros & S Tierney 'The Presumption of Innocence and the Human Rights Act' (2004) 67 MLR 402; V Tadros 'Rethinking the Presumption of Innocence' (2007) 1 *Criminal Law and Philosophy* 193; RA Duff 'Strict Liability, Legal Presumptions, and the Presumption of Innocence' in AP Simester (ed) *Appraising Strict Liability* (OUP, Oxford 2005) 125.

[4] The key academic proponent of this approach is Paul Roberts: P Roberts 'The Presumption of Innocence Brought Home? Kebilene Deconstructed' (2002) 118 *LQR* 41; P Roberts 'Drug Dealing and the Presumption of Innocence: The Human Rights Act (almost) Bites' (2002) 6 *E & P* 17; P Roberts, 'Strict Liability and the Presumption of Innocence: An Exposé of Functionalist Assumptions' in AP Simester (ed) *Appraising Strict Liability* (OUP, Oxford 2005) 151; P Roberts 'Criminal Procedure,

leaves the substance of the criminal law unaffected but extends procedural protection to defendants by requiring the prosecution to bear the burden of proof with respect to the core aspects of an offence. The core of an offence is signified by terms such as 'elements' or 'gravamen'. Regardless of the terms used, the narrow procedural approach entails that there is no breach of the presumption of innocence, even in a *prima facie* sense, if the burden of proof is imposed on the defendant with respect to a peripheral matter. Part C discusses the broad procedural approach.[5] The broad procedural approach requires the prosecution to prove all matters that are necessary for conviction. On this approach, no distinction is drawn between the core and peripheral aspects of an offence. If the defendant is confronted with a burden of proof in respect of any matter relevant to conviction there is an interference with the presumption of innocence.

This chapter argues in favour of the broad procedural approach to the presumption of innocence. Underlying the broad procedural approach is the understanding that rules of criminal liability, whether derived from statute or the common law, demarcate an area of criminal prohibition. The presumption of innocence requires the prosecution to prove beyond reasonable doubt that the defendant falls within the area of the criminal prohibition: otherwise, he or she must not be convicted. The proposition that no person should be subject to criminal sanctions unless he or she has breached a criminal prohibition is integral to the rule of law. Under this approach, all reverse burdens constitute a *prima facie* interference with the presumption of innocence. Whether the reverse burden is inconsistent with Article 6(2) will depend on the extent to which it is appropriate to place limits on the presumption.

A. Substantive Approach

The substantive approach extends the scope of the presumption of innocence so that it may be used to adjudicate on the substantive content of the criminal law. If an offence as defined by statute or the common law does not include a sufficient degree of culpability or blameworthiness to justify a criminal conviction and punishment, the presumption is breached. This view is commonly adopted in support of the argument that strict liability offences are contrary to the presumption of innocence.[6] Strict liability offences are those in which there is at least one aspect

the Presumption of Innocence and Judicial Reasoning under the Human Rights Act' in H Fenwick, G Phillipson & R Masterman (eds) *Judicial Reasoning Under the UK Human Rights Act* (CUP, Cambridge 2007) 377.

[5] Key articles include: BD Underwood 'The Thumb on the Scales of Justice: Burdens of Persuasion in Criminal Cases' (1977) 86 *YLJ* 1299; HA Ashford & DM Risinger 'Presumptions, Assumptions and Due Process in Criminal Cases: A Theoretical Overview' (1969) 79 *YLJ* 165; D Dripps 'The Constitutional Status of the Reasonable Doubt Rule' (1987) 75 *California Law Review (Cal LR)* 1665.

[6] Jeffries & Stephan (see n 3 above) 1371–76; Tadros & Tierney (see n 3 above) 422–24. See the discussion below at text accompanying notes 44–52.

of the *actus reus* that does not have a corresponding *mens rea* requirement.[7] As the argument goes, if the prosecution has not proved *mens rea*, it has not proved a sufficient basis for conviction and punishment. While much of the discussion below relates to strict liability, it will nevertheless become clear that the substantive approach to the presumption of innocence has consequences for every aspect of the definition of criminal offences, not just those relating to *mens rea*. This Part deals first with the English cases on strict liability and Article 6(2) and then addresses the academic argument in support of the substantive approach to the presumption of innocence.

1. Rejection in the English Cases

The starting point for English cases on the presumption of innocence is almost always the decision of the Strasbourg court in *Salabiaku v France*.[8] In that case, the Strasbourg Court stated that Contracting States under the ECHR are entitled 'to define the constituent elements' of offences and, in principle could 'penalise a simple or objective fact as such, irrespective of whether it results from criminal intent or negligence.'[9] This quote appears to support the view that Article 6(2) does not have a substantive scope and cannot be used to rein in strict liability offences. However, the Court went on to apply a 'reasonable limits' test to what was arguably a strict liability offence, suggesting that Article 6(2) is capable of controlling such offences.[10] *Salabiaku* is, at best, equivocal as to whether Article 6(2) applies to strict liability offences.[11]

Despite its ambiguous nature, the English courts have relied upon *Salabiaku* as authority for the proposition that Article 6(2) does not control the substance of the criminal law and accordingly does not impact on strict liability offences.[12] The first notable case was the decision of the Divisional Court in *Barnfather v Islington Education Authority*.[13] The defendant in that case was convicted under section 444(1) of the Education Act 1996 as the parent of a child who failed to attend school regularly. Section 444(1) stated: 'If a child of compulsory school age who is a registered pupil at a school fails to attend regularly at the school, his parent is guilty of an offence.' The offence was one of strict liability, providing no defence

[7] This is the definition adopted by S Green 'Six Senses of Strict Liability: A Plea for Formalism' in AP Simester (ed) *Appraising Strict Liability* (OUP, Oxford 2005) 1, 9–10. That work rejects other definitions of strict liability as insufficiently precise. See also D Husak 'Varieties of Strict Liability' (1995) 8 *Canadian Journal of Law and Jurisprudence* 189.

[8] *Salabiaku v France* (App No 10589/83) (1991) 13 EHRR 379.

[9] Ibid [27].

[10] Ibid [28].

[11] The proper interpretation of *Salabiaku* is discussed in greater detail in Ch 4. Ch 4 argues that a careful reading of the Strasbourg cases reveals several instances in which Art 6(2) has been given substantive scope. This chapter explains why that approach is wrong in principle.

[12] In addition to the cases discussed below, see *obiter dicta* in *R v Daniel* [2003] 1 Cr App R 6 (CA) [34] (Auld LJ); *R v Muhamad* [2003] QB 1031 (CA) [32] (Dyson LJ); *R (Grundy & Co Excavations Ltd)) v Halton Division Magistrates Court* (2003) 167 JP 387 (QBD) [52]–[54] (Clarke LJ).

[13] *Barnfather v Islington Education Authority* [2003] 1 WLR 2318 (QBD).

of due diligence. A parent would be guilty of the offence even if he or she did not know and had no means of knowing about the truancy of the child.[14]

In the Divisional Court, Maurice Kay J began his discussion of the presumption of innocence by stating: 'At first sight it is not obvious how Art 6(2) might impact on the issue of a strict liability offence. Its subject matter appears to be procedural and evidential rather than substantive.'[15] His Honour was confirmed in this view following an analysis of the Strasbourg and English cases.[16] Similarly, Elias J agreed that Article 6(2) 'does not impose any restrictions on the power of Parliament to create strict liability offences.'[17] It followed that the courts could not use the HRA to import a defence into a strict liability offence or make a declaration of incompatibility because of the lack of a defence.[18]

The rejection of the substantive approach to Article 6(2) was confirmed by the House of Lords in *R v G*.[19] In that case, the defendant, a 15-year-old boy, had pleaded guilty to sexual intercourse with a 12-year-old girl, contrary to section 5 of the Sexual Offences Act 2003 (SOA). Section 5 made it an offence for a male to have sexual intercourse with a child under the age of 13, regardless of the consent of the child. Further, it was irrelevant under section 5 whether the defendant knew or had reason to know that the child was under 13. Section 5 consequently created an offence of strict liability in relation to knowledge of the age of the victim.[20] By contrast, section 9 of the SOA created an offence of sexual touching of a child under 16. Under that section, it was necessary for the prosecution to prove that the defendant did not 'reasonably believe' the child was 16 or over. The defendant appealed against his conviction contending that section 5 was incompatible with Article 6(2).

In the Court of Appeal, Lord Phillips CJ had stated: 'The presumption of innocence is a presumption that one is not guilty of whatever may be the elements of a criminal offence. One must not confuse innocence of a criminal offence with innocence of blameworthy conduct.'[21] This conclusion was resoundingly affirmed in the House of Lords. Lord Hoffman considered that, to the extent that *Salabiaku* supported a substantive conception of Article 6(2), it was an 'unfortunate case' that ought to be 'ignored'.[22] His Lordship stated that Article 6(2) requires a person 'to be presumed innocent of the offence but does not say anything about what

[14] *Cf* s 444(1A) which requires the prosecution to prove, beyond reasonable doubt, that the parent had no reasonable justification for not causing the child to attend school: *R (P) v Liverpool City Magistrates* [2006] EWHC 887 (Admin) [23]–[24] (Collins J).

[15] Ibid [12].

[16] Ibid [17]–[25].

[17] Ibid [34].

[18] Ibid. The two judges were divided on the question of whether s 444(1) would have been proportionate had Art 6(2) applied. Maurice Kay J held it was proportionate: ibid [32]. Elias J held it was not: ibid [57].

[19] *R v G* [2008] 1 WLR 1379 (HL).

[20] Lord Hope observed that the *mens rea* element was the deliberate act of penetration: ibid [20].

[21] *R v G* [2006] 1 WLR 2052 (CA) [36]. The Court of Appeal decision was followed in *S v DPP* [2006] EWHC 2231 (Admin) [13] (Walker J); *R v Deyemi* [2007] EWCA Crim 2060 [26]–[27] (Latham LJ).

[22] [2008] 1 WLR 1379 (HL) [6].

the mental or other elements of the offence should be.'[23] Lord Hope considered that both in its civil and in its criminal applications Article 6 is concerned with procedure and not with substance.[24] His Lordship stated:[25]

> Article 6(2), like article 6(3), must be read in the context of article 6(1). The article as a whole is concerned essentially with procedural guarantees to ensure that there is a fair trial, not with the substantive elements of the offence with which the person has been charged . . . Close attention is paid to the requirements of a fair trial. But it is a matter for the contracting states to define the essential elements of the offence with which the person has been charged. So when article 6(2) uses the words 'innocent' and 'guilty' it is dealing with the burden of proof regarding the elements of the offence and any defences to it. It is not dealing with what those elements are or what defences to the offence ought to be available.

While the allocation of the burden of proof is a procedural matter, the issues that must be established to secure a conviction are a matter of substance and outside the scope of Article 6(2). It follows that Article 6(2) cannot be used to review the substance of the criminal law.

Finally, some assistance as to the meaning of the presumption of innocence may be found in the Privy Council decision in *Khan v Trinidad*.[26] In that case, the Privy Council, interpreting the Constitution of Trinidad and Tobago, held that the presumption of innocence is not a substantive protection. The defendant in *Khan* challenged the felony murder rule, which had been reintroduced by a statutory provision in Trinidad and Tobago. Under the statute, a person—engaged in the commission of an 'arrestable offence involving violence' in the course of which someone was killed—was liable to be convicted of murder, even if the killing was unintentional. The defendant was convicted of murder as one of four men who had taken part in a robbery which had resulted in fatal injuries to the victim. On appeal, it was argued that the felony murder rule breached the presumption of innocence, enshrined in section 5(2)(f) of the Constitution, because it relieved the prosecution of the need to prove the requisite *mens rea* for murder.[27]

Lord Bingham delivered the speech for the majority of the Privy Council. His Lordship stated:[28]

23 Ibid [4].

24 Ibid [27]. See also *R v Gemmell* [2003] 1 Cr App R 23 (CA) [33] (Dyson LJ, for the Court), rev'd, on a different point, in *R v G* [2004] 1 AC 1034 (HL); *Matthews v Ministry of Defence* [2003] 1 AC 1163 (HL) [3] (Lord Bingham). See also [25] (Lord Hoffmann), [51] (Lord Hope), [77] (Lord Millett), [142] (Lord Walker); *R (Kehoe) v Secretary of State for Work and Pensions* [2006] 1 AC 42 (HL) [41] (Lord Hope).

25 Ibid [27]. Two other members of the House agreed with Lord Hoffmann and Lord Hope on this point: ibid [41] (Baroness Hale), [63] (Lord Mance). Lord Carswell expressed no view on the issue.

26 *Khan v Trinidad* [2005] 1 AC 374 (PC).

27 Ibid 377 (P Thornton and R Trowler, for the defendant). It was also argued that the felony murder rule was inconsistent with 'the due process of law' protected by s 4(a) and 'the protection of the law' guaranteed by s 4(b): ibid 376. The Privy Council rejected this argument, while accepting that an 'unreasonable or oppressive' rule might breach the 'due process of law': ibid [11] (Lord Bingham). On the meaning of 'due process of law' see also: *Thomas v Baptiste* [2000] 2 AC 1 (PC) 21–22, 32–33 (Lord Millett). *Cf Lewis v AG of Jamaica* [2001] AC 50 (PC) 85 (Lord Slynn).

28 Ibid [14].

> The presumption of innocence is perhaps the most fundamental principle underlying the administration of the criminal law. It places on the prosecution, fairly and squarely, the duty of proving guilt. But it does not control the ingredients of the offence which the prosecution must prove to establish guilt.

It followed that the statute under review did not infringe the presumption of innocence since it defined what needed to be proved and required the prosecution to prove it. Lord Bingham stated that a provision requiring the defendant to establish some ground of exoneration might, depending on the precise statutory context, infringe the presumption of innocence. But the presumption of innocence did not permit a challenge to the substance of the law.[29]

The current state of English authority on Article 6(2), coupled with the decision of the Privy Council in *Khan*, precludes the adoption of a substantive approach to the presumption of innocence. This has the effect of preventing Article 6(2) from being employed in an argument against an unfair, illiberal or overly broad rule. However, it also means that the courts do not become enmeshed in difficult and inherently controversial questions about the proper scope of the criminal law. It seems unthinkable that the English courts will use Article 6(2) to arrogate to themselves the capacity to review and rewrite the substantive rules of criminal law. Nevertheless, some powerful arguments have been made in academic circles for a substantive approach to the presumption of innocence. The following section addresses these arguments.

2. Case for a Substantive Approach

While the English courts have not been attracted to the substantive approach, it has received ardent support from academics in various jurisdictions.[30] In England, Victor Tadros and Stephen Tierney have written an article supporting the substantive approach to Article 6(2).[31] In the United States, John Jeffries and Paul Stephan have written a highly influential article supporting the substantive approach, in response to cases under the 'due process' clause of the US Constitution.[32] This

[29] Ibid. The majority of the Privy Council held, however, that the availability of the death sentence when intention to kill had not been proved could constitute a 'cruel and unusual treatment or punishment' contrary to s 5(2)(b) of the Constitution: The majority declined to hold the death penalty would always be disproportionate, but nevertheless quashed the death sentence on the defendant and ordered a re-sentencing: ibid [18] (Lord Bingham). Lord Steyn (dissenting) held that s 2A was invalid to the extent that it authorised the death penalty for felony murder: ibid [40]. Lord Millett (dissenting) held that s 2A was invalid to the extent that it authorised the imposition of the death penalty in circumstances where it had not previously been authorised: ibid [55]. By contrast, the Canadian Supreme Court has held that ss 7 and 11(d) of the Canadian Charter will not permit a murder conviction unless the prosecution has proved (at least) the objective foreseeability of death: *R v Vaillancourt* [1987] 2 SCR 636.

[30] See the articles collected in n 3 above.

[31] Tadros & Tierney (see n 3 above).

[32] Jeffries & Stephan (see n 3 above). For important US cases see: *Re Winship*, 397 US 358 (1970); *Mullaney v Wilbur*, 421 US 684 (1975); *Patterson v New York*, 432 US 197 (1977).

section will use the arguments of Tadros and Tierney and Jeffries and Stephan as representative of the academic case in favour of the substantive approach.

Supporters of the substantive approach argue that it would be absurd to hold that a reverse burden defence breaches the presumption of innocence, but a strict liability offence does not.[33] For instance, Tadros and Tierney observe that a reverse burden with respect to *mens rea* is generally recognised as an interference with the presumption of innocence.[34] However, if the *mens rea* requirement is simply removed altogether, there is no breach of the presumption on the procedural approach. Tadros and Tierney state:[35]

> That leads to the absurd conclusion that a reverse onus of proof in a defence to an offence of strict liability may be held incompatible with article 6(2) where *the very same offence* will be regarded as compatible as a whole if no such defence exists *at all*.

Tadros and Tierney argue that strict liability offences are introduced not because *mens rea* is regarded as morally irrelevant but because it is difficult for the prosecution to prove. By warranting the conviction of some persons who are not morally at fault, in order to ensure the conviction of those who are, the legislature interferes with the presumption of innocence.[36] Tadros and Tierney argue there is an interference with the presumption of innocence whenever an offence is constructed in such a way as to permit convictions for conduct which the offence was not designed to control.[37]

Similarly, Jeffries and Stephan respond to the perceived absurdity of a standard that permits the complete elimination of a fault requirement but not the reversal of the burden of proof as to that requirement. They begin by stating that the requirement of proof beyond reasonable doubt seeks to prevent the injustice of convicting an 'innocent' person.[38] However, in their view, 'guilt' and 'innocence' are not simply a matter of the definition adopted by the legislature; rather they are 'substantive concepts'.[39] Jeffries and Stephan state:[40]

> A constitutional policy to minimize the risk of convicting the 'innocent' must be grounded in a constitutional conception of what may constitute 'guilt'. Otherwise, 'guilt' would have to be proved with certainty, but the legislature could define "guilt" as it pleased, and the grand ideal of individual liberty would be reduced to an empty promise.

Jeffries and Stephan later contend that the problem at which the presumption of innocence is directed is the 'excessive or unwarranted imposition of criminal liability'.[41] The evil of convicting moral innocents arises whenever the prosecution

[33] See also Paizes (see n 3 above) 412.
[34] Tadros & Tierney (see n 3 above) 423.
[35] Ibid (original emphasis).
[36] Ibid.
[37] Ibid 417–18.
[38] Jeffries & Stephan (see n 3 above) 1347.
[39] Ibid.
[40] Ibid.
[41] Ibid 1359.

has not had to prove a sufficient basis for conviction and punishment. This is the case whether the prosecution is relieved of its burden by shifting it to the defence, or by eliminating a matter altogether. This evil can be cured only by a rule that relates the requirement of proof beyond reasonable doubt to the substantive content of the criminal law.[42] The authors propose that the presumption of innocence should be read 'to assert a constitutional requirement of proof beyond reasonable doubt of a constitutionally adequate basis for imposing the punishment authorised.'[43]

At this point, it becomes necessary for supporters of the substantive approach to take a position on what would be a sufficient basis for conviction and punishment. Typically, it is contended that some degree of *mens rea* is essential to the culpability of any defendant and therefore must be included as an element of every offence. Tadros and Tierney use strict liability offences as the prime example of offences which interfere with the presumption of innocence on the substantive approach but not on the procedural approach.[44] They define strict liability offences as those which do not require proof of *mens rea*.[45] Beyond this, the authors do not provide much guidance on what they consider to be the necessary features of criminal liability under Article 6(2).[46]

Jeffries and Stephan acknowledge that the task of identifying a sufficient basis for conviction and punishment is 'more than a little forbidding'.[47] Nevertheless, they proceed to sketch out a 'highly tentative' background to the question of the required minima for criminal liability.[48] They identify three requirements: *actus reus*, *mens rea* and proportionality in punishment.[49] Of these three requirements, it is the *mens rea* criterion that would be called upon to perform most of the work in protecting the presumption of innocence. Criminal offences with no *actus reus* are virtually unheard of in Anglo-American law,[50] while offences without *mens rea* are relatively commonplace.[51] Further, while excessive sentences may breach a

[42] Ibid 1359.

[43] Ibid 1365. A further characteristic of this approach is that, provided the prosecution has proved an adequate basis for conviction and punishment, it would be acceptable to reverse the burden of proof with respect to a 'gratuitous' defence: ibid 1358–59. See also Tadros & Tierney (see n 3 above) 418–20.

[44] Tadros & Tierney (see n 3 above) 422–24.

[45] Ibid 422

[46] Tadros has discussed the theoretical requirements of criminal responsibility in other published work: V Tadros *Criminal Responsibility* (OUP, Oxford 2005). However, he has never made the case for incorporating these theoretical requirements into a substantive conception of 'guilt' under Art 6(2).

[47] Jeffries & Stephan (see n 3 above) 1366.

[48] Ibid.

[49] Ibid 1370–76.

[50] English law has a small class of 'status offences' in which there is no requirement of *actus reus*: eg Education Act 1996, s 444(1) (being the parent of a truant child). This offence might also be characterised as an instance of vicarious liability. *R v Larsonneur* (1933) 24 Cr App R 74 (CCA) in which the defendant was prosecuted for being an illegal alien after she was transported against her will onto English territory is sometimes cited as an example of a status offence: D Ormerod *Smith & Hogan: Criminal Law* 11th edn (OUP, Oxford 2005) 73–75. There is controversy over the correct interpretation of this case: see Roberts (2005) (see n 4 above) 152 fn 8 and the authorities collected therein.

[51] A Ashworth & M Blake 'The Presumption of Innocence in English Criminal Law' [1996] Crim LR 306, 309. The authors found that roughly half of all offences triable in the Crown Court did not have a *mens rea* requirement corresponding to each element of the *actus reus*.

requirement of proportionality in punishment,[52] it adds nothing to assert that excessive sentences also breach the presumption of innocence. Consequently, on the substantive approach, the requirement of *mens rea* is called upon to perform the bulk of the work in protecting defendants from unfair convictions.

The argument that the presumption of innocence imposes a requirement of *mens rea*, and therefore has a role in controlling strict liability offences, is highly appealing. From the point of view of substantive justice, there is a significant problem with strict liability offences. The defendant is subject to liability even though he or she did not have a culpable state of mind at the time of the infringing conduct or did not cause the relevant state of affairs.[53] People who act with *mens rea* are 'sufficiently aware of what they are doing, and of the consequences it may have, that they can fairly be said to have chosen the behaviour and its consequences.'[54] Therefore, it is argued that a culpable state of mind is a prerequisite for the imposition of a criminal sanction in any system of criminal justice which treats the defendant as an autonomous individual capable of choosing between alternative actions.[55] Accordingly, it would seem an eminently positive development to use Article 6(2) to control strict liability offences and avoid abuses of the criminal law. Strict liability offences could be controlled with the simply stated rule that every part of the *actus reus* of an offence must have a corresponding element of *mens rea*.

While the rule is simple to state there are two controversies surrounding its application. First, there is considerable academic disagreement over whether there need always be correspondence between *actus reus* and *mens rea*.[56] For instance, it has been suggested that the principle of 'moral luck' requires people to take responsibility for the good or bad consequences of their conduct, even if those consequences are unintended or unforeseen.[57] Second, the degree of *mens rea* required for certain offences is controversial; in particular, there is disagreement

[52] Article 3 of the ECHR prohibits 'inhuman or degrading treatment of punishment'. This may imply a requirement of proportionality in punishment: *Weeks v UK* (App No 9787/82) (1988) 10 EHRR 293 [47]. See also D van Zyl Smit & A Ashworth 'Disproportionate Sentences as Human Rights Violations' (2004) *MLR* 541. In *Khan v State of Trinidad and Tobago* [2005] 1 AC 374 (PC), the Privy Council held that the death penalty for homicide, in the absence of proof of intention to kill, could be a disproportionate punishment.

[53] See HL Packer, 'Mens Rea and the Supreme Court' [1962] *Supreme Court Review*107, 109; L Alexander 'Reconsidering the Relationship Among Voluntary Acts, Strict Liability and Negligence in Criminal Law' (1990) *Social Philosophy and Policy* 84, 86.

[54] A Ashworth *Principles of Criminal Law* 5th edn (OUP, Oxford 2006) 158.

[55] Ibid 159.

[56] J Horder 'A Critique of the Correspondence Principle in Criminal Law' [1995] Crim LR 759; B Mitchell 'In Defence of a Principle of Correspondence' [1999] *Crim LR* 195; J Horder 'Questioning the Correspondence Principle—A Reply' [1999] *Crim LR* 206; N Lacey 'A Clear Concept of Intention: Elusive or Illusory?' (1993) 56 *MLR* 621; JA Laing, 'The Prospects of a Theory of Criminal Culpability: Mens Rea and Methodological Doubt' (1994) 14 *OJLS* 57; J Gardner 'Criminal Law and the Uses of Theory: A Reply to Laing' (1994) 14 OJLS 217; J Horder 'Intention in the Criminal Law: A Rejoinder' (1995) 58 *MLR* 678; RA Duff 'Codifying Criminal Fault: Conceptual Problems and Presuppositions' in IH Dennis (ed) *Criminal Law and Justice* (Sweet & Maxwell, London 1987) 93; J Gardner & H Jung 'Making Sense of Mens Rea: Antony Duff's Account' (1991) 11 *OJLS* 559

[57] AM Honoré, *Responsibility and Fault* (Hart Publishing, Oxford 1999); K Simons 'When is Strict Criminal Liability Just?' (1997) 87 *Journal of Criminal Law and Criminology* 1075, 1105–20.

over whether negligence should suffice.[58] Notwithstanding these controversies, a rule requiring correspondence between *actus reus* and *mens rea* would be relatively certain and easy to apply. Judges are already accustomed to applying a *mens rea* requirement, due to the common law rule of interpretation that every offence includes *mens rea*, unless the contrary intention appears from a statute.[59] Further, such a rule would be easily implemented under the HRA by using s 3 to re-interpret offending criminal legislation to include *mens rea*.

However, the argument in favour of the substantive approach begins to look less appealing when it is recognised that *mens rea* alone is not a sufficient indicator of the appropriateness of imposing criminal liability. Criminal law theorists recognise that in addition to culpability, the concept of criminality must include some notion of 'wrongfulness'.[60] The idea of wrongfulness guides the decision about what conduct to criminalise in the first place.[61] Some theory of wrongfulness is necessary to explain why killing should be criminalised, or assault or rape.[62] Further, excuses and justifications play an important role in delineating the boundaries of wrongfulness for the purpose of criminal offences. A killing in self-defence, for example, may be intentional and yet not wrongful, and therefore not a proper subject of criminalisation. One can easily adapt the arguments of the substantivists so that the presumption of innocence extends not only to strict liability offences but also to a wide variety of defences. If it is a breach of the presumption of innocence to reverse the burden of proof with respect to self-defence, it must also be a breach of the presumption to eliminate self-defence altogether. Otherwise, the presumption of innocence would provide no genuine protection for the defendant who acts in legitimate self-defence. On the substantive approach, the confines of the presumption must expand to insist upon wrongfulness, as well as *mens rea*.

In addition to wrongfulness, the criminal law must take account of the capacity of the defendant to bear responsibility for his or her acts. Considerations such as insanity, diminished responsibility or intoxication play a role in distinguishing the guilty from the non-guilty in criminal trials. It has even been suggested that people who lack the capacity for empathy cannot be held responsible for their crimes.[63]

[58] J Hall 'Negligent Behavior Should be Excluded from Penal Liability' (1963) 63 *Columbia Law Review (Columb LR)* 632; A Ashworth 'Taking the Consequences' in S Shute, J Gardner & J Horder (eds) *Action and Value in Criminal Law* (OUP, Oxford 1993) 107. Arguing the opposite case are J Horder 'Two Histories and Four Hidden Principles of Mens Rea' (1997) 113 LQR 95; S Gardner 'The Importance of Majewski' (1994) 14 *OJLS* 279; J Horder 'Cognition, Emotion and Criminal Culpability' (1990) 106 LQR 469; C Wells 'Swatting the Subjectivist Bug' [1982] *Crim LR* 209.

[59] *B (A Minor) v DPP* [2000] 2 AC 428 (HL) 460 (Lord Nicholls), 470 (Lord Steyn), 478 (Lord Hutton).

[60] J Gardner 'Wrongs and Faults' in AP Simester (ed) *Appraising Strict Liability* (OUP, Oxford 2005) 51, esp 68–69.

[61] D Husak 'Limitations on Criminalization and the General Part of Criminal Law' in S Shute & AP Simester (eds) *Criminal Law Theory: Doctrines of the General Part* (OUP, Oxford 2002) 13, 28–29.

[62] See J Gardner & S Shute 'The Wrongness of Rape' in J Horder (ed) *Oxford Essays in Jurisprudence: Fourth Series* (OUP, Oxford 2000) 193.

[63] P Arenella 'Convicting the Morally Blameless: Reassessing the Relationship Between Legal and Moral Accountability' (1992) *UCLA Law Review*1511.

Firm ideas about when it is appropriate to hold a person responsible for his or her conduct must be brought into play in considering the scope of these considerations. If the substantive approach is to insist that the morally innocent must not be convicted, it would need to explain when a person's mental state is such that they could be regarded as morally innocent. Again, this aspect of innocence is separate from *mens rea* and the substantive approach requires a greatly expanded concept of innocence in order to take account of it.

Further, liberal theorists postulate that only conduct which is harmful to others should be subject to criminal prohibition.[64] A theory of criminal liability must decide if the causing of harm to others is a necessary precondition of criminal liability and, and if it is, calibrate the 'harm principle' in the appropriate way. This would require engagement with controversial theories of what for these purposes constitutes 'harm'.[65] One class of offences sometimes thought to pose problems for the 'harm principle' is inchoate offences.[66] Inchoate offences target conduct that is not harmful in itself but may lead to harm.[67] The most prominent examples are attempts, conspiracies and incitements. These offences, by definition, do not harm anyone since it is not necessary to prove that harmful conduct has been carried out. Similarly, offences of possession are inchoate offences since the act of possession does not cause harm (although it may result in harm at a later point).[68] Possessing a knife in a public place, for example, is a criminal act yet it is not obviously wrongful and, provided that the conduct is limited to possession, does not cause harm.[69] The person who possesses a knife could therefore, on one view, be regarded as 'innocent'. A substantive approach to the presumption of innocence would need to develop a theory to explain whether, and if so when, inchoate offences are a proper subject of criminal sanctions.

The attempt to extend the scope of the presumption of innocence to cover strict liability offences quickly results in further expansion. In addition to a theory of *mens rea*, one must develop a theory of wrongfulness, capacity and harmfulness. It becomes clear that what is required under the substantive approach is a fully comprehensive theory of criminal liability.[70] There is currently no complete theory of criminal responsibility that garners widespread support.[71] The need for

[64] The most well known proponent of this position is JS Mill *On Liberty* (Penguin, Harmondsworth 1974) (original 1859).

[65] See J Feinberg *The Moral Limits of the Criminal Law: Harm to Others* (OUP, Oxford 1984).

[66] Gardner & Shute (see n 62 above) 216–17; AP Simester and A von Hirsch 'Rethinking the Offense Principle' (2002) 8 *Legal Theory* 269, 283–87.

[67] See A Ashworth 'Defining Criminal Offences without Harm' in P Smith (ed) *Criminal Law: Essays in Honour of JC Smith* (Butterworths, London 1987) 7; J Horder 'Crimes of Ulterior Intent' in AP Simester & ATH Smith (eds) *Harm and Culpability* (Clarendon Press, Oxford 1996) 153.

[68] Roberts describes these as 'substantive inchoates' to distinguish them from attempts, conspiracies and incitements: Roberts (2002) *LQR* (see n 4 above) 55–57.

[69] Roberts (2005) (see n 4 above) 166–67.

[70] A Ashworth 'Four Threats to the Presumption of Innocence' (2006) 10 E & P 241, 254–55; Roberts (2005) (see n 4 above) 156–57; J Spencer & A Pedain 'Approaches to Strict and Constructive Liability in Continental Criminal Law' in AP Simester (ed) *Appraising Strict Liability* (OUP, Oxford 2005) 237, 280;

[71] *Cf* Tadros and Tierney (see n 3 above) 411 n 28.

such a theory should put us on notice that the presumption of innocence is being asked to expand well beyond any historical understanding of the doctrine.[72]

Even if such a theory were possible it would seem anomalous for the theory to be developed and implemented by the courts, rather than by the legislature. The courts have historically had a role in developing common law offences and have a continued role in refining and developing existing offences.[73] Despite this, the courts have recently refrained from creating new offences and left this role entirely to the legislature.[74] There are two reasons why the legislature, in general, is better suited to making the rules of criminal liability. First, the legislature does not need to create a general theory of criminal liability in order to enact criminal laws. It can consider each instance on its merits and then make adjustments and refinements through legislation taking into account the success of the model adopted. Second, the legislature has the force of democratic authority behind it so that the criminal laws enacted may be said to have a degree of popular assent. Certainly, there are limits on what a democratic legislature may do consistently with the HRA. But this does not mean that the democratic legislature should be limited by a judicially constructed theory of criminal liability.

If a complete theory of criminal liability is too ambitious a project for the courts, one possible response is to limit the substantive approach so that it insists only upon *mens rea*. This would require the identification of something unique about the *mens rea* requirement that makes it indispensable to the presumption of innocence. If there is something unique about *mens rea*, it might be possible to restrict the substantive approach so as to insist upon *mens rea* but not every other aspect of a comprehensive theory of criminal liability. A substantive approach limited in this way might be more attractive to the courts.

One possibility is that *mens rea* helps to put potential defendants on notice that they are 'about to enter the realms of possible criminality'.[75] Without a *mens rea* requirement, people can be found guilty of crimes without an adequate opportunity to avoid breaking the law. Such people are 'innocent' in the sense that nothing they could have done would have avoided their falling afoul of the criminal prohibition. By contrast, a law that is unfair because it criminalises conduct that is not wrongful nevertheless advertises itself to potential defendants so that they can avoid becoming liable. An offence of eating pizza, for example, might be said to involve no wrongfulness. However, provided the offence carries the *mens rea* requirement of knowledge that the thing eaten is pizza, only people who act with the requisite knowledge can come within the offence. People therefore have the ability to avoid committing the offence by not eating anything they know is pizza.[76]

[72] Some of those who accept that strict liability offences are contrary to the presumption of innocence nevertheless urge caution in using Art 6(2) to control other aspects of substantive criminal law: S Trechsel *Human Rights in Criminal Proceedings* (OUP, Oxford 2005) 158.

[73] Ashworth (see n 54 above) 7.

[74] *Knuller v DPP* [1973] AC 435 (HL) 457–58 (Lord Reid), 464–65 (Lord Morris), 490 (Lord Simon), 496 (Lord Kilbrandon).

[75] Gardner & Shute (see n 62 above) 215. See also Trechsel (see n 72 above) 157 n 16.

[76] This example is taken from Husak (see n 61 above) 28–29.

Seen in this way, strict liability offences deprive people of the opportunity to avoid contravening the criminal law and are therefore an especially pernicious form of unjust offence.

There are two responses to this. First, even in the case of strict liability offences people do have a form of notice that they may be entering the realm of a criminal prohibition. They know that when engaged in certain types of conduct they will be held strictly liable for anything that goes wrong. For example, in a jurisdiction with a felony murder rule, people who commit violent offences ought to be on notice that if death results from their acts, they will be liable for murder. Second, to the extent that a *mens rea* requirement seeks to ensure that only those with a choice to behave otherwise are liable, it is not clearly distinguishable from other features of criminal responsibility. Justificatory defences also operate to protect those defendants who are deprived of choice in avoiding the criminal prohibition. For example, a person who assaults another in self-defence may be said to have no means of avoiding committing the crime, since the only other option is to permit the assault by the assailant (assuming there is no opportunity to retreat). Similarly, excusing defences operate to bring persons who lack a genuine choice in their actions outside the realms of criminal liability.[77] People who act under a delusion of insanity, or as automatons or under a mistake of fact or under the threat of coercion are deprived of the opportunity to make a genuine choice concerning their actions.[78] Hence, while it is true that strict liability offences are pernicious, they are not uniquely so. There is nothing about *mens rea* that makes it essential to a properly functioning presumption of innocence.

It follows that if the English courts were to recognise a requirement of *mens rea*, it would need to be derived from a principle distinct from the presumption of innocence. Convictions in the absence of culpability do offend against a principle of justice: the principle that there should be no punishment without culpability.[79] This is a separate principle from the presumption of innocence and it is not contained within the ECHR.[80] Until there is a constitutional basis for such a principle in English law, the courts ought not to divine it from the presumption of

[77] See HLA Hart *Punishment and Responsibility* (Clarendon Press, Oxford 1968) 22 arguing that the recognition of excuses is necessary to limit criminal sanctions to conduct that is 'the outcome of . . . free choice'.

[78] Ibid 28–53.

[79] Ashworth (see n 70 above) 253; A Ashworth 'Case and Comment: R v G' [2006] *Crim LR* 930, 933.

[80] Such a principle is found in other jurisdictions. The Canadian Supreme Court has derived a requirement of *mens rea* from the 'principles of fundamental justice' protected by s 7 of the Canadian Charter of Rights and Freedoms: *Re BC Motor Vehicle Act* [1985] 2 SCR 486, 513–15 (Lamer J, for the majority); *R v Vaillancourt* [1987] 2 SCR 636, 653–54 (Lamer J, for the majority).The German Constitutional Court recognises the need for *mens rea* in all offences. The requirement is derived from the protection of 'human dignity' in Art 2(1) of the Basic Law: see Spencer & Pedain (see n 70 above) 237. Spencer & Pedain note that German (and French) law have been able to dispense with strict liability offences because the rules of criminal procedure in those countries make it easier to prove fault: ibid 269.

innocence.[81] It follows that the English courts have been right to reject the substantive approach to the presumption of innocence.

If the presumption of innocence is a procedural protection, it consequently does nothing to assist a morally innocent person who is prosecuted under an unfair or over-expansive law. In chapter two, it was argued that one of the rationales for the presumption of innocence was to protect the innocent from wrongful conviction. It does not follow, however, that a purely procedural interpretation of the presumption of innocence fails to meet this rationale. Even as a procedural protection, the presumption of innocence protects the innocent because there is considerable overlap between moral innocence and legal innocence. To the extent that legal prohibitions mirror our intuitions regarding moral innocence, the insistence that the prosecution must prove that the defendant has contravened a legal prohibition will protect the morally innocent. Legal prohibitions do not always match our intuitions concerning blameworthiness. Strict liability offences are an obvious example. But they often do match especially in the case of traditional offences such as murder, rape and theft. Further, a procedural conception of the presumption of innocence meets the rationale of promoting the rule of law by insisting that there should be no conviction in the absence of proof that a person has contravened a pre-ordained legal prohibition. A procedural conception of the presumption of innocence therefore responds to both rationales for the presumption.

3. Other Constraints on Unfair Offences

While Article 6(2) does not impose constraints on the substance of the criminal law this does not mean that there are no constraints on unfair offences in English law or under the ECHR. To begin with, strict liability offences are constrained in English law by virtue of a well-established rule of statutory interpretation that all offences are to be read so as to include *mens rea*, unless the contrary intention appears.[82] If Parliament wishes to exercise its power to create strict liability offences, the intention to eliminate *mens rea* must appear either expressly or by necessary implication.[83] The effect of this rule is that strict liability offences may be enacted only by deliberate drafting techniques, and anyone familiar with the relevant law will be able to understand the strict liability nature of the crime.

Further, other provisions of the ECHR impose substantive constraints on criminal law prohibitions. Laws that criminalise homosexual acts are a breach of the right to privacy in Article 8 and the right to freedom from discrimination in Article 14.[84] Laws that criminalise certain forms of speech may be a breach of the right to

[81] See Roberts (2005) (see n 4 above) 193.

[82] *Fowler v Padget* (1798) 7 Term Rep 509, 514 (Lord Kenyon CJ); *Brend v Wood* (1946) LT 306, 307 (Lord Goddard CJ); *Warner v MPC* [1969] 2 AC 256 (HL) 271 (Lord Reid); *Sweet v Parsley* [1970] AC 132 (HL) 148 (Lord Reid), 152 (Lord Morris)

[83] *B (A Minor) v DPP* [2000] 2 AC 428 (HL) 460 (Lord Nicholls), 470 (Lord Steyn).

[84] *Dudgeon v UK* (App No 7525/76) (1982) 4 EHRR 149; *Norris v Ireland* (App No 10581/83) (1991) 13 EHRR 186.

freedom of expression in Article 10.[85] Retroactive laws will run afoul of Article 7 and laws with disproportionate punishments could run afoul of the prohibition on inhuman and degrading treatment in Article 3.[86]

In addition to these constraints, Alan Michaels proposes an approach to human rights protections which would bring some categories of strict liability offences within the boundaries of ECHR control.[87] His approach seizes upon the characteristic that *mens rea* places persons on notice that they are about to enter the area of a criminal prohibition.[88] If the field is one in which a human rights protection guarantees freedom to the individual, the absence of warning that a person is about to traverse the boundaries of a criminal prohibition would breach the protected right. An offence of strict liability imposes a side constraint on the exercise of the protected right by exposing people to the risk of criminal prosecution, even when they have acted without *mens rea*. Michaels states that the way to determine the compatibility of a strict liability offence is to consider whether the offence would pass muster without the aspect of the offence to which strict liability attaches.[89]

> According to the principle of constitutional innocence, strict liability is constitutional when, but only when, the intentional conduct covered by the statute could be made criminal by the legislature. In other words, strict liability runs afoul of the Constitution if the other elements of the crime, with the strict liability element excluded, could not themselves be made a crime. Otherwise, strict liability is constitutional.

This approach does not create an independent restriction on strict liability, but rather draws on other rights-based restrictions to establish the parameters of permissible strict liability.[90]

Michaels uses the example of a Californian statute which criminalised possession of an obscene book in a place where books were sold.[91] The offence had no requirement of knowledge or intention with respect to the obscene nature of the book and no defence of due diligence. Michaels argues this offence breached the right to freedom of speech because a person innocently engaged in the selling of books could be caught within the criminal prohibition. Applying the 'constitutional innocence' principle, the only intentional conduct that needed to be committed to constitute the crime was selling books. However, an offence of selling books would manifestly be inconsistent with the right to freedom of

[85] S Turenne 'The Compatibility of Criminal Liability with Freedom of Expression' [2007] Crim LR 866.

[86] *Weeks v UK* (App No 9787/82) (1988) 10 EHRR 293 [47].

[87] AC Michaels 'Imposing Constitutional Limits on Strict Liability: Lessons from the American Experience' in AP Simester (ed) *Appraising Strict Liability* (OUP, Oxford 2005) 219. The approach is based on Michaels' arguments concerning the compatibility of strict liability offences with the US Constitution: see AC Michaels, 'Constitutional Innocence' (1999) *Harv L Rev* 829.

[88] Michaels (2005) ibid 225–26.

[89] Ibid 221–22.

[90] Ibid 222.

[91] Ibid 222. The example is drawn from *Smith v California*, 361 US 147 (1959) where the US Supreme Court held the offence was unconstitutional.

expression. Consequently, the strict liability offence was inconsistent with the US Constitution.

If adopted under the HRA, this argument could bring some strict liability offences into conflict with ECHR rights. It is useful to investigate how this argument would apply to the decision in *R v G*.[92] In that case, the offence was one of sexual intercourse with a girl under the age of 13. There was no requirement that the defendant knew the age of the victim and no defence of reasonable mistake as to age. The offence was therefore one of strict liability with respect to the age of the victim.[93] On Michaels' argument, the compatibility of the offence with Article 8 would be determined by considering whether the offence would pass muster in the absence of the aspect to which strict liability attached, that is, the age of the victim. In the absence of this element, the offence would be one of having sexual intercourse, and such an offence would clearly be incompatible with Article 8.[94] Just as the strict liability offence of possessing an obscene book has a 'chilling effect' on free speech, the strict liability offence of sexual intercourse with a girl aged 13 impedes freedom within the private realm of sexual conduct. Under the HRA, the courts would very likely conclude that the interference with sexual freedom was proportionate to the legitimate objective of protecting under-aged persons from sexual predation.[95] However, if it were deemed disproportionate, the offence could be brought into line with Article 8 by reading in an appropriate *mens rea* element, such as absence of reasonable belief the girl was aged over 13.

The availability of such arguments to rein in the worst excesses of over-criminalisation shows that it is not necessary to permit the presumption of innocence to expand beyond all recognition. There are existing constraints on unfair offences, including strict liability offences, without requiring Article 6(2) to operate as a vehicle for the judicial implementation of a comprehensive, but inherently controversial, theory of criminal liability.

[92] *R v G* [2008] 1 WLR 1379 (HL). A similar analysis could be applied to the offence considered in *Barnfather v Islington Education Authority* [2003] 1 WLR 2318 (QBD). Criminalising parents for the truancy of their children could be a breach of the right to family life protected by Art 12, although it would be necessary to consider whether the interference was proportionate to the objective of ensuring attendance at school: see Michaels (2005) (see n 87 above) 233.

[93] The Court of Appeal acknowledged that an offence of this nature could on 'particular facts' breach the right to privacy under Art 8, which includes a right to engage in consensual sexual conduct *R v G* [2006] 1 WLR 2052 (CA) [46] (Lord Phillips CJ, for the Court).

[94] Michaels (2005) (see n 87 above) 232.

[95] See *R v G* [2008] 1 WLR 1379 (HL) 1383 [7] (Lord Hoffmann): 'The other ground of appeal is that the conviction violated the defendant's right of privacy under article 8. This is, on the face of it, an astonishing proposition. Is it really being suggested that a young person under 18 has a human right to have undisturbed sexual intercourse with a child under 13? If anything is likely to bring human rights into disrepute, it is such a claim.'

B. Narrow Procedural Approach

Rejecting the substantive approach to the presumption of innocence means that Article 6(2) cannot be used to re-write substantive rules of criminal liability. On a procedural approach to the presumption, the courts need be concerned only with aspects of the offence which appear from the statute. In determining the scope of the presumption of innocence, the next question to be asked is whether there are some matters relevant to conviction with respect to which the burden of proof can be placed on the defendant. The narrow procedural approach requires the prosecution to prove only the 'core' of the offence. With respect to peripheral matters, it would permit reversal of the burden of proof. In contrast, under the broad procedural approach, the prosecution must prove every matter necessary for conviction, whether part of the core or the periphery of the offence. This Part first considers the approach of the English courts to the relevance of the 'gravamen' of the offence. It then contends with the academic arguments in favour of the narrow procedural approach. Discussion of the broad procedural approach is postponed to Part C.

1. Confusion in the English Cases

The idea that criminal offences have an identifiable 'core' which must be proved by the prosecution was introduced in the first case decided under the HRA concerning reverse burdens of proof. In *Kebilene*,[96] a challenge was brought to the consent by the DPP to a prosecution under section 16A(1) of the Prevention of Terrorism (Temporary Provisions) Act 1989, which made it an offence to have possession of any article in circumstances giving rise to a 'reasonable suspicion' that the article was held for a purpose connected with terrorism. Possession could be established by proof of physical proximity to the articles or by occupation or use of premises in which the articles were kept.[97] A defendant could avoid conviction by proving that he or she had no knowledge of the presence of the articles or did not have control over the articles.[98] Further, it was a defence to prove that the article was not possessed for a terrorist purpose.[99] In the Divisional Court, Lord Bingham sought to identify the conduct that was in fact prohibited by the offence. His Lordship adopted the term 'gravamen' to describe the conduct at which the offence was directed. His Lordship stated:[100]

> The gravamen of the offence charged by section 16A is the possession of articles, in themselves innocent, for terrorist purposes. The crucial ingredients of the offence are in

96 *R v DPP, ex p Kebilene* [2000] 2 AC 326 (HL).
97 Section 16A(4)
98 Section 16A (4).
99 Section 16A (3).
100 [2000] 2 AC 326 (QBD) 344 (Lord Bingham). See also 356 (Laws LJ). Sullivan J agreed with both judgments: 357.

reality possession (the actus reus) and the terrorist purpose (the mens rea). But neither of these crucial ingredients need be proved by the prosecution to the criminal standard to secure a conviction.

Lord Bingham's identification of the gravamen (or 'crucial ingredients') of the offence did not depend upon the language or structure of the statute. By searching for the gravamen, Lord Bingham cut across the formal layout of the offence to identify the conduct that was in fact prohibited by section 16A. According to Lord Bingham, since the prosecution did not need to prove either possession or the terrorist purpose, the reversal of the burden offended the presumption of innocence 'in a blatant and obvious way'.[101] In the House of Lords, the discussion of Article 6(2) was *obiter*, and added little to the understanding of the aspects of an offence that must be proved by the prosecution.[102]

The problem of what the prosecution must prove arose again in *R v Lambert.*[103] In that case, a reverse burden imposed under the Misuse of Drugs Act 1971 was analysed. Section 5(3) made it an offence to be in possession of a controlled drug with intent to supply. Previous authority had held that the *mens rea* associated with possession was knowledge that something was possessed, but it was not necessary to prove that the defendant had knowledge that the thing possessed was a controlled drug.[104] However, section 28(2) of the 1971 Act made it a defence for the defendant to prove that he or she neither knew, nor suspected, nor had reason to suspect that the thing possessed was a controlled drug. The House of Lords was required to determine whether this reverse persuasive burden was consistent with Article 6(2).

In determining what the prosecution is required to prove in accordance with the presumption of innocence, the House of Lords disapproved of reliance upon the language and structure of the statute and, in particular, the distinction between 'elements' and 'defences'. Lord Steyn stated that it would be hopelessly formalistic to rely upon the language of the statute to determine the applicability of the presumption of innocence. His Lordship stated:[105]

[101] Ibid 344 (Lord Bingham). The Divisional Court also held that the reverse burden applied to the offence of collection or possession of information for terrorist purposes (s 16B) was incompatible with the presumption of innocence: ibid 344 (Lord Bingham), 356 (Laws LJ). By the time the case reached the House of Lords, the defendant charged under s 16B was no longer involved in the appeal.

[102] Lord Hope (at 381) used similar language to Lord Bingham in describing the offence under s 16A: '[T]he essence of the offence is the possession of articles for a terrorist purpose.' Lord Hobhouse (at 398) referred, briefly, to 'a need to look beyond the bare words of the statute . . . concerning the identification of the essential criminality which the prosecution must prove . . .' Neither judge clarified the significance of these concepts for the purposes of the scope of the presumption.

[103] *R v Lambert* [2002] 2 AC 545 (HL).

[104] *R v McNamara* (1988) 87 Cr App R 246 (CA).

[105] [2002] 2 AC 545 (HL) [35]. Lord Steyn quoted *R v Whyte* [1988] 2 SCR 3, 18 (Dickson CJ, for the Court): 'The exact characterization of a factor as an essential element, a collateral factor, an excuse, or a defence should not affect the analysis of the presumption of innocence. It is the final effect of a provision on the verdict that is decisive.' By contrast, the US Supreme Court has apparently been willing to draw distinctions based on the structure of the offence: compare *Mullaney v Wilbur*, 421 US 684, 698 (1975) (Powell J) with *Patterson v New York*, 432 US 197, 205–10 (1977) (White J, for the majority). See also *Martin v Ohio*, 480 US 228 (1987); *Sandstrom v Montana*, 442 US 510 (1979).

> The distinction between constituent elements of the crime and defensive issues will sometimes be unprincipled and arbitrary. After all, it is sometimes simply a matter of which drafting technique is adopted: a true constituent element can be removed from the definition of the crime and cast as a defensive issue whereas any definition of an offence can be reformulated so as to include all possible defences within it. It is necessary to concentrate not on technicalities and niceties of language but rather on matters of substance.

For Lord Steyn, the decisive factor was that knowledge of possession of a controlled drug bore directly on the 'moral blameworthiness' of the defendant and that this factor alone justified the maximum possible penalty of life imprisonment.[106] Lord Steyn concluded: 'In my view there is an inroad on the presumption even if an issue under section 28 is in strict law regarded as a pure defence.'[107] On this approach to Article 6(2), the distinction between elements and defences was not crucial. What mattered was whether the defendant could be convicted even though the prosecution had not proved every aspect necessary for criminal liability.

By contrast, in *R v S*,[108] the Court of Appeal came very close to holding that a reverse burden with respect to an exculpatory 'defence' would never be a breach of the presumption of innocence. The defendant in that case was charged with infringing a trade mark by selling counterfeit goods contrary to section 92 of the Trade Marks Act 1994. Under section 92(5) it was a defence to show that the defendant believed on reasonable grounds that the use made of the trade mark was not an infringement. Rose LJ, on behalf of the Court of Appeal, held that dishonesty was not an 'essential element'[109] or part of the 'gravamen'[110] of the offence. Section 92, according to Rose LJ, was intended to capture infringements of trade marks even when the infringement was not dishonest.[111] Consequently, the reverse burden in section 92(5) did not infringe the presumption of innocence. Rose LJ went so far as to say that Article 6(2) 'has no application'.[112] Rose LJ evidently had misgivings about this conclusion, however, and His Lordship stated that he 'would not regard it as satisfactory to rest the ultimate decision in this case solely on that basis.'[113] Accordingly, he went on to consider whether the reverse burden in section 92(5) was proportionate to the objective of controlling trade mark infringement, concluding that it was.[114]

In *Johnstone*,[115] the House of Lords subjected section 92(5) to a further review. Lord Nicholls stated that section 92(5) constituted a *prima facie* derogation from the presumption of innocence because it set out facts which the defendant was required to prove in order to avoid conviction.[116] Hence, Lord Nicholls was not

[106] Ibid.
[107] Ibid. See also [17] (Lord Slynn), [185] (Lord Hutton). *Cf* [153] (Lord Clyde).
[108] *R v S* [2003] 1 Cr App R 35 (CA).
[109] Ibid [34].
[110] Ibid [30].
[111] Ibid.
[112] Ibid [34].
[113] Ibid [35].
[114] Ibid [49].
[115] *R v Johnstone* [2003] 1 WLR 1736 (HL).
[116] Ibid [47].

attracted to the view that there was no breach of the presumption of innocence merely because the reverse burden related to a 'defence'. The compatibility of the reverse burden had to be determined applying the proportionality analysis. In this process, the relative importance of the matters which the defendant was required to prove was nevertheless significant. Lord Nicholls stated: 'The extent and nature of the factual matters required to be proved by the accused, and their importance relative to the matters required to be proved by the prosecution, have to be taken into account.'[117] Lord Nicholls consequently considered it relevant to the proportionality inquiry that section 92 created an offence of 'near absolute liability' and that intent to infringe the trademark need not be proved.[118] This was one of six factors that Lord Nicholls considered in concluding that the reverse burden was proportionate and therefore compatible with Article 6(2).[119]

A division over the scope of the presumption of innocence arose in the House of Lords in the joined decisions in *Sheldrake v DPP* and *AG's Reference (No 4 of 2002)*.[120] In the former case, the House of Lords considered the offence created by section 5(1)(b) of the Road Traffic Act 1988 of being drunk in charge of a motor vehicle. Section 5(2) of the same Act permitted a 'defence' if it could be proved that the circumstances were such that there was no likelihood of the defendant driving the vehicle while his or her blood alcohol level was over the prescribed limit. Lord Bingham, who wrote the majority decision in both joined appeals, disapproved of the view that the likelihood of driving was part of the gravamen of the offence.[121] Lord Bingham explained that the purpose of Parliament had been to criminalise those people who failed to divest themselves of the power of driving while under the influence of alcohol. Even if there was no likelihood of the defendant driving, he or she would still 'fall squarely within the class of those whose conduct Parliament has . . . legislated to criminalise.'[122] However, having determined that the likelihood of driving was not an essential ingredient of the offence, Lord Bingham nevertheless recognised that section 5(2) constituted a *prima facie* breach of Article 6(2). Lord Bingham stated: 'It may not be very profitable to debate whether section 5(2) infringes the presumption of innocence. It may be assumed that it does.'[123] Hence, in the view of Lord Bingham (with whom the majority agreed) there could be a *prima facie* breach of the presumption of innocence even when the reverse burden did not relate to the gravamen or an essential element.

This approach contrasts with the minority judgment of Lord Rodger in the second of the joined appeals, *AG's Reference (No 4 of 2002)*.[124] In that case, the defendant was charged with membership of Hamas, and professing to membership

[117] Ibid [50].
[118] Ibid [52].
[119] Ibid.
[120] *Sheldrake v DPP* and *AG's Reference (No 4 of 2002)* [2005] 1 AC 264 (HL).
[121] Ibid [40]. The Divisional Court below had held unanimously that it was part of the gravamen: *Sheldrake v DPP* [2004] QB 487 (QBD) [30] (Clarke LJ), [92] (Henriques J), [142] (Jack J).
[122] Ibid [40].
[123] Ibid [41].
[124] *AG's Reference (No 4 of 2002)* Ibid.

of Hamas, a proscribed terrorist organisation, contrary to section 11(1) of the Terrorism Act 2000. Under section 11(2), it was a defence for a person to prove that the organisation was not proscribed when he or she became a member, and that the person had not taken part in its activities since it was proscribed. Lord Rodger concluded that the conduct at which the offence was aimed was complete once it was shown that the defendant was either a member of a terrorist organisation or had professed membership in the organisation. The purpose of criminalising membership in a terrorist organisation was to prevent public demonstrations of support for terrorism and to disrupt terrorist networks.[125] The purpose of prohibiting people from making claims of membership in an organisation (even false claims) was to prevent an exaggerated impression of the strength of the organisation in question.[126] It followed that the defences in section 11(2) did not bring defendants outside the purpose of the offence. For Lord Rodger, there was not even a threshold breach of Article 6(2) because the prosecution was required to prove every element related to the purpose of the offence.[127] The defences in section 11(2) were nothing more than a form of 'favourable treatment' for certain defendants.[128]

Hence, we can see that according to Lord Rodger, a defence would not breach the presumption of innocence, even in a *prima facie* sense, if the prosecution had already proved the essential ingredients of the offence. This was an example of the narrow procedural approach to the presumption of innocence. By contrast, Lord Bingham had concluded that a reverse burden would constitute a *prima facie* interference with the presumption even if it related to something outside the gravamen of the offence. This was an example of the broad procedural approach to the presumption. As Lord Bingham wrote on behalf of the majority in the case, his reasons must be regarded as binding on all lower courts. However, this issue was not discussed in any great detail, especially by Lord Bingham, and consequently it is conceivable that a later decision of the House might revisit this aspect.

In *R v Chargot Limited*,[129] the House of Lords did not expressly revisit the question of gravamen, although the circumstances of the case undoubtedly raised the issue of what matters constituted the core of the offence. In that case, Chargot Limited, one of its directors and a related company had been charged under section 33(1)(a) of the Health and Safety at Work Act 1974 with breaches of certain duties imposed by the Act. Specifically, it was alleged that the defendants had breached the duty imposed by section 2(1) to ensure, as far as was reasonably practicable, the health and safety of employees at work and had also breached the duty imposed by section 3(1) to ensure, so far as reasonably practicable, that non-employees were not exposed to risks to their health and safety. Section 40 of the Act placed the persuasive burden on the defendants to prove that they had taken all reasonably practicable steps to ensure a safe workplace.

125 Ibid [62].
126 Ibid [63].
127 Ibid [65].
128 Ibid [69]. See also [71].
129 *R v Chargot Limited* [2009] 1 WLR 1 (HL).

In analyzing this statutory framework, Lord Hope found that to enliven sections 2(1) and 3(1) the prosecution needed only to demonstrate that the health or safety of an employee had been compromised or that a non-employee had been exposed to a risk. As a matter of statutory construction, it was not necessary for the prosecution to prove the acts or omissions on the part of the employer that led to those results.[130] Lord Hope went on to find that the reverse burden imposed by section 40 with respect to whether the defendant had taken all reasonably practicable steps to ensure a safe workplace was proportionate and justifiable.[131]

Lord Hope did not expressly address whether the issue of reasonably practicable steps was part of the gravamen or core of the offence. However, Lord Hope held, in effect, that the objective fact that an employee's health and safety had been compromised, or that a non-employee had been exposed to a health and safety risk, was a sufficient basis upon which to mount a prosecution. This suggests Lord Hope regarded those facts as constituting the core of the offence, while the question whether the employer had taken all reasonably practicable steps to prevent those results was only a subsidiary matter, such that placing the persuasive burden on the defendants with respect to it was not unfair. It is submitted that this conclusion is highly questionable, since the taking of reasonably practicable steps to prevent risks to health and safety is the only conduct that an employer can undertake to ensure a safe workplace. It is the failure to take those steps which makes the employer morally culpable and a proper subject of criminal liability, not the objective fact that an accident has occurred in the workplace. In any case, as Lord Hope did not expressly address the issue of gravamen, he cannot be taken to have departed from the view of Lord Bingham as expressed in *Sheldrake* that every reverse burden is a *prima facie* interference with the presumption of innocence.

2. Case for a Narrow Procedural Approach

The House of Lords decisions discussed above lean towards the view that all reverse burdens constitute a *prima facie* interference with the presumption of innocence, and that the compatibility of the burden must be determined under the proportionality analysis. This section investigates the arguments concerning the narrow procedural approach in a systematic fashion, drawing upon the relevant academic commentary. Although it is not always clear from the cases, the narrow procedural approach takes various guises depending on the method used to distinguish core aspects of the offence from peripheral aspects. Three different approaches will be discussed below: (a) a formal distinction between the core and periphery of an offence, mirroring the distinction between 'elements' and 'defences'; (b) a substantive distinction based on identifying the 'gravamen' of an

[130] Ibid [21]. Lord Hoffmann, Lord Scott and Lord Neuberger agreed with Lord Hope. Lord Brown wrote his own concurring judgment.

[131] Ibid [30].

offence; and (c) a proposal for distinguishing offence aspects from defence aspects by reference to 'prima facie' wrongfulness.

(a) Elements and Defences

Paul Roberts has argued that the presumption of innocence requires the prosecution to prove the 'elements' of an offence, but that the persuasive burden can be placed on the defendant with respect to 'defences'.[132] He developed this view in response to the decisions of the House of Lords in *Kebilene* and *Lambert*. As we have seen, in *Kebilene*, Lord Bingham looked past the formal features of the statute under review and instead identified the 'gravamen' of the offence.[133] For Roberts, this way of characterising the offence charged in *Kebilene* was fundamentally flawed because it failed to recognise the distinction between 'elements' and 'defences'.

Roberts insists that there were two elements to the offence create by section 16A: (i) being in possession of any article; and (ii) a reasonable suspicion that the article is possessed for a terrorist purpose. Possession for a terrorist purpose and knowledge of or control over the article were not elements of the offence. Rather, they were defences that came to be proved after the elements had already been established. In Roberts' view, when the section 16A offence is broken down into its component parts, there is no interference with the presumption of innocence 'since the prosecution shoulders the full probative burden of proof on both positive elements of the offence'.[134] Hence, according to Roberts, 'the relevant offence does not even raise a threshold issue of compatibility with Article 6(2).'[135]

Similarly, Roberts has argued that the reverse persuasive burden with respect to knowing possession of a controlled drug, held inconsistent with Article 6(2) in *Lambert*, did not implicate the presumption of innocence.[136] Roberts emphasises that under section 5(3) of the Misuse of Drugs Act 1971, the mental element of possession was complete upon proof that the defendant knew he or she was in possession of something, even if the defendant did not know it was a controlled drug.[137] It followed that knowledge the substance was a controlled drug was not an element of the offence but rather a defence. As such, it was not an interference with the presumption of innocence to place the burden of proof with respect to knowledge onto the defendant. According to Roberts, the House of Lords analysis of the compatibility of section 28 with Article 6(2) 'should have been pre-empted by this threshold consideration'.[138]

[132] Roberts (2002) *LQR* (see n 4 above); Roberts (2002) *E & P* (see n 4 above). Roberts also rejects the substantive approach to Art6(2): Roberts (2002) *LQR* (see n 4 above) 48–49, 68–70; Roberts (2002) *E & P* (see n 4 above) 22; Roberts & Zuckerman 384, 387.

[133] See above text accompanying footnotes 96–101.

[134] Roberts (2002) *LQR* (see n 4 above) 50.

[135] Ibid 43.

[136] Roberts (2002) *E & P* (see n 4 above).

[137] Ibid 22–23.

[138] Ibid 25.

As these examples show, Roberts sees the distinction between 'elements' and 'defences' as dependent upon the language and structure of the relevant legislation. Roberts has buttressed his argument by attempting to show why attention must be paid to the statutory characterisation of the different aspects of criminal liability.[139] He argues against those who suggest 'functional equivalence' between evidentiary devices and the substantive criteria of criminal liability.[140] According to Roberts, there is 'a communicative dimension that invests the legislature's choice of statutory language, patterns and models of offence structure, conceptual distinctions, and drafting tools and techniques with nuanced moral salience.'[141] He argues that Parliament should be allowed the full range of conceptual tools and legislative techniques to determine the rules of criminal liability with appropriate finesse.[142] This means that judges should recognise a difference between the defining elements of an offence and an affirmative defence, applying the language and structure of the relevant statute. Judges would be failing to give effect to the message intended by a statute if they reinterpreted a criminal offence to insist that the prosecution should not only prove the elements but also disprove any defences. This argument is directed principally at supporters of a substantive approach to the presumption of innocence but it also operates as an argument against a broad procedural approach.

Roberts' plea for clear definitions of criminal offences is no doubt commendable. The difficulty is that there is nothing to suggest that the legislature uses different drafting techniques with anything like the degree of deliberation that Roberts supposes. Criminal legislation ought to define an area of a criminal prohibition with clarity so that citizens can conduct their lives and organise their affairs in order to avoid contravening the prohibition, and so that courts have clear rules to apply in deciding whether a criminal boundary has been traversed. However, there is no rule of statutory drafting that the legislature will always put the substance of a criminal prohibition into the definition of an offence, leaving exculpatory matters for later sections. The choice to use one drafting technique rather than another is often a matter of convenience or ease of phrasing. In some instances, aspects of an offence may be divided out into separate sub-sections so that the field of prohibited conduct is more clearly expressed. In other instances, one element of an offence may be separated out in order to facilitate the imposition of a persuasive burden on the defendant with respect to that element.

[139] Roberts (2005) (see n 4 above).

[140] According to Roberts, 'functionalists' assert that a strict liability offence is 'functionally equivalent' to a reverse onus clause: Roberts (2005) (see n 4 above) 153, 168–69. He then proceeds to show how reverse onus clauses operate differently to strict liability offences: ibid 172. This misconceives the argument of the substantivists who in general do not assert the functional equivalence of procedural devices and the substantive law. For example, Ronald Allen's case for functional similarity is limited to a comparison of various procedural devices, such as affirmative defences, burdens of production, judicial comment, presumptions and inferences: Allen (see n 3 above). The argument of the substantivists is not that strict liability offences function in an equivalent way to offences subject to reverse onuses, but that both share the same flaw by putting the morally innocent in danger of conviction.

[141] Ibid 191.

[142] Ibid 194.

In terms of the impact upon the substance of the criminal prohibition there is no difference between describing a matter as an element and describing is as a defence. Any condition qualifying an offence could always be redrafted so as to be included within the initial definition of the offence, and any definitional element could be couched as a qualifying defence.[143] Regardless of the drafting technique used, the question ought always to be whether the defendant has been proved to come within the area of the criminal prohibition. Both 'elements' and 'defences' are essential in defining the area of a criminal prohibition. A person who is entitled to rely upon a defence does not come within the criminal prohibition, just as a person who has not performed one of the elements of the offence does not come within it. Provisions that have the effect of placing a persuasive burden on the defendant allow conviction even though criminality (however criminality has been defined) has not been proved.

Roberts' proposition that there is a salient difference between 'elements' and 'defences' might be defended if we were to treat statutes creating criminal offences as a set of rules about what the prosecution must prove and what the defence must prove. On this view, one purpose of the statute is to communicate to the court that if the prosecution can prove certain matters, and the defence is unable to prove other matters, then the defendant is liable to conviction. Another purpose of the statute is to communicate to individuals that they should engage in certain conduct only if they are in a position to prove that they fall within an exception to criminality. This is an impoverished and misleading understanding of statutes creating criminal offences. Statutes communicate both to the courts and the public by expressing shared standards of conduct that the community expects all people to follow. Together, the offence and defence aspects of the statute tell the individual what may and may not be done. For example, when communicating to individuals in the community, the statute does not say that it is illegal to possess items in circumstances that create a reasonable suspicion of a terrorist purpose, unless you can prove you have no terrorist purpose. Rather, the statute informs individuals in the community that it is illegal to possess items for a terrorist purpose. The question of who must prove what in the course of a criminal trial is a matter of procedure. The presumption of innocence, as a procedural guarantee, requires that the prosecution should prove that the defendant falls within the bounds of criminality.

It might well be preferable if Parliament drafted all offences so that every aspect of criminality necessary for conviction was contained within one section, making the substance of the criminal prohibition clear and easily ascertainable, both to the courts and the public.[144] However, Parliament has never adopted such a practice and there is nothing to suggest that it will in the future. Therefore, the language and structure of a statute is not a reliable guide to the placement of the burden of proof. Any attempt to distinguish between prosecution and defence aspects of

[143] G Williams 'Offences and Defences' (1982) 2 *Legal Studies* 233, 252–56.

[144] Although it might still be more convenient to place defences of general application together in one place so that they need not be repeated alongside each offence.

criminal liability based upon formal criteria is therefore doomed to fail. There might, however, be an inherent difference of substance between prosecution and defence aspects. The following sections investigate whether any such difference could operate as a guide to the placement of the burden of proof.

(b) Gravamen

Due to the formalistic nature of the distinction between 'elements' and 'defences' the cases often use the term 'gravamen' to signify the core of an offence. The search for the 'gravamen' of an offence cuts across the formal structure of the statute creating the offence. However, it is not always clear what is meant by 'gravamen'. Two alternatives present themselves. Gravamen might mean the part of the offence which makes the conduct wrongful and therefore suitable for criminal sanctions. Alternatively, it might mean the conduct which the offence is intended to control; that is, the gravamen of the offence depends upon its purpose. The two alternatives will overlap to the extent that the purpose of an offence is to control wrongful conduct. However, an offence may have the purpose of controlling conduct that is not itself wrongful. It is necessary to investigate whether either approach to identifying the gravamen of an offence is doctrinally sound, and if so whether it could be used as the basis for allocating the burden of proof.

The first approach to identifying the 'gravamen' is to look for the aspects of the offence which relate to 'moral blameworthiness'. This approach is suggested by the decision of Lord Steyn in *Lambert*.[145] In that case, Lord Steyn held that the reverse burden in section 28 breached the presumption of innocence because knowledge that the substance possessed was a controlled drug was a matter 'directly bearing on the moral blameworthiness of the accused'.[146] Similarly, in *AG's Reference (No 4 of 2002)*,[147] Lord Bingham held it was a breach of the presumption of innocence to impose a reverse burden with respect to the time of joining a proscribed organisation and involvement in its activities since proscription. One reason for this was that in the absence of proof relating to these matters the conduct of the defendant could not reasonably 'be regarded as blameworthy or such as should properly attract criminal sanctions'.[148] It is necessary to investigate whether the notion of 'moral blameworthiness' could be used to identify the gravamen of an offence. If so, on the broad procedural approach, reverse burdens with respect to matters of moral blameworthiness would interfere with the presumption of innocence, but other reverse burdens would not.

The problem with this approach is that it rests on an assumption that the legislature should criminalise only morally blameworthy conduct. To this extent, the courts run into a similar problem to that discussed under the substantive

[145] [2002] 2 AC 545 (HL).
[146] Ibid [35].
[147] *AG's Reference (No 4 of 2002)*[2005] 1 AC 264 (HL).
[148] Ibid [47].

approach: what is morally blameworthy conduct, or what conduct can properly be made the subject of criminal sanctions? This is a highly controversial question. Further, it fails to recognise that there may be degrees of wrongfulness. Proof from the prosecution of certain aspects of an offence may establish one degree of wrongfulness, while a reverse burden defence relates to a different degree of wrongfulness. Hence, a person might be thought morally blameworthy for failing to ensure that he or she did not come into possession of drugs, but blameworthy to a greater degree for deliberately taking possession of drugs.[149] The search for 'moral blameworthiness' does not assist us in deciding which degree of blameworthiness it would be proper for the legislature to criminalise. The identification of aspects of an offence which go to "moral blameworthiness" is too nebulous and uncertain a method to apply as the touchstone for assessing the compatibility of a reverse burden with the presumption of innocence.

The second approach to identifying the 'gravamen' involves a search for the 'purpose' of an offence. Tadros and Tierney treat the term 'gravamen' as synonymous with the purpose for which the offence was created.[150] While the authors recognise that the legislature, in creating an offence, may have more than one purpose,[151] and concede there might be difficulties in finding the purpose of an offence, they state it is nevertheless a general principle useful for structuring the reasoning of the court.[152] They argue, for example, that the offence of possession for a terrorist purpose was not intended to convict people about whom there was merely a reasonable suspicion, but rather people who actually had a terrorist purpose. Hence, the gravamen of that offence included the terrorist purpose and to reverse the burden with respect to that aspect was a breach of the presumption of innocence.[153] According to Tadros and Tierney, it could not have been part of the purpose of the legislature to convict people, and expose them to a possible ten year prison sentence, upon suspicion alone since such a purpose would be 'absurdly illiberal'.[154]

This final aspect of their reasoning suggests that the test of 'purpose' resolves into an investigation of what conduct the legislature could reasonably have intended to criminalise. This is because, in the investigation of legislative 'purpose', the authors assume that the legislature would not have intended to criminalise conduct that was not wrongful or culpable.[155] The obvious problem with this is that the legislature may have intended to criminalise people whose conduct was not wrongful or culpable. For instance, the legislature may have been content

[149] See *R v Lambert, Ali and Jordan* [2002] QB 1112 (CA) [24] (Lord Woolf CJ), arguing that the offence of possession was intended 'to make the defendant responsible for ensuring that he does not take into his possession containers which in fact contain drugs.'

[150] Tadros & Tierney (see n 3 above) 410. Tadros advanced the case for this conception again in Tadros (see n 3 above).

[151] Ibid.

[152] Ibid 416 fn 36.

[153] Ibid 411.

[154] Ibid 413.

[155] Ibid 411.

to criminalise people whose possession of articles raised a reasonable suspicion of a terrorist purpose, in order to prevent people from putting themselves into that position. By preventing people from possessing articles in circumstances that give rise to a reasonable suspicion of a terrorist purpose, the legislature would very effectively control terrorist conduct. Identifying the purpose of the legislature depends upon a policy judgment concerning what conduct it would be proper for the legislature to criminalise.

Such a judgment carries all the controversy and uncertainty associated with the substantive approach. An analysis of some of the offences considered by the English courts illustrates the potential for irresolvable disagreement over the purpose of an offence. For instance, in relation to the offence of being drunk in charge of a motor vehicle, Tadros and Tierney argue that the purpose is to prevent people from being in charge of a motor vehicle when they are intoxicated and there is a risk they might drive while still unfit.[156] Hence, the likelihood of driving is part of the gravamen of the offence. But an equally convincing explanation of the purpose of the offence, offered by the House of Lords in *Sheldrake*,[157] is that people are to be expected to put it out of their power to drive while intoxicated. We have already seen that Lord Bingham characterised the gravamen of the offence in this way.[158] Lord Carswell also stated that the risk of driving was not part of the gravamen of the offence. His Lordship stated: 'Being drunk in charge of a motor vehicle while over the limit is in itself such an anti-social act that Parliament has long since made it an offence. A person who has drunk more than the limit should take steps to put it out of his power to drive.'[159] While it might be more wrongful if there was a likelihood of driving, the failure to divest oneself of the power to drive while intoxicated could itself be regarded as a proper target of the legislation.

In the same way, Tadros and Tierney argue that it was not part of the purpose of the offence in section 11(1) of the Terrorism Act 2000 to capture people who fell within the exceptions in section 11(2).[160] Section 11(1) created the offence of membership or professing to membership in a proscribed organisation. Section 11(2) created an exception if the defendant joined the organisation after it was proscribed and had not taken part in its activities since it was proscribed. It is possible the legislature did not intend that such people should be convicted. But it is equally possible that such people were intended to be caught within the offence. As Lord Rodger demonstrated, it may well have been the purpose of the offence to capture those who were members of terrorist organisations, even though they joined before proscription and had not since actively participated, because this would disrupt terrorist networks.

To identify the 'gravamen' of an offence, the courts must adopt a theory of wrongfulness that may or may not coincide with the aspect of the conduct which

156 Ibid 410–11.
157 [2005] 1 AC 264 (HL).
158 See text accompanying notes 120–23 above,.
159 Ibid [84] (Lord Carswell).
160 Tadros & Tierney (see n 3 above) 421.

the legislature had considered wrongful. There is no suitable way of determining the 'gravamen' of the offence that does not depend upon controversial theories of wrongfulness. Further, we might ask why we should have regard to the putative 'gravamen' of the offence rather than the area of the criminal prohibition that the legislature has in fact laid down in the statute. For example, the inclusion of a defence for people who joined an organisation before it was proscribed and have not since participated in its activities shows that such people do not come within the scope of the criminal prohibition. That is, it is not criminal to have joined a terrorist organisation before it was proscribed, provided a person does not subsequently participate. Searching for the gravamen of the offence takes the focus off the language of the statute and switches to far more nebulous factors. A rule that states that the prosecution must (at least as a *prima facie* matter) prove all aspects of a criminal prohibition is a far more certain means of analysing statutes than a search for the gravamen.

(c) Offence and Defence Aspects

Kenneth Campbell argues that there is a conceptual distinction between offence and defence elements.[161] He argues in favour of this by building upon the definitions of justifications and excuses.[162] Justificatory defences include self-defence, prevention of crime, some cases of necessity and the exercise of lawful authority. In each of these cases, the act causes some harm, and there is a *prima facie* reason for not performing the act, but the harm is outweighed by the countervailing reasons for committing the act. Excusing defences include such things as insanity, automatism, mistake and intoxication. In these cases, there is no suggestion that the conduct of the defendant was justified on balance. There were no reasons for acting as the defendant did but the defendant may be excused from full criminal liability because of his or her condition.[163] Campbell generalises from these definitions to explain the distinction between offence and defence elements. Campbell states:[164]

[161] K Campbell 'Offence and Defence' in IH Dennis (ed) *Criminal Law and Justice* (Sweet & Maxwell London 1987) 73

[162] Campbell relies, in particular on P Robinson 'Criminal Law Defenses: A Systematic Analysis' (1982) 82 *Columb LR* 199. Further discussion of this distinction can be found in GP Fletcher *Rethinking Criminal Law* (OUP, Oxford 2000) ch 7; GP Fletcher 'The Nature of Justification' in S Shute, J Gardner & J Horder (eds) *Action and Value in Criminal Law* (Clarendon Press, Oxford 1993) 175; J Gardner *Offences and Defences: Selected Essays in the Philosophy of Criminal Law* (OUP, Oxford 2007); RA Duff 'Rule Violations and Wrongdoings' in S Shute & AP Simester (eds) *Criminal Law Theory: Doctrines of the General Part* (OUP, Oxford 2002) 47; V Tadros *Criminal Responsibility* (Oxford, OUP 2005) 117; J Horder *Excusing Crime* (OUP, Oxford 2004).

[163] Campbell (see n 161 above) 77. Campbell also includes nonexculpatory or public policy defences. This includes such things as time bar, unfitness to plead, autrefois acquit and diplomatic immunity. Defences in this class say nothing about the defendant's culpability.

[164] Ibid 79.

> Take any set of rules which completely defines the incidence of liability in respect of any act. That subset which completely defines the scope of that against which the law takes there to be a *prima facie* reason is the offence part. That subset which completely defines the scope of exonerating conditions is the defence part.

Hence, offence aspects are conduct against which there is a *prima facie* reason to act, and defence aspects are those things which either outweigh the *prima facie* reason (justifications) or excuse the conduct due to the characteristics of the defendant at the time of the conduct (excuses). Campbell accepts that this conceptual distinction does not make it easy to define the offence and defence aspects since the underlying value judgments concerning when there is a *prima facie* reason against certain conduct are controversial.[165]

This may be a useful means for understanding the difference between 'offence' and 'defence' elements. However, we are here concerned with whether it is a sound basis for allocating the burden of proof. Campbell accepts that the distinction is not conclusive of the allocation of the burden of proof since, in his view that 'will turn on more basic arguments about the balancing of individual rights or interests against those of the public.'[166] Campbell nevertheless believes that the distinction is not 'toothless' in this area.[167] However, it is difficult to see how this distinction between offence and defence could have any relevance to the allocation of the burden of proof. A criminal trial is not concerned with whether there was a *prima facie* reason against the defendant acting in the way he or she did. The trial is concerned with whether the defendant was entitled within the law to have acted in that way, all things taken into account. Placing the burden of proof on the defendant once the prosecution has established a *prima facie* reason why the defendant's conduct was wrong would place the defendant at risk of conviction despite the fact that on balance, the conduct was not wrongful.

It might be argued, however, that the distinction between justifications and excuses is relevant to the allocation of the burden of proof, even if the distinction between offence and defence elements is not. When the defendant's conduct is 'justified' it is because, all the circumstances having been taken into account, the conduct was not wrongful. For example, a killing in self-defence is not wrongful and indeed might even be thought laudable. However, if the defendant's conduct is merely excused, the conduct is still wrongful. It is just that there is some absence of comprehension or capacity on the part of the defendant that makes it inappropriate for the defendant to be held responsible. If the defendant is allocated the burden of proof with respect to an 'excuse', the prosecution has already established the wrongfulness of the conduct. The risk of convicting a person whose conduct was non-wrongful has been eliminated. That is to say, the conduct falls within the area of the criminal prohibition, even though the defendant lacked

165 Ibid 84.
166 Ibid 85.
167 Ibid.

some quality necessary for culpability. Hence, it might be argued that reverse burdens are acceptable for excuses but not for justifications.

The problem with this is that while excuses do not negate wrongfulness, they do negative the capacity for responsibility. If the law has determined that certain classes of people ought not to be treated as responsible for their acts, proof that the person does not come within that class is part and parcel of proving that the defendant is a proper subject of criminal sanction. We must therefore refine our understanding of the area of criminal prohibition to include the capacity of the defendant. Nevertheless, it may be the case that the degree of interference with the presumption of innocence is less if the defendant is required to bear the burden of proof with respect to an excuse. Once the prosecution has proved the wrongfulness of the act, it could be said there is reduced risk of convicting the 'innocent'. I will return to this contention in Chapter Six as part of a discussion about whether it is appropriate to reverse the burden of proof in respect of duress and insanity.

C. Broad Procedural Approach

Having considered and rejected various methods for limiting the matters that must be proved by the prosecution we are left in the position that the prosecution must prove all matters necessary for a criminal conviction: the broad procedural approach. The broad procedural approach is premised on the notion that statutes and common law rules demarcate an area of criminal prohibition. The area of the criminal prohibition is defined by the entirety of the 'offence package',[168] including all aspects, whether described as elements, defences, excuses or justifications. A defendant either falls within the area of the criminal prohibition or does not. If the defendant is required to carry the burden of proof, he or she may be convicted in the absence of proof that his or her conduct was within the criminal prohibition. By insisting that the prosecution prove all aspects necessary for conviction, the broad procedural approach extends the maximum protection to the innocent. Further, the broad procedural approach enhances respect for the rule of law.[169] It permits the legislature to make the rules concerning criminal responsibility. But, having made those rules, the legislature is not permitted to manipulate criminal procedures in order to bring about the conviction of people who have not been proven to fall within the area of the criminal prohibition.

There are two principal objections to the broad procedural approach to the presumption of innocence: (1) the argument that the 'greater power' to create strict liability includes the 'lesser power' to reverse the burden of proof; and (2) the concern that the broad procedural approach might encourage the legislature to create more strict liability offences. I will respond to each of these arguments below.

[168] G Williams 'The Logic of "Exceptions"' (1988) 47 *Cambridge Law Journal* 261, 280.
[169] See Dripps (see n 5 above) 1718.

1. Greater Power Includes the Lesser

One major reason given for supporting a distinction between 'elements' and 'defences' is that if the legislature has the power to enact an offence without providing a defence, it must also have the power to enact the offence subject to a defence, but with a reverse burden. That is, the 'greater power' to eliminate the defence must include the 'lesser power' to create the defence but reverse the burden of proof.[170] Another way of putting this is that, if the offence is consistent with the presumption of innocence without any defence, it cannot fall afoul of the presumption if a concession is made to the defendant by allowing the defence.[171] Lord Rodger (dissenting) in *AG's Reference (No 4 of 2002)*[172] made this point in relation to the offence of membership or professing to membership in a terrorist organisation. Lord Rodger stated:[173]

> The defence in section 11(2) can be seen as relaxing the rigour of the offence in section 11(1) for defendants in these particular circumstances. If section 11(1) itself contains nothing to infringe article 6(1) or (2), then nothing in section 11(2), which serves only to improve the defendant's situation, can precipitate a violation of article 6(1) or (2). If that were not so, Parliament could remove the violation by deleting the defence—and yet this would be to the defendant's obvious disadvantage.

Following this reasoning, Lord Rodger, held that the reverse burden for the defence in section 11(2) did not even raise a threshold issue of interference with the presumption of innocence.

The same argument appears in a minority judgment of Kentridge AJ in *S v Coetzee*,[174] a decision of the Constitutional Court of South Africa. The Constitutional Court there considered section 332(5) of the Criminal Procedure Act which deemed the director of a corporation to be liable for the acts of the corporation, unless the director could prove that he or she did not take part in the commission of the acts and could not have prevented them. A majority of the Constitutional Court held that section 332(5) was invalid because it breached the presumption of innocence.[175] Kentridge AJ dissented on the validity of section 332(5). He stated:[176]

> The legislature did not in fact choose to create an absolute vicarious liability. It chose to mitigate what would otherwise have been the harshness of the provision, by permitting

[170] Jeffries & Stephan (see n 3 above) 1345. According to Jeffries and Stephan, this is a reason for rejecting any kind of procedural approach to the presumption of innocence. See also *Ferry v Ramsey*, 277 US 88, 94 (1928) (Holmes J).

[171] Roberts (2002) LQR (see n 4 above) 57; PW Ferguson 'Proof of Innocence' (2004) 36 *Scots Law Times* 223, 227.

[172] [2005] 1 AC 264 (HL).

[173] Ibid [71].

[174] *S v Coetzee* 1997 (3) SA 527 (CC).

[175] Ibid [46] (Langa J), [62] (Mahomed DP), [137] (Mokgoro J), [195] (O'Regan J), [220] (Sachs J). *Cf* [130] (Madala J) holding that the reverse burden was justifiable.

[176] Ibid [88]. See also at [93].

> an accused director or servant to escape liability upon proof, on a balance of probabilities, of the two exempting factors . . . As a matter of logic and common sense I find it difficult to accept that in thus rendering the impact of the section less severe than it would otherwise have been, the legislature was thereby rendering a trial under the subsection less fair than it would otherwise have been.

This was an invocation of the 'greater power includes the lesser' argument. According to Kentridge AJ, if the legislature had the power to create an absolute vicarious liability, it must also have the power to ameliorate the harshness of the law by providing an exculpatory defence subject to a reverse burden.[177]

The fundamental objection to the 'greater power includes the lesser' argument is that the power to pass strict liability offences is not a 'greater' power than a power to impose reverse burdens. The two are simply different types of power. On the broad procedural approach, the legislature has the power to control the rules of criminal liability. That is, it has power over the substantive content of the law. However, the legislature does not have the power, consistently with the presumption of innocence, to require the defendant to prove certain matters in order to avoid conviction. In a system that gives protected status to the presumption of innocence, the legislature does not have the power to manipulate rules of procedure. The proposition that the legislature can create strict or vicarious liability, but cannot reverse the burden of proof is consonant with the rule of law. People may not be subjected to the sanctions or stigma of criminal prosecution unless, following rules of fundamental fairness, they have been proved to have contravened an existing prohibition. The presumption of innocence can be understood quite comprehensibly as limiting the power of the legislature to make procedural alterations, but not limiting the power of the legislature over the substance of the law.

2. Risk of More Strict Liability Offences

The second objection to the broad procedural approach is that, if courts begin to 'read down' persuasive burdens of proof, the legislature may respond by eliminating defences, or by not creating defences in the first place. As the argument goes, the legislature may be willing to ameliorate a harsh rule of law, but only to the extent of allowing a person to be acquitted if he or she can prove the applicable defence. If the legislature is deprived of the option of a reverse burden of proof, it may prefer to leave the harsh law intact.[178] Lord Woolf made this point in the Privy Council decision *AG of Hong Kong v Lee Kwong-kut*.[179] His Lordship stated:[180] 'It would not assist the individuals who are charged with offences if,

[177] Two of the judges in the case responded to this argument by suggesting that the legislature did not have the power to create absolute vicarious liability because it would breach the right to freedom and security of the person, protected by s 11: ibid [57] (Mahomed P), [160] (O'Regan J).

[178] Roberts (2002) *E & P* (see n 4 above) 29; Roberts & Zuckerman 386, 389.

[179] *AG of Hong Kong v Lee Kwong-kut* [1993] AC 951 (PC).

[180] Ibid 975.

because of the approach adopted to "statutory defences" by the courts, the legislature, in order to avoid the risk of legislation being successfully challenged, did not include in the legislation a statutory defence to a charge.' An over-zealous implementation of the presumption of innocence might be deemed a Pyrrhic victory for defenders of the innocent if it resulted in a proliferation of strict liability offences.

Fears of the legislature permitting a proliferation of strict liability as a result of over-zealous reading down of reverse burdens are difficult to substantiate, especially as the UK legislature enthusiastically created strict liability offences well before the HRA. Since the introduction of the HRA and the capacity of the courts to read down persuasive burdens, one response of the legislature has been expressly to create evidential burdens.[181] However, even if statutory draftsmen did start removing or limiting defences, rather than allowing the prosecution to bear the full burden of proof, this might well be preferable.

If the legislature wishes to make it more difficult for defendants to avail themselves of defences, it ought to implement this policy through the substance of the criminal law, not through manipulation of procedure. When a reverse burden is used in statutory drafting it makes the liability of the defendant depend upon his or her capacity to present evidence rather than on the substantive merits in the case.[182] One would expect some degree of correlation between the availability of evidence and the culpability of a defendant, since the defendant who is in fact entitled to a defence is more likely to be able to prove this than the defendant who is not entitled: the facts giving rise to the defence either exist or they do not. However, the correlation is imperfect since even a person entitled to a defence may not be able to prove it. This is especially so in fields of life where people do not conduct their affairs expecting to be required to produce exculpatory evidence relating to a crime. Following this reasoning, it is less fair to make the liability of defendants contingent upon the ability to produce evidence than to make liability depend on the substantive content of the law.

A further problem with reverse burdens is that they can obfuscate the substance of a criminal prohibition. A prime example of this is the offence of being drunk 'in charge' of a motor vehicle. In the first instance, 'in charge' means having the ability to operate the vehicle and a person can, accordingly be convicted even though outside the vehicle if in possession of the keys. Upon closer examination, however, it is not unlawful for an intoxicated person to be in or around his or her motor vehicle and in a position to drive. This is because the defendant is not to be convicted if he or she can prove there was no likelihood of driving. To the ordinary person unfamiliar with the intricacies of statutory drafting, it would not be clear that he or she is liable to conviction for being intoxicated in the vicinity of a car while in possession of the keys, unless they can prove there was no likelihood of driving. A strict liability offence making likelihood of driving irrelevant to the offence would be less ambiguous.

[181] See Terrorism Act 2000, s 118(2); Regulation of Investigatory Powers Act 2000, s 53(5); Sexual Offences Act 2003, s 75(2).

[182] Underwood (see n 5 above) 1321.

In the context of criminal statutes, there are two salutary effects of making the potential liability of a defendant both clear and unambiguous. First, the impact of the statute becomes subject to the democratic oversight of the legislature. If an offence on its face is one of strict liability or makes a person criminally responsible in the absence of wrongfulness or moral blameworthiness, this will be visible to the legislature upon the passage of the bill. If upon scrutiny the prohibition is thought to be unfair the legislature can insist upon changes or decline to pass the bill. The democratic processes of Parliament impose a constraint on the promulgation of bad laws. A government that wishes to enact a law that potentially criminalises the innocent should be required to do so openly, rather than hiding the potential for injustice behind the procedural device of a reverse burden.[183] In this way, the government must 'squarely confront what it is doing and accept the political cost'.[184] Further, if an unjust offence is passed and moral innocents are convicted, the offence will be a clearly advertised target for reform.[185] By contrast, if moral innocents are convicted because they cannot satisfy the burden of proof, it is not clear that moral innocents are being convicted. The procedural mechanism of the reverse burden hides the true reason for the conviction.

Second, the clear definition of the area of a criminal prohibition allows people to plan their affairs and conduct themselves so as to avoid contravening the prohibition. Barbara Underwood puts this argument in terms of 'fair notice'. She argues that procedural devices can subvert the fair notice that a person might expect from the law. She gives an example.[186] If possession of marijuana is a crime but presence in a house containing marijuana is not a crime then a person might, in reliance on the law, engage in the innocent conduct of associating with marijuana smokers. However, if presence in a house containing marijuana creates a presumption of possession until the defendant proves the contrary, there is a substantial risk of conviction created by the non-criminal act of associating with marijuana smokers. As Underwood states:[187]

> The criminal law is meant to operate as a guide to conduct, announcing serious penalties for certain acts, announcing minor penalties for other acts, and offering people the opportunity to avoid sanctions altogether by avoiding prohibited conduct . . . It is reasonable to expect people to guide their conduct by the prohibitions and penalties of the substantive law. It is rather less reasonable to expect them to know about the subtleties of rules of proof.

To amplify this point, it might be added that ordinary people do not read statutes in order to become familiar with the criminal law. They rely on other people, such as lawyers and government agencies, to explain the effect of the law and it is implausible that these explanations will include reference to procedural niceties.

[183] Roberts (2005) (see n 4 above) 184.
[184] *R v Secretary of State for the Home Department; ex p Simms* [2000] 2 AC 115 (HL) 131 (Lord Hoffmann).
[185] Roberts (2005) (see n 4 above) 183.
[186] Underwood (see n 5 above) 1324.
[187] Ibid.

Rather, people are advised on what they are entitled to do within the law. To return to the example of being drunk in charge of a motor vehicle, if the defence that there was no likelihood of driving were removed, this would at least have the benefit of being clear. People familiar with the law would understand that they must not be in or around their motor vehicle while their blood alcohol content is over the prescribed limit. This shows that a proliferation of strict liability offences may in fact have some advantages over reverse burdens which have a tendency to disguise the harsh effects of the law.

D. Conclusion

This Chapter has argued in favour of the broad procedural approach to the presumption of innocence. It has done so first by rejecting the substantive approach. The substantive approach to the presumption of innocence would require a complete theory of criminal law that is controversial and outside the expertise and constitutional remit of the courts. A procedural approach to Article 6(2) allows the legislature to make the rules of criminal liability, whether fair or not, subject of course to other constraints on unfair offences that can be derived from the ECHR. A procedural approach insists, however, that having made the rules, the legislature must not attempt to use procedural mechanisms to water down the requirement of proof. Further, this chapter has argued that the broad procedural approach is preferable to the narrow procedural approach. This is because there is no satisfactory method for distinguishing core aspects of an offence from peripheral aspects. The broad procedural approach sees the law as setting out various criminal prohibitions and requires the prosecution to prove that the defendant falls within one or more of those prohibitions. The requirement of proof that the defendant has breached a criminal prohibition is vital to protect those whose conduct has not brought them within the criminal prohibition. It is also vital to the promotion of the rule of law since it helps to ensure that the government cannot take punitive action against an individual unless the person has been proved to come within the pre-ordained legal conditions for the imposition of conviction and punishment. The following chapter considers the approach taken to the presumption of innocence in Strasbourg, where regular acceptance of reverse burdens appears to undermine both the protection of the innocent and the promotion of the rule of law.

4

The Presumption in Strasbourg

THE PURPOSE OF this chapter is to analyse the Strasbourg cases on Article 6(2) with a view to determining what principles may be discerned and applied by the English courts.[1] Part A below outlines the various formulations adopted by the Strasbourg Court to describe what it means to be presumed innocent until proven guilty. Part A will also consider the extent to which the Strasbourg Court treats Article 6(2) as capable of controlling the substantive rules of criminal law. Part B of this chapter will discuss the Strasbourg approach to limitation of the presumption of innocence. It will be shown that the Strasbourg Court applies a proportionality analysis to measures that infringe Article 6(2) and generally permits reasons of community interest to be invoked to justify the infringement. By contrast, in relation to other Article 6 rights the Strasbourg Court has been reluctant to permit the community interest to operate as a reason for limitation. It will be suggested that aspects of the stricter approach taken in relation to other Article 6 rights ought also to be applied to the presumption of innocence.

[1] As a preliminary matter, Art 6(2) applies only when a person is 'charged with a criminal offence'. Since this book is concerned with the reversal of the burden of proof in criminal trials, the meaning of this phrase will not be addressed here. Detailed analysis can be found in B Emmerson, A Ashworth & A McDonald *Human Rights and Criminal Justice* 2nd edn (Sweet & Maxwell, London 2007) ch 4; S Stavros *The Guarantees for Accused Persons Under Article 6 of the European Convention on Human Rights* (Martinus Nijhoff, Dordrecht 1993) ch 1; DJ Harris, M O'Boyle & C Warbrick *The Law of the European Convention on Human Rights* (Butterworths, London 1995) 166–73; S Trechsel *Human Rights in Criminal Proceedings* (OUP, Oxford 2005) ch 2; P van Dijk et al *Theory and Practice of the European Convention on Human Rights* 4th edn (Intersentia, Oxford 2006) 511–56. As to the meaning of 'criminal', the House of Lords has held that the hearing for the imposition of an Anti-Social Behaviour Order (ASBO) is a civil hearing, and consequently Art 6(2) does not apply. The House of Lords held, nevertheless, that given the seriousness of the allegations made in an ASBO hearing, the required standard of proof would be proof beyond reasonable doubt: *R (McCann) v Crown Court of Manchester* [2003] 1 AC 787 (HL). For academic commentary see S MacDonald 'The Nature of the Anti-Social Behaviour Order—R (McCann & Others) v Crown Court at Manchester' (2003) 66 *MLR* 630; C Bakalis 'Anti-Social Behaviour Orders—Criminal Penalties or Civil Injunctions' (2003) 62 *CLJ* 583; A Ashworth 'Social Control and "Anti-Social Behaviour": The Subversion of Human Rights?' (2004) 120 *LQR* 263; A Ashworth 'Four Threats to the Presumption of Innocence' (2006) 10 *E & P* 241, 270–74. As to the meaning of 'charge', the Privy Council and House of Lords have held that proceedings for the confiscation of the proceeds of crime do not entail a 'charge' so that Art 6(2) is inapplicable in such cases: *McIntosh v Lord Advocate* [2003] 1 AC 1078 (PC) [25] (Lord Bingham); *R v Rezvi; R v Benjafield* [2003] 1 AC 1099 (HL) 1152 (Lord Steyn); *R v Briggs Price* [2009] UKHL 19 [40] (Lord Phillips), [64] (Lord Rodger), [13] (Lord Mance), *cf* [94] (Lord Brown). See also *Phillips v UK* (App No 41087/98) ECHR 5 July 2001; *Grayson and Barnham v UK* (App No 19955/05) ECHR 23 September 2008.

Section 2(1) of the HRA requires English courts to 'take into account' all decisions of the Strasbourg Court when interpreting rights protected under the ECHR. Accordingly, the Strasbourg approach to Article 6(2) is relevant for the English courts when applying the presumption of innocence.[2] In *Alconbury*, Lord Slynn stated that: 'In the absence of some special circumstances it seems to me that the court should follow any clear and constant jurisprudence of the [Strasbourg Court].'[3] However, the direction to 'take into account' the Strasbourg jurisprudence does not make those decisions binding in the same sense as decisions of the superior courts in the UK.[4] In particular, when decisions of the Strasbourg Court are based on a misunderstanding of some aspect of English law, the English courts do not regard themselves as bound by the Strasbourg case-law.[5] This chapter will suggest that the Strasbourg Court often fails to appreciate that a burden of proof in English law allocates the risk of non-persuasion, and accordingly that a defendant may be convicted due to an inability to satisfy the burden. English courts ought to be cautious in following the Strasbourg cases to the extent that they routinely permit the reversal of the burden of proof.

A. The Content of the Presumption

The Strasbourg Court has adopted various formulations to define the content of the presumption of innocence. This Part discusses three ways in which the content of the right has been defined: (1) a principle prohibiting official decisions

[2] Second Reading of Lord Chancellor (Lord Irvine of Lairg) Hansard HL (series 5) vol 582 col 1230 (3 November 1997): 'It is entirely appropriate that our courts should draw on the wealth of existing jurisprudence on the Convention.' See also R Masterman, 'Section 2(1) of the Human Rights Act 1998: Binding Domestic Courts to Strasbourg?' [2004] *PL* 725; R Masterman 'Aspiration or Foundation? The Status of the Strasbourg Jurisprudence and the "Convention Rights" in Domestic Law' in H Fenwick, R Masterman & G Phillipson (eds) *Judicial Reasoning under the UK Human Rights Act* (CUP, Cambridge 2007) 57.

[3] *R (Alconbury) v Secretary of State for the Environment, Transport and the Regions* [2003] 2 AC 295 (HL) [26] (Lord Slynn). See also *R (Anderson) v Secretary of State for the Home Department* [2003] 1 AC 837 (HL) [18] (Lord Bingham); *Kay v Lambeth LBC* [2006] 2 AC 465 (HL) [28] (Lord Bingham); *R (Purdy) v DPP* [2009] UKHL 45 [34] (Lord Phillips).

[4] *Kay v Lambeth LBC* [2006] 2 AC 465 (HL) [40]–[44] (Lord Bingham), [50] (Lord Nicholls), [62] (Lord Hope), [121] (Lord Scott), [177] (Lord Walker), [178] (Baroness Hale); *R (RJM) v Secretary of State for Work and Pensions* [2009] 1 AC 311 (HL) [64] (Lord Neuberger). See also Home Office, *Rights Brought Home: The Human Rights Bill* (Cm 3782) (HMSO, London 1997) [2.4]: "(although these will not be binding)". Geoffrey Hoon MP, Parliamentary Secretary to the Lord Chancellor's Department, explained that the phrase 'must take into account' did not mean that domestic courts were obliged to follow Strasbourg jurisprudence and therefore resisted an amendment which would have substituted 'may take into account'. The amendment was withdrawn: Hansard HC (series 6) vol 313, cols 388–415 (3 June 1998). See also the Lord Chancellor (Lord Irvine of Lairg) in the Committee stage of the Bill in the House of Lords: Hansard HL (series 5) vol 583 cols 514–15 (18 November 1997).

[5] *R v Spear* [2003] 1 AC 734 (HL) [12]–[13] (Lord Bingham), [65]–[66] (Lord Rodger); *R v Lyons* [2003] 1 AC 976 (HL) [46] (Lord Hoffmann); *Kay v Lambeth LBC* [2006] 2 AC 465 (HL) [28] (Lord Bingham).

reflecting guilt in the absence of a prior judicial determination; (2) a principle placing the burden of proof on the prosecution and giving the defendant the benefit of any doubt; and (3) a principle requiring presumptions of fact or law to be confined within reasonable limits. The second of these formulations, concerning the burden of proof, is more in line with the common law understanding of the presumption of innocence. However, it is the third formulation, concerning 'presumptions', that has become the standard means in Strasbourg cases for describing the content of the right protected by Article 6(2). This Part will explore the consequences of the Strasbourg Court's different understanding of the presumption of innocence, including its use of Article 6(2) to control the substantive content of the criminal law.

1. Official Decisions Reflecting Guilt

In the Strasbourg Court, a common and influential formulation of the presumption of innocence states that an official decision should not reflect the opinion that the defendant is guilty, unless the guilt of the defendant has previously been determined according to law. This definition originates from the decision in *Minelli v Switzerland*.[6] In that case, the applicant had been charged with criminal defamation and ordered to pay two thirds of the costs of the private prosecutor, even though, due to the expiry of a limitation period, the case against the applicant was dismissed. The applicant alleged that the costs order was a breach of Article 6(2) because it involved an informal finding that the defendant had been guilty of the crime. The Strasbourg Court stated:[7]

> In the Court's judgment, the presumption of innocence will be violated if, without the accused's having previously been proved guilty according to law and, notably, without his having had the opportunity of exercising his rights of defence, a judicial decision concerning him reflects an opinion that he is guilty. This may be so even in the absence of any formal finding; it suffices that there is some reasoning suggesting that the court regards the accused as guilty.

The Strasbourg Court noted that the costs order was made on the basis that, in the absence of the limitation period, the prosecution would 'very probably have led to the conviction' of the applicant.[8] It followed that the Swiss court had made a determination of the guilt of the defendant, even though he had not had the benefit of the guarantees in Article 6. The apportionment of costs on the basis of the applicant's assumed guilt was therefore in contravention of the presumption of innocence.

Cases following *Minelli* have drawn a distinction between decisions that reflect a determination of guilt and decisions that reflect a continuing state of suspicion concerning the defendant. The former will breach the presumption of innocence,

6 *Minelli v Switzerland* (App No 8660/79) (1983) 5 EHRR 554.
7 Ibid [37].
8 Ibid [38].

whereas the latter will not. For instance, the Strasbourg Court has approved the domestic practice of denying compensation to a defendant when a criminal proceeding is discontinued but he or she is subject to a 'continuing state of suspicion' concerning the offence.[9] By contrast, if the proceedings ended as a result of an acquittal, rather than as a result of discontinuance, a decision reflecting the guilt of the defendant would not be permitted. In *Sekanina v Austria*,[10] the Strasbourg Court stated:[11]

> The voicing of suspicions regarding an accused's innocence is conceivable as long as the conclusion of criminal proceedings has not resulted in a decision on the merits of the accusation. However, it is no longer admissible to rely on such suspicions once an acquittal has become final.

Hence, the Strasbourg Court gave a strong warning that judicial decisions should not be based on continuing suspicion surrounding the defendant once a trial had resulted in acquittal.[12] Following this principle, the Strasbourg Court has held that, once a defendant is acquitted of an offence, it is impermissible to assume that the defendant has benefited from that offence for the purposes of a criminal confiscation proceeding.[13]

The *Minelli* formulation has since been expanded so that the strictures concerning decisions that reflect guilt apply not only to courts but also to public authorities. Accordingly, in *Allenet de Ribemont v France*,[14] the applicant successfully claimed a breach of Article 6(2) after the Minister of the Interior and two senior police officers informed a press conference that the applicant, who was under arrest, had instigated a murder. The Strasbourg Court held that Article 6(2) imposed obligations 'not only on criminal courts determining criminal charges but also on other authorities'.[15] The Strasbourg Court's decision that Article 6(2) applies to acts by public authorities other than courts greatly expands its potential scope. The Strasbourg Court goes so far as to emphasise 'the importance of the choice of words by public officials in their statements before a person has been tried and found guilty of an offence.'[16] Consequently, even prosecutors in the course of commencing a prosecution or conducting a trial are required to observe the presumption of innocence.[17]

[9] *Nölkenbockhoff v Germany* (App No 10300/83) (1987) 10 EHRR 163; *Lutz v Germany* (App No 9912/82) (1987) 10 EHRR 182; *Englert v Germany* (App No 10282/83) (1987) 13 EHRR 392.

[10] *Sekanina v Austria* (App No 13126/87) (1994) 17 EHRR 221.

[11] Ibid [30]. Applied in *Hussain v UK* (App No 8866/04) (2006) 43 EHRR 22.

[12] This could have consequences for the practice in English law of allowing evidence of conduct in respect of which the defendant was acquitted to be admitted in a subsequent case as similar fact evidence: *cf R v Z* [2000] 2 AC 483 (HL).

[13] *Geerings v Netherlands* (App No 30810/03) (2007) 46 EHRR 1222 [47]–[51].

[14] *Allenet de Ribemont v France* (App No 15175) (1995) 20 EHRR 557.

[15] Ibid [33].

[16] *Daktaras v Lithuania* (App No 42095/98) (2002) 34 EHRR 60 [41]. See also *Böhmer v Germany* (App No 37568/97) (2004) 38 EHRR 19 [54].

[17] Ibid. This should be contrasted with the earlier view in *Pfunders Case (Austria v Italy)* (1963) 6 Yearbook ECHR 740, 784 that the conduct of a prosecutor would breach Art 6(2) only if the court appeared to endorse the prosecutor's inflammatory or insulting language. If the *Minelli* formulation

It is clear that the cases decided under the *Minelli* formulation of the presumption of innocence are far removed from the situation of a reverse burden of proof in a criminal trial. These decisions relate to very specific circumstances in which the defendant is treated as guilty despite the absence of a conclusive judicial determination. They consequently have little relevance to the question of reverse burdens and the English courts rightly have not focused on them in reverse burdens cases.

2. Burden of Proof

A second formulation of the right protected by Article 6(2) refers to the allocation of the burden of proof. This formulation originated in the 1963 decision of the Strasbourg Commission in *Pfunders Case.*[18] In that case, the Austrian Government alleged that the Italian courts had denied the presumption of innocence to six young men who had been convicted of the murder of an Italian customs officer. The Commission gave some general guidance on the meaning of Article 6(2):[19]

> This text, according to which everyone charged with a criminal offence shall be presumed innocent until proved guilty according to law, requires firstly that court judges in fulfilling their duties should not start with the conviction or assumption that the accused committed the act with which he is charged. In other words, the onus to prove guilt falls upon the Prosecution, and any doubt is to the benefit of the accused. Moreover, the judges must permit the latter to produce evidence in rebuttal. In their judgment they can find him guilty only on the basis of direct or indirect evidence sufficiently strong in the eyes of the law to establish his guilt.

It is significant that the Commission regarded the placement of the burden of proof as another way of stating that the court should not start the proceedings with an assumption of guilt. The perceived equivalence between these two standards suggests the Commission did not regard it as important that the burden of proof (that is, the risk of non-persuasion) remain on the prosecution throughout the trial. Provided that the court did not begin with an assumption of guilt, but required the prosecution to present evidence of guilt, a subsequent reversal of the burden of proof on a single issue or series of issues might still be compatible with Article 6(2). Hence, the reference to the burden of proof in *Pfunders* might be taken as referring to the overall burden of proving guilt, rather than the burden of proof with respect to specific issues. It is difficult to apply the *Pfunders* formulation in the English context because English law understands the burden of proof as relating to discrete issues.[20]

were applied strictly to all public authorities, it would be impermissible to commence any prosecutions because the presentation of an indictment would reflect an opinion that the defendant is guilty. This cannot be the correct interpretation of Art6(2): Trechsel (see n 1 above) 161.

[18] (1963) 6 Yearbook ECHR 740.

[19] Ibid 782.

[20] Cross & Tapper 140: '[T]he expression "burden of proof" is meaningless unless it is used with reference to a particular issue.'

The formulation of the presumption of innocence emphasising the burden of proof has been recognised in only a small number of Strasbourg cases.[21] In *Lingens v Austria*,[22] the Commission considered whether a reversal of the burden of proof was a breach of Article 6(2). The applicants were two journalists who were convicted of defamation after describing a politician as a liar in a newspaper article. The Austrian Penal Code required the applicants to prove the truth of their statement in order to avoid conviction. The applicants alleged that there was a breach of Article 6(2) because they had been convicted even though the court was not convinced beyond doubt of the falsity of their allegation. The Commission noted that the prosecutor was required to prove the existence of a defamatory statement and that there was no shifting of the burden of proof on this matter.[23] There was, however, a shifting of the burden of proof as it applied to the 'special defense' concerning the truth of the statement at issue.[24] The Commission stated:[25]

> This in no way means that the accused has to prove his innocence because he can only be considered as innocent if he has not committed the offence. The offence as conceived in the applicable provisions of the Penal Code, however, can even be committed by a true statement: What exculpates is not the objective truth of a defamatory statement, but ability to prove its truth. In this way the law intends to compel the author of such statements to make sure in advance that what is being said can also be proven as true, i.e., it imposes a particular standard of care on everybody who makes defamatory statements in the press.

The Strasbourg Court consequently endorsed the idea that, provided the prosecution proved the substance of the offence, it would be permissible to reverse the burden of proof in respect of a special defence. A reversal of the burden of proof on such a defence did not raise even a threshold issue of a breach of the presumption of innocence.[26] This approach to the presumption of innocence does not provide the maximum protection to defendants since it permits conviction when the prosecution has not proved every aspect necessary for conviction.

Most recently, the importance of the burden of proof was recognised in *Telfner v Austria*.[27] In that case, the applicant was charged with causing injury by negligence in a car accident. The victim had been able to identify the type and registration number of the car but was unable to identify the driver, or even to say whether the driver was male or female. At trial, the police evidence suggested that

[21] In addition to the two cases discussed below, see *Barberà, Messegué and Jabardo v Spain* (App No 10588/83) (1988) 11 EHRR 360 [77]. In this case, however, the Strasbourg Court later applied the *Minelli* formula and held there was no breach of the presumption of innocence because the presiding judge had not, during the trial, taken decisions or demonstrated an attitude reflecting the guilt of the defendant: ibid [101].

[22] *Lingens v Austria* (App No 8803/79) (1982) 4 EHRR 373.

[23] Ibid 390.

[24] Ibid 390–91.

[25] Ibid 391.

[26] See also the similar case of *BT v Norway* (App No 16269/90) EComHR 1 April 1992.

[27] *Telfner v Austria* (App No 33501/96) (2002) 34 EHRR 7.

the applicant was the main user of the car but that it was also driven at times by his mother and his sister. The applicant denied driving the car at the time in question but gave no other evidence. He was convicted and alleged that he had suffered a breach of Article 6(2). The Strasbourg Court stated:[28]

> Article 6(2) requires, *inter alia*, that when carrying out their duties, the members of a court should not start with the preconceived idea that the accused has committed the offence charged; the burden of proof is on the prosecution, and any doubt should benefit the accused. Thus, the presumption of innocence will be infringed where the burden of proof is shifted from the prosecution to the defence.

The Strasbourg Court found the only evidence against the applicant was that he was the main user of the car and that the trial court had drawn adverse inferences from the applicant's silence as to his whereabouts on the night of the accident. The Strasbourg Court held that the evidence presented did not constitute a case against the defendant which would have called for an explanation from him.[29] The Strasbourg Court concluded: 'In requiring the applicant to provide an explanation although they had not been able to establish a convincing prima facie case against him, the courts shifted the burden of proof from the prosecution to the defence.'[30] Consequently, there was a breach of Article 6(2).

The crucial factor in *Telfner* was the reversal of the burden of proof before the prosecution had established a *prima facie* case. This was held to breach the presumption of innocence because the court was able to convict on evidence that was not sufficient to constitute proof. The protection accorded to defendants by the decision in *Telfner* is limited because it would allow the reversal of the burden of proof once the prosecution has established a *prima facie* case. A *prima facie* case does not constitute proof of all the matters that are necessary for conviction. Consequently, the approach taken in *Telfner* does not prevent reversal of the burden of proof on discrete issues.[31]

These cases suggest that, as far as the Strasbourg organs are concerned, the presumption of innocence does not require the burden of proof to remain on the prosecution throughout the trial and in relation to all matters necessary for conviction. In one case, the Commission has even gone so far as to say that Article 6(2) 'does not . . . lay down any specific rights in relation to the standard or burden of proof.'[32] There are several reasons why the Strasbourg Court lays such little emphasis on the burden of proof. Most importantly, the role of the burden of proof is quite different in continental systems from its role under the common law.[33]

[28] Ibid [15].

[29] The reference to evidence that 'calls for an explanation' suggests the Strasbourg Court was heavily influenced by cases on the right to silence.

[30] Ibid [18]. See also *Blum v Austria* (App No 31655) ECHR 3 February 2005 [28]–[29].

[31] See also *H v UK* (App No 15023/89) EComHR 4 April 1990 and *Robinson v UK* (App No 20858/92) EComHR 5 May 1993 holding, respectively, that reversal of the burden of proof on insanity and diminished responsibility did not breach Art6(2).

[32] *Steel v UK* (App No 24838/94) EComHR 9 April 1997 [71].

[33] See Trechsel (see n 1 above) 167.

Continental systems do not regard the burden of proof as determinative of the risk of non-persuasion, since it is always for the court to determine whether facts are established.[34] Mirjan Damaška argues that this is due to the inquisitorial system in which the role of the judge alters the two-party format on which rules concerning the allocation of the burden of proof are predicated.[35] When continental courts speak of a 'burden of proof' they usually mean that one party is responsible for introducing evidence, an obligation similar to the evidential burden in English law.[36] Placing the burden on the defendant to produce evidence is not the same as presuming the guilt of the defendant, since the court is always required to keep an open mind.[37] In continental systems, the protection of the innocent is facilitated not by the allocation of the formal burden of proof but by the principle of *in dubio pro reo*, which requires doubt to be resolved in favour of the defendant.[38]

The continental attitude towards the burden of proof is evident in the work of Stefan Trechsel. He states that the allocation of the burden of proof is 'of negligible importance in practice'.[39] He goes on to state: 'It is highly unlikely that a court would state that the accused's conviction is based on the fact that he or she failed to prove his or her innocence.'[40] This statement is unsupportable if the burden of proof is envisaged as allocating the risk of non-persuasion, as it is in English law. When the defendant bears the burden of proof, the court may indeed base a conviction on the failure of the defendant to discharge that burden, even if the court is not convinced of guilt beyond reasonable doubt.

A further reason why the Strasbourg Court underemphasises the burden of proof is that it has, since its early cases, found the presumption of innocence to be an aspect of the overall right to fair trial under Article 6(1).[41] While English lawyers tend to conceive of the presumption of innocence as a rule placing the burden on the prosecution and requiring proof beyond reasonable doubt, the Strasbourg Court treats it as an equivalent to the general principle of fair trial. Hence, it is common for the Strasbourg Court to explain that it will discuss alleged infringements of Article 6(1) and Article 6(2) together or that, having made a

[34] JES Fawcett, *The Application of the European Convention on Human Rights* 2nd edn (Clarendon Press, Oxford 1987) 180; F Jacobs *The European Convention on Human Rights* (Clarendon Press, Oxford 1975) 113.

[35] MR Damaška *Evidence Law Adrift* (New York: Yale University Press, 1997) 81–84.

[36] Ibid.

[37] The Strasbourg Court recognised in *Hardy v Ireland* (App No 23456/94) EComHR 29 June 1994 that placing the evidential burden on the defendant did not breach Art6(2).

[38] GP Fletcher 'Two Kinds of Legal Rules: A Comparative Study of Burden-of-Persuasion Practices in Criminal Cases' (1968) 77 *Yale Law Journal* 880. See also J Hatchard, B Huber & R Vogler *Comparative Criminal Procedure* (BIICL, London 1996) 28 (France), 112 (Germany). The Strasbourg Commission discussed the relationship between *in dubio pro reo* and the presumption of innocence in *Lingens v Austria* (App No 8803/79) (1982) 4 EHRR 373, 390.

[39] Trechsel (see n 1 above) 167.

[40] Ibid.

[41] *Deweer v Belgium* (App No 6903) (1979) 2 EHRR 439 [56]. See, more recently, *Grayson and Barnham v UK* (App No 19955/05) ECHR 23 September 2008 [39].

ruling under Article 6(1), it is unnecessary to consider Article 6(2).[42] The Strasbourg Court equates the presumption of innocence with a range of fair trial rights: it requires that adverse inferences not be drawn from silence unless the evidence calls for an explanation,[43] that the court be independent and impartial,[44] that the defendant be informed of the charge,[45] and that the defendant be entitled to the privilege against self-incrimination.[46] By conflating each of these fair trial rights with the presumption of innocence, the Strasbourg Court has lost sight of the sense in which the presumption is a distinct principle requiring the prosecution to prove its case to a sufficient standard of certainty.[47]

To regard the presumption of innocence in Article 6(2) as a right subsumed within the right to a fair trial in Article 6(1) is contrary to the structure of the ECHR which places the presumption of innocence in a separate paragraph. This suggests there is something distinct about the presumption of innocence that might otherwise not be included in the general principle of fair trial. At the least, it requires that the presumption of innocence be treated as a separate right capable of breach even if other guarantees in Article 6 are protected.

The subsumption of Article 6(2) within Article 6(1) also belies the drafting history of the ECHR which reveals a process in which the presumption of innocence was deliberately removed to its own paragraph.[48] In the early stages of drafting, the provision of the ECHR dealing with the presumption of innocence was identical to Article 11(1) of the Universal Declaration of Human Rights.[49] Article 11(1) states: 'Everyone charged with a penal offence has the right to be presumed innocent until proved guilty according to law in a public trial at which he has had all the guarantees necessary for his defence.' On this formulation, the presumption of innocence is closely linked to other 'guarantees' necessitated by the general principle of fair trial. However, the UK representative in the Committee of Experts was concerned that the initial Draft Convention merely enumerated rights without

[42] *Bonisch v Austria* (App No 8658/79) (1987) 9 EHRR 191 [37]; *Delta v France* (App No 11444/85) (1993) 16 EHRR 574 [38]; *Funke v France* (App No 10828/84) (1993) 16 EHRR 297 [45]; *Västbergat Taxi Aktiebolag and Vulic v Sweden* (App No 36985/97) ECHR 23 July 2002 [108]; *Radio France v France* (App No 53984) (2005) 40 EHRR 29 [24].

[43] *Telfner v Austria* (App No 33501/96) (2002) 34 EHRR 7 [18].

[44] *Austria v Italy (Pfunders Case)* (1963) 6 Yearbook ECHR 740, 782.

[45] *Barberà, Messegué and Jabardo v Spain* (App No 10588/83) (1988) 11 EHRR 360 [77].

[46] *Saunders v UK* (App No 19187/91) (1997) 23 EHRR 313 [68]; *Heaney and McGuinness v Ireland* (App No 34720/97) (2001) 33 EHRR 12 [40]; *Quinn v Ireland* (App No 36887/97) ECHR 21 December 2000 [40].

[47] *Cf McIntosh v Lord Advocate* [2003] 1 AC 1078 (PC) [31] (Lord Bingham): 'In some cases the acceptability of a reverse onus provision will turn not on consideration of the provision in the abstract but on its application in a particular case. The right to a fair trial, guaranteed by Art 6(1), will ensure that any reverse onus provision is fairly applied in the given case.'

[48] In general, the Strasbourg Court has placed little reliance on the *travaux preparatoires* of the Convention: but see *Lawless v Ireland* (App No 332/57) (1979–80) 1 EHRR 15 [14]; *James v UK* (App No 8793/79) (1986) 8 EHRR 123 [64]; *Johnston v Ireland* (App No 9697/82) (1987) 9 EHRR 203 [52]; *Marckx v Belgium* (App No 6833/74) (1979–80) 2 EHRR 330 [63].

[49] See Council of Europe *Collected Edition of the "Travaux Preparatoires" of the European Convention on Human Rights, Vol III* (Martinus Nijhoff, The Hague 1977) 222, Art 3(3)(c); 236, Art 2(3)(c).

defining them.[50] Accordingly, the UK proposed an alternative draft with more detailed exposition of each right.[51] In the first version of the UK draft, the presumption of innocence operated as an overriding principle from which were derived other guarantees such as the right to be informed of the charge, the right to counsel, the right to examine witnesses and the right to an interpreter.[52] Later that same day, the UK representative proposed amendments in the Committee of Experts so that the presumption of innocence occupied a provision of its own, and the other guarantees were contained in a new paragraph within the same Article.[53]

On 16 March 1950, the Committee of Experts presented two alternative Draft Conventions to the Committee of Ministers.[54] One draft (known as Alternative A)[55] closely followed the UDHR and the provision dealing with the presumption of innocence was identical to Article 11(1).[56] Alternative B was the draft promoted by the UK in which the presumption of innocence and other fair trial rights took the form proposed by the UK in the Committee of Experts.[57] A Conference of Senior Officials held at Strasbourg between 8 and 17 June 1950 substantially adopted the UK-sponsored Alternative B with some compromise components taken from Alternative A.[58] Hence, the presumption of innocence was retained in its own provision and other fair trial rights were separately defined. With some minor amendments, this was the version of the Convention ultimately signed in Rome on 4 November 1950.[59] The drafting history shows that, due to the

[50] Ibid 256.

[51] Ibid 280.

[52] Ibid 284, Art 8(2): 'Everyone charged with a penal offence has the right to be presumed innocent until proved guilty according to law. In the determination of any criminal charge against him, everyone is entitled: (a) to be informed promptly of the nature and cause of the accusation against him; (b) to defend himself in person or through legal assistance of his own choosing and, if he has not sufficient means to pay for such assistance, to be given it free when the interests of justice so require; (c) to examine or have examined witnesses against him and to obtain compulsory attendance of witnesses on his behalf; (d) to have free assistance of an interpreter if he cannot understand or speak the language used in court.'

[53] Ibid 290, Art8(2): 'Everyone charged with a penal offence has the right to be presumed innocent until proved guilty according to law.' The other guarantees were removed to a separate Art8(3).

[54] Council of Europe *Collected Edition of the "Travaux Preparatoires" of the European Convention on Human Rights, Vol IV* (Martinus Nijhoff, The Hague 1977) 2.

[55] On 9 March 1950, the UK draft was designated Alternative A and the UDHR-inspired draft was designated Alternative B. It is unclear why the designations were subsequently reversed: ibid 312 (Alternative A), 320 (Alternative B).

[56] Ibid 52, Art 2(3)(c).

[57] Ibid 60, Art 7(2).

[58] On 14 June 1950, an amended version of Alternative B was set out. In the provision dealing with the presumption of innocence, the word 'penal' was replaced with the word 'criminal': ibid 186, Art 8(2): 'Everyone charged with a criminal offence has the right to be presumed innocent until proved guilty according to law.' On 15 June 1950, the Conference of Senior Officials produced one draft of the Convention, substantially conforming to Alternative B (the British draft). The wording for the presumption of innocence adopted on 14 June 1950 was retained: ibid 222, Art 6(2). On 17 June 1950, the Conference of Senior Officials adopted its final report to the Committee of Ministers, appending a Draft Convention. The wording of the presumption of innocence was unchanged from 15 June 1950: ibid 278, Art 6(2).

[59] The wording of the presumption of innocence was retained in identical form to the draft of 17 June 1950 throughout most of the subsequent processes: see Council of Europe *Collected Edition of the "Travaux Préparatoires" of the European Convention on Human Rights, Vol V* (Martinus Nijhoff, The Hague 1977) 80, Art 6(2); 124, Art 6(2); 150, Art 6(2). Council of Europe *Collected Edition of the*

insistence of the UK, the presumption of innocence was not subsumed within or deemed to be constitutive of other fair trial rights. The presumption of innocence stood alone as a separately defined guarantee with its own distinct content. In its case law on Article 6(2), the Strasbourg Court has given insufficient attention to the distinct nature of the presumption of innocence.

3. Presumptions Confined Within Reasonable Limits

In the Strasbourg Court, the most common way of defining the content of the right to be presumed innocent is the instruction that presumptions of fact or law must be confined within reasonable limits. This formulation originated in *Salabiaku v France*[60] and has been quoted, paraphrased and repeated regularly since that time, both by the Strasbourg Court and by English courts. In *Salabiaku*, the applicant had been found in possession of a trunk containing 10kg of herbal seed cannabis and was convicted of the customs offence of importing prohibited goods. The French statute in question provided that a person in possession of prohibited goods would be deemed liable for the offence of smuggling. There was a limited defence of *force majeure* which applied only to a circumstance that was not attributable to the defendant and which it was 'absolutely impossible for him to avoid' such as the 'absolute impossibility of knowing the contents of a package'.[61] Before the Strasbourg Court, the applicant alleged that this 'almost irrebuttable' presumption was in contravention of Article 6(2). The Strasbourg Court stated:[62]

> Presumptions of fact or law operate in every legal system. Clearly, the Convention does not prohibit such presumptions in principle. It does, however, require the Contracting States to remain within certain limits in this respect as regards the criminal law . . . Article 6(2) does not therefore regard presumptions of fact or law provided for in the criminal law with indifference. It requires States to confine them within reasonable limits which take into account the importance of what is at stake and maintain the rights of the defence.

The Court went on to hold that the presumption created for the purpose of the customs offence was consistent with Article 6(2). The reason for this was that the French courts enjoyed a 'genuine freedom of assessment'[63] in deciding the guilt of the defendant and 'were careful to avoid resorting automatically to the pre-

"Travaux Préparatoires" of the European Convention on Human Rights, Vol VI (Martinus Nijhoff, The Hague 1977) 204, Art 6(2); 245–46, Art 6(2). In the Final Text of the Convention, adopted at Rome on 4 November 1950, Art 6(2) had been altered (for unknown reasons) to its present form: Council of Europe *Collected Edition of the "Travaux Préparatoires" of the European Convention on Human Rights, Vol VII* (Martinus Nijhoff, The Hague 1977) 54, Art 6(2): 'Everyone charged with a criminal offence shall be presumed innocent until proved guilty according to law.'

60 *Salabiaku v France* (App No 10589/83) (1991) 13 EHRR 379.
61 Ibid [19].
62 Ibid [28].
63 Ibid [29].

sumption'.[64] The fact that the French courts did not resort automatically to the presumption suggests that the defendant was not burdened with the risk of non-persuasion and would have been given the benefit of any doubt.[65] This is not the case in English law when a defendant is subject to a persuasive burden.

The statement quoted above has become the standard formulation for the right protected by Article 6(2) in cases involving reversal of the burden of proof. From the perspective of the common law, it is unusual that a formulation dealing with 'presumptions' has become the dominant means of understanding the presumption of innocence, rather than a formulation concerned with the burden of proof. Nevertheless, there is an undeniable connection between presumptions and reverse burdens. In English criminal law, statutes often use the language of presumption when imposing a burden on a defendant. Even when the language of presumption is not used, there is a sense in which reverse burdens always involve a presumption. The matter which the defendant must prove will be presumed against the defendant until the burden of proof is satisfactorily discharged. Hence, the directive that 'presumptions' of fact or law must be contained within reasonable limits is capable of being adapted to any situation in which a reverse burden is imposed.[66]

Despite the directive that presumptions must be contained within 'reasonable limits' there is not a single case either from the Strasbourg Court or the Commission in which a 'presumption' has been held to contravene Article 6(2).[67] The main reason for this is that the Strasbourg organs generally conclude that the rights of the defendant are maintained provided the defendant has an opportunity to present evidence in order to show the presumption is incorrect.

Even before *Salabiaku*, the Strasbourg Commission had upheld a reverse burden largely on the basis that the presumption created thereby could be overcome by evidence to the contrary. In *X v UK*,[68] the applicant was convicted of living on the immoral earnings of a prostitute. He alleged that reliance upon a statutory presumption in obtaining his conviction was a breach of Article 6(2). The statute stated that: 'a man who lives with or is habitually in the company of a prostitute ... shall be presumed to be knowingly living on the earnings of prostitution unless he proves the contrary.' The Strasbourg Commission rejected the complaint stressing that the presumption would only be made once the prosecution had

[64] Ibid [30]. See also *Pham Hoang v France* (App No 13191/87) (1993) 16 EHRR 53, concerning the application of the same provision of French law.

[65] *Cf Porras v Netherlands* (App No 49226/99) ECHR 18 January 2000 in which it is arguably clearer that the presumption relied upon was discretionary and therefore did not alter the burden of proof.

[66] *Cf Sheldrake v DPP; AG's Reference (No 4 of 2002)* [2005] 1 AC 264 (HL) [76] (Lord Rodger, dissenting) apparently suggesting that the *Salabiaku* formulation could apply only if the reverse burden was created using the language of presumptions.

[67] This conclusion is based on a search of the HUDOC website (www.echr.coe.int/echr) for all judgments and decisions of the Strasbourg organs citing *Salabiaku*. Of the 68 cases citing *Salabiaku* (as at 29 September 2009), none reached a finding that a 'presumption' went beyond reasonable limits (although some found breaches of other Article 6 rights).

[68] *X v UK* (App No 5124/71) EComHR 19 July 1972; (1972) 42 Collection of Decisions 135.

proved the circumstance that the defendant was habitually in the company of a prostitute. The presumption did not contravene Article 6(2) because it was 'neither irrebuttable nor unreasonable'.[69] The opportunity given to the defendant to prove that he was not living on immoral earnings ensured there was no breach of Article 6(2), even though under English law the defendant bore the risk of non-persuasion on this point.

Following *Salabiaku*, the Strasbourg Court has routinely found that Article 6(2) is not breached because the court retains a 'genuine freedom of assessment'. For example, in *AG v Malta*,[70] the applicant was a company director convicted after customs forms signed in the name of his company were found to contain false declarations. A Maltese statute provided that if an offence was committed by a body corporate, the director of the body would 'be guilty of that offence unless he proves that the offence was committed without his knowledge and that he exercised all due diligence to prevent the commission of the offence.' The applicant alleged that the provision was inconsistent with Article 6(2). After stating the effect of the impugned provision, the Commission concluded that: 'The applicant was therefore provided under the legislation with the possibility of exculpating himself.'[71] Finally, the Commission found that the 'Maltese courts enjoyed a genuine freedom of assessment' in assessing whether the defendant had proved his defence.[72] On the Commission's reasoning, allowing the defendant the opportunity to prove certain facts in order to avoid conviction was not a breach of the presumption of innocence.

Similarly, in *Bates v UK*,[73] the applicant was charged with having a dangerous dog, specifically a pit bull terrier, in a public place, contrary to section 1 of the Dangerous Dogs Act 1991. Section 5(5) of that Act stated that if the prosecution alleged the dog was one to which the Act applied, the court was to presume it was such a dog unless the defendant proved otherwise. The applicant was convicted after failing to produce evidence as to the breed of the dog. The Strasbourg Commission regarded it as significant that section 5(5) of the Act provided an opportunity to the defendant to adduce evidence at the trial hearing as to the dog's breeding.[74] Therefore, even though the defendant faced a potential penalty of six months' imprisonment, the Commission held that 'given the opportunity expressly provided to the defence to rebut the presumption of fact' the complaint under Article 6(2) was manifestly ill-founded.[75] Again, the Commission did not regard the reversal of the burden of proof as problematic, provided the defendant was given the opportunity to satisfy the burden.

[69] Ibid.
[70] *AG v Malta* (App No 16641/90) EComHR 10 December 1991.
[71] Ibid.
[72] Ibid.
[73] *Bates v UK* (App No 26280/95) EComHR 16 January 1996. See also, considering the same statutory provision, *Brock v UK* (App No 26279/95) EComHR 16 January 1996; *Foster v UK* (App No 28846/95) EComHR 16 January 1996; *Bullock v UK* (App No 29102/95) EComHR 16 January 1996.
[74] Ibid.
[75] Ibid.

A series of cases decided in relation to Article 5(1) of the Austrian Code of Administrative Offences has adopted similar reasoning. Article 5(1) laid down a rule that in the criminal offences to which it applied, negligence would be sufficient to establish guilt. Further, once the conduct constituting the offence was proven, there was to be a presumption of negligence unless the defendant proved that he or she was not at fault. Considering this presumption, the Strasbourg Commission stated:[76]

> The Commission finds that the second sentence of Article 5(1) of the Code of Administrative Offences is no more than a statutory repetition of the common sense proposition that where a person does a prohibited action, or fails to do something which he is under a duty to do, the conclusion can reasonably be drawn that he has contravened the provision at issue, unless he can show that he was not at fault.

In these cases, the Strasbourg organs have not been concerned that the defendant is required to prove the absence of negligence. This is regarded as a 'common sense' position consistent with Article 6(2). As in the other cases discussed above, the Strasbourg organs take the view that the rights of the defence are adequately protected provided the defendant is permitted to present his or her case.

A deeply counterintuitive result follows from these cases. Reverse burdens of proof will virtually never contravene the presumption of innocence since a defendant subject to a reverse burden always has the opportunity, at least in theory, to satisfy the burden. This characteristic of the Strasbourg approach to Article 6(2) was observed by Lord Rodger, dissenting, in *Sheldrake v DPP*.[77] Lord Rodger stated:[78]

> It is clear, however—not least from the decision of the European Court in *Salabiaku v France* . . . that, if the law provides for a defence and the defendant is free to deploy his case in support of that defence before the trial court, then the mere fact that the onus is on him to establish the facts giving rise to the defence does not constitute a violation of article 6(2) or make his trial unfair for the purposes of article 6(1) . . . What matters is that the tribunal assesses the facts with an open mind, without any preconception of the defendant's guilt. In addition, in a case like the present, the rights of the defence are fully respected. The defendant is free to give evidence himself, and to lead the evidence of other witnesses, in support of the defence.

No other English judge has drawn these conclusions from the Strasbourg cases, but they flow inexorably from a long series of decisions.

There may be two exceptions to the rule that a reversal of the burden of proof will not breach Article 6(2). First, following the authority of *Telfner v Austria*,[79] a

[76] *Proksch v Austria* (App No 18724/91) EComHR 18 October 1994. See also *Bruckner v Austria* (App No 21442/93) ECom HR 18 October 1994; *Müller v Austria* (No 1) (App No 12555/03) ECHR 5 October 2006 [34]; *TH v Austria* (App No 19116/91) EComHR 13 October 1993; *Müller v Austria* (No 2) (App No 28034/04) ECHR 18 September 2008 [40]. And see (involving a different statute) *Resch v Austria* (App No 21585/93) EComHR 18 October 1994.

[77] *Sheldrake v DPP* [2005] 1 AC 264 (HL).

[78] Ibid [71], [76].

[79] (App No 33501/96) (2002) 34 EHRR 7.

reverse burden would contravene the presumption of innocence if it were introduced before the prosecution had established a *prima facie* case. The most extreme example would be a reverse burden of proof on all the aspects of the offence once the prosecution had proved the identity of the defendant. The Strasbourg Court would very likely find that a presumption of this nature was not within 'reasonable limits'. Second, a reverse burden might infringe Article 6(2) if the burden related to something about which the defendant could not reasonably be expected to provide proof.[80] In such a case, there would be no genuine opportunity to rebut the presumption created by the reverse burden. Outside of these extreme situations, reverse burdens will virtually always be acceptable as far as the Strasbourg Court is concerned. For English lawyers, the suggestion that reverse burdens of proof do not, in general, infringe the presumption of innocence because the defendant has the opportunity to mount a defence is surprising. Either the Strasbourg Court does not regard the burden of proof as a mechanism for allocating the risk of non-persuasion, or it does not appreciate the objectionable nature of burdening the defendant with this risk. In either case, English courts should be cautious when seeking to apply the Strasbourg decisions to domestic law.

If the conclusions of the Strasbourg cases were to be applied in English law, it would unravel the understanding of the presumption of innocence that has stood since *Woolmington v DPP*.[81] Rather than needing to fall within a specific common law or statutory exception, or needing to be justified as proportionate to a legitimate objective, all reverse burdens would be acceptable provided the defendant had the opportunity to present exonerating evidence. The result would be that defendants could be convicted in the absence of proof beyond reasonable doubt. Indeed, defendants could be convicted simply because they were unable to prove their innocence on the balance of probabilities. This would result in an unacceptable risk of wrongful convictions and would undermine the rule of law principle that only those who are proven to have contravened the criminal law should be subject to its penalties. To the extent that the Strasbourg Court understands the concept of a burden of proof in a manner different from the common law, the English courts should not regard themselves as bound by its decisions.

4. Article 6(2) and Substantive Law

The cases discussed in the previous section held that there was no contravention of Article 6(2) because the defendant had the opportunity present evidence to overcome a presumption. That is, the Strasbourg organs held that the presumptions in question were within 'reasonable limits' because they were rebuttable. This suggests that the Strasbourg Court might find a breach of Article 6(2) if the impugned presumption was irrebuttable. Irrebuttable presumptions are a method

[80] C Ovey, R White *Jacobs and White: The European Convention on Human Rights* 4th edn (Oxford, OUP, 2006) 202.

[81] *Woolmington v DPP* [1935] AC 462 (HL).

of creating substantive rules of law.[82] By suggesting that an irrebuttable presumption might contravene Article 6(2), the Strasbourg cases imply that Article 6(2) is capable of controlling the substantive content of the law.

The leading authority on the substantive scope of Article 6(2) is *Salabiaku v France.*[83] In that case, the Strasbourg Court stated:[84]

> [I]n principle the Contracting States remain free to apply the criminal law to an act where it is not carried out in the normal exercise of one of the rights protected under the Convention and, accordingly, to define the constituent elements of the resulting offence. In particular, and again in principle, the Contracting States may, under certain conditions, penalise a simple or objective fact as such, irrespective of whether it results from criminal intent or from negligence.

The assertion that States are permitted to 'define the constituent elements of the . . . offence' suggests that Article 6(2) does not affect the substantive rules of criminal law. The next sentence confirms, more specifically, that Article 6(2) does not prevent the creation of strict liability crimes, that is, crimes with no requirement of criminal intent or negligence. However, a degree of ambiguity is introduced by the phrases 'in principle' and 'under certain conditions'. These phrases imply that Article 6(2) could impose some limits on the capacity of States to control the substantive content of the criminal law.[85] They might suggest that strict liability crimes are permissible, provided they comply with the requirements of Article 6(2).

The idea that the presumption of innocence could have consequences for the substantive content of the criminal law is supported by a further statement in *Salabiaku* regarding the interpretation of the phrase 'according to law'. The most obvious and natural interpretation of this phrase is that a person charged with a criminal offence is to be presumed innocent until proved guilty of an offence as defined by the domestic law of a contracting state.[86] The Strasbourg Court, however, stated that the meaning of 'according to law' should not be limited in this way.[87]

> [T]he national legislature would be free to strip the trial court of any genuine power of assessment and deprive the presumption of innocence of its substance, if the words "according to law" were construed exclusively with reference to domestic law. Such a situation could not be reconciled with the object and purpose of Article 6, which, by protecting the right to a fair trial and in particular the right to be presumed innocent, is intended to enshrine the fundamental principle of the rule of law.

[82] See Ch 1, p 13.
[83] *Salabiaku v France* (App No 10519/83) (1991) 13 EHRR 379.
[84] Ibid [27].
[85] *Cf R v G* [2008] 1 WLR 1379 (HL) [28] (Lord Hope), suggesting that 'under certain conditions' was affirming the proposition that acts protected by substantive rights in the ECHR could not be criminalised.
[86] See A Ashworth 'Four Threats to the Presumption of Innocence' (2006) 10 *E & P* 241, 252; P Mirfield 'Silence, Innocence and Human Rights' in P Mirfield & R Smith (eds) *Essays for Colin Tapper* (LexisNexis, London 2003) 126, 133. *Cf Ong Ah Chuan v Public Prosecutor* [1981] AC 648 (PC) 670–71 (Lord Diplock) on the meaning of 'in accordance with law' under the Singaporean Constitution.
[87] (App No 10519/83) (1991) 13 EHRR 379 [27].

It is not clear what the Strasbourg Court envisaged as included within the 'fundamental principle of the rule of law'. The Court may have intended only that certain procedural protections could not be removed, such as those which would deprive the courts of the ability to make a genuine assessment of the guilt of a defendant. However, if the 'fundamental principle of the rule of law' includes a requirement that only those who are culpable should be punished, then Article 6 in general and Article 6(2) in particular would constrain the substance of the criminal law.

Immediately following its statement on the interpretation of 'according to law', the Strasbourg Court went on to state that 'presumptions of fact or law' must be confined within 'reasonable limits'.[88] Unfortunately, the Court did not clarify the kind of 'presumption' that was subject to this 'reasonable limits' test. On one usage, presumptions of fact are discretionary presumptions, while presumptions of law are mandatory presumptions.[89] Mandatory presumptions may be either rebuttable or irrebuttable. Irrebuttable presumptions are a means of creating substantive rules of law.[90] If the 'reasonable limits' test was intended to apply to irrebuttable presumptions, the result would be that Article 6(2) has at least a limited capacity to govern the substance of the criminal law.

A further ambiguity in *Salabiaku* derives from confusion over the type of offence that was examined in that case. Some authors have suggested that the offence examined in *Salabiaku* was one of strict liability.[91] If this were the case, the Strasbourg Court would have applied its 'reasonable limits' test to a strict liability offence. In one sense, the offence of smuggling in *Salabiaku* was almost certainly one of strict liability. There was no requirement that the defendant have knowledge that he or she was in possession of smuggled goods. However, a limited defence of *force majeure* applied when the box came into the possession of the defendant as a result of forces outside of his control or when it was 'impossible' to know the contents of the box. This defence could be regarded as importing *mens rea* in the form of negligence or failure to exercise due diligence. If the defendant could have discovered the contents of the box, but did not, this would constitute sufficient culpability to support a conviction.[92] *Salabiaku* is a highly unsatisfactory

[88] Ibid [28].

[89] See PJ Schwikkard & SE van der Merwe *Principles of Evidence* 2nd edn (Juta Law, Lansdowne 2002) 469–71.

[90] See Ch 1, p 13.

[91] J Spencer & A Pedain 'Approaches to Strict and Constructive Liability in Continental Criminal Law' in AP Simester (ed) *Appraising Strict Liability* (OUP, Oxford 2005) 237, 263, 269. Spencer & Pedain provide a convenient summary of the different classes of offences under French law and show that the customs offence at issue in *Salabiaku* would have been considered a strict liability offence: ibid 256–57. Similarly, the applicant's complaint before the Commission in *Salabiaku v France* (App No 10519/83) EComHR 16 April 1986 stated: 'Under the French classification of offences, customs offences, including that provided for in Art 392 of the Customs Code are offences of "absolute" or "strict" liability.' See also Mirfield (see n 86 above) 133.

[92] *Cf* Trechsel (see n 1 above) 171–72: 'Customs legislation requires persons who take possession of imported goods to make sure that the customs formalities have been complied with. In other words, they are under a specific obligation of carefulness. It is not reasonable to expect the customs' authorities to prove the 'negative fact' that the necessary care was not applied. On the other hand, going

authority on the question of whether Article 6(2) applies to strict liability offences.[93] However, a number of other Strasbourg cases suggest that Article 6(2) has a substantive scope and, for example, is capable of applying to strict liability offences.

For instance, in *Hansen v Denmark*,[94] the applicant was the managing director of a transport company. He was fined because one of his drivers exceeded the maximum daily driving period, in contravention of an EU regulation. The ECJ and the Danish courts found that the imposition of strict (or vicarious) liability on the managing director was compatible with Article 6(2) and the applicant applied to Strasbourg. The Strasbourg Court quoted the comments from *Salabiaku* concerning the need to confine presumptions within 'reasonable limits'.[95] This constituted an assumption that strict liability offences were within the ambit of Article 6(2) and had to comply with the 'reasonable limits' test. The Strasbourg Court went on to conclude that the imposition of vicarious liability was reasonable in the circumstances. One English judge has described *Hansen v Denmark* as an aberration that 'appears rapidly to have achieved a degree of obscurity'.[96] However, there are a number of other cases in which substantive rules of law have been examined under the 'reasonable limits' test.

Selvanayagam v UK[97] is a striking case in which the Strasbourg Court applied the 'reasonable limits' test to a rule of substantive law. In that case, the applicant was an animal rights protester who had been restrained by a High Court injunction from going on or near a certain mink farm. Despite the injunction, the applicant conducted protests outside the mink farm and was subsequently charged with harassment under section 2 of the Protection from Harassment Act 1997. Her defence was that engaging in these protests had been 'reasonable' within the meaning of the Act. The Divisional Court rejected this defence on the ground that an action could not be regarded as reasonable if it was in breach of an injunction. This decision by the Divisional Court took the form of a substantive rule of law. Regardless of any facts tending to show that a protest was reasonable, the defence of reasonableness was not available to a defendant who acted in contravention of an injunction. Nevertheless, the Strasbourg Court applied the 'reasonable limits' test before deciding there was no breach of Article 6(2). The Strasbourg Court concluded that 'any presumption of law that arose out of the judgment of the Divisional Court . . . was within reasonable limits, took account of the importance

through the required formalities leaves traces which it is easy to produce in evidence. To take possession of imported goods without such proof is connected with a risk. Creating this risk is the offence—it is usually proved without difficulty.'

[93] *R v G* [2008] 1 WLR 1379 (HL) [5]–[6]: 'My Lords, I think that judges and academic writers have picked over the carcass of this unfortunate case so many times in attempts to find some intelligible meat on its bones that the time has come to call a halt. The Strasbourg court, uninhibited by the doctrine of precedent or the need to find a ratio decidendi, seems to have ignored it . . . I would recommend your Lordships to do likewise.'

[94] *Hansen v Denmark* (App No 28971/95) ECHR 16 March 2000.

[95] Ibid.

[96] *Barnfather v Islington Education Authority* [2003] 1 WLR 2318 (QBD) [22] (Maurice Kay J).

[97] *Selvanayagam v UK* (App No 57981/00) ECHR 12 December 2002.

of what was at stake and maintained the rights of the defence.'[98] Had the Strasbourg Court concluded that the rule applied by the Divisional Court was not within 'reasonable limits' it would presumably have declared it incompatible with Article 6(2).

A further case in which the 'reasonable limits' test was applied to a substantive rule of law is *Brown v UK*.[99] In that case, the applicant was a shareholder and director of a Sunday newspaper which published the name of the complainant in a rape case, contrary to section 4(1) of the Sexual Offences (Amendment) Act 1976. He was convicted by the English courts on the basis of section 4(5) of the Act which made any 'proprietor, editor or publisher' of a newspaper liable for the publication. Section 5(5) provided a defence if the defendant could prove that he was not aware, did not suspect and had no reason to suspect that publication would include the prohibited material. The magistrates found that the applicant did not know or suspect that the offending article was to be published, but had reason to suspect because he always visited the offices of the newspaper in the days preceding publication. The applicant alleged before the Strasbourg Court that the conviction was an unjustified restriction of the freedom of speech, contrary to Article 10, and a breach of Article 6(2). The Court held there was no violation of Article 10 because the defendant had the opportunity to prove that he was not at fault in the publication.

As to the alleged breach of the presumption of innocence, the UK argued that since Article 6(2) did not prohibit strict liability crimes it could not *a fortiori* prohibit the reversal of the burden of proof so as to allow defendants to avoid criminal liability by showing the exercise of due care. The Strasbourg Court reiterated that: 'Contracting States may, in principle and under certain conditions, penalize a simple or objective fact as such, irrespective of whether it results from criminal intent or from negligence.' However, the Court noted that in order to obtain a conviction under section 4(5) of the Act, it was necessary for the prosecution to prove all the requisite elements of that section. Further, the defendant was able to escape liability if he or she could prove that they were in no way at fault in connection with the offending article. The Strasbourg Court stressed that the existence of the defence in section 5(5) prevented the offence of publication from breaching Article 6(2). Far from being problematic for Article 6(2), the defence, even though subject to a reverse burden, is what saved it from being contrary to Article 6(2). Since the presumption of liability might have been incompatible in the absence of the available defence, it follows that that the Strasbourg Court treated Article 6(2) as capable of controlling strict liability offences.[100]

The treatment of reverse burdens and strict liability offences in the Strasbourg Court leads to the counterintuitive conclusion that reverse burdens will nearly always be compatible with Article 6(2), whereas strict liability offences are more

[98] Ibid.

[99] *Brown v UK* (App No 44223/98) ECHR 2 July 2002.

[100] See also the very similar case of *Radio France v France* (App No 53984/00) (2005) 40 EHRR 29.

problematic. Both aspects of this conclusion are at odds with the best understanding of the presumption of innocence. The presumption of innocence has long been understood in English law to require, in the usual case, that the prosecution should bear the persuasive burden on each issue relevant to conviction. Departures from this practice need to fall within an established statutory or common law exception. To the extent that the Strasbourg organs adopt a different understanding of the burden of proof to that which applies in English law, English courts should depart from the Strasbourg jurisprudence. Further, the best understanding of the presumption requires it to be seen as a procedural protection rather than a substantive protection,[101] and accordingly, the English courts should not follow the practice of using Article 6(2) to control rules of substantive law. To apply Article 6(2) to the substance of the criminal law would be an unjustified intrusion by the courts into the constitutional duties of the legislature.

B. Limitation of Article 6 Rights

As we have seen, the Strasbourg Court has held that the presumption of innocence can be restricted by 'presumptions of fact or law', provided those presumptions are confined within 'reasonable limits'. This Part will focus on the use by the Strasbourg Court of the community interest as a justification for limiting the right protected by Article 6(2), and draw a contrast with the approach taken to other Article 6 rights. Section one will set out some of the key cases in which considerations of the community interest have been used to justify the limitation of the presumption of innocence. Section two will show that, while considerations of the community interest are not treated as irrelevant in respect of other Article 6 rights, a series of principles is applied to ensure greater protection for these rights. Section two will also consider whether aspects of this approach can be adapted to protect the presumption of innocence against limitations in the name of community interest.

1. Community Interest Under Article 6(2)

As stated above, the *Salabiaku* formula requires 'presumptions' to be confined 'within reasonable limits which into account the importance of what is at stake and maintain the rights of the defence.'[102] This 'reasonable limits' test bears a resemblance to a test of proportionality. The use of proportionality under Article 6(2) was expressly confirmed in *Janosevic v Sweden.*[103] In that case, the applicant

[101] See Ch 3.
[102] (App No 10589/83) (1991) 13 EHRR 379 [28].
[103] *Janosevic v Sweden* (App No 34619/97) (2004) 38 EHRR 22.

had alleged that the Swedish procedure for imposing tax surcharges imposed 'an almost insurmountable burden of proof'[104] on the taxpayer. In upholding the procedure, the Strasbourg Court stated: '[T]he Contracting States are required to strike a balance between the importance of what is at stake and the rights of the defence; in other words, the means employed have to be reasonably proportionate to the legitimate aim sought to be achieved.'[105] A notable aspect of this statement is the implication that the 'importance of what is at stake' refers to the interest of the community in pursuing a 'legitimate aim'. Earlier cases following *Salabiaku* had implied that it was the interests of the applicant that were 'at stake', in particular the potential for a severe penalty.[106] *Janosevic* confirmed that the effect of the *Salabiaku* formula was to require an investigation of the proportionality or 'balance' between an individual right and the community interest. The statements to this effect in *Janosevic* have been quoted or paraphrased in two later cases.[107]

By holding that the community interest is relevant to the 'balancing' exercise under Article 6(2), the Strasbourg Court opened the way to the limitation of the presumption in order to protect the community interest. For instance, in *Västbergat Taxi Aktiebolag and Vulic v Sweden*,[108] the Strasbourg Court considered a reverse burden of proof on the question of liability for tax surcharges. The Court considered that the reverse burden could be justified because of the importance to the State of maintaining a sound system of taxation. The Court stated:[109]

> The Court also has regard to the financial interests of the State in tax matters, taxes being the State's main source of income. A system of taxation principally based on information supplied by the taxpayer would not function properly without some form of sanction against the provision of incorrect or incomplete information, and the large number of tax returns that are processed annually coupled with the interest in ensuring a foreseeable and uniform application of such sanctions undoubtedly require that they be imposed according to standardised rules.

In effect, the Strasbourg Court held that the reverse burden as to liability for the tax surcharge made such an important contribution to the effectiveness of the tax system that it outweighed the right of the applicant to be presumed innocent.

Similarly, the Strasbourg Commission has held that the importance of environmental protection can outweigh the right to be presumed innocent. In *Maatschap v Netherlands*,[110] the Commission considered whether the use of flat rates to calculate manure production contravened the presumption of innocence. The Commission upheld the statutory presumption and in doing so had 'regard to the

[104] Ibid [77].
[105] Ibid [101].
[106] *Bates v UK* (App No 26280/95) EComHR 16 January 1996. *Brock v UK* (App No 26279/95) EComHR 16 January 1996; *Foster v UK* (App No 28846/95) EComHR 16 January 1996; *Bullock v UK* (App No 29102/95) EComHR 16 January 1996.
[107] *Västberga Taxi Aktiebolag and Vulic v Sweden* (App No 36985/97) ECHR 23 July 2002 [113]; *Falk v Netherlands* (App No 66273/01) ECHR 19 October 2004.
[108] (App No 36985/97) ECHR 23 July 2002.
[109] Ibid.
[110] *Maatschap v Netherlands* (App No 31463/96) EComHR 21 May 1997.

aim and purpose of the environmental legislation and the obvious technical difficulties in determining manure production in individual cases'.[111] In other words, the Commission held it was permissible to penalise the defendant for excess manure production, even if the defendant had, in fact, not exceeded the manure production limits. This restriction of the defendant's rights was permissible because it advanced the community interest in maintaining a regulatory regime for environmental protection.

The invocation of the community interest as a justification for the restriction of the defendant's rights is fundamentally unsound. It allows the community interest to 'trump' the right of the defendant to be presumed innocent until proven guilty. In the cases discussed above, the Strasbourg organs have allowed these restrictions without regard to the unfairness this imposes on the defendant. The effect of this is that, if the community interest is sufficiently important, the right of the defendant to be presumed innocent can simply be ignored. This approach to the presumption of innocence is at odds with the wording of the Article 6(2), which is expressed in unqualified terms. This may be contrasted with Articles 8–11 of the ECHR which expressly permit limitations on protected rights when it is 'necessary in a democratic society'. Further, the Strasbourg Court's recourse to the community interest when applying Article 6(2) is at odds with its approach when applying other Article 6 rights. The following section sets out the important features of this approach.

2. Community Interest and Other Article 6 Rights

For the most part, the rights protected by Article 6 of the ECHR are expressed in unqualified terms. There is no overarching provision allowing the limitation of Article 6 rights when the community interest requires it. Despite this, some Strasbourg cases have stated that the search for balance between the general interest of the community and the rights of the individual is 'inherent in the whole of the Convention'.[112] English cases have referred to these decisions to support proportionate limitations on Article 6 rights.[113] Similarly, Stephanos Stavros states that courts applying Article 6 'often have to pronounce on the tension between the opposing values of increased protection for the accused and interests of the community in the apprehension and punishment of criminals in the context of an efficiently administered system of justice.'[114] Accordingly, he accepts that rights under Article 6 can be subject to limitation in order to advance the 'opposing legitimate interests of society'.[115]

[111] Ibid. See also *Klein Poelhuis v Netherlands* (App No 34970/97) EComHR 21 May 1997.

[112] *Cossey v UK* (App No 10843/84) (1991) 13 EHRR 622 [37]; *Sporrong and Lönnroth v Sweden* (App No 7151/75) (1983) 5 EHRR 35 [69]; *Soering v UK* (App No 14038/88) (1989) 11 EHRR 439 [89]; *Rees v UK* (App No 9532/81) (1986) 9 EHRR 56 [37].

[113] *Brown v Stott* [2003] 1 AC 681 (PC) 704–06 (Lord Bingham); *R v DPP; ex p Kebilene* [2000] 2 AC 326 (HL) 384 (Lord Hope).

[114] Stavros (see n 1 above) 340.

[115] Ibid 344.

However, with the exception of cases under Article 6(2), the Strasbourg Court has in fact resisted attempts to limit Article 6 rights by reference to the community interest.[116] For example, in *Teixeira de Castro v Portugal*,[117] the Strasbourg Court stated: 'the right to a fair administration of justice . . . holds such a prominent place that it cannot be sacrificed for the sake of expedience.'[118] As will be seen below, there are many references to 'proportionality', 'balance' or 'weighing' in the Article 6 cases. In addition, there are statements that Article 6 rights are not 'absolute' which suggests that they may give way to other concerns. However, the Strasbourg Court avoids allowing the community interest to hobble individual rights by applying a series of principles. First, rules are laid down for the content of rights which, regardless of the countervailing community interest, cannot be breached. Second, if a trial right is limited there must be 'adequate safeguards' to ensure protection of the interests of the defendant. Third, regardless of the public interest, there are numerous statements that the 'very essence' of Article 6 rights may not be restricted. Each of the principles will be discussed below and illustrated by reference to specific Article 6 rights.

(a) Rules Defining the Content of a Right

The delineation of the content of a right by the use of clear rules can be illustrated by reference to the right to silence. Although not mentioned in Article 6, the Strasbourg Court has held that the 'right to remain silent under police questioning and the privilege against self-incrimination are generally recognized standards which lie at the heart of the notion of a fair procedure under Article 6.'[119] In Strasbourg, the leading cases on the right to silence deal with the question of whether adverse inferences can be drawn from the failure of the defendant to answer questions under police questioning or to give evidence at trial.

In a series of cases, the Strasbourg Court has held that the right to silence is not 'absolute'.[120] The question of whether the drawing of adverse inferences from silence is compatible with Article 6 must be 'determined in the light of all the circumstances of the case, having particular regard to the situations where inferences may be drawn, the weight attached to them by the national courts in their assessments of the evidence and the degree of compulsion inherent in the situation.'[121]

[116] This reading of the Strasbourg cases is advanced by A Ashworth *Human Rights, Serious Crime and Criminal Procedure* (Sweet & Maxwell, London 2002) ch 2. See also A Ashworth 'Criminal Proceedings After the Human Rights Act: The First Year' [2001] *Crim LR* 855, 864–68; A Ashworth 'Security, Terrorism and the Value of Human Rights' in L Lazarus & B Goold (eds) *Security and Human Rights* (Hart Publishing, Oxford 2007) 203. See also M Redmayne 'Rethinking the Privilege Against Self-Incrimination' (2007) 27 *OJLS* 209, 229.

[117] *Teixeira de Castro v Portugal* (App No 25829/94) (1999) 28 EHRR 101.

[118] Ibid [36].

[119] *Murray v UK* (App No 18731/91) (1996) 22 EHRR 29 [45].

[120] Ibid [47]; *Averill v UK* (App No 36408/97) (2001) 31 EHRR 36 [44]; *Beckles v UK* (App No 44652/98) (2003) 36 EHRR 13 [57]; *Quinn v Ireland* (App No 36887/97) ECHR 21 December 2000 [47]; *Heaney and McGuinness v Ireland* (App No 34720/97) (2001) 33 EHRR 12 [47].

[121] (App No 18731/91) (1996) 22 EHRR 29 [47].

The Strasbourg Court has also stated that it is necessary to find the appropriate 'balance' between the right of the defendant to remain silent and the drawing of appropriate inferences from silence.[122] Hence, it follows that the right to silence can be subject to limitation: suspects and defendants are not entitled to remain silent in all circumstances without attracting the prospect of adverse inferences.

Significantly, however, the Strasbourg Court does not use proportionality as the touchstone of compliance with the right to silence. Rather, the Strasbourg Court has laid down rules determining when adverse inferences may be drawn from silence. In general, the silence of the defendant 'in situations which clearly call for an explanation' may be 'taken into account in assessing the persuasiveness of the evidence adduced by the prosecution'.[123] Further, in respect of silence under police questioning, an adverse inference may be drawn only if there is no plausible explanation for the defendant's silence other than guilt.[124] Finally, it is impermissible 'to base a conviction solely or mainly on the accused's silence or on a refusal to answer questions or to give evidence himself.'[125]

By applying these rules, the Strasbourg Court avoids the process of 'balancing' the rights of the defendant against the community interest. The rules focus on whether fairness to the defendant has been maintained. If the drawing of an adverse inference from silence is consistent with fairness to the defendant, then it is permissible; if it is not fair, then it is impermissible. The rules applied by the Strasbourg Court determine whether the criterion of fairness has been met. This contrasts with a proportionality analysis in which the compatibility of an action with the Convention is determined by balancing the community interest against the interest of the defendant.

The use of rules to define the boundaries of the right to silence helps to ensure that considerations of the community interest do not place the defendant at risk of unfair conviction. It is worth considering briefly whether aspects of this 'rule-based' approach to determinations of compatibility could be applied to the presumption of innocence. In English law, the presumption of innocence can be expressed as the rule that the prosecution must prove the guilt of the defendant beyond reasonable doubt. It would be possible to enforce this rule without recognising exceptions: every persuasive burden on a defendant would breach the presumption of innocence. Such a rule would be capable of simple application and would ensure that the right of the defendant to be presumed innocent is never 'balanced' away in the name of community interest.

However, an absolute rule of this nature might be thought excessive since the extent to which the presumption of innocence contributes to the protection of

[122] *Condron v UK* (App No 35718/97) (2001) 31 EHRR 1 [58]. See also *Averill v UK* (App No 36408/97) (2001) 31 EHRR 36 [45].

[123] Ibid.

[124] *Beckles v UK* (App No 44652/98) (2003) 36 EHRR 13 [59], [62].

[125] (App No 18731/91) (1996) 22 EHRR 29 [47]. See also *Condron v UK* (App No 35718/97) (2001) 31 EHRR 1 [56]; *Averill v UK* (App No 36408/97) (2001) 31 EHRR 36 [45]; *Beckles v UK* (App No 44652/98) (2003) 36 EHRR 13 [58].

defendants differs depending on the circumstances. The presumption of innocence may be less important when the risk of wrongful conviction is low or when the penalty upon conviction is minimal.[126] In recognition of these scenarios, the courts could develop rules designed to ensure that the persuasive burden can be reversed only when the interests of the defendant are implicated in an attenuated way. Candidate rules might include a rule that the persuasive burden should not be reversed if the defendant faces possible imprisonment, or a rule that the persuasive burden should not be reversed until the prosecution has proved some degree of criminality or wrongfulness. Considerations of proportionality could still come into play after these rules have been applied. Provided that the rights of the defendant are sufficiently protected, it might be permissible to reverse the burden of proof if there is a compelling reason for doing so. The application of rules would however pre-empt arguments about the community interest in any cases where the interests of the defendant would be unfairly prejudiced. The work of developing these rules constitutes the bulk of the work in deciding when reverse burdens of proof are acceptable. Chapter Six approaches the problem of reverse burdens in this manner.

(b) Adequate Safeguards

As well as the rules defining the content of the right to silence, the Strasbourg Court insists upon 'safeguards' whenever the trial court proposes to draw an adverse inference from silence.[127] The doctrine of 'safeguards' provides further protection for the rights of defendants and ensures that the community interest is not permitted to prevail against those rights. In the context of the right to silence, four 'safeguards' are listed: (1) the defendant must be given a warning regarding the legal effect of silence; (2) a *prima facie* case must be established before an inference is drawn from silence; (3) the trial judge or jury must be left a discretion on whether to draw an adverse inference; and (4) the discretion must be reviewable on appeal.[128] Each of these safeguards contributes to the overall goal of ensuring that the defendant is given a fair trial.

The insistence upon 'safeguards' has also played a role in respect of other Article 6 rights. Notably, the Strasbourg Court has applied the 'safeguards' principle in some instances where it has been willing to acknowledge the importance of the community interest. In these cases, the safeguards are intended to ensure that, notwithstanding the competing community interest, the rights of the defendant are adequately protected.

This can be seen, for example, in decisions concerning the right of the defendant to disclosure of all information relevant to the case. The Strasbourg Court has held that the public interest in protecting witnesses or keeping secret methods of

[126] See Ch 2, pp 48–51.
[127] (App No 18731/91) (1996) 22 EHRR 29 [51].
[128] Ibid.

criminal investigation must be 'weighed against' the right of the accused to disclosure of information relevant to the case. In *Rowe and Davis v UK*,[129] the Strasbourg Court stated:[130]

> In any criminal proceedings there may be competing interests, such as national security or the need to protect witnesses at risk of reprisals or keep secret police methods of investigation of crime, which must be weighed against the rights of the accused. In some cases it may be necessary to withhold certain evidence from the defence so as to preserve the fundamental rights of another individual or to safeguard an important public interest.

Despite this, measures restricting the rights of the defence to see material relevant to the case would only be permissible if 'strictly necessary'.[131] Further, 'in order to ensure that the accused receives a fair trial, any difficulties caused to the defence by a limitation on its rights must be sufficiently counterbalanced by the procedures followed by the judicial authorities.'[132] Hence, for example, the prosecution could not withhold evidence of its own volition but had to apply to the trial judge who could then consider whether concealment was justified.[133]

The requirement for adequate safeguards can also be seen in cases concerning the right of a defendant to confront witnesses, protected by Article 6(3)(c). This right has been relied upon to challenge domestic laws which permit evidence from anonymous witnesses. When reviewing domestic law for compatibility with Article 6(3)(c), the Strasbourg Court does not regard the community interest as irrelevant. For instance, in *Kostovski v Netherlands*,[134] the Strasbourg Court stated that the importance of the struggle against organised crime was 'not without force'.[135] However, the Strasbourg Court also stated: 'The right to a fair administration of justice holds so prominent a place in a democratic society that it cannot be sacrificed to expediency.'[136] The Strasbourg Court in that case held that a conviction based 'to a decisive extent' on anonymous evidence would be inconsistent with a fair trial.[137] Hence, even if the community interest in controlling crime was relevant, it could never be invoked when this would result in unfairness to the defendant.

A different calculation concerning the community interest was employed in *Doorson v Netherlands*.[138] The applicants in that case had been convicted of drug-dealing. At trial, two witnesses were permitted to remain anonymous for fear of reprisals. The Strasbourg Court noted that Article 6 did not explicitly require the interests of witnesses to be taken into account, but that witnesses had rights to life,

[129] *Rowe and Davis v UK* (App No 28901/95) (2000) 30 EHRR 1.
[130] Ibid [61].
[131] Ibid.
[132] Ibid. See also *Jasper v UK* (App No 27052/95) (2000) 30 EHRR 441 [52]; *Fitt v UK* (App No 29777/96) (2000) 30 EHRR 480 [45]; *Atlan v UK* (App No 36533/97) ECHR 19 June 2001 [40].
[133] Ibid [63].
[134] *Kostovski v Netherlands* (App No 11454/85) (1989) 12 EHRR 434.
[135] Ibid [44].
[136] Ibid [44]. See also *Windisch v Austria* (App No 12489/86) (1991) 13 EHRR 281 [30].
[137] Ibid.
[138] *Doorson v Netherlands* (App No 20524/92) (1996) 22 EHRR 330.

liberty and security of person under Article 8 of the Convention.[139] Hence, the Strasbourg Court stated: 'principles of fair trial . . . require that in appropriate cases the interests of the defence are balanced against those of witnesses or victims called upon to testify.'[140] These reasons were regarded as sufficient in *Doorson* to permit the witnesses to remain anonymous. It is notable that the 'balancing' involved in *Doorson* was a balancing of the rights of the defendants against the rights of another identifiable set of people. It was not a balancing against the general community interest in obtaining convictions. Further, the Strasbourg Court considered it important that 'counterbalancing procedures' were in place to protect the rights of the defendant, such as permitting defence counsel to question the witnesses.[141]

In subsequent cases, the Strasbourg Court has reinforced the principle that if the right to confront witnesses is restricted by allowing evidence from anonymous witnesses, it is necessary for sufficient safeguards to be put in place to protect the rights of the defendant.[142] If prosecution witnesses remain anonymous this will mean the defence is faced with abnormal difficulties. Accordingly, it is necessary that 'the handicaps under which the defence labours be sufficiently counterbalanced by the procedures followed by the judicial authorities.'[143] For example, the defendant must 'be given an adequate and proper opportunity to challenge a witness against him either when he was making his statements or at a later stage of the proceedings.'[144] Further, 'a conviction should not be based either solely or to a decisive extent on anonymous statements'.[145] Insistence upon 'adequate safeguards' operates to protect defendants when an Article 6 right is restricted.

It is very difficult to apply the doctrine of 'adequate safeguards' to the presumption of innocence. The principle that the defendant must not be convicted unless his or her guilt has been proved to a sufficient standard of certainty is itself a safeguard intended to protect the innocent. If that principle is restricted through the use of a reverse burden, there is no 'safeguard' that can operate to ensure that the defendant is not convicted in the absence of sufficiently certain evidence. Hence, while the doctrine of 'adequate safeguards' is important in the protection of many Article 6 rights, it is unlikely to assist in protecting the right to be presumed innocent.

(c) Very Essence

The idea that Article 6 rights have a core content which cannot be restricted, regardless of the circumstances, was introduced in cases concerning the right of

139 Ibid [70].
140 Ibid.
141 Ibid [73].
142 *Van Mechelen v Netherlands* (App No 21363/93) (1997) 25 EHRR 647 [54]; *Taal v Estonia* (App No 13249/02) ECHR 22 November 2005 [31].
143 (App No 21363/93) (1997) 25 EHRR 647 [54].
144 (App No 13249/02) ECHR 22 November 2005 [31].
145 Ibid.

access to the courts. The Strasbourg Court has repeatedly held that the right of access to courts is not absolute and there is room for limitation of the right by implication.[146] There are express references to proportionality between the aim to be achieved and the rights of the defendants.[147] However, there must be no limitation of the 'very essence' of the right.[148] Hence, while the interests of the community may be invoked under the proportionality analysis, there must be no limitation of the 'very essence' of the right of access to a court. For example, the community interest could not be invoked to prevent an entire class of claimants from accessing the courts, as this would infringe the 'very essence' of the right.[149]

The concept of the 'very essence' of a right has also been relied upon in cases dealing with the privilege against self-incrimination. Reliance upon the concept of 'very essence' has occurred against the backdrop of extensive discussion of the relevance of the community interest. In *Funke v France*,[150] the applicant had been convicted and fined for refusing to disclose bank statements wanted by customs officials. He alleged the conviction constituted a breach of the privilege against self-incrimination protected under Article 6. The Commission stated:[151]

> The Commission cannot choose to ignore the special character of inquiries of an economic and financial nature, which the customs authorities are required to conduct with the aim of protecting the country's vital economic interests. These inquiries are difficult to handle in more than one respect, since they concern a sensitive area, namely a State's economic policy, which includes protection of financial balance in public accounts.

In accordance with this quote, the Commission was prepared to limit the privilege against self-incrimination when an important objective of the state was concerned. On the Commission's view, even an economic objective could be sufficient to justify the limitation of an Article 6 right. The Commission stated: '[U]nder the Convention system, there is an inherent balance between the legitimate interests of the community, on the one hand, and the individual rights it protects on the

[146] *Golder v UK* (App No 4451/70) (1979–90) 1 EHRR 524 [38]; *Winterwerp v Netherlands* (App No 6301/73) (1979–80) 2 EHRR 387 [60]; *Ashingdane v UK* (App No 8225/78) (1985) 7 EHRR 528 [57]; *Lithgow v UK* (App No 9006/80) (1986) 8 EHRR 329 [194]; *Fayed v UK* (App No 17101/90) (1994) 18 EHRR 393 [65]; *Stubbings v UK* (App No 22083/93) (1996) 23 EHRR 213 [50]; *Societe Levages Prestations v France* (App No 21920/93) (1997) 24 EHRR 351 [40]; *Tinnelly & Sons Ltd and McElduff v UK* (App No 20390/92) (1999) 27 EHRR 249 [72]; *Osman v UK* (App No 23452/94) (2000) 29 EHRR 245 [147]; *Brualla Gomez de la Torre v Spain* (App No 26737/95) (2001) 33 EHRR 1341 [33]; *Devlin v UK* (App No 29545/95) (2002) 34 EHRR 43 [29]; *Devenney v UK* (App No 24265/94) (2002) 35 EHRR 24 [23].

[147] Ibid.

[148] Ibid.

[149] See also *Murray v UK* (App No 18731/91) (1996) 22 EHRR 29 [66] holding that the right of access to a lawyer could not be denied 'whatever the justification for denial'.

[150] *Funke v France* (App No 10828/84) (1993) 16 EHRR 297.

[151] Ibid [C63]. But see the dissenting opinion: ibid 320: 'The Commission considers that the presumption of innocence and the fairness of the proceedings were respected because . . . it is necessary to take into account "the special character of inquiries of an economic and financial nature." . . . Art 6 provides certain guarantees in criminal cases, without making any distinctions within the area of criminal law . . . The law on road traffic offences and the law on customs offences are branches of criminal law and all the elements of protection afforded by Art 6 are thus applicable.'

other.'[152] In the Strasbourg Court, however, this line of reasoning was disapproved. The Strasbourg Court held that the applicant's conviction constituted a breach of the privilege against self-incrimination and that the 'special features of customs law cannot justify such an infringement'.[153]

Similarly, in *Saunders v UK*,[154] the Court rejected the argument that the public interest in fighting corporate crime could be a ground for infringing the privilege. In that case, the applicant had been convicted of offences arising out of an illegal share support scheme after a trial at which documents compulsorily acquired in an earlier investigation were used against him. The UK government argued that the complexity of corporate fraud and the vital public interest in the investigation and punishment of those responsible justified a restriction of the privilege against self-incrimination. The Commission stated that the guarantees in Article 6 'must apply equally to alleged company fraudsters as to those accused of other types of fraud, rape, murder or terrorist offences. Further, there can be no legitimate aim in depriving someone of the guarantees necessary in securing a fair trial.'[155] The Strasbourg Court agreed stating:[156]

> [T]he general requirements of fairness contained in Article 6, including the right not to incriminate oneself, apply to criminal proceedings in respect of all types of criminal offences without distinction, from the most simple to the most complex. The public interest cannot be invoked to justify the use of answers compulsorily obtained in a non-judicial investigation to incriminate the accused during the trial proceedings.

Hence, *Funke v France* and *Saunders v UK* established that neither the needs of customs officials nor the importance of investigating corporate fraud could justify a limitation on the privilege against self-incrimination.

The protection given to the privilege against self-incrimination is buttressed by the principle that the 'very essence' of the right can never be restricted. In *Heaney v Ireland*,[157] the applicants had been convicted of refusing to answer questions concerning an explosion at a British army checkpoint in Derry. The Court held that the 'security and public order concerns relied on by the Government cannot justify a provision which extinguishes the very essence of the applicants' rights to silence and against self-incrimination guaranteed by Article 6(1) of the Convention.'[158] The Court in *Heaney* did not hold that security and public order concerns were irrelevant. Rather they could not be relied upon to justify a provision that extinguished the 'very essence' of the right.

The same idea appears in *Jalloh v Germany*.[159] In that case, the applicant had been held down by police officers while a doctor administered a salt solution

[152] Ibid [C64].
[153] Ibid [44].
[154] *Saunders v UK* (App No 19187/91) (1997) 23 EHRR 313.
[155] Ibid [C71].
[156] Ibid [74].
[157] *Heaney v Ireland* (App No 34720/97) (2001) 33 EHRR 12.
[158] Ibid [57].
[159] *Jalloh v Germany* (App No 54810/00) (2007) 44 EHRR 32.

through a stomach tube and an apormorphine injection in order to induce the applicant to regurgitate a bag of heroin. The Strasbourg Court first held that the privilege against self-incrimination applied to the contents of a person's stomach. The Court then considered whether the public interest in controlling drugs offences could justify an infringement of the privilege:[160]

> [W]hen determining whether the proceedings as a whole have been fair the weight of the public interest in the investigation and punishment of the particular offence at issue may be taken into consideration and be weighed against the individual interest that the evidence against him be gathered lawfully. However, public interest concerns cannot justify measures which extinguish the very essence of an applicant's defence rights . . .

The Strasbourg Court in *Jalloh v Germany* appeared more willing than in previous cases to consider the importance of the public interest in the investigation and punishment of a crime. However, under no circumstances could the pursuit of the public interest justify an offence that breached the 'very essence' of a defendant's rights.

The 'very essence' doctrine has been criticised on the ground that it is impossible to identify the 'very essence' of a right without reference to the competing community interest.[161] On this view, the determination that the 'very essence' of a right has been breached is merely a statement of a conclusion reached using considerations of balancing.[162] This criticism sometimes appears justified. For instance, in *Jalloh v Germany*, the Court conflated its consideration of the 'very essence' with considerations of whether the community interest justified forced regurgitation of evidence. The conclusion that the community interest did not justify this action ran parallel to the conclusion that the 'very essence' of the right was breached.

In other instances, however, the idea of 'very essence' makes more sense. For instance, the prosecution of a defendant for refusing to answer questions strikes at the heart of the privilege against self-incrimination. If a person cannot refuse to answer questions without risking prosecution, he or she is entirely denied the privilege against self-incrimination. Similarly, outside of Article 6, the 'very essence' doctrine is used in respect of rights that can be entirely denied. For example, the 'very essence' doctrine appears in the context of the right to marry,[163] the right to vote[164] and the right to an education.[165] In each of these instances, one can envisage situations in which a person is entirely deprived of these rights. Such a deprivation cannot be justified on grounds of community interest because the right would then be worthless.

[160] Ibid [97].

[161] J Rivers 'Proportionality and Variable Intensity of Review' (2006) 65 *CLJ* 174, 186–87.

[162] Ibid.

[163] *F v Switzerland* (App No 11329/85) (1987) 10 EHRR 411 [32]; *Rees v UK* (App No 9532/81) (1986) 9 EHRR 56 [50]; *B v UK* (App No 36536/02) (1996) 42 EHRR 11 [34].

[164] *Ahmed v UK* (App No 22954/93) (1998) 29 EHRR 1 [75]; *Py v France* (App No 66289/01) (2006) 42 EHRR 26 [47].

[165] *Campbell and Cosans v UK* (App No 7511/76) (1982) 4 EHRR 293 [41]; *Sahin v Turkey* (App No 44774/98) ECHR 10 November 2005 [154].

It might be possible to adapt something of the 'very essence' doctrine to the presumption of innocence. For instance, it could be said that the very essence of the presumption of innocence is breached when (a) there is an unacceptable risk that an innocent person will be convicted; and (b) the penalty upon conviction is imprisonment. This is the core area of the presumption of innocence and should not be subject to limitation, whatever the competing public interest consideration. However, this leaves proportionality to operate in situations where there is a minimal risk of wrongful conviction, or where imprisonment is not the penalty. While these protections for the right to be presumed innocent can be expressed in the language of 'very essence', it is not clear that this language, in itself, adds much to a determination of the compatibility of reverse burdens with Article 6(2). All the work remains to be done in deciding what is the 'very essence' of the right.

C. Conclusion

This chapter has argued that there are many problematic aspects in the Strasbourg approach to Article 6(2). There are three areas under Article 6(2) in which the English courts should depart from the Strasbourg jurisprudence. The first is in relation to the burden of proof. It is very probable that in cases from England concerning reverse burdens the Strasbourg Court has not understood that the burden of proof allocates the risk of non-persuasion to the defendant. Consequently, English courts should take a more rigorous approach to enforcing the presumption of innocence when a burden of proof is imposed on the defendant. Second, the English courts should not use Article 6(2) to control rules of substantive law. Third, the English courts should not follow the flexible approach of the Strasbourg Court when the presumption of innocence is infringed by a reverse burden. Rather the UK courts should insist that reasons of community interest not be employed except in cases where the risk of wrongful conviction is minimal or the consequences of conviction relatively trivial. In these cases, a proportionality analysis may be used to determine the compatibility of a reverse burden with Article 6(2). The following chapter will discuss the approach to proportionality taken by the English courts and make specific suggestions for improvement.

5

Proportionality and the Presumption

IN CHAPTER FOUR, it was argued that the Strasbourg Court has been too quick to resort to a proportionality analysis to decide whether a reverse burden of proof is compatible with Article 6(2). Some restrictions on the presumption of innocence are never justifiable, regardless of the contribution to the public interest. Nevertheless, it was conceded that in cases where limitation of the presumption of innocence is appropriate some form of proportionality analysis may be used to determine the proper extent of the limitation. Further, both the Strasbourg Court and the English courts have continually employed a proportionality inquiry as the touchstone of compliance with Article 6(2). For these reasons, it is important to understand the principles of proportionality and explain how they might apply in the context of reverse burdens of proof. If proportionality is to be used under Article 6(2), it should, at the least, be applied in a coherent fashion, and in a manner that avoids unnecessary interference with the presumption of innocence.

The purpose of this chapter is to outline a conceptually coherent and normatively attractive method for the use of proportionality in the context of criminal procedure. Part A will analyse the use by English courts of the doctrine of proportionality in cases concerning reverse burdens. It will be shown that English courts have vacillated between an approach to proportionality that emphasises 'necessity' and an approach that emphasises reasonableness or 'balance'. Part B will demonstrate the conceptual distinction between these approaches and argue in favour of a necessity-focused approach. This approach is more coherent from a methodological perspective and more appropriate in the context of criminal law as a starting point for the degree of deference to be accorded to parliament. Part B will also show how a necessity-focused approach to proportionality can assist in determining the compatibility of a reverse burden of proof with Article 6(2). Specifically, it will be argued that a reverse burden of proof can be justified only if the legitimate objective could not be met using an evidential burden.

A. Confusion in the English Cases

In *Kebilene*,[1] the first case on reverse burdens under the HRA, there was a tentative suggestion that the presumption of innocence was not subject to any kind of proportionality test. Lord Cooke stated:[2]

> To introduce concepts of reasonable limits, balance or flexibility, as to none of which art 6.2 says anything, may be seen as undermining or marginalizing the philosophy embodied in the straightforward provision that everyone charged with a criminal offence shall be presumed innocent until proven guilty according to law.

Had this statement been accepted in the courts, all reverse burdens would have fallen afoul of Article 6(2) regardless of considerations of community interest imported through a proportionality test. However, since that time the House of Lords has repeatedly quoted from *Salabiaku* to the effect that presumptions of fact and law are permissible provided they are confined within 'reasonable limits'.[3] Accordingly, the application of a proportionality analysis has become standard practice in cases concerning reverse burdens.

This section examines the approach of English courts to proportionality in the context of reverse burdens. It reveals that the House of Lords initially treated proportionality as involving a test of 'necessity'. Under this test, a reverse burden would be compatible with Article 6(2) only if there were no alternative means to overcome the problems of proof that might face the prosecution if it were required to prove a matter beyond reasonable doubt. In particular, the necessity-focused version of the proportionality inquiry insisted that a persuasive burden should not be used if the problems of the prosecution could be avoided by imposing an evidential burden on the defendant.

By contrast, in another line of cases, the House of Lords treated proportionality as involving a test of 'reasonableness' or 'balance'. In accordance with this version of proportionality, it was unnecessary to consider whether alternative measures could be employed to solve the prosecutorial problems of proof. A reverse burden was to be treated as compatible with Article 6(2) if it was reasonable in the circumstances and struck the right balance between the rights of the individual and the interest of the community. In *Sheldrake*,[4] Lord Bingham dismissed the divergence between a 'necessity' test and a 'balance' test as a difference of emphasis.[5]

[1] *R v DPP; ex p Kebilene* [2000] 2 AC 326 (HL).

[2] Ibid 373.

[3] The comments of the Strasbourg Court in *Salabiaku v France* (App No 10589/83) (1991) 13 EHRR 379 [28] have been quoted and endorsed by the House of Lords in *Brown v Stott* [2003] 1 AC 681 (PC) 693 (Lord Bingham); *McIntosh v Lord Advocate* [2003] 1 AC 1078 (PC) [30] (Lord Bingham); *R v DPP; ex p Kebilene* [2000] 2 AC 326 (HL) 384 (Lord Hope); *R v Lambert* [2002] 2 AC 545 (HL) [34] (Lord Steyn), [87] (Lord Hope), [150] (Lord Clyde); *R v Johnstone* [2003] 1 WLR 1736 (HL) [48] (Lord Nicholls); *Sheldrake v DPP; AG's Reference (No 4 of 2002)* [2005] 1 AC 264 (HL) [12] (Lord Bingham).

[4] *Sheldrake v DPP; AG's Reference (No 4 of 2002)* [2005] 1 AC 264 (HL).

[5] Ibid [30].

However, as this Part will show, the two versions of proportionality differ both in the questions that the court must ask and, at times, in the results that are produced. Generally, when a court applies a 'necessity' test it finds that a reverse burden is inconsistent with Article 6(2), and when it applies a 'balance' test, it finds a reverse burden is within reasonable limits.

1. Necessity Approach

A necessity-focused approach to proportionality was adopted as the orthodoxy for English courts following the decision of the House of Lords in *Lambert*.[6] In that case, the defendant was arrested in the car park of a train station in possession of a duffle bag containing two kilograms of cocaine worth over £140,000. He claimed that he had been paid to collect the bag and did not know that it contained drugs. He was charged with possession of a controlled drug with intent to supply, contrary to section 5(3) of the Misuse of Drugs Act 1971. Section 28(2) provided a defence to the charge if the defendant proved that he neither knew, nor suspected, nor had reason to suspect, that the bag contained a controlled drug. It was accepted that, on ordinary principles of construction, section 28(2) imposed a persuasive burden on the defendant in relation to the question of knowledge.[7]

The majority of the House of Lords ultimately decided the case on the basis that the HRA did not have retrospective effect and therefore did not apply to the defendant.[8] However, the comments made *obiter* in relation to Article 6(2) are highly informative and have been widely followed.[9] The language used by Lord Steyn made necessity the principal element of the proportionality inquiry. His Lordship stated: 'The burden is on the state to show that the legislative means adopted were not greater than necessary.'[10] His Lordship went on to state: 'The principle of proportionality requires the House to consider whether there was a pressing necessity to impose a legal rather than evidential burden on the accused.'[11] Further, his Lordship stated '[T]he burden of showing that *only* a reverse legal burden can overcome the difficulties of the prosecution in drugs cases is a heavy one.'[12] Lord Steyn concluded that it was not necessary to impose a persuasive burden on a

[6] *R v Lambert* [2002] 2 AC 545 (HL).

[7] Ibid [17] (Lord Slynn), [72] (Lord Hope), [182] (Lord Hutton).

[8] Ibid [10] (Lord Slynn), [116] (Lord Hope), [148] (Lord Clyde), [175] (Lord Hutton). Lord Steyn dissented on this point: ibid [28]–[29]. On the question of retrospectivity, *Lambert* was affirmed, despite some misgivings, in *R v Kansal (No 2)* [2002] 2 AC 69 (HL) [10] (Lord Slynn), [21] (Lord Lloyd), [27] (Lord Steyn), [102] (Lord Hutton). *Cf* Lord Hope dissenting: [75]. The Strasbourg Court subsequently found a breach of art 6(1): *Kansal v UK* (App No 21413/02) (2004) 39 EHRR 31. On retrospectivity of the HRA, see also *R v Benjafield* [2003] 1 AC 1099 (HL) [1] (Lord Slynn), [2] (Lord Browne-Wilkinson), [6] (Lord Steyn), [15] (Lord Hope), [16] (Lord Hutton); ID MacPhail, 'Human Rights, Burden of Proof, Retrospectivity and Precedent in the House of Lords' (2002) 61 *CLJ* 1.

[9] The comments were treated as binding in *R v Carrera* [2002] EWCA Crim 2527; *Sheldrake v DPP* [2004] QB 487 (QBD) [20] (Clarke LJ).

[10] [2002] 2 AC 545 (HL) [37] (Lord Steyn).

[11] Ibid [38].

[12] Ibid (emphasis in original).

defendant in order to pursue the legitimate objective of securing convictions for drug offences. One reason for this was that failure by the defendant to offer any satisfactory explanation for possession of the unauthorised drugs would itself be an important piece of circumstantial evidence that the defendant was aware of the contents of the container.[13] A further reason was that, under section 34 of the Criminal Justice and Public Order Act 1994, adverse inferences could be drawn if the defendant failed to mention his or her explanation for possession when questioned or charged.[14] An evidential burden was consequently sufficient to prevent the majority of offenders from escaping conviction.[15]

Lord Hope's characterisation of the proportionality inquiry was more difficult to discern but, like Lord Steyn, he adopted the language of necessity. Lord Hope stated:[16]

> It is now well settled that the principle which is to be applied requires a balance to be struck between the general interest of the community and the protection of the fundamental rights of the individual. This will not be achieved if the reverse onus provision goes beyond what is necessary to accomplish the objective of the statute.

This statement by Lord Hope includes a reference to balance, but does not treat that element as the determinative factor in the proportionality inquiry. Rather, balance is treated as an overarching principle, and the question to be asked by the court is whether the measure adopted by parliament in pursuit of its objective 'goes beyond what is necessary'. Lord Hope reasoned that the objective of penalising unauthorised drug use could be met effectively with an evidential burden. The evidential burden was not merely 'illusory'.[17] It would relieve the prosecution of the burden of proving knowledge, except in cases where the defendant produced some evidence of a lack of knowledge.[18]

Counsel for the defendant in *Lambert* had submitted that necessity was the 'dominant test'.[19] The choice by Lord Steyn and Lord Hope to employ the language of necessity was therefore a deliberate endorsement of that language to describe the question involved in the proportionality inquiry. The question which the court was to ask was not merely whether community interest and the rights of the individual had been rightly balanced, but whether the measure adopted by the legislature was necessary in pursuit of a legitimate objective. If a less-restrictive method for pursuing that objective was available, the approach taken by Parliament could not be regarded as necessary and the legislation would fail the proportionality inquiry. Specifically, if the objectives of the legislature could be achieved by imposing only an evidential burden on the defendant, a persuasive

[13] Ibid [39].
[14] Ibid.
[15] Ibid [41].
[16] Ibid [88].
[17] Ibid [90].
[18] See also: ibid [17] (Lord Slynn); [153]–[157] (Lord Clyde). *Cf* Lord Hutton (dissenting), holding a persuasive burden was necessary: ibid [193]–[198].
[19] Ibid 550–51.

burden would be disproportionate.[20] The House of Lords consequently would have been prepared to read down the language of section 28(2) so that it imposed an evidential burden rather than a persuasive burden.[21]

Following *Lambert*, the lower courts were highly inconsistent in their approach to proportionality. Some decisions used the language of necessity to describe the proportionality inquiry. For instance, in *Carass*,[22] the Court of Appeal stated that: '[T]he proper approach has to be that if a reverse legal burden is to be imposed on an accused it must be . . . demonstrated why a legal or persuasive burden rather than an evidential burden is necessary.'[23] Having stated the test in this way, the Court of Appeal concluded that an evidential burden would have been sufficient to resolve the prosecution's problems of proof, and accordingly that the reverse persuasive burden should be read as an evidential burden.[24] In *Davies*,[25] the Court of Appeal made reference to the need for 'fair balance' but appropriately directed itself to the necessity of the legal burden.[26] It concluded that a persuasive burden was necessary because an evidential burden would permit a large number of defendants in the most serious cases to escape conviction, thus undermining the efficacy of a regulatory health and safety framework intended to protect the public.[27]

By contrast, other cases decided after *Lambert* focused only on whether a reverse persuasive burden was 'reasonable' or 'balanced'. In *L v DPP*,[28] the Divisional Court considered a charge of possession of a bladed article in a public place, contrary to s 139(1) of the Criminal Justice Act 1988. Section 139(4) placed a persuasive burden on a defendant 'to prove that he had good reason or lawful authority for having the article with him in a public place.' In considering the compatibility of this reverse burden with Article 6(2), Pill LJ asked only whether a 'fair balance' had been struck.[29] He reasoned that there was a strong public interest in bladed articles not being carried in public and that it was not 'obviously offensive'

[20] Similarly, the South African Constitutional Court has struck down a persuasive burden on a defendant because an evidential burden was a 'less invasive means': *S v Manamela* 2000 (3) SA 1 (CC) [49]. See also *S v Singo* 2002 (4) SA 858 (CC) [40].

[21] The decision in *Lambert* to read down s 28(2) was followed in *R v Carrera* [2002] EWCA Crim 2527; *R v Lang and Deadman* [2002] EWCA Crim 298; *R v Forsyth* [2001] EWCA Crim 2926 and in Scotland in *Henvey v HM Advocate* 2005 SLT 384 (HCJ). In each of these cases, it was held that misdirection on the burden of proof had caused a miscarriage of justice and the conviction was overturned.

[22] *R v Carass* [2002] 1 WLR 1714 (CA).

[23] Ibid [60] (Waller J).

[24] Ibid [61] (Waller J). *Carass* was followed, with some misgivings on the question of proportionality in *R v Daniel* [2003] 1 Cr App R 6 (CA) [25], [31] (Auld LJ). It was overruled by a five-judge panel of the Court of Appeal in *AG's Reference (No 1 of 2004)* [2004] 1 WLR 2111 (CA) [84] (Lord Woolf CJ). In *Sheldrake v DPP; AG's Reference (No 4 of 2002)* [2005] 1 AC 264 (HL) [32], Lord Bingham agreed that *Carass* had been wrongly decided. As can be seen below at text accompanying nn 54–64, the courts in these latter cases appeared to approve the 'balance' approach to proportionality.

[25] *R v Davies* [2003] ICR 586 (CA).

[26] Ibid [10] (Tuckey LJ).

[27] Ibid [24]–[31] (Tuckey LJ). See also *R v Drummond* [2002] 2 Cr App R 25 (CA) applying the necessity test but finding a reverse persuasive burden proportionate. *Drummond* was followed in *DPP v Ellery* [2005] EWHC 2513 (Admin).

[28] *L v DPP* [2003] QB 137 (QBD).

[29] Ibid [26]–[27].

to require an individual to prove good reason.[30] In a brief judgment, Poole J agreed with Pill LJ stating simply that the reverse burden was 'a proportionate measure' and 'well within reasonable limits'.[31] Neither judge turned his attention to whether a reverse persuasive burden was necessary.[32]

This decision was affirmed in *Matthews*[33] following a complete review of the relevant authorities. The Court of Appeal in *Matthews* described the question as whether a persuasive burden rather than an evidential burden was 'justified'.[34] As in *L v DPP*, the court failed to appreciate that the test, following *Lambert*, was not one of justification but of necessity. To state that a persuasive burden is 'justified' is only to state that there is a legitimate objective in sight. The proportionality inquiry, in the formulation adopted in *Lambert*, requires the court to consider whether the means adopted is necessary, and there is no necessity if there is another available measure that is less restrictive of a protected right.

2. Balance Approach

Part of the confusion as to the correct test to be applied in the proportionality inquiry was the result of the approach to proportionality outlined by Lord Hope in *Kebilene*.[35] This was the first case in which an English court was called upon to confront the impact of Article 6(2) on reverse burdens. A group of Algerian nationals had been charged with possession of chemical containers, radio equipment, manuals, credit cards and sums of money which the police suspected were to be used for the purpose of assisting terrorist acts in Algeria. The charges were brought under section 16A(1) of the Prevention of Terrorism (Temporary Provisions) Act 1989, which made it an offence to have possession of any article in circumstances giving rise to a 'reasonable suspicion' that the article was held for a purpose connected with terrorism. Section 16A(3) stated: 'It is a defence for a person charged with an offence under this section to prove that at the time of the alleged offence the article in question was not in his possession for [a terrorist purpose].' The defendants argued that this reverse persuasive burden was contrary to the presumption of innocence and challenged as unlawful the consent of the DPP to their continuing prosecution.

The House of Lords held that the decision of the DPP to consent to a prosecution was not amenable to judicial review and could not be undermined on the basis of Article 6(2).[36] Lord Hope was the only member of the House to consider

30 Ibid [27].

31 Ibid [31].

32 In *Sheldrake v DPP* [2004] QB 487 (QBD) [71], Clarke LJ stated: 'It is not easy to see where in L's case the court considered the crucial question, which is not whether a reverse onus can be justified but whether, that being the case, it is necessary to provide for a persuasive and not simply an evidential burden.'

33 *R v Matthews* [2004] QB 690 (CA).

34 Ibid [16] (Field J).

35 *R v DPP; ex p Kebilene* [2000] 2 AC 326 (HL).

36 Ibid 368 (Lord Steyn), 372 (Lord Cooke), 376 (Lord Hope), 397 (Lord Hobhouse).

proportionality issues at length.[37] His Lordship criticised the Divisional Court for concluding, without any consideration of proportionality and balance, that section 16A breached the presumption of innocence.[38] His Lordship held that even if there were a *prima facie* breach of the presumption of innocence 'that will not lead inevitably to the conclusion that the provision is incompatible with Article 6(2) of the Convention.'[39] According to Lord Hope, the implementation of the fundamental principles embodied in the ECHR involves 'questions of balance between competing interests and issues of proportionality.'[40] The competing interests referred to by Lord Hope were 'the demands of the general interest of the community and the protection of the fundamental rights of the individual'.[41] As to the interests of the community, it was important to take account of the 'special nature of terrorist crime and the threat which it poses to a democratic society'.[42] As to the rights of the individual, Lord Hope considered it was not 'immediately obvious' that the defendant was faced with an 'unreasonable burden'.[43]

Throughout his speech, Lord Hope considered only whether a reverse burden was reasonable and at no point did his Lordship consider whether it was necessary. Further, according to Lord Hope, it was important to remember that there was an area of judgment within which the judiciary ought to defer, on democratic grounds, to the considered opinion of the legislature.[44] This may be taken as supporting the view that, where there is a range of means and methods available to pursue a legitimate objective, the legislature is not confined to selecting the method which will have the least impact on fundamental rights. Given his conclusion that the decision of the DPP was not amenable to judicial review, Lord Hope opined that: 'It would not be appropriate to resolve the difficult question whether the balance between the needs of society and the presumption of innocence has been struck in the right place.'[45] Lord Hope's outline of the approach to proportionality did not include any element of necessity and appeared to reduce the proportionality inquiry to one of mere 'balance'. Its presence among the precedents which later courts were called on to consider may be regarded as a reason for the confusion in the Court of Appeal over the correct approach to proportionality.

Lord Hope's approach to the proportionality inquiry was resurrected by the House of Lords in *Johnstone*.[46] In that case, a parcel of 519 bootleg CDs addressed to the defendant was mistakenly delivered to the wrong address. The recipient

[37] Lord Steyn limited himself to stating that the impact of art 6(2) was 'undecided and entirely open at all levels in the criminal proceedings': ibid 372. Lord Hobhouse noted there were 'arguable points' to be made in relation to art 6(2): ibid 397–98. As discussed above, Lord Cooke doubted whether 'concepts of reasonable limits, balance or flexibility' could undermine the presumption of innocence: ibid 373.

[38] Ibid 385–86.

[39] Ibid 380.

[40] Ibid 381.

[41] Ibid 384.

[42] Ibid 381.

[43] Ibid 387.

[44] Ibid 381.

[45] Ibid 387.

[46] *R v Johnstone* [2003] 1 WLR 1736 (HL).

reported the parcel to a record company, leading to a police search of the defendant's home and the discovery of some 500 further bootleg CDs and cassettes. The defendant was charged with possession of, and intention to sell, material infringing a trade mark, contrary to section 92(1)(c) of the Trade Marks Act 1994. Section 92(5) made it a defence for a person 'to show that he believed on reasonable grounds that the use of the sign in the manner in which it was used . . . was not an infringement of the registered trademark.' Writing the leading judgment, with which the other members of the House agreed, Lord Nicholls did not refer to the proportionality approach adopted in *Lambert.* Instead, His Lordship stated in relation to Article 6(2):[47]

> [A] reasonable balance has to be held between the public interest and the interests of the individual. In each case it is for the state to show that the balance held in the legislation is reasonable. The derogation from the presumption of innocence requires justification . . . [F]or a reverse burden of proof to be acceptable there must be a compelling reason why it is fair and reasonable to deny the accused person the protection normally guaranteed to everyone by the presumption of innocence.

Lord Nicholls made no reference to 'necessity' instead focusing upon whether a 'reasonable balance' had been held or whether the reverse burden was 'fair and reasonable'. By omitting any reference to 'necessity', Lord Nicholls altered the focus of the proportionality inquiry so that there was no requirement to consider the availability of alternative options. A reverse persuasive burden could be 'reasonable' even if an evidential burden would have been sufficient to resolve the evidential problems faced by the prosecution. Further, Lord Nicholls shifted the focus from necessity by emphasising the deference to be given to the decision of Parliament. His Lordship stated:[48]

> In evaluating these factors the court's role is one of review. Parliament, not the court, is charged with the primary responsibility for deciding, as a matter of policy, what should be the constituent elements of a criminal offence . . . The court will reach a different conclusion from the legislature only when it is apparent the legislature has attached insufficient importance to the fundamental right of an individual to be presumed innocent until proved guilty.

The emphasis on deference suggests that the legislature is not obliged to adopt the least restrictive means available for pursuing a legitimate objective. Provided that the legislature chooses from within a range of reasonable options, that decision will not be challenged by the courts. Determining whether an option is within the reasonable range turns, in Lord Nicholls' approach, on whether it strikes a reasonable balance between the interests of the community and the fundamental rights of the individual.

Lord Nicholls concluded that the persuasive burden imposed by section 92(5) was justified and reasonable. A 'compelling' reason for this conclusion was that

[47] Ibid [48]–[49].
[48] Ibid [51].

those who trade in brand products need to be aware of counterfeit products, and counter the risk by keeping records and dealing with reputable suppliers. Another reason was that it would be difficult for the prosecution to prove that a trader acted dishonestly, especially as those who supply traders would be hard to trace and unwilling to co-operate with investigators.[49] There was no suggestion in Lord Nicholls' speech that he had considered whether a persuasive burden on the defendant was necessary to alleviate problems of proof and whether an evidential burden would have sufficed.

It does not necessarily follow that Lord Nicholls would have reached a different result in *Johnstone* if he had applied a necessity-focused version of proportionality. *Johnstone* affirmed the earlier decision of the Court of Appeal in *R v S*.[50] That decision held that it was 'necessary, justified and proportionate'[51] for section 92(5) to impose a legal burden on the defendant. It was clear from its judgment that the Court of Appeal in *R v S* turned its mind to the question of whether an evidential burden would have sufficed to fulfill the objective pursued by the legislation, although some of the factors it considered were not obviously relevant to that inquiry.[52] Two crucial factors were (a) that an effective and workable regulatory regime could not sensibly depend on the prosecution proving in every case that a trader acted dishonestly and (b) that the prosecution would be faced with insurmountable evidential difficulties if it needed to prove dishonesty beyond reasonable doubt, including difficulty in locating witnesses concerned in the supply chain.[53] While the distinction between 'necessity' and 'balance' may not have been crucial to the result in *Johnstone*, it has been important in other cases discussed below, most notably, *Sheldrake*.

3. A 'Difference of Emphasis'

The distinction between the approach to proportionality endorsed in *Lambert* and the approach followed in *Johnstone* was identified by the Court of Appeal in *AG's Reference (No 1 of 2004)*.[54] The Court of Appeal referred to a 'significant difference in emphasis' between the approaches of Lord Steyn and Lord Nicholls and noted that, in practice, Lord Steyn's approach was much more likely to result in the reduction of a persuasive burden to an evidential burden.[55] The Court of Appeal preferred the approach of Lord Nicholls on the basis that it was more 'flexible' and reflected the intent of the HRA in achieving a balance between the role of Parliament and the courts.[56] The Court of Appeal went on to emphasise that, while both speeches were *obiter*, Lord Nicholls' was later in time and was endorsed by the

[49] Ibid [52]–[53].
[50] *R v S* [2003] 1 Cr App R 35 (CA).
[51] Ibid [47] (Rose LJ).
[52] Ibid [48] (Rose LJ).
[53] Ibid.
[54] *AG's Reference (No 1 of 2004)* [2004] 1 WLR 2111 (CA).
[55] Ibid [38] (Lord Woolf CJ).
[56] Ibid.

other members of the House. The Court consequently recommended that until the position was clarified by the House of Lords, lower courts should follow the approach of Lord Nicholls.[57] The balance approach to proportionality was evident in the ten elements of guidance provided to assist lower courts in adjudicating on the validity of reverse burdens.[58] It is significant that having endorsed and adopted the approach of Lord Nicholls, the Court of Appeal proceeded to hold that all but one[59] of the reverse burdens under consideration were reasonable and proportionate, and therefore not incompatible with Article 6(2).[60]

The recognition of the difference between the necessity and balance approaches to proportionality was undermined by the subsequent decision of the House of Lords in two joined appeals, *Sheldrake v DPP* and *AG's Reference (No 4 of 2002)*.[61] The leading speech was delivered by Lord Bingham. Each member of the House agreed with his exposition of the applicable law, even those who disagreed as to the outcome.[62] Lord Bingham denied that there was an inconsistency between the approach to proportionality adopted in *Lambert* and that in *Johnstone*. His Lordship considered that any differences of emphasis were 'explicable by the difference in the subject matter of the two cases.'[63] Lord Bingham thus appeared to endorse both approaches leaving the doctrine of proportionality in a state of confusion. According to Lord Bingham, 'the opportunity given to the defendant to rebut the presumption, maintenance of the rights of the defence, flexibility in application of the presumption, retention by the courts of a power to assess evidence, the importance of what is at stake and the difficulty which a prosecutor may face in the absence of a presumption' were all relevant factors in a judgment on reasonableness or proportionality.[64] However, since Lord Bingham failed to clarify the correct approach to the proportionality test, the significance of each of these factors was left uncertain.

In the application of the legal principles to the facts of the two cases under appeal, Lord Bingham appeared to use a 'balance' approach rather than a 'necessity' approach. In the first of the appeals, *Sheldrake v DPP*, the defendant was found at 8:40 pm drunk and asleep at the wheel of his car in a car park adjacent to a public house. He was charged with being in charge of a motor vehicle in a public place with a blood alcohol ratio over the prescribed limit, contrary to section 5(1)(b) of the Road Traffic Act 1988. Under section 5(2), it was a defence to prove that there

57 Ibid.

58 Ibid [52] (Lord Woolf CJ).

59 Section 352 of the Insolvency Act 1986 was disproportionate in the manner in which it applied to the offence under s 357(1): ibid [90]. However, it was proportionate in the manner in which it applied to the offence under s 353(1)(b): ibid [95].

60 The other provisions found to be proportionate were Protection from Eviction Act 1977, s 1(2); Homicide Act 1957, s 4; and Criminal Justice and Public Order Act 1994, s 51(7).

61 *Sheldrake v DPP* and *AG's Reference (No 4 of 2002)* [2005] 1 AC 264 (HL).

62 Lord Steyn and Lord Phillips agreed with Lord Bingham without adding any further reasons: ibid [55], [56]. Lord Rodger agreed with the 'general exposition of the applicable case law' as outlined by Lord Bingham: ibid [57]. Lord Carswell agreed with Lord Rodger and added some further observations of his own: ibid [79].

63 Ibid [30].

64 Ibid [21].

was no likelihood of driving the vehicle while over the prescribed limit. The defendant gave evidence that he had made efforts to arrange alternative transport home, but the magistrates were not satisfied, on the balance of probabilities, that there was no likelihood of his driving and he was convicted. In relation to the proportionality of the reverse burden, Lord Bingham stated: 'I do not regard the burden placed on the defendant as beyond reasonable limits or in any way arbitrary.'[65] Lord Bingham concluded by stating: 'I do not think that imposition of a legal burden went beyond what was necessary.'[66] It followed that it was proportionate to place the persuasive burden on the defendant and that the provision should be read to that effect.[67] However, this conclusion was reached without any discussion of whether an evidential burden would have sufficed.

When Lord Bingham's conclusion is compared to the decision of the Divisional Court in *Sheldrake*,[68] it is readily apparent that the distinction between the necessity and balance approaches is more than a 'difference of emphasis'. In the Divisional Court, Clarke LJ undertook a careful consideration of the correct approach to the proportionality inquiry. Clarke LJ noted that questions of 'fair balance' between the general interest of the community and the fundamental rights of the individual would always arise.[69] However, the proper weight to be attached to each interest was to be decided following a test of necessity. Following *Lambert*, Clarke LJ stated that: 'The question is therefore whether it is necessary to construe section 5(2) as imposing a legal burden of proof and not an evidential burden.'[70] Leaving no doubt as to his views, Clarke LJ stated that: 'The test is not a lower test such as whether it was reasonable to do so.'[71] Jack J agreed and added: '[I]n deciding whether the section is proportionate it is necessary to look at the alternative to having a legal burden on the defendant.'[72] Applying a necessity test, Clarke LJ and Jack J made a finding that an evidential burden would be an effective alternative and concluded that there was no necessity to impose a persuasive burden. Accordingly the provision was incompatible with Article 6(2) and had to be read down under s 3 of the HRA to impose only an evidential burden.[73] It is

[65] Ibid [41].

[66] Ibid.

[67] As to the interpretation of s 5(2) of the Road Traffic Act, Sheldrake has been followed in *CPS v Thompson* [2007] EWHC 1841 (Admin) [7]; *Orrock v Procurator Fiscal* [2008] HCJAC 65 [9] (Lord Wheatley), [20]–[23] (Lord Reed).

[68] *Sheldrake v DPP* [2004] QB 487 (QBD).

[69] Ibid [36].

[70] Ibid [45].

[71] Ibid [84].

[72] Ibid [144].

[73] Henriques J (dissenting) appeared to agree that the test was one of necessity and turned his mind to whether an evidential burden would suffice. However, he also emphasised that, in considering whether a reverse burden is necessary 'the court should show deference to the judgment of Parliament if appropriate': ibid [131]. This could be taken as suggesting that Parliament is not obliged to adopt the least restrictive means, which would be a watering down of the necessity test. Having emphasised this factor, Henriques J held that the persuasive burden was justified and proportionate: ibid [133]. Prior to its reversal in the House of Lords, the view of the majority in the Divisional Court was followed in *DPP v Janman* [2004] EWHC 101 (Admin) [14].

significant that, when applying a necessity-focused test, the majority of the Divisional Court concluded that the measure imposed by the legislature was not proportionate. By contrast, all members of the House of Lords, applying a 'balance' test found that the measure was proportionate. The capacity of the two tests to lead to different results suggests that there is a substantive distinction between a 'balance' focused proportionality test and a 'necessity' focused test.

In the second of the joined appeals to the House of Lords, *AG's Reference (No 4 of 2002)*,[74] the defendant was charged with membership of Hamas, and professing to membership of Hamas, a proscribed terrorist organisation, contrary to section 11(1) of the Terrorism Act 2000. Under section 11(2), it was a defence for a person to prove that the organisation was not proscribed when he or she became a member, and that the person had not taken part in its activities since it was proscribed. Lord Bingham held that: 'The crucial question is . . . whether . . . imposition of a legal burden on a defendant in this particular situation is a proportionate and justifiable legislative response to an undoubted problem.'[75] Lord Bingham did not address attention to whether a persuasive burden was necessary. However, he regarded the burden as disproportionate because it might be impossible for a defendant to prove that he had not taken part in the activities of the organisation, especially if relevant evidence was abroad and hard to adduce.[76] The lack of precision displayed by Lord Bingham in identifying the correct questions for a court to ask under Article 6(2) leaves the law in a confused and unsatisfactory state.

Following *Sheldrake*, the decisions of the lower courts concerning Article 6(2) reveal a continued uncertainty as to the nature of the proportionality test.[77] In *R v Makuwa*,[78] the defendant entered the UK from the Democratic Republic of Congo using a doctored passport. She was charged with using a false instrument contrary to section 3 of the Forgery and Counterfeiting Act 1981 and raised the defence provided by section 31 of the Immigration and Asylum Act 1999. That section provided a defence to the charge if a refugee could show that he or she presented to the authorities without delay, had good cause for illegal entry to the UK, and had made a claim of asylum as soon as reasonably practicable. The defendant was convicted after the trial judge directed the jury that the defendant needed to

[74] *AG's Reference (No 4 of 2002)* [2005] 1 AC 264 (HL).

[75] Ibid [50].

[76] Ibid [51]. Lord Rodger and Lord Carswell dissented as to the compatibility of s 11(2) of the Terrorism Act 2000 and art 6(2) ECHR. Lord Rodger considered, for the reasons discussed in Ch 3, that the presumption of innocence was not infringed by s 11(2) so that issues of proportionality did not arise: ibid [65]. Lord Carswell agreed with Lord Rodger, but also held the provision was proportionate: ibid [92]. On the interpretation of s 11(2) of the Terrorism Act 2000, *AG's Reference (No 4 of 2002)* was followed in *R v Brogan* [2004] NICC 27 [36] (Gillen J).

[77] Following *Sheldrake*, many cases dealing with art 6(2) have asked whether the reverse burden is 'fair' and 'reasonable' or strikes a proper balance: *McLean v Carnegie* 2006 SLT 40 (HCJ) [9]; *R v Navabi and Embaye* [2005] EWCA Crim 2865 [12], [29]; *R v McQuade* [2005] NI 331 (CA); *Clarke v R* [2008] EWCA Crim 651 [26]. In each of these cases, the reverse burden in question was found to be compatible with art 6(2). *Cf Okendiji v Government of the Commonwealth of Australia* [2005] EWHC 471 (Admin) [15]–[27].

[78] *R v Makuwa* [2006] 2 Cr App R 11 (CA).

prove these matters on the balance of probabilities. The Court of Appeal agreed with this direction.[79] The Court of Appeal quoted passages from *Sheldrake* and *Johnstone* to the effect that reverse burdens must be contained within 'reasonable limits'[80] and must be 'fair and reasonable'.[81] However, the principal reason for the decision was that the statutory offence would be 'rendered largely ineffective' if the burden on the defendant was only evidential.[82] Hence, despite using the language of reasonableness, the Court of Appeal concluded that a reverse persuasive burden was proportionate because it was necessary.

In *R v Keogh*,[83] the Court of Appeal considered a reverse burden imposed by section 2(3) of the Official Secrets Act 1989. The defendant had acquired possession of a confidential record of a meeting between the Prime Minister and the President of the United States, and had allowed the record to be passed on to others. He was charged under section 2 of the Act with making a damaging disclosure of information relating to defence. Section 2(3) required him to prove that he did not know and had no reasonable cause to believe, that the information related to defence or that its disclosure would be damaging. The Court of Appeal discussed the compatibility of this reverse burden under the heading of 'necessity'.[84] It was concluded that a persuasive burden was not necessary since the prosecution could undermine the defence by showing the defendant had 'reasonable cause to believe' the information had the relevant characteristics.[85] This was a question of objective fact that did not depend upon knowledge held by the defendant.[86] Accordingly, the reverse burden was to be read as an evidential burden.

In *DPP v Wright*,[87] the defendant had been charged with hunting a wild mammal with a dog contrary to section 1 of the Hunting Act 2004. It was not an offence to hunt with a dog, provided the hunting came within one of the exemption conditions in Schedule 1 to the Act. The High Court held that, as a matter of construction, section 1 and Schedule 1 imposed only an evidential burden on the defendant with respect to the exemption conditions.[88] Nonetheless, the High Court was clear that, had those provisions imposed a persusasive burden on the defendant 'that would be an oppressive, disproportionate, unfair, and in particular unnecessary intrusion upon the presumption of innocence in Article 6 of the Convention.'[89] The prospect had been raised that the legislation would become unworkable if the prosecutor was required to negative all of the exemptions. However, the High Court emphasised that a persuasive burden was not necessary

[79] Although it found the trial judge had erred by imposing the burden on the defendant of proving that she was, in fact, a refugee: ibid [26] (Moore-Brick LJ).
[80] Ibid [29].
[81] Ibid [31].
[82] Ibid [36].
[83] *R v Keogh* [2007] 1 WLR 1500 (CA).
[84] Ibid [26] (Lord Phillips CJ).
[85] Ibid [29].
[86] Ibid.
[87] *DPP v Wright* [2009] EWHC 105 (Admin).
[88] Ibid [89].
[89] Ibid [85].

to alleviate this concern, since the imposition of an evidential burden would force the defendant to reveal his or her case.[90]

The most recent pronouncement of the House of Lords on the proportionality of reverse burdens is *R v Chargot Limited*.[91] In that case, the House of Lords followed *R v Davies*[92] in holding that it was not disproportionate to require a defendant to prove that he or she had taken all reasonably practicable steps to ensure a safe workplace. While Lord Hope discussed the compatibility of the reverse burden under the heading 'proportionality', his Lordship gave no guidance as to the application of the proportionality test except to say that 'the justifiability of any infringement of the presumption of innocence cannot be resolved by any rule of thumb, but on examination of all the facts and circumstances of the particular provision as applied in the particular case.'[93] Needless to say, the limited discussion in *R v Chargot Limited* does little to clear up the confusion in the cases between a necessity-based approach to proportionality and an approach premised on balance.

The divergence in the English decisions concerning the proportionality test under Article 6(2) has led to a great deal of confusion. This confusion not only undermines the authority of the reasoning in the cases, but also leads to conflicting results. The following part aims to provide greater analytical clarity to the concept of proportionality and makes a case for a 'necessity' focused approach when proportionality is applied in the context of criminal procedure.

B. The Nature of the Proportionality Inquiry

Following the lead of the Strasbourg Court, many of the English decisions concerning rights under the ECHR are infused with the language of proportionality. In understanding proportionality, assistance can be derived from the decisions of other jurisdictions that apply the doctrine. In particular, Germany,[94] the ECJ[95]

[90] Ibid [87]. Further, the prosecution needed only to prove that one condition out of five was not satisfied in order to demonstrate that the exemption in sch 1 did not apply.

[91] *R v Chargot Limited* [2009] 1 WLR 1 (HL).

[92] *R v Davies* [2003] ICR 586 (CA).

[93] [2009] 1WLR 1 (HL) [28].

[94] English-language discussion of the German principle of proportionality, or Verhältnismäsigkeit, may be found in R Alexy & J Rivers (trans) *A Theory of Constitutional Rights* (OUP, Oxford 2002) ch 3 and Postscript; J Schwarze, *European Administrative Law* (Sweet & Maxwell, London 1992) 685–92; N Emiliou, *The Principle of Proportionality in European Law: A Comparative Study* (Kluwer Law International, London 1996) 23–66; M Singh, *German Administrative Law in Common Law Perspective* 2nd edn (Springer, London 2001) 160–67; J Jowell & A Lester, 'Proportionality: Neither Novel nor Dangerous' in J Jowell & D Oliver (eds) *New Directions in Judicial Review* (Stevens & Sons, London 1988) 51, 52–54.

[95] Case 331/88 *R v Minister for Agriculture, Fisheries and Food; ex p Fedesa* [1990] ECR I-4023 [13]–[14]; Joined Cases C-27/00 and C-122/00 *R v Secretary of State for the Environment, Transport and the Regions; ex p Omega Air Ltd* [2002] ECR I-2569 [62]; Case C-180/96 *United Kingdom v Commission* [1998] ECR I-2265 [96]. For academic commentary see G de Búrca, 'The Principle of Proportionality

and Canada[96] have adopted a nuanced and structured approach to the proportionality inquiry. The preliminary stage in this approach is to identify a legitimate objective in pursuit of which a protected right has been restricted. Following the identification of a legitimate objective, the proportionality inquiry is typically divided into three levels: suitability, necessity and proportionality in the strict sense (or 'balance'). An altered version of this approach, amalgamating the necessity and balance aspects, was adopted by the Privy Council in *de Freitas*.[97] That formulation has since been quoted and endorsed by the House of Lords in decisions under the HRA,[98] although not in any of the decisions concerning reverse burdens. While the English courts have referred to the structured model of proportionality, the application of the precise proportionality criteria has often been brief and superficial.

The purpose of this part is to explain the nature of each stage in the proportionality inquiry and apply this understanding to the example of reverse burdens. Section one below will discuss the meaning of a legitimate objective and make

and its Application in EC Law' (1993) 13 *Yearbook of European Law* 105; P Craig & G de Búrca *EU Law: Text, Cases and Materials* 3rd edn (OUP, Oxford 2003) 371–379; T Tridimas, *The General Principles of EC Law* (OUP, Oxford 1999) chs 3–4; T Tridimas, 'Proportionality in Community Law: Searching for the Appropriate Standard of Scrutiny' in E Ellis (ed) *The Principle of Proportionality in the Law of Europe* (Hart Publishing, Oxford 1999) 65.

[96] *R v Oakes* [1986] 1 SCR 103, 138–39. The three-level approach was affirmed by the Supreme Court of Canada in *Chaoulli v Quebec (AG)* [2005] 1 SCR 791 [48]. For academic commentary see P Hogg *Constitutional Law of Canada (Looseleaf)* 5th edn (Thomson Carswell, Toronto 2007) ch 38; E Mendes 'The Crucible of the Charter: Judicial Principles v. Judicial Deference in the Context of Section 1' (2005) 27 *Supreme Court Law Review*, 2nd series 47. In *AG for Hong Kong v Lee Kwong-kut* [1993] AC 951 (PC) 972–73, Lord Woolf held that the Canadian approach to proportionality need not normally be applied under the Hong Kong Constitution but could provide 'useful general guidance in a case of difficulty'. This passage was quoted with approval in *R v DPP; ex p Kebilene* [2000] 2 AC 326 (HL) 386 (Lord Hope).

[97] *De Freitas v Permanent Secretary of Ministry of Agriculture, Fisheries, Lands and Housing* [1999] 1 AC 69 (PC) 80 (Lord Clyde): In determining whether a limitation is arbitrary or excessive the court should ask itself whether: '(i) the legislative objective is sufficiently important to justify limiting a fundamental right; (ii) the measures designed to meet the legislative objective are rationally connected to it; and (iii) the means used to impair the right or freedom are no more than is necessary to accomplish the objective.' This formulation was taken from Zimbabwean cases: *Nyambirai v National Social Security Authority* [1996] 1 LRC 64, 75 (Gubbay CJ); *Retrofit (Pvt) Ltd v Posts and Telecommunications Corporation* [1996] 4 LRC 489, 506 (Gubbay CJ).

[98] *R v A (No 2)* [2002] 1 AC 45 (HL) [38] (Lord Steyn); *R (Daly) v Secretary of State for the Home Department* [2001] 2 AC 532 (HL) [27] (Lord Steyn); *R v Shayler* [2003] 1 AC 247 (HL) [33] (Lord Bingham); *A v Secretary of State for the Home Department* [2005] 2 AC 68 (HL) [30] (Lord Bingham); *R (Pretty) v DPP* [2002] 1 AC 800 (HL) [93] (Lord Hope); *Huang v Secretary of State for the Home Department* [2007] 2 AC 167 (HL) [19] (Lord Bingham); *Tweed v Parades Commission for Northern Ireland* [2006] UKHL 53; [2007] 1 AC 650 (HL) [35] (Lord Carswell); *AS (Somalia) v Secretary of State for the Home Department* [2009] UKHL 32; [2009] 1 WLR 1385 (HL) [18] (Lord Hope). The use of the three-level approach to proportionality in administrative law is discussed in P Craig *Administrative Law* 5th edn (Sweet & Maxwell, London 2003) 622; A Lester 'Developing Constitutional Principles of Public Law' [2001] *PL* 684, 689–93. The search for a legitimate objective followed by a three level proportionality test is proposed as a standard formulation for UK courts in M Fordham & T de la Mare 'Identifying the Principles of Proportionality' in J Jowell & J Cooper (eds) *Understanding Human Rights Principles* (Hart, Oxford 2001) 27, 28; J Jowell 'Beyond the Rule of Law: Towards Constitutional Judicial Review' [2000] *PL* 671, 679–80; D Hoffman & J Rowe *Human Rights in the UK: An Introduction to the Human Rights Act 1998* (Pearson Longman, London 2003) 90.

some suggestions as to how the legitimate objective of a reverse burden of proof may be identified. Section two will analyse 'suitability', 'necessity' and 'balance' with a view to highlighting the differences between each stage of the proportionality inquiry. Section three will explain the connection between the different levels of the proportionality inquiry and the concept of judicial deference to the decisions of the legislature. It will be argued that a 'necessity' focused proportionality inquiry fixes the degree of deference in the most appropriate fashion for judicial decisions in the context of criminal procedure.

4. Legitimate Objective

The identification of a legitimate objective, in pursuit of which a protected right has been infringed, is a threshold requirement for the application of a proportionality test. In the absence of a legitimate objective, there can be no justification for the infringement of a protected right, since there is no competing interest capable of taking precedence over the protected right. Articles 8–11 of the ECHR expressly enumerate the objectives that may justify limitation or restriction of the respective rights. The enumerated objectives are expressed in general terms so that the range of objectives that may qualify as legitimate is exceptionally broad. In respect of most Article 6 rights, including the presumption of innocence, there is no express enumeration of legitimate objectives.[99] The result is that, to the extent that proportionality applies under Article 6, there are few limits to the objectives that might, in theory, qualify as legitimate.

Judges characterising the legitimate objective in reverse burdens cases regularly identify suppression of the conduct in question as the relevant objective for the purpose of a proportionality test. For example, in *Kebilene*,[100] Lord Hope stated that the purpose of the terrorist offence in question was 'to spare the lives of innocent people and to avoid the massive damage and dislocation to ordinary life which may follow from explosions which destroy or damage property.'[101] In *Lambert*,[102] Lord Hutton stated that there was a justification for a reverse burden in a drug trafficking offence because: 'The taking of controlled drugs is a great social evil which causes widespread suffering and the possession of controlled drugs with intent to supply is a grave and frequently committed offence which ensures the continuation of this social evil.'[103] In *Sheldrake*,[104] Lord Bingham stated that the legitimate objective of a reverse burden in relation to a traffic offence was 'the prevention of death, injury and damage caused by unfit drivers.'[105]

[99] The only exception is the right to a public hearing, which may be limited in certain specified circumstances: see art 6(1) ECHR.
[100] [2000] 2 AC 326 (HL).
[101] Ibid 387.
[102] [2002] 2 AC 545 (HL).
[103] Ibid [190].
[104] [2005] 1 AC 264 (HL).
[105] Ibid [41].

However, these characterisations are too simplistic. Under any proportionality analysis, the focus must be placed upon the justification for the impugned measure. Hence, when a reverse burden is challenged as being contrary to Article 6(2), it is not the criminal prohibition that needs justification, but rather the use of the reverse burden. The legitimate objective must be capable of justifying the decision to place the burden of proof on the defendant, in a departure from the ordinary rule imposing the burden of proof on the prosecution. An example of a legitimate objective might be the avoidance of wrongful acquittals due to the difficulty of proving certain matters, or the risk that a defendant might invent false defences. In *Lambert*,[106] Lord Steyn properly identified the legitimate objective of the reverse burden of proof created by section 28 of the Misuse of Drugs Act 1971. His Lordship stated:[107]

> I am satisfied that there is an objective justification for some interference with the burden of proof . . . The basis for this justification is that sophisticated drug smugglers, dealers and couriers typically secrete drugs in some container, thereby enabling the person in possession of the container to say that he was unaware of the contents. Such defences are commonplace and they pose real difficulties for the police and prosecuting authorities.

This identification of the 'justification' by Lord Steyn focused upon the problems of proof that the prosecution could face and the risk of defences that were false but hard to disprove. It was not enough merely to recount the scourge of drug trafficking as a reason for reversing the burden of proof. Of course, focus upon the justification for the reverse burden does not mean that the conduct at which the criminal prohibition is aimed is entirely irrelevant. The avoidance of wrongful acquittals might be regarded as more important in cases where the damage to society caused by the prohibited conduct is great. However, for the purposes of the proportionality test, the focus must be upon the justification for the reverse burden, not the justification for criminalising the prohibited conduct.

Further, it must be recognised that the prosecution faces problems of proof in all cases. The objective of reversing the burden to avoid ordinary problems of proof cannot be accepted as legitimate because such an objective would involve a direct contradiction of the presumption of innocence. In other contexts, the Canadian Supreme Court has held that an objective will not be legitimate if it is directly contradictory to a protected right. Applying this principle, the Canadian Supreme Court held that a Sunday trading law introduced in order to enforce religious observance could not be justified, since the objective itself was directly contradictory to religious freedom.[108] Just as religious motives cannot be a justification for limitation of the freedom of religion, the ease that would be created by reversing the burden of proof cannot be used to justify limitation of the presumption of innocence. The legitimate objective must involve some factor going beyond

[106] [2002] 2 AC 545 (HL).
[107] Ibid [36].
[108] *R v Big M Drug Mart* [1985] 1 SCR 295. *Cf R v Edwards Books and Arts* [1986] 2 SCR 713, in which Sunday trading laws introduced for a secular purpose were upheld.

the ordinary problems of proof. For instance, there may be cases in which the defendant has exclusive access to information which is relevant to the crime. In such cases, there would be a legitimate objective in imposing some form of burden on the defendant to bring that information before the court. The relevant question will be whether an evidential burden or a persuasive burden is necessary to resolve the problem of proof.

In addition, the avoidance of expense or inconvenience which the prosecution would encounter in proving certain matters is not, in itself, a legitimate objective capable of justifying reversal of the burden of proof. In general, the avoidance of inconvenience or the saving of money should not be capable of justifying the infringement of a protected right.[109] The choice of one means over another as the method for pursuing a legitimate objective may be influenced by considerations of expense of inconvenience, but these considerations are not, in themselves, the objective pursued.[110] The relevant question is at what point the expense or inconvenience becomes sufficiently great to justify the use of a more expedient measure that infringes a protected right. Taken alongside another objective, such as the need to ensure that vast numbers of guilty persons are not acquitted due to a problem of proof, considerations of expense or inconvenience which the prosecution might face in the absence of a reverse burden are relevant. The following section will assist in understanding at what point in the inquiry these kinds of considerations should come into play.

2. Suitability, Necessity and Balance

The division of the proportionality inquiry into the three stages of suitability, necessity and proportionality in the strict sense assists by identifying in precise terms the questions that a court must ask. A brief explanation of each stage is useful at this point: (1) Suitability is concerned with whether the measure in issue is objectively capable of contributing towards the pursuit of the legitimate objective. It is sometimes expressed as a requirement that there be a rational connection between the means adopted and the objective pursued. (2) Necessity is concerned with whether the measure adopted in pursuit of the objective results in the least possible impairment of the protected right. The court will ask itself whether any less restrictive alternative measures were available that could have been adopted in pursuit of the objective. (3) Proportionality in the strict sense asks whether the extent of interference with a protected right is in proper proportion to the contribution of the measure to the legitimate objective. This is the stage at which considerations of 'balance' between competing interests are most visible. For convenience, I will refer to this level of the inquiry as the 'balance' stage.

[109] See *Singh v Minister of Employment and Immigration* [1985] 1 SCR 177, 218–19 (Wilson J); *R v Lee* [1989] 2 SCR 1384, 1420 (Wilson J), 1391 (Lamer J).

[110] This is the approach of the Canadian Supreme Court: *Newfoundland (Treasury Board) v NAPE* [2004] 3 SCR 381 [59]–[76] (Binnie J).

This section will make two general points concerning the three stages of proportionality. First, while considerations of 'balance' are most evident in the final stage of proportionality, they are in fact present in all three stages. This is because proportionality is always concerned with the attempt to resolve a conflict between competing principles. Second, drawing on comparative material, it will be shown that, in its practical application, the proportionality inquiry tends to focus on one of the three stages. The inquiry functions differently depending on whether the focus rests upon 'suitability', 'necessity' or 'balance'. Hence, while the three levels of proportionality are usually depicted as consecutive stages in a single inquiry, they can also be envisaged as distinct tests.

Seen in this way, it becomes apparent that Lord Steyn in *Lambert* was applying a proportionality test that emphasised the 'necessity' stage of the inquiry. His Lordship insisted that the legislature adopt the least restrictive means to pursue its legitimate objective, using an evidential burden when it would suffice rather than a persuasive burden. By contrast, Lord Nicholls in *Johnstone* was applying a test that emphasised the 'balance' stage of the inquiry. Lord Nicholls did not ask whether there was a less restrictive means to achieve the legitimate objective, but only whether, in general terms, the measure adopted was 'fair', 'reasonable' or 'balanced'.

The remainder of this chapter is devoted to the question of whether the courts should adopt a 'necessity' test or 'balance' test when applying proportionality in the context of reverse burdens, setting aside, for the moment, questions concerning whether or when it is appropriate to engage in a proportionality inquiry at all. In deciding between these two tests, it will be relevant to consider which method of asking the proportionality question brings the relevant issues into sharpest focus. This section will argue that, in addition to the obvious point that a 'necessity' test provides greater protection to the individual, that test is also more conceptually coherent than the balance test. The arguments employed in this section are relevant not only in the context of reverse burdens, but more generally in all fields where proportionality is applied. Section three below returns to considerations that apply more specifically in the field of criminal justice.

(a) Suitability

The first aspect of the proportionality inquiry is the consideration of whether the measure adopted is a suitable means for pursuing the legitimate objective, or whether it has a 'rational connection'[111] to the legitimate objective. This aspect of proportionality gives effect to the principle that a protected right ought not to be infringed unless there is some corresponding contribution to the community interest. Satisfaction of 'suitability' involves the factual or causative demonstration of a 'rational connection' and leaves little room for evaluative argument concerning the balance between the community interest and individual rights. However,

[111] *R v Edwards Books and Art* [1986] 2 SCR 713, 770; *R v Oakes* [1986] 1 SCR 103, 139.

considerations of balance may arise in cases where there is uncertainty regarding the contribution of the measure to the fulfillment of the objective. The more important the protected right or the greater the degree of interference the more clearly the evidence would need to establish a contribution.[112] Conversely, the more significant the objective, the more the court may be willing to make a finding of suitability based on abstract reasoning without requiring compelling evidence.[113]

It is possible to apply the proportionality inquiry so that it is limited to the 'suitability' stage.[114] When the proportionality inquiry is applied in this way it is necessary to show only that there is a rational connection between the means adopted and the objective pursued. A proportionality inquiry limited to 'suitability' would be comparable to the *Wednesbury*[115] test of unreasonableness, traditionally applied in administrative law. In accordance with that test, the court was permitted to interfere with an administrative decision only if it was 'so unreasonable that no reasonable authority could ever have come to it'.[116] Since the introduction of the HRA, the House of Lords has departed from *Wednesbury* and held that the court is required 'to assess the balance which the decision maker has struck, not merely whether it is within the range of rational or reasonable decisions.'[117] A proportionality test that stops at the suitability or 'rational connection' stage has therefore been disapproved under the HRA.

Further, in the context of reverse burdens, none of the English courts have restricted their inquiries to whether the measure adopted is 'suitable'. A persuasive

[112] The Strasbourg Court has stressed that justification for infringement of certain rights must be 'convincingly established': *Vogt v Germany* (App No 17851/91) (1995) 21 EHRR 205 [52]; *Observer and Guardian v UK* (App No 13585/88) (1991) 14 EHRR 153 [59]; *Ahmed v UK* (App No 22954/93) (1998) 29 EHRR 1 [55]; *Buck v Germany* (App No 41604/98) (2006) 42 EHRR 21 [44]; *Barthold v Germany* (App No 8734/79) (1985) 7 EHRR 383 [58].

[113] The Canadian Supreme Court has held that a rational connection based on 'reason', 'logic' or 'common sense' would suffice even though the evidence was not 'scientifically measurable': *RJR-Macdonald v Canada* [1995] 3 SCR 199 [156]–[158] (McLachlin J, for the majority), [85] (La Forest J, for the minority). See also *R v Butler* [1992] 1 SCR 452, 503 ('reasonable to presume' that there is a causal connection between obscenity and violence against women); *Ross v New Brunswick School District No. 15* [1996] 1 SCR 825 [101] ('reasonable to anticipate' that there is a causal relationship between anti-Semitic activity by schoolteacher outside school and discriminatory attitudes within school).

[114] For example, the ECJ will decline to hold that a community measure is unlawful unless the measure is 'manifestly inappropriate': Case 331/88 *R v Minister for Agriculture, Fisheries and Food; ex p Fedesa* [1990] ECR I-4023 [14]; Case C-11/00 *Commission v European Central Bank* [2003] ECR I-7147 [157]. The ECJ has adopted various similar phrases: Case 40/72 *Schroeder v Germany* [1973] ECR 125 [14]: 'obviously inappropriate'; Case 138/78 *Stolting v Hauptzollant Hamburg-Jonas* [1979] ECR 713 [7]: 'patently unsuited'; Case 59/83 *Biovilac v EEC* [1984] ECR 4057 [17]: 'manifestly unsuitable'. By contrast, when reviewing the legality of a national measure, the ECJ applies the 'less restrictive alternative' test: Case 124/81 *Commission v United Kingdom* [1983] ECR 203 [13]; Case 72/83 *Campus Oil Limited v Minister for Industry and Energy* [1984] ECR 2727 [37]; Case C367/89 *Richardt and 'Les Accessoires Scientifiques'* [1991] ECR I-4621 [20]; Case 13/78 *Joh Eggers Sohn & Co v Freie Hansestadt Bremen* [1978] ECR 1935 [30].

[115] *Associated Provincial Picture Houses Ltd v Wednesbury Corporation* [1948] 1 KB 223 (CA).

[116] Ibid 230 (Lord Greene MR).

[117] *R (Daly) v Secretary of State for the Home Department* [2001] 2 AC 532 (HL) 547 (Lord Steyn).

burden on the defendant will always be a 'suitable' means for avoiding problems of proof that may be faced by the prosecution. A persuasive burden which relieves the prosecution of the risk of non-persuasion is, by definition, objectively capable of contributing to the legitimate objective of alleviating problems of proof. If the inquiry ceased at the suitability stage, all persuasive burdens would be proportionate. Accordingly, in deciding which level of the inquiry to focus upon, the realistic choice is between 'necessity' and 'balance'

(b) Necessity

'Necessity' gives effect to the principle that a measure infringing a right ought not to be permitted if another measure is available that will make the same contribution to the fulfilment of the objective while having less impact upon the protected right. Consequently, the focus of the 'necessity' aspect is directed towards the availability of a less restrictive alternative measure that would make a comparable contribution to the objective. The 'less restrictive alternative' test is illustrated by cases before the ECJ in which the prohibition on the sale of a product was defended on grounds of public health. The ECJ has consistently held that the complete prohibition of a product is not necessary when the public health concerns can be addressed by the alternative measure of affixing an appropriate label to the product in question.[118] When applying the 'less restrictive alternative' test, the court will make its own evaluation of the alternative measures available. The 'necessity' aspect of proportionality consequently provides a high degree of protection to individual rights by curtailing any measure which could be replaced by a less restrictive measure.

There are two considerations which lead to complications in the application of the 'necessity' aspect of the test. First, it will nearly always be possible to identify an alternative measure that is less restrictive of a protected right, provided the legislature is willing to sacrifice some degree of efficacy in the fulfilment of the legitimate objective.[119] Consequently, the efficacy of alternative measures is a variable that must be taken into account, in addition to the impact upon the protected right. Second, an alternative measure might be more expensive or inconvenient than the impugned measure. If the degree of expense or inconvenience is sufficient it will permit the conclusion that it is not 'reasonable' or 'practicable' for the legislature to adopt the alternative measure.[120] The presence of variables in the form of efficacy and practicability ensures that the application of the necessity test will never be rigid or mechanical. It will be necessary for the court to have regard to the

[118] Case 174/84 *Commission v Germany* [1987] ECR 1227 [28]; Case 261/81 *Walter Rau Lebensmittelwerke v De Smedt* [1982] ECR 3961 [12], 3981 (Reischl AG); Case 120/78 *Rewe-Zentrale AG v Bundesmonopolverwaltung für Branntwein* [1979] ECR 649 [13].

[119] P Chapman 'The Politics of Judging: Section 1 of the Charter of Rights and Freedoms' (1986) 24 *Osgoode Hall Law Journal* 867, 883; Mendes (see n 96 above) 87.

[120] Case 104/75 *De Peijper* [1976] ECR 613 [18].

importance of the legitimate objective and the degree of interference with the protected right in order to reach conclusions on whether a reduction in efficacy or greater expense and inconvenience ought to be tolerated in order to afford more protection to the infringed right. Considerations of 'balance' between the community interest and individual rights will therefore be unavoidable in the vast majority of cases in which the 'necessity' aspect is applied.[121]

The contours of the 'necessity' test in the context of reverse burdens are easy to identify. The court must make a decision about whether the less restrictive measure of an evidential burden would suffice to meet the problems of proof faced by the prosecution. If an evidential burden would suffice, a provision placing the persuasive burden on the defendant will be disproportionate. It is unavoidable that the answer to this question will involve evaluative considerations. An evidential burden is easier for a defendant to satisfy than a persuasive burden and consequently, where an evidential burden is used, it is reasonable to assume that more defendants, including some who are in fact guilty, will escape conviction. The use of an evidential burden is a less efficacious means of enforcing a criminal prohibition than a persuasive burden. The court must therefore evaluate whether the reduction in efficacy is a sufficient problem to make it 'necessary' to impose a persuasive burden on the defendant.[122] Further, when the prosecution is faced with a persuasive burden, it is likely that greater resources will be required to collect the evidence and present it in court. This expense is a further variable, in addition to efficacy, that comes into play under the question of 'necessity'.

(c) Balance

Proportionality in the strict sense, or balance, has the potential to extend the protection afforded to individual rights beyond what is accorded by 'suitability' and 'necessity' alone. This aspect dictates that, even when a measure is suitable and necessary for the fulfilment of a legitimate objective, it must not be adopted if the impact upon a protected right is disproportionate to the contribution of the measure to the realisation of the objective. However, in practice, proportionality in the strict sense rarely operates as an independent check upon the infringement of a right. This is because, if the legitimate objective is sufficiently important, in principle, to justify some limitation of the right, and no alternative measure is reasonably available, it will be difficult to conclude that the impact of the measure is excessive in the circumstances. Consequently, in Canada, the third aspect has

[121] Canadian cases emphasise the importance of 'context' in the necessity test: *R v Jones* [1986] 2 SCR 284, 300; *Andrews v Law Society of British Columbia* [1989] 1 SCR 143, 184–85; *Black v Law Society of Alberta* [1989] 1 SCR 591, 627–28; *Edmonton Journal v Alberta (AG)* [1989] 2 SCR 1326, 1355–56, 1380; *McKinney v University of Guelph* [1990] 3 SCR 229, 280–81; *Dickason v University of Alberta* [1992] 2 SCR 1103, 1122.

[122] For the purposes of argument, I am setting aside here the more general point that, unless there is a reduced risk of wrongful conviction or the consequences of conviction are minimal, the court ought not to introduce considerations of community interest through a proportionality inquiry.

rarely had an impact upon the outcome of a case,[123] and the 'necessity' aspect is usually the focus of the inquiry.[124] Similarly, in the ECJ, the third aspect is often 'folded' back into the 'necessity' aspect[125] and the Court will ask only whether the measure is 'appropriate' and 'necessary'.[126] The formulation of the proportionality test adopted in *de Freitas* omitted proportionality in the strict sense as a separate component of the inquiry.[127] Therefore, despite its theoretical potential, proportionality in the strict sense rarely operates as a cumulative criterion in conjunction with 'suitability' and 'necessity'.

Julian Rivers criticises the reduction of the proportionality inquiry to a test of suitability and necessity.[128] He argues that by focusing on the necessity aspect, and the search for the least-restrictive alternative, the proportionality inquiry becomes a test of 'mere efficiency'.[129] The necessity test, according to Rivers, assumes that whatever is necessary to achieve a legitimate objective will be justified regardless of the impact upon human rights.[130] In Rivers' conception of proportionality, questions of balance between competing interests should be excluded from the necessity stage of the inquiry, and postponed to the balance stage where they can

[123] Hogg observes that the third level of the proportionality analysis 'has never had any influence on the outcome of any case': Hogg (see n 96 above) [38–43]. Two cases appear to have turned on the 'balance' aspect, but both could have been decided under the 'necessity' aspect: *New Brunswick v G* [1999] 3 SCR 46 [98]; *R v Sharpe* [2001] 1 SCR 45 [110].

[124] Hogg (see n 96 above) [38–36]; Mendes (see n 96 above) 87; R Clayton 'Regaining a Sense of Proportion: The Human Rights Act and the Proportionality Principle' [2001] *European Human Rights Law Review (EHRLR)* 504, 521. *Cf Chaoulli v Quebec (AG)* [2005] 1 SCR 791 [48] (Deschamps J): 'It is the minimal impairment analysis that has proven to be the most delicate stage in the instant case. The other stages cannot, however, be bypassed.'

[125] Craig & de Búrca (see n 95 above) 372. See also Tridimas, *General Principles of EC Law* (see n 95 above) 92; Tridimas, 'Proportionality in Community Law' (see n 95 above) 68; Fordham & de la Mare (see n 98 above) 41; W Van Gerven, 'The Effect of Proportionality on the Actions of Member States of the European Community: National Viewpoints from Continental Europe' in E Ellis (ed) *The Principle of Proportionality in the Laws of Europe* (Hart Publishing, Oxford 1999) 37, 60; J Usher, *General Principles of EC Law* (Longman, New York 1998) 40; F Jacobs, 'Recent Developments in the Principle of Proportionality in European Community Law' in E Ellis (ed) *The Principle of Proportionality in the Laws of Europe* (Hart Publishing, Oxford 1999) 1, 2.

[126] Case C-19/92 *Kraus v Land Baden-Württenberg* [1993] ECR I-1663 [32]; Case C-106/91 *Ramrath v Ministre de la Justice* [1992] ECR I-3351 [29]–[30]; Case C-11/00 *Commission v European Central Bank* [2003] ECR I-7147 [156]; Case C-491/01 *British American Tobacco (Investments) and Imperial Tobacco* [2002] ECR I-11453 [122]. A variant formulation asks whether the means employed 'correspond to the importance of the aim' and are 'necessary': Case 66/82 *Fromançais SA v Fonds d'Orientation et de Régularisation des Marchés Agricoles (FORMA)* [1983] ECR 395, 404 [8]; Case 47/86 *Roquette Frères v ONIC* [1987] ECR 2889 [19]; Case 56/86 *Sociéte pour l'exportation des sucres* [1987] ECR 1423 [28]; Case 281/84 *Zuckerfabrik Bedburg v Council* [1987] ECR 49 [36]; Case C-358/88 *Oberhausener Kraftfutterwerk Wilhelm Hopermann GmbH v Bundesanstalt für landwirtschaftliche Marktordnung* [1990] ECR I-1687 [13]. A further variation is found in Case C-159/90 *Society for the Protection of Unborn Children Ireland Ltd v Grogan* [1991] ECR I-4685, 4719–20 (Van Gerven AG): a measure must be 'useful', 'indispensable' and not 'disproportionate'.

[127] *De Freitas v Permanent Secretary of Ministry of Agriculture, Fisheries, Land and Housing* [1999] 1 AC 69 (PC) 80 (Lord Clyde). More recently, the House of Lords re-inserted that requirement: *Huang v Secretary of State for the Home Department* [2007] 2 AC 167 (HL) [19] (Lord Bingham).

[128] J Rivers 'Proportionality and Variable Intensity of Review' (2006) 65 *CLJ* 174.

[129] Ibid 190.

[130] Ibid.

be addressed 'separately and openly'.[131] However, the necessity stage would become virtually redundant if considerations of balance were removed. It would be very rare to find an alternative measure that makes the same contribution to the fulfillment of the legitimate objective as the impugned measure. Compounding the problem, Rivers urges that courts should defer to legislative or administrative decision-makers on the question of whether an alternative measure makes a comparable contribution to the objective.[132] The result of applying the test in this way would be that that the necessity stage is passed over and all the evaluative work is left to be done under the auspices of 'balance'. That is, the test would resolve into a question about whether the proper 'balance' has been struck.

This is the approach that is routinely taken in the Strasbourg Court. There, the proportionality inquiry is commonly described as the search for a 'fair balance' between the rights of the individual and the interests of the community.[133] Steven Greer states that: '[I]n most cases which reach the European Court of Human Rights, the principles of suitability and necessity will already have been answered in the affirmative, and . . . [the] . . . neat tripartite test will, therefore, have collapsed into a single "balancing question" '.[134] The Strasbourg Court has been reluctant to apply a 'least-restrictive means' test. In one case under Article 10, the first instance Chamber insisted that states are required to minimise the interference with rights 'by trying to find alternative solutions and by generally seeking to achieve their aims in the least onerous way as regards human rights'.[135] However, the Grand Chamber overturned the decision and rejected the insistence on the least-restrictive means, stating that states 'must in principle be left a choice between different way and means' of meeting the obligation to respect rights.[136] In one case under Article 6(3)(d), the Strasbourg Court has stated that measures restricting

[131] Ibid.

[132] Ibid 199–200.

[133] *Belgian Linguistic Case (Merits)* (App No 1474/62) (1968) 1 EHRR 252, 282; *Sporrong and Lönnroth v Sweden* (App No 7151/75) (1983) 5 EHRR 35 [69]; *Soering v UK* (App No 14038/88) (1989) 11 EHRR 439 [89]; *Sheffield and Horsham v UK* (App No 22885/93) (1999) 27 EHRR 163 [41]; *Powell and Rayner v UK* (App No 9310/81) (1990) 12 EHRR 355 [41]; *Rees v UK* (App No 9532/81) (1986) 9 EHRR 56 [37]; *Gaskin v UK* (App No 10454/83) (1989) 12 EHRR 36 [42]; *Hokkanen v Finland* (App No 19823/92) (1994) 19 EHRR 139 [55]; *Kroon v The Netherlands* (App No 18535) (1994) 19 EHRR 263 [31]; *Katte Klitsche de la Grange v Italy* (App No 12539/86) (1994) 19 EHRR 368 [42]; *Jacobsson v Sweden* (App No 10842/84) (1989) 12 EHRR 56 [55]; *Barfod v Denmark* (App No 11508/85) (1991) 13 EHRR 493 [29]. The same idea is prevalent throughout the decisions of the House of Lords under the HRA: *R v A (No 2)* [2002] 1 AC 45 (HL) [91] (Lord Hope); *R (ProLife Alliance) v BBC* [2004] 1 AC 185 (HL) [137] (Lord Walker); *R (Razgar) v Secretary of State for the Home Department* [2004] 2 AC 368 (HL) [20] (Lord Bingham); *R (Roberts) v Parole Board* [2005] 2 AC 738 (HL) [14] (Lord Bingham); *Kay v Lambeth LBC* [2006] 2 AC 465 (HL) [32] (Lord Bingham); *R (Countryside Alliance) v AG* [2007] UKHL 52; [2008] 1 AC 719 (HL) [155] (Lord Brown); *R (Wellington) v Secretary of State for the Home Department* [2008] UKHL 72 [23] (Lord Hoffmann), [57] (Lord Carswell); *Re E (A child)* [2009] 1 AC 536 (HL) [48] (Lord Carswell); *Austin v Commissioner of Police of the Metropolis* [2009] UKHL 5; [2009] 1 AC 564 (HL) [27] (Lord Hope); *Trent Strategic Health Authority v Jain* [2009] UKHL 4; [2009] 1 All ER 957 (HL) [13] (Lord Scott).

[134] S Greer '"Balancing" and the European Court of Human Rights: A Contribution to the Habermas-Alexy Debate' (2004) 63 *CLJ* 412, 433.

[135] *Hatton v UK* (App No 36022/97) (2002) 34 EHRR 1 [97].

[136] *Hatton v UK* (App No 36022/97) (2003) 37 EHRR 28 [123].

the right to confront witnesses 'should be strictly necessary' and that '[i]f a less restrictive measure can suffice then that measure should be applied.'[137] However, this statement has not been followed in any subsequent cases.[138] To the extent that proportionality is applied under Article 6, it is limited to a consideration of whether the correct 'balance' has been struck.[139]

When 'balance' operates as the exclusive and substantive test in the proportionality inquiry there are serious methodological problems. One objection to a 'balance' approach is that the competing principles 'balanced' in the proportionality inquiry are 'incommensurable'.[140] That is, there is no accepted unit of measurement that can be used to place value upon both principles. Community interest and individual rights cannot be expressed in a common currency and therefore cannot be weighed against each other. Even competing individual rights cannot be expressed in a common currency.

Robert Alexy has responded to the objection that the competing principles involved in the 'balancing' process are incommensurable. He argues that common value can be ascribed to competing principles by adopting a unitary point of view based on the constitution.[141] For example, the value of two competing rights can be determined based on the importance attributed to each right under the constitution.[142] Similarly, the value of an individual right relative to a community interest can be determined by assessing the constitutional value of each.[143] Alexy acknowledges that there may be disputes about the value attributed to various principles under any constitution, but insists that these arguments can be resolved by recourse to reason and argument.[144]

[137] *Van Mechelen v Netherlands* (App No 21363/93) (1997) 25 EHRR 647 [58].

[138] In *Jasper v UK* (App No 27052/95) (2000) 30 EHRR 441, 476–79 Judge Hedigan (dissenting) quoted *Van Mechelen* regarding the existence of a 'less restrictive measure' and applied that test to find that the procedure governing disclosure was not compatible with art 6(1) and art 6(3)(d). The majority, which did not refer to the 'less restrictive measure' test, found the procedure was compatible. See the related judgment in *Fitt v UK* (App No 29777/96) (2000) 30 EHRR 480. In *Visser v Netherlands* (App No 26668/95) ECHR 14 February 2002 [43] the reference to 'less restrictive measure' in *Van Mechelen* was quoted by the Court together with other paragraphs from that judgment. However, the Court in *Visser* did not proceed to consider alternative measures that might have been taken.

[139] See eg *Jalloh v Germany* (App No 54810/00) (2007) 44 EHRR 32 [97]. See Ch 4 for more detailed discussion of the use of proportionality under art 6.

[140] See C Sunstein 'Incommensurability and Valuation in Law' (1994) 92 *Michigan Law Review* 779; M Alder 'Law and Incommensurability: Introduction' (1998) 146 *University of Pennsylvania Law Review* 1169; F Schauer 'Commensurability and its Constitutional Consequences' (1994) 45 *Hastings Law Journal* 785, 790; D Meyerson 'Why Courts Should not Balance Rights against the Public Interest' (2007) 31 *Melbourne University Law Review* 873, 887.

[141] R Alexy 'On Balancing and Subsumption: A Structural Comparison' (2003) 16 *Ratio Juris* 433, 442.

[142] Alexy uses the Titanic case BVerfGE vol 86, 1 to illustrate balancing. That case involved a conflict between individual rights — freedom of expression and individual personality in the context of a defamation claim: ibid 437–39.

[143] Alexy also uses the Tobacco case BVerfGE vol 95, 179 to illustrate balancing. The conflict in that case was between the individual right of tobacco producers to pursue their profession without interference and the benefit to the community that would be provided by a law imposing compulsory health warnings on cigarette packets: ibid 437.

[144] Ibid 442.

The suggestion of using the constitution as a common reference point to assign value to different principles holds some promise. Where the competing principles take the form of two (or more) individual rights, it is conceivable to assign a constitutional value to each right based on some common idea about why rights are valuable. This seems especially plausible under the German Basic Law, with which Alexy is principally concerned, and which uses the concept of human dignity as a common reference point.[145] Under other frameworks, such as the HRA, there is no explicit textual basis for a common reference point, but it conceivably could be supplied by a liberal idea such as autonomy.[146] However, this would require an explicitly political and evaluative model capable of capturing the importance of rights. The common reference point would no doubt be highly controversial under the HRA and judges in England would be unlikely to perform the task of enunciating the common reference point. Any common reference point would be left unstated or even shift from case to case. Hence, the 'balancing' of the rights within an ostensible common scale would become a smokescreen obscuring the true reasons for a decision.

The idea is even less promising when an individual right must be balanced against a competing community interest. This is where the problem of incommensurability is most acute. It is unclear how the value of a community interest can be expressed in constitutional terms. Even a comprehensive constitution like the German Basic Law does not give expression to every community interest that could legitimately be pursued by a government. A limited quasi-constitutional document like the HRA gives little indication of a scale for valuing community interests. Even under Articles 8–11 of the ECHR, which expressly enumerate legitimate objectives, the expression given to community interests is in the most general of terms. Hence, there is no common baseline from which to judge the importance of the protected right against the community interest.

The incommensurability objection to balance may partially be answered by a reminder that 'balance' is a metaphor.[147] Judges applying a 'balance' test are not placing two incommensurable values onto the scales, but rather asking whether, in the circumstances, the adoption of a particular measure in pursuit of the community interest is 'reasonable', having regard to the impact upon individual rights. However, when the proportionality question is posed in this way there is an immanent danger that the reasons for the decision will be non-transparent or irrational. Accordingly, Jurgen Habermas has complained that 'weighing takes place either arbitrarily or unreflectively'.[148]

In response, Alexy has sought to show how a balancing process can operate rationally. Alexy characterises the degree of interference with the protected right as either 'light', 'moderate' or 'serious'.[149] He then characterises the degree to

[145] German Basic Law, art 1.
[146] See J Raz *The Morality of Freedom* (Clarendon Press, Oxford 1986) chs 14, 15.
[147] Rivers (see n 128 above) 201.
[148] J Habermas, W Regh (trans), *Between Facts and Norms* (Polity Press, Cambridge 1996) 259.
[149] Alexy (see n 141 above) 440.

which the legitimate objective or competing right would be compromised in the absence of the impugned measure as either 'light', 'moderate' or 'serious'.[150] Having made these characterisations, Alexy argues it is possible to make the requisite judgments concerning balance using the tripartite scale. For instance, a 'light' infringement of a protected right would be justified if the prejudice to the competing interest in the absence of the impugned measure would be either 'moderate' or 'serious'. Alexy argues that these characterisations are not irrational or based on prejudice because they are to be made following argument from both sides and must be supported by reasons.[151] This defence of rational balancing suffers from the same flaw as the defence to the charge of incommensurability. The classification of infringements as 'light', 'moderate' or 'serious' requires a common scale in which to express the value of each interest. Unless there is such a clearly articulated common scale there can be no basis for the characterisations upon which Alexy's model depends.

Further, to state that the interests of the community and the rights of individuals must be fairly balanced does not provide courts, or potential parties before the courts, with any means of determining when the balance is reached. How significant must the community interest be before interference with an individual right is justified? Must the community interest overwhelmingly outweigh an individual right, or is a mere preponderance of interest sufficient? A 'balance' test does not provide a consistent threshold for determining when the infringement of a protected right is justified. Instead, the threshold depends on the variable and vague criteria of 'reasonableness' or 'fairness'. A concept of proportionality that is methodologically sound must go beyond the notion of 'balance' and apply more precise criteria for evaluating the justification for limitation of rights.

Each of these problems with a 'balance' approach to proportionality is alleviated (though not eliminated) under the 'necessity' approach. While the 'necessity' test includes considerations of balance it is not reducible to a test of 'balance'. Rather than inquiring whether a measure is 'fair' or 'reasonable', the 'necessity' test focuses attention upon the specific question of whether there are any alternative means of pursuing the legitimate objective. In order to conclude that a measure is necessary, the court must examine any proposed alternative measures and explain why each could not have replaced the impugned measure. This inquiry is sharply focused and the conclusions must be expressed openly, exposing the explanation for the decision and discouraging arbitrary reasoning. The need to make evaluative judgments informed by considerations of balance regarding the practicability or efficacy of an alternative measure is not removed, but the foundation of these judgments is more likely to be rational and open.

Further, judges are not required to develop a common baseline for understanding the importance of human rights before applying the necessity test. Each case can be evaluated on its own merits. The 'necessity' test determines the threshold at

[150] Ibid 444–45.
[151] Ibid 439.

which the infringement of a protected right may be justified. A measure infringing a protected right may be justified only when necessary or, in other terms, when there is no alternative measure available to meet the legitimate objective. 'Necessity' consequently provides a methodologically consistent means of adjudicating upon the justification for an infringement. From the methodological point of view, a 'necessity' focused proportionality test is preferable. It might be argued, however, that a 'necessity' test involves inappropriate judicial intrusion in the realm of the legislative or administrative decision-maker. The following section addresses this problem.

3. Proportionality and the Problem of Deference

Commentators[152] and courts[153] have directed considerable attention to the degree of deference which a court reviewing a measure under the HRA ought to accord to the original decision-maker. Less attention has been paid to the questions that must be asked in a proportionality inquiry, although it can be seen that there is an important connection between these two matters.[154] As discussed in the preceding section, the three levels of proportionality may be conceived of as three distinct tests. Each test allows a greater or lesser degree of discretion to the decision-maker and, inversely, a greater or lesser degree of protection for individual rights. In

[152] A selection of recent works includes: TRS Allan 'Human Rights and Judicial Review: A Critique of "Due Deference"' (2006) 65 *CLJ* 671; R Clayton, 'Judicial Deference and Democratic Dialogue: The Legitimacy of Judicial Intervention under the Human Rights Act 1998' [2004] *PL* 33; R Edwards 'Judicial Deference Under the Human Rights Act' (2002) 65 *MLR* 859; R Ekins 'Judicial Supremacy and the Rule of Law' (2003) 119 *LQR* 127; C Gearty 'Reconciling Parliamentary Democracy and Human Rights' (2002) 118 *LQR* 248; C Gearty *Principles of Human Rights Adjudication* (OUP, Oxford 2004) 117–45; J Jowell 'Judicial Deference and Human Rights: A Question of Competence' in P Craig and R Rawlings (eds) *Law and Administration in Europe: Essays in Honour of Carol Harlow* (Oxford University Press, Oxford 2003) 67; F Klug, 'Judicial Deference Under the Human Rights Act' [2003] *EHRLR* 125; M Hunt 'Sovereignty's Blight: Why Contemporary Public Law Needs the Concept of 'Due Deference" in N Bamforth and P Leyland (eds) *Public Law in a Multi-Layered Constitution* (Hart Publishing, Oxford 2003) 337; D Pannick & A Lester (eds) *Human Rights: Law and Practice* 2nd edn (Lexis Nexis, London 2004) 95–100; J Laws 'The Limitations of Human Rights' [1998] *PL* 254; D Pannick, 'Principles of Interpretation of Convention Rights under the Human Rights Act and the Discretionary Area of Judgment' [1998] *PL* 545.

[153] The following is a selection of House of Lords decisions dealing with deference: *A v Secretary of State for the Home Department* [2005] 2 AC 68 (HL) [29] (Lord Bingham), [80] (Lord Nicholls), [107]–[108] (Lord Hope), [116] (Lord Hope), [176]–[177] (Lord Rodger), [196] (Lord Walker), [226] (Baroness Hale); *Brown v Stott* [2003] 1 AC 681 (PC) 703 (Lord Bingham), 710–11 (Lord Steyn); *R (ProLife Alliance) v BBC* [2004] 1 AC 185 (HL) [75]–[76] (Lord Hoffmann); *R v Lichniak* [2003] 1 AC 903 (HL) [14] (Lord Bingham); *Secretary of State for the Home Department v Rehman* [2003] 1 AC 153 (HL) [62] (Lord Hoffmann); *R (Alconbury) v Secretary of State for the Environment, Transport and the Regions* [2003] 2 AC 295 (HL) [129] (Lord Hoffmann); *R (Daly) v Secretary of State for the Home Department* [2001] 2 AC 532 (HL) [28] (Lord Steyn); *R v DPP; ex p Kebilene* [2000] 2 AC 326 (HL) 380–81 (Lord Hope); *R (Pretty) v DPP* [2002] 1 AC 800 (HL) [57] (Lord Steyn), [120] (Lord Hobhouse). In the Court of Appeal, there is an influential discussion of deference in the dissenting judgment of Laws LJ in *International Transport Roth GmbH v Secretary of State for the Home Department* [2003] QB 728 (CA) [69]–[87].

[154] See Rivers (see n 129 above).

determining which level of the inquiry to focus upon, the level of deference which the court considers should be accorded to the legislature is a crucial factor.

A proportionality inquiry that focuses upon suitability will allow the most discretion to the legislature. Under the 'suitability' aspect, the court is concerned only with whether the measure does, in fact, make a contribution towards the achievement of the legitimate objective. The legislature is free to choose any method that contributes to the objective, regardless of the impact upon individual freedoms, and consequently there is a broad area of discretion. The area of discretion is curtailed if the court focuses on the 'balance' aspect. Under this aspect, the measure chosen must not only contribute to the legitimate objective, but must also be reasonable, taking into account the contribution of the measure to the fulfillment of the objective and the degree of interference with the protected right. However, the legislature still has a considerable discretion on the 'balance' test. A range of measures might satisfy the test of 'balance', each having a different impact on individual rights. The legislature would be permitted to choose any of the measures within this range. A proportionality inquiry focusing upon the 'necessity' aspect imposes the greatest restrictions on the discretion of the legislature. The legislature is required to choose the measure that has the least impact upon individual rights. Consequently, a proportionality inquiry focused on 'necessity' leaves minimal discretion to the legislature and results in minimal deference on the part of the courts.[155]

It is notable that in its decisions on reverse burdens in which a 'balance' approach was applied, the House of Lords emphasised that the role of the court was one of review, and that deference should be given to legislative decisions.[156] This emphasis sits well with the 'balance' approach to proportionality because that approach allows the legislature to choose from a range of measures. On the 'balance' approach, the legislature may impose a persuasive burden on the defendant, even if an evidential burden would suffice, provided that, in the view of the court, it is reasonable to do so. On the necessity approach, a persuasive burden is never to be permitted in any case where an evidential burden would suffice.

[155] In theory, the legislature is left with some discretion under a 'necessity' focused approach. In the abstract, it is possible to conceive of a situation in which two or more measures make the same contribution to a legitimate objective, and have the same impact upon protected rights. In such a case, the legislature would be free to select either means in pursuit of the objective. More often, the discretion of the legislature will be found in the area in which there is uncertainty regarding the contribution of a measure and its impact upon protected rights. In some cases, the limits of human knowledge or the unavailability of evidence will prevent the court from reaching a firm conclusion on the contribution of a measure, or its impact. In other cases, there may be evaluative uncertainty regarding which of several alternative measures provides the best protection for individual rights. In all such cases, the court could resolve the uncertainty by deferring to the decision already made by the legislature: see Alexy (see n 94 above) 410–16; J Rivers 'Proportionality, Discretion and the Second Law of Balancing' in G Pavlakos (ed) *Law, Rights and Discourse: The Legal Philosophy of Robert* Alexy (Hart, Oxford 2007) 167.

[156] *R v DPP; ex p Kebilene* [2000] 2 AC 326 (HL) 381 (Lord Hope); *R v Johnstone* [2003] 1 WLR 1736 (HL) [51] (Lord Nicholls). *Cf Sheldrake v DPP; AG's Reference (No 4 of 2002)* [2005] 1 AC 264 (HL) [31] (Lord Bingham). See also *AG's Reference (No 1 of 2004)* [2004] 1 WLR 2111 (CA) [52] (Lord Woolf CJ).

With a clear understanding of the differing degrees of deference associated with the 'balance' and 'necessity' approaches, it is possible to decide which approach is most appropriate in the field of criminal procedure and evidence. The appropriate degree of deference may vary between different fields such as economic or social policy on the one hand and criminal evidence and procedure on the other.[157] An approach to proportionality which leaves a considerable discretion to the legislature will be appropriate only if a corresponding degree of deference is called for in that field. In general, there are four justifications given for deference by the courts to the legislature: (1) the democratic legitimacy of the legislature; (2) the role assigned to the courts by the Westminster system, in which Parliament is sovereign; (3) the comparative lack of expertise of the court on certain questions; and (4) the institutional limitations of judicial decision-making. Each of these justifications must be assessed to determine the extent to which they carry weight in the context of criminal procedure and evidence.

The first objection to a system of judicial review of legislative decisions is that 'elected legislators have a far greater democratic mandate than unelected judges'.[158] Similarly, when a system of judicial review is adopted, as it has been under the HRA, it is argued that the courts should demonstrate respect for the democratic legitimacy of parliament by according deference to parliamentary action.[159] One response to the democratic justification for deference is to observe that the HRA is itself a product of the democratically elected legislature.[160] By applying the HRA, the courts are simply giving effect to the expressed wishes of the legislature. Another response is that a fully-flourishing democracy is one in which fundamental rights, including those of unpopular minorities, are protected.[161] Hence, as Dworkin argues, while democracy requires that the legislature be given primary responsibility for questions of policy, the courts are the guardians of fundamental rights, which come under the category of principles.[162] The need for courts to stand as the guardians of human rights is at its highest in the context of procedural rights in a criminal trial. In the criminal justice system, the power of the democratic state is brought to bear against an individual in circumstances which place his or her physical freedom at stake. Democratic legitimacy cannot

[157] *R v DPP; ex p Kebilene* [2000] 2 AC 326 (HL) [381 (Lord Hope); *Libman v Quebec (AG)* [1997] 3 SCR 569 [59]–[62].

[158] Ekins (see n 152 above) 144.

[159] *Brown v Stott* [2003] 1 AC 681 (PC) 703 (Lord Bingham); *International Transport Roth GmbH v Secretary of State for the Home Department* [2003] QB 728 (CA) [82]–[83] (Laws LJ); *R (Alconbury) v Secretary of State for the Environment, Transport and the Regions* [2003] 2 AC 295 (HL) [69]–[70] (Lord Hoffmann), [60] (Lord Nolan), [144] (Lord Clyde); Hunt (see n 152 above) 354; *Irwin Toy v Quebec (AG)* [1989] 1 SCR 927, 993.

[160] A Ashworth *Human Rights, Serious Crime and Criminal Procedure* (Sweet & Maxwell, London 2002) 71–72.

[161] Ibid 72–73. See also J Laws, 'Law and Democracy' [1995] *PL* 72, 81; *Reyes v R* [2002] 2 AC 235 (PC) [26] (Lord Bingham).

[162] R Dworkin, *Takings Rights Seriously* (Duckworth, London 1977) 22. See also TRS Allan, *Constitutional Justice: A Liberal Theory of the Rule of Law* (OUP, Oxford 2001) 280; J Jowell 'Judicial Deference: Servility, Civility or Institutional Capacity?' [2003] *PL* 592.

take priority over the moral imperative of ensuring that a trial is conducted in accordance with a fair procedure.

The second justification for deference to the legislature rests on the concern that overly expansive judicial review undermines the principle of parliamentary sovereignty and replaces it with a principle of judicial supremacy.[163] This concern is related to the problem of democratic legitimacy, since the primary moral justification for parliamentary sovereignty is that parliament is democratically accountable to the electorate.[164] Under the Westminster system the role of parliament is to deliberate and pass legislation and the role of the courts is to interpret that legislation in accordance with the intention of parliament and to apply it as law. If the courts step too far outside this role, for example, by arrogating to themselves the power to re-write legislation under section 3 of the HRA, the constitutional compact will be broken. An argument for deference relating to the proper role of the courts vis-à-vis parliament cannot be dismissed as ill-founded. However, this argument is at its weakest in the field of criminal justice since the role of the courts in determining the admissibility of evidence and the correct procedures has long been accepted. In the Westminster system, matters of criminal procedure have traditionally been treated as a 'paradigm of the judiciary's special responsibility'.[165]

The third reason for deference by courts to the legislature is that the courts do not have the expertise to make decisions in complex and technical areas of policy.[166] Questions concerning economic policy, social policy and the distribution of finite resources may fairly be regarded as areas where the expertise of the legislature is greater than that of the courts. When the legislature lacks expertise in a certain area, it can commission experts to investigate the matter unlike the courts which are limited, for the most part, to the evidence adduced by the parties. Accordingly, there is a respectable argument that courts should exercise caution before intervening in complex social and economic decisions. By contrast, the field of criminal justice is one in which, by virtue of their day-to-day involvement, the courts can rightly proclaim a degree of expertise equal to or greater than that possessed by the legislature. Courts have a sense of the consequences of procedural practices by virtue of their constant exposure to them. For instance, the courts understand the likely consequences in terms of additional evidence if the prosecution is required to shoulder the burden of proof on a particular matter.

The fourth reason for deference by courts to the legislature is that the adversarial process and the techniques of judicial investigation are ill-suited to the determination of certain questions.[167] Some questions involve 'polycentric disputes' affecting

[163] Ekins (see n 152 above).

[164] Ibid) 144; K Ewing & C Gearty, 'Rocky Foundations for Labour's New Rights' [1997] *EHRLR* 146, 147–48.

[165] *International Transport Roth GmbH v Secretary of State for the Home Department* [2003] QB 728 (CA) [77] (Laws LJ).

[166] Ibid [87] (Laws LJ); Jowell (see n 152 above) 72–73; Jowell (see n 162 above) 598; Hunt (see n 152 above) 353; Pannick (see n 152 above) 550.

[167] Jowell (see n 162 above) 80.

a large number of disparate interests.[168] The adversarial process, by its nature, is not capable of taking complete account of the interests of every group with a stake in the resolution of the dispute. In many contexts, this consideration might induce the courts to defer to decisions of the legislature which has a greater capacity for deliberation, negotiation and the reaching of a fair compromise between the competing interests. However, the overarching feature of criminal trials is that the state is the 'singular antagonist of the individual'.[169] The interests at stake in a criminal trial are normally apparent, with the interest of the state in obtaining conviction set against the interest of the defendant in avoiding it. The adversarial process is capable of taking each of these interests into account. There is no reason to assume that a legislature, in imposing a persuasive burden on a defendant, has access to information that cannot adequately be assessed by the court.

It follows that, whatever the appropriate degree of deference in other areas of law, the strictest standards of review ought to apply when a legislative measure infringes upon fundamental rights in a criminal trial.[170] There is, of course, no bright-line distinction between the field of criminal justice and other areas of policy since the 'criminal law regulates a whole swathe of social and economic life in the United Kingdom.'[171] For instance, in recent times, the infringement of rights in the criminal field has been justified by reference to national security. While the criminal law is paradigmatically a question for the courts, national security is similarly a question for the executive.[172] However, as has already been argued in this book, the right of the defendant to fair procedures overrides the general interest of the community. A necessity-focused proportionality inquiry gives effect to the need to reduce the discretion available to the legislature and increase the oversight of the courts. Considerations of the appropriate level of deference, together with the methodological benefits discussed in section two, therefore support the adoption by English courts of a necessity-focused approach to the proportionality inquiry, in preference to a 'balance' approach.

[168] L Fuller 'The Forms and Limits of Adjudication' (1978) 92 *Harvard Law Review* 353; JWF Allison 'Fuller's Analysis of Polycentric Disputes and the Limits of Adjudication' [1994] *CLJ* 367; JWF Allison *A Continental Distinction in the Common Law: A Historical and Comparative Perspective on English Public Law* (Clarendon Press, Oxford 1996) ch 9. See also Allan (see n 162 above) 188–92 (supporting deference in polycentric disputes).

[169] *Iriwin Toy Ltd v Quebec (AG)* [1989] 1 SCR 927, 994; *R v Laba* [1994] 3 SCR 965, 1009 (Sopinka J, for the Court).

[170] N Blake 'Importing Proportionality: Clarification or Confusion' [2002] *EHRLRRJR-Macdonald v Canada* [1995] 3 SCR 199 277; *Libman v Quebec* (AG) [1997] 3 SCR 569 [59]–[62]; *Irwin Toy v Quebec (AG)* [1989] 1 SCR 927, 993–94; *McKinney v University of Guelph* [1990] 3 SCR 229, 304–05; *Stoffman v Vancouver General Hospital* [1990] 3 SCR 483, 521.

[171] Edwards (see n 152 above) 864.

[172] *International Transport Roth GmbH v Secretary of State for the Home Department* [2003] QB 728 (CA) [77] (Laws LJ).

C. Conclusion

This chapter has argued that, to the extent that it is appropriate for the courts to apply a proportionality test under Article 6(2), they should apply a test that focuses upon the 'necessity' of the reverse burden of proof. The reason for this is two-fold. First, the 'necessity' test is more conceptually coherent than a 'balance' test. The 'balance' test depends upon arbitrary and often unstated claims about reasonableness or fairness. By contrast, the 'necessity' test focuses attention sharply on whether alternative means will suffice to meet the legitimate objective. Specifically, in the context of reverse burdens, it focuses attention on whether an evidential burden would suffice. Second, the 'necessity' test fixes the degree of deference to the legislature at the appropriate level. Individuals are protected by the insistence that the legislature pursue its legitimate objectives in a manner that imposes the least possible restriction on rights. The following chapter will analyse each of the factors relevant to the allocation of the burden of proof, taking into account the extent to which those factors either implicate the values protected by the presumption of innocence or are relevant to a necessity focused proportionality inquiry.

6

Allocating the Burden of Proof

SINCE THE INTRODUCTION of the HRA, the English courts have identified a large number of factors that are potentially relevant to the allocation of the burden of proof. This chapter will describe the approach of the English courts to each of these factors, and also analyse that approach in order to reach conclusions about the proper weight to be attributed to each factor. The English courts have tended to treat each of the factors discussed below as relevant to the proportionality inquiry. This book has argued that proportionality ought to be applied to determine the compatibility of a reverse burden only when the rationale of protecting the innocent from wrongful conviction is attenuated. However, even if the rationale of protecting the innocent is attenuated, the rationale of promoting the rule of law continues to operate. Consequently, it does not follow in such cases that all limitations of the presumption of innocence are permissible. A proportionality inquiry must be applied to determine whether limitation of the presumption of innocence is indeed justified, taking into account the legitimate purpose for reversing the burden of proof, the need to maintain the rule of law, and the residual interest of the defendant in avoiding wrongful conviction. Some of the factors discussed below are relevant because, when present, they suggest the attenuation of the rationale of protecting the innocent. Other factors are relevant to the inquiry into the proportionality of a reverse burden.

Part A of this chapter will consider the relevance the English courts have ascribed to the seriousness of an offence. Following on from the conclusions reached in Chapter Two, it will be maintained that the seriousness of the offence cannot justify reversal of the burden of proof. Part B will show that when the potential punishment for an offence is severe the necessity for protecting the rights of the defendant is at its highest. In particular, when imprisonment is a potential penalty reverse burdens ought not usually to be permitted, unless there is a minimal risk of wrongful conviction. Part C will argue that when an offence is intended to facilitate a regulatory framework there may be a greater justification for a reverse burden, although this factor cannot be determinative. Part D will consider the relative ease of proof between prosecution and defence as a ground for reversing the burden of proof. Part E will consider the argument that there is a lesser infringement of the presumption of innocence if the prosecution is required to prove some degree of wrongfulness, or sufficient facts to make the guilt of the defendant highly likely, before the burden of proof is reversed.

A. Seriousness of the Offence

In Chapter Two, it was argued that the threat to society posed by serious offences should not be relied upon to justify limitation of the presumption of innocence. Nevertheless, the English cases have placed some degree of emphasis on the seriousness of the offence when considering the compatibility of a reverse burden with Article 6(2).

Focus on the seriousness of the offence was evident in *Kebilene*,[1] the first English case dealing with reverse burdens under the HRA. In that case, the defendants had been charged with possessing items for a terrorist purpose and were faced with the persuasive burden of proving the absence of such a purpose. Lord Hope stated that one of the relevant considerations in any case involving a reverse burden was the 'the nature of the threat faced by society which the provision is designed to combat . . .'[2] In relation to the specific threat of terrorism, Lord Hope stated: 'Society has a strong interest in preventing acts of terrorism before they are perpetrated—to spare lives of innocent people and to avoid the massive damage and dislocation to ordinary life which may follow from explosions which destroy or damage property.'[3] Lord Cooke did not express any clear view but suggested that the Strasbourg Court 'may be prepared to treat terrorism as a special subject'.[4] Hence, both Lord Hope and Lord Cooke intimated that the serious threat posed by terrorist offences could be a relevant consideration in determining the compatibility of a reverse burden. However, neither explained the precise relevance of this factor.

Similarly, in *Lambert*,[5] the threat of drugs was considered a relevant consideration in determining the compatibility of a reverse burden with Article 6(2). Lord Clyde stated that 'there is a serious consideration of the public interest in the discouragement of what is well recognized as a grave social evil, the unlawful distribution of drugs.'[6] Lord Hutton considered that the 'threat posed by drugs to the welfare of society' was so grave that, combined with the difficulty of rebutting a defence of ignorance as to the nature of the thing possessed, a reverse persuasive burden with respect to the defendant's knowledge was reasonable.[7] Hence, in the first two House of Lords cases on reverse burdens, the threat of terrorism and the threat of serious drug crime were regarded as relevant factors in determining whether a reverse burden was permissible. However, in neither case was the seriousness of the offence alone regarded as a proper ground for reversing the burden of proof.

[1] *R v DPP; ex p Kebilene* [2000] 2 AC 326 (HL).
[2] Ibid 386 (Lord Hope).
[3] Ibid 387.
[4] Ibid 373.
[5] *R v Lambert* [2002] 2 AC 545 (HL).
[6] Ibid [153].
[7] Ibid [190], [193].

In other cases, the control of less serious, but possibly more prevalent, offences has been given as a reason for reversing the burden of proof. For example, in *L v DPP*,[8] Pill LJ stated that there was 'a strong public interest in bladed articles not being carried in public without good reason' and that Parliament was entitled 'to deter the carrying of bladed or sharply pointed articles in public to the extent of placing the burden of proving a good reason on the carrier.'[9] In *R v S*[10] and *Johnstone*,[11] the courts listed the need to protect consumers from counterfeit products as a reason for requiring defendants charged with infringement of trademarks to prove their belief, on reasonable grounds, that their use of the trademark was not an infringement. In the same way, the problems associated with drink driving have been cited in support of a statute requiring a defendant to prove an absence of likelihood of driving when found in an intoxicated state in or near a motor vehicle.[12] Further, 'the very serious threat to the proper administration of criminal justice' posed by the intimidation of witnesses, has been highlighted to justify a reverse burden requiring a defendant to prove an absence of intention to pervert or interfere with the course of justice, following an assault on a witness.[13] And finally, as a justification for requiring persons charged with offering illegal immigration advice to prove their qualifications, a court has cited the need:[14]

> to combat the menace of unqualified (and potentially unscrupulous or incompetent) so called 'advisers' preying on the vulnerable and thereby undermining public confidence in the system available for those seeking immigration services or advice . . .

The interests of the community in controlling certain offences have therefore regularly been highlighted as part of the process of justifying reverse burdens of proof. Usually, however, the seriousness of the offence has not, on its own, been capable of supporting a reverse burden. The evidential problems that might be faced by the prosecution have also been influential factors.

The significance of the community interest in suppressing crimes, especially serious crime, was again considered by the House of Lords in *AG's Reference (No 4 of 2002)*.[15] That case involved the offence of membership in or professing to membership in a terrorist organisation. In the Court of Appeal,[16] Latham LJ had stated that 'there is a manifest public interest in the suppression of terrorism which requires effective measures which can meet the threat to society.'[17] However, in the House of Lords, Lord Bingham stated that: 'While security considerations must always carry weight, they do not absolve member states from their duty to

[8] *L v DPP* [2003] QB 137 (QBD).
[9] Ibid [27].
[10] *R v S* [2003] 1 Cr App R 35 (CA) [48] (Rose LJ).
[11] *Johnstone* [2003] 1 WLR 1736 (HL) [52] (Lord Nicholls).
[12] *Sheldrake v DPP* [2004] QB 487 (QBD) [112] (Henriques J, dissenting).
[13] *AG's Reference (No 1 of 2004)* [2004] 1 WLR 2111 (CA) [147] (Lord Woolf CJ, for the Court).
[14] *Clarke v R* [2008] EWCA Crim 651 [29] (Leveson LJ).
[15] *AG's Reference (No 4 of 2002)* [2005] 1 AC 264 (HL).
[16] *AG's Reference (No 4 of 2002)* [2003] EWCA Crim 762; [2005] 1 AC 264 (CA).
[17] Ibid [42].

ensure that basic standards of fairness are observed.'[18] If the serious threat posed by terrorism does not absolve states of the duty to ensure basic standards of fairness, *a fortiori* the less serious threat posed by knife crimes, counterfeit trading, drink driving etc does not absolve the state of its duty to observe standards of fairness.

Lord Bingham's statement in *AG's Reference (No 4 of 2002)* may be compared with his earlier statement in *McIntosh v Lord Advocate.*[19] There Lord Bingham stated:[20]

> The general interest of the community in suppressing crime, however important, will not justify a state in riding roughshod over the rights of a criminal defendant . . . But it is not irrelevant. Nor is the position of the defendant. In weighing the balance between the general interest of the community and the rights of the individual, it will be relevant to ask . . . what public threat the provision is directed to address . . .

This statement declares that the community interest cannot justify unfairness to the accused, but nevertheless insists that the community interest is relevant in determining what level of rights the defendant may expect. There is a fundamental illogic in this reasoning. If it is unfair to the defendant to deprive him or her of some aspect of the right to a fair trial, the deprivation of that right cannot be made fair simply because there is a conflicting community interest. Hence, if it is unfair to the defendant to relieve the prosecution of the need to prove certain matters beyond reasonable doubt, the importance to the community of suppressing a certain crime cannot negate the unfairness.

If the nature of the threat posed to society by serious crime is relevant, it must be on the basis that sometimes unfairness to the defendant will be justified in order to pursue the public interest. As was argued in Chapter Two, unfairness to the defendant cannot be justified by reference to the community interest in suppressing serious crime. Hence, proportionality should not be used to justify limitation of the presumption of innocence if that would result in unfairness to the accused, for example, by posing an unacceptable risk of wrongful conviction. However, even if this argument is rejected, and proportionality is used to assist in determining the compatibility of a reverse burden of proof, the seriousness of the offence should play no part in the proportionality inquiry.

If the seriousness of the offence is relevant to the proportionality inquiry it must be on the basis that, when the offence is serious, the need to deter criminal conduct, secure convictions and maintain the integrity of the criminal prohibition is greater, meaning that greater limitations on the presumption of innocence are justified. However, proportionality requires the interest in suppressing crime to be balanced against the interest of the defendant. When the offence is serious, the interest of the defendant in avoiding wrongful conviction is also increased. This

[18] Ibid [51]. See also ibid [21] (Lord Bingham): 'Security concerns do not absolve member states from their duty to observe basic standards of fairness.'

[19] *McIntosh v Lord Advocate* [2003] 1 AC 1078 (PC).

[20] Ibid [31].

point was made by Sachs J in the Constitutional Court of South Africa in *S v Coetzee*.[21] His Honour stated:[22]

> There is a paradox at the heart of all criminal procedure, in that the more serious the crime and the greater the public interest in securing convictions of the guilty, the more important do constitutional protections of the accused become. The starting point of any balancing enquiry where constitutional rights are concerned must be that the public interest in ensuring that innocent people are not convicted and subjected to ignominy and heavy sentences, massively outweighs the public interest in ensuring that a particular criminal is brought to book. Hence the presumption of innocence, which serves not only to protect a particular individual on trial, but to maintain public confidence in the enduring integrity and security of the legal system. Reference to the prevalence and severity of a certain crime therefore does not add anything new or special to the balancing exercise. The perniciousness of the offence is one of the givens, against which the presumption of innocence is pitted from the beginning, not a new element to be put into the scales as part of a justificatory balancing exercise. If this were not so, the ubiquity and ugliness argument could be used in relation to murder, rape, car-jacking, housebreaking, drug-smuggling, corruption . . . the list is unfortunately almost endless, and nothing would be left of the presumption of innocence, save, perhaps, for its relic status as a doughty defender of rights in the most trivial of cases.

This statement has met considerable approval in the English courts.[23] In *Lambert*,[24] Lord Steyn quoted Sachs J and concluded: 'The logic of this reasoning is inescapable.'[25] To summarise, the seriousness of the offence, at first glance, appears relevant to the 'balancing' inquiry in the proportionality test. The more serious the offence, the more compelling is the community interest in prevention, deterrence and punishment. However, at the same time, the individual on trial has an increased interest in avoiding wrongful conviction, since the consequences in terms of punishment and censure are more severe. In terms of a 'balance' between the community interest and individual rights, the seriousness of the offence has no net impact. Hence, even if a proportionality inquiry is applied, the seriousness of the offence should be regarded as irrelevant. Rather than focusing on the seriousness of the offence, courts must focus upon matters that are relevant to problems of proof, or upon matters which suggest the interests of the defendant are not seriously threatened.

21 *S v Coetzee* 1997 (3) SA 527 (CC).

22 Ibid [220].

23 It is cited with approval in *R v Lambert* [2002] 2 AC 545 (HL) [34] (Lord Steyn); *McIntosh v Lord Advocate* [2003] 1 AC 1078 (PC) [31] (Lord Bingham); *R v Johnstone* [2003] 1 WLR 1736 (HL) [48]–[49] (Lord Nicholls). See also *DPP v Wright* [2009] EWHC 105 (Admin) [68]: 'We note that other versions of this paradox may be constructed. A version espoused by [counsel] is; the less serious the crime, the less important constitutional protection of the accused becomes. But again: the less serious the crime, the lesser the public interest in securing convictions of the guilty; and therefore the lesser the need for a legal burden of proof on the accused. There is a danger, of course, that these become just word games.'

24 [2002] 2 AC 545 (HL).

25 Ibid [34].

B. Penalty

This part will show that the penalty associated with the offence is relevant and in some cases may be determinative when considering the compatibility of a reverse burden with Article 6(2). There is, of course, a correlation between the seriousness of an offence and the penalty associated with that offence. However, we should be clear at the outset that it is the consequences of conviction, in particular the penalty,[26] and not the seriousness of the offence itself, that have an impact on the allocation of the burden of proof. The penalty associated with an offence is relevant because the impact upon the rights of the defendant will be greater if he or she is subjected to more serious consequences.

The English courts have emphasised the penalty associated with the offence when determining the compatibility of a reverse burden, but their approach has been neither consistent nor principled.[27] In *Lambert*,[28] the potential penalty upon conviction for an offence of possessing a controlled drug with intent to supply was life imprisonment. This penalty was an important factor contributing to Lord Steyn's *obiter dictum* that a reverse burden with respect to knowledge of the contents of the package was incompatible with Article 6(2). According to Lord Steyn, the high maximum penalty suggested that knowledge of the controlled drug was an important part of the offence so that it would be unacceptable to allow a conviction in the absence of proof of knowledge.[29] Lord Steyn concluded it was unreasonable that 'a guilty verdict may be returned in respect of an offence punishable by life imprisonment even though the jury may consider that it is reasonably possible that the accused had been duped.'[30]

One other case has relied (in part) on the severity of the penalty as a reason for finding that a reverse burden is not compatible with Article 6(2). In *AG's Reference (No 4 of 2002)*,[31] the offence of membership or professing to membership in a terrorist organisation carried a potential penalty of ten years imprisonment. The defendant could escape conviction by proving that he or she had joined the organisation before it was proscribed and had not taken part in its activities since proscription. Lord Bingham described the penalty of ten years' imprisonment as 'severe' and included it amongst a list of six reasons for holding that the reverse burden was incompatible with Article 6(2).[32] This suggests that the severity of the

[26] While the stigma and censure associated with a conviction should not be ignored, it will normally be difficult to determine the degree of stigma and censure attached to crimes, and the degree will in any case very depending on the circumstances of the crime. Focus should therefore be placed on the penalty: P Hogg *Constitutional Law of Canada (Looseleaf)* 5th edn (Thomson Carswell, Toronto 2007) [47]–[34] fn 171 (criticising the focus on stigma in Canadian cases under s 7 of the Charter).

[27] See IH Dennis 'Reverse Onuses and the Presumption of Innocence: In Search of Principle' [2005] *Crim LR*901, 913–14.

[28] [2002] 2 AC 545 (HL).

[29] Ibid [35].

[30] Ibid [38].

[31] [2005] 1 AC 264 (HL).

[32] Ibid [51].

penalty is relevant to the determination of compatibility but is just one factor to be weighed among many. In three other cases involving a penalty of imprisonment, it has been held that a reverse burden was unjustifiable, although no emphasis was placed in those cases on the severity of the penalty.[33]

If the possibility of imprisonment militates against the reversal of the burden of proof, the absence of that possibility may make a reverse burden easier to justify. When the penalty for an offence is minimal, the interest of the defendant in avoiding wrongful conviction is reduced (but not abrogated), so that the rationale for the presumption of innocence is attenuated. In some cases, the non-custodial nature of the penalty has been emphasised as a reason supporting the imposition of a reverse burden. In *Davies*,[34] the Court of Appeal considered an offence of failing to comply with the obligation to conduct a business so as not to expose others to risks to their health or safety. The relevant statute provided for a defence if the business operator could prove that all reasonably practicable steps had been taken to ensure health and safety. Tuckey LJ emphasised that the only available penalty upon conviction was a monetary fine and noted that the absence of a risk of imprisonment was 'undoubtedly an important factor in deciding whether Parliament has struck the right balance in this legislation.'[35] Similarly, in *Grundy & Co Excavations Ltd*,[36] the Court of Appeal considered an offence of felling trees without a licence, the penalty for which was a fine. Reverse burdens with respect to the available defences were held to be compatible with Article 6(2), in part because 'the offence involves only a monetary penalty'.[37] Finally, in *International Transport Roth v Home Secretary*,[38] the Court of Appeal considered a penalty of £2000 imposed on truck drivers for each illegal entrant into the UK concealed in a truck at a UK border crossing. The penalty could be avoided if the truck driver proved that he or she had no knowledge of the illegal entrant, or reasonable grounds to suspect concealment, and had put in place a system to prevent concealment. Simon Brown LJ held that the reverse burden was not inconsistent with Article 6(2) (although he held the scheme overall was inconsistent with Article 6(1)).[39] In reaching this decision, Simon Brown LJ distinguished *Lambert* since that case involved a penalty of life imprisonment, while the instant case involved only a financial penalty.[40]

[33] *R v Keogh* [2007] 1 WLR 1500 (CA); *R v Carass* [2002] 1 WLR 1714 (CA); *R v Daniel* [2003] 1 Cr App R 6 (CA). The latter two cases were overruled by a five-judge panel of the Court of Appeal in *AG's Reference (No 1 of 2004)* [2004] 1 WLR 2111 (CA) [84] (Lord Woolf CJ, for the Court). The House of Lords has since agreed that these cases were wrongly decided: *Sheldrake v DPP; AG's Reference (No 4 of 2002)* [2005] 1 AC 264 (HL) [32] (Lord Bingham).

[34] *R v Davies* [2003] ICR 586 (CA).

[35] Ibid [19]. The House of Lords reached the same conclusion in respect of the statute, but emphasising differing reasons in *R v Chargot Limited* [2009] 1 WLR 1 (HL).

[36] *R (Grundy & Co Excavations Ltd) v Halton Division Magistrates Court* (2003) 167 JP 387 (QBD).

[37] Ibid [66].

[38] *International Transport Roth v Home Secretary* [2003] QB 728 (CA).

[39] Ibid [46]. Jonathan Parker LJ held the reverse burden itself was disproportionate: ibid [182]. Laws LJ (dissenting) held the reverse burden was not disproportionate nor was the overall scheme unfair, and referred to the trivial nature of the penalty in support: ibid [93].

[40] Ibid [44].

Taken on their own, the cases discussed above might suggest a pattern by which reverse burdens will be inconsistent with Article 6(2) whenever imprisonment is a possible penalty, and consistent when the penalty is non-custodial. However, this pattern is breached by numerous cases in which reverse burdens have been upheld in respect of offences carrying custodial sentences ranging from three months to life-imprisonment.[41] Most notably, in *Johnstone*,[42] the House of Lords upheld a reverse burden associated with an offence of trademark infringement carrying a possible penalty of ten years' imprisonment. Lord Nicholls acknowledged that: 'The more serious the punishment which may flow from conviction, the more compelling must be the reasons [for a reverse burden].'[43] Nevertheless, the House of Lords held, *obiter*, that a reverse burden with respect to knowledge of the infringement was a proportionate limitation on the presumption of innocence. Accordingly, the English courts have not adopted a rule about the allocation of the burden of proof based on the possibility of a custodial sentence.

If there were to be such a rule, it would be controversial whether the court should focus its attention on the maximum potential penalty, or on the penalty usually applied. This issue was raised in *R v S*[44] where the Court of Appeal considered the same statutory reverse burden that was later upheld in *Johnstone*. In *R v S*, Rose LJ noted that the potential penalty for the offence was as high as ten years. However, Rose LJ considered it acceptable to look to the penalty normally imposed rather than the potential penalty. Rose LJ stated:[45]

> That the maximum available sentence under s 92 is as much as 10 years—quite apart from the prospects of an unlimited fine and confiscation orders—cannot be overlooked . . . it is, indeed, an important point. But we do not think it unprincipled also to have regard to the reality of the matter: which is that most cases under s 92 are brought in the magistrates' court and, of those, the majority result (in the case of conviction) in a fine.

Rose LJ went on to cite the conviction figures for the period from 1998 to 2000 which revealed that fewer than 10 percent of the convictions for infringement of trade mark resulted in an immediate custodial sentence, and that there was no sentence longer than five years.[46] The low actual sentences imposed for the offence were therefore held to be a factor supporting the imposition of a reverse burden of proof.[47]

[41] *Parker v DPP* (2000) 165 JP 213 (6 months); *R v Drummond* [2002] 2 Cr App R 25 (CA) (10 years); *R v S* [2003] 1 Cr App R 35 (CA) (10 years); *L v DPP* [2003] QB 137 (QBD) (2 years); *R v Matthews* [2004] QB 690 (CA) (2 years); *AG's Reference (No 1 of 2004)* [2004] 1 WLR 2111 (CA) (various offences, ranging from 2 years to automatic life sentence); *Sheldrake v DPP* [2005] 1 AC 264 (HL) (3 months); *DPP v Barker* (2004) 168 JP 617 (QBD) (6 months); *Clarke v R* [2008] EWCA Crim 651 (2 years). The maximum penalties listed with each case are those available when the trial is upon indictment.

[42] [2003] 1 WLR 1736 (HL).

[43] Ibid [50].

[44] [2003] 1 Cr App R 35 (CA).

[45] Ibid [48].

[46] Ibid.

[47] Similarly, in the Divisional Court in *Sheldrake*, Henriques J (dissenting) was prepared to uphold a reverse burden relying in part on the fact that, while there was a possible penalty of three months imprisonment, the standard sentence recommended in Wilkinson's Road Traffic Offences was a fine on level 4 and 10 penalty points: *Sheldrake v DPP* [2004] QB 487 (QBD) [96]–[97].

The question of whether courts should focus on the actual or maximum penalties when considering the justifiability of reverse burdens is an important issue of principle. On the one hand, focusing on the maximum penalty would result in more reverse burdens being read as evidential and therefore provide greater protection for the presumption of innocence. On the other hand, focusing on the penalties actually imposed would involve a more realistic appraisal of the likely degree of interference with the presumption. The best argument in support of having regard to the maximum penalty is that, in allocating the burden of proof, the court is interpreting a statute to decide whether a burden should be read as evidential or persuasive. The court is not deciding whether there is a breach of the presumption of innocence in individual cases. The interpretation of the statute must take into account the highest penalty available so that the interpretation of the statute cannot result in unfairness. Some support for this approach may be found in the Strasbourg cases under Article 6 on the meaning of 'criminal', where the Court focuses on the potential penalty, rather than the actual or most likely penalty.[48]

Andrew Ashworth has stated that: 'It ought surely to be insisted that, where deprivation of liberty is a possible penalty, there is no place for a reversal of the burden of proof.'[49] It would be possible for the courts to adopt a rule stating that reverse burdens must not be used when there is a possible penalty of imprisonment. Such a rule would have certain advantages. It would clarify that the presumption of innocence cannot be compromised when the liberty of the defendant is at stake. Since the deprivation of liberty is the most severe consequence imposed upon conviction, the interests of defendants would be protected in an important way. Further, a prohibition on reverse burdens in cases where imprisonment is a possible penalty would be a clear rule, capable of simple application by the courts. It would bypass the need for a great deal of difficult and convoluted analysis of the context of offences. Lower courts could apply the rule with certainty. It would be clear to statutory drafters and legislators alike that a reverse burden associated with an offence carrying a sentence of imprisonment will always be treated by the courts as an evidential burden.

The application of this rule would involve two forms of practical difficulty. First, some reverse burdens apply to more than one offence. One offence to which the burden applies might carry a penalty of imprisonment, while the other does not.[50] The 'imprisonment' rule would require the statutory provision creating the reverse burden to be read differently with respect to each offence. This leads to the difficult conclusion that the same words in a statutory provision must be read dif-

[48] *Engel v Netherlands* (App No 5100/71) (1979) 1 EHRR 647 [85]; *Demicoli v Malta* (App No 13057/87) (1992) 14 EHRR 47 [34].

[49] A Ashworth 'Four Threats to the Presumption of Innocence' (2006) 10 *E & P* 241, 262.

[50] See eg Health and Safety at Work Act 1974, s 40 which requires the defendant to prove that reasonably practicable steps were taken to avoid committing an offence under the Act. Section 40 applies to every offence under the Act. Under s 33, some offences carry a maximum penalty of a fine, while others a maximum penalty of between six months and two years imprisonment.

ferently depending on the offence to which the provision is applied. While this result is linguistically problematic, it is still relatively certain. The Court of Appeal has already interpreted one reverse burden provision as imposing a persuasive burden in respect of one offence, but an evidential burden in respect of another.[51]

The second complication is that some offences carry an offence of imprisonment if tried on indictment, but only a fine if tried in the Magistrates' Court. The statutory provision might need to be read differently depending on the method of the trial. In *R v Hunt*,[52] Lord Griffiths referred to this factor as a reason for insisting that the allocation of burdens of proof should be the same in trials on indictment as in summary trials. His Lordship stated: 'The law would have developed on absurd lines if in respect of the same offence the burden of proof today differed according to whether the case was heard by the magistrates or on indictment.'[53] However, the necessity for equiparation between trials on indictment and summary trials is not as clear as it may seem. It is not wholly unprincipled to suggest that a choice should be allowed between trial on indictment, which carries a heavier potential penalty, but also a greater degree of procedural protection, and summary trial, which carries a lesser penalty, but without the procedural protection. Further, if equiparation between the magistrates' courts and the higher courts is desirable, it could be achieved by insisting that each statutory reverse burden is interpreted according to the penalty that would be imposed in the higher courts. Hence, practical problems that might be caused by a general rule prohibiting reverse burdens in respect of imprisonable offences are not sufficient to undermine the case in favour of such a rule.

Nevertheless, there is a reason of principle for eschewing an inflexible prohibition on reverse burdens in cases where imprisonment is a potential penalty. It was argued above that a minimal penalty makes a reverse burden more likely to be justified because the rationale of protecting the innocent is attenuated.[54] However, this rationale is also attenuated when the risk of wrongful conviction is low. This might occur, for example, in cases where the defendant, if innocent, could discharge the burden with ease or where the defence allowed to the defendant is inherently improbable. These situations are considered in parts D and E, below. In these situations, even if there is a potential penalty of imprisonment, it could be argued that limits on the presumption of innocence are acceptable. Hence, before it can be concluded that a reverse burden is impermissible, it must also be considered whether there is a low risk of wrongful conviction. The possibility of imprisonment as a penalty is a strong indicator that reversal of the burden of proof is unacceptable. But it should not be determinative in every case.

[51] In *AG's Reference (No 1 of 2004)* [2004] 1 WLR 2111 (CA), the Court of Appeal held that the burden imposed by s 352 of the Insolvency Act 1986 was to be read as a persuasive burden when applied to the offence created by s 353(1)(b), but an evidential burden when applied to the offence created by s 357(1): ibid [90], [95].

[52] *R v Hunt* [1987] AC 352 (HL).

[53] Ibid 373.

[54] See Ch 2.

C. Regulatory Offences

There has been a persistent suggestion both in English cases and in cases from other jurisdictions that it is more justifiable to impose a burden of proof on a defendant if the offence is of a regulatory nature rather than truly criminal. As will be seen below, it is not possible to draw a clear distinction between 'regulatory' offences and offences that are 'truly criminal'. However, for the purposes of discussion, a rough distinction can be drawn between the two types of offences.[55] Criminal offences are those which involve conduct that is so reprehensible that it ought to be prohibited completely. Common examples of such crimes are murder, sexual assault, fraud, robbery and theft. By contrast, regulatory offences relate to conduct that has the potential to create conditions dangerous to others, but which is not so obviously wrongful that it should be prohibited in its entirety. A regulatory regime is imposed in order to ensure that the relevant activity is carried out in a way that minimises the risk of harm. Typical examples of regulatory regimes include workplace health and safety, environmental protection, licensing regimes and road traffic codes.

There are two features commonly associated with regulatory offences that are said to be relevant to the allocation of the burden of proof: (1) that regulatory offences may carry minimal penalties and minimal censure; and (2) that regulatory regimes rely upon strict compliance for their efficacy, such that reversal of the burden of proof will sometimes be necessary. The following two sections consider these features in turn.

1. Minimal Censure and Penalty

The tentative definition of regulatory offences adopted above suggests that such offences are regarded as less serious and do not involve true moral culpability. Regulatory offences, it has been said, often 'carry with them no social disgrace or infamy'[56] and involve 'no real moral stigma or obloquy'.[57] Since the offence is less serious, the consequences for the defendant in terms of penalty and censure will be reduced. As discussed in part B above, when the consequences of conviction are minor, the rationale of protecting the innocent is attenuated and limitations on the presumption of innocence are easier to justify. If an offence carries a minimal penalty and a low degree of censure, the reversal of the burden is more likely to be acceptable. This is true of any offence, whether or not it is characterised as regulatory. Significantly, however, the fact that an offence takes place within a regulatory

[55] See *R v The Wholesale Travel Group Inc* [1991] 3 SCR 154, 218–20 (Cory J).

[56] *R v Lambert* [2002] 2 AC 545 (HL) [154] (Lord Clyde). Cited with approval in *R v S* [2003] 1 Cr App R 35 (CA) [48] (Rose LJ, for the Court).

[57] *R (Grundy & Co Excavations Ltd) v Halton Division Magistrates Court* (2003) 167 JP 387 (QBD) [66] (Clarke LJ).

regime may bear no relation to the censure, stigma or penalty associated with the offence. Some regulatory offences attract high penalties including imprisonment,[58] and for the purposes of allocating the burden of proof, it is the penalty, rather than the characterisation of the offence that is more important.

Further, regulatory offences do not always attract a lesser degree of censure and stigma. The distinction between regulatory offences and true crimes might be thought to mirror the distinction between offences *malum in se* and offences *malum prohibitum*. Offences are said to be *malum in se* 'when they criminalize conduct that would be considered morally wrongful even if not prohibited' while offences are *malum prohibitum* 'when they criminalize conduct that is considered morally wrongful, if at all, primarily because it is prohibited.'[59] However, it does not follow from this that all regulatory offences involve a low degree of moral culpability.[60]

First, some regulatory regimes are intended to facilitate co-operation in a field where multiple actors are operating.[61] Non-compliance with the regime reduces the efficacy of co-operation and is consequently morally wrongful. For example, driving on the right side of the road is not morally wrongful in a pre-regulatory environment, but once a system is established (either by custom or by law) requiring driving on the left it may become so. Second, a regulatory regime is usually adopted to pursue a certain value such as protection of the public or the environment. The pursuit of this value provides a reason for complying with the regulation that is independent of the regulation itself.[62] Protecting the environment, protecting employees from a dangerous workplace, or protecting the public from unsafe products are all valuable goals, and the failure to comply with obligations imposed in pursuit of those goals is itself morally culpable.[63] Third, failure to comply with a regulatory regime can have serious consequences for other people.

[58] See Trade Marks Act 1994, s 92(1)(c), treated as having a regulatory character in *R v S* [2003] 1 Cr App R 35 (CA) [48] (Rose LJ).

[59] S Green 'Six Senses of Strict Liability: A Plea for Formalism' in AP Simester (ed) *Appraising Strict Liability* (OUP, Oxford 2005) 1, 9, fn 38. Coke CJ understood this distinction as reflecting the divergence between common law and statute: *Case of Proclamations* (1612) 12 Co Rep 74, 76. William Blackstone drew the distinction along similar lines to Green: W Blackstone *Commentaries on the Laws of England: Book the First* (Clarendon Press, Oxford 1765) 54, 57. Jeremy Bentham scathingly criticised Blackstone's distinction: 'This is the first occasion of our hearing of the acute distinction between *mala in se*, and *mala prohibita*; which being so shrewd and sounding so pretty, and being made in Latin, has no sort of occasion to have any meaning to it: accordingly it has none.' J Bentham *A Comment on the Commentaries* (Clarendon Press, Oxford 1928) (original 1776) 80. The distinction has been treated with ambivalence or even outright rejected in various cases: *Regazzoni v K.C. Sethia (1944) Ltd* [1958] AC 301 (HL) 306 (Lord Reid); *Bensley v Bignold* (1822) 5 B & Ald 335, 341 (Best J); *Aubert v Maze* (1801) 2 Bos & Pul 371, 375 (Rooke J); *Jackson v Harrison* (1978) 138 CLR 438 (HCA) 455 (Mason J).

[60] See S Green, Stuart P, 'Why It's a Crime to Tear the Tag off a Mattress: Overcriminalization and the Moral Content of Regulatory Offences' (1997) 46 *Emory Law Journal* 1533.

[61] J Finnis 'The Authority of Law in the Predicament of Contemporary Social Theory' (1985) 1 *Notre Dame Journal of Law, Ethics & Public Policy* 115, 136. See also J Finnis, *Natural Law and Natural Rights* (Oxford: Clarendon Press, 1980) chs 9, 10.

[62] AP Simester & S Shute 'On the General Part in Criminal Law' in S Shute & AP Simester (eds) *Criminal Law Theory: Doctrines of the General Part* (OUP, Oxford 2002) 1, 10–11. See also J Raz *The Authority of Law: Essays on Law and Morality* (Oxford: Oxford University Press, 1979) 248–249.

[63] D Hamer 'The Presumption of Innocence and Reverse Burdens: A Balancing Act' (2007) 66 *CLJ* 142, 149.

For example, in *R v Davies*[64] and in *R v Chargot Limited*,[65] the employer's failure to maintain a safe workplace resulted in a death. Therefore, it will not always be true that regulatory offences involve a low degree of censure and stigma.

Another factor that might be thought to distinguish regulatory offences from the truly criminal is that the former category involves conduct that is not prohibited in its entirety, while the latter involves conduct that is always wrongful. Regulatory regimes provide guidelines within certain spheres of social or commercial activity, while criminal offences prohibit the activity altogether. Following this distinction, it might be thought that regulatory offences will always carry a lower degree of censure and stigma because the offender has fallen short of a standard in performing an otherwise permissible act, rather than engaging in an act that is always wrongful. This may be true in some cases. However, it is not a sure ground for distinguishing serious and non-serious offences. Drug offences, for example, are part of a regime for the regulation of dangerous substances. It is recognised that sometimes possession or sale of drugs is not wrong and should not be criminal.[66] However, drug offences in the absence of the qualifying conditions are usually regarded as among the most serious of offences. The degree of censure and stigma associated with an offence must be determined independently of whether the offence is characterised as regulatory.

The label attached to an offence ought not to affect the allocation of the burden of proof. When allocating the burden of proof, what is 'ultimately important are not labels . . . but the values at stake in the particular context.'[67] The severity of the penalty reflects what is at stake for the defendant and is therefore relevant to the allocation of the burden of proof. By contrast, the characterisation of the offence as regulatory is not a helpful guide.

2. An Effective Regulatory Regime

It has been argued that when an offence takes place within a regulatory regime it is necessary for the defendant to bear the burden of proof with respect to some matters in order for the regime to be workable. For example, in *R v S*,[68] Rose LJ, considering a reverse burden in an offence of trademark infringement, stated that: 'an effective and workable regime in this context cannot sensibly depend on proof by the prosecution in every case of a trader's absence of belief on reasonable grounds that the goods were genuine . . .'[69] Similarly, Cory J in the Canadian Supreme Court has stated that:[70]

[64] [2003] ICR 586 (CA).
[65] [2009] 1 WLR 1 (HL).
[66] See Misuse of Drugs Act 1971, s 7.
[67] *R v The Wholesale Travel Group Inc* [1991] 3 SCR 154, 209 (La Forest J, dissenting). See also *S v Coetzee* 1997 (3) SA 527 (CC) [43] (Langa J).
[68] [2003] 1 Cr App R 35 (CA).
[69] Ibid [48].
[70] *R v The Wholesale Travel Group Inc* [1991] 3 SCR 154, 246–47 (Cory J).

> [T]he enforcement of regulatory offences would be rendered virtually impossible if the Crown were required to prove negligence beyond a reasonable doubt . . . Governments would be forced to devote tremendous expenditure, in terms of monetary and human resources, to regulatory enforcement mechanisms. Armies of investigators and experts would be required in order to garner sufficient evidence to establish negligence or disprove due diligence beyond a reasonable doubt . . .

The enforcement of many regulatory regimes is in the hands of an agency with a limited budget and the requirement to establish certain elements of an offence beyond reasonable doubt could not be met within those constraints.[71] Given that regulatory regimes often provide great benefit to the public in terms of protection from dangerous conduct, it might be regarded as unacceptable to allow a regime to collapse because of a want of proof.

There is a need to be highly cautious of this argument as it is closely aligned with the proposition that the individual right to be presumed innocent must sometimes be subjugated to the community interest. As argued in Chapter Two, the public benefit that can be derived from the enforcement of a criminal prohibition cannot be used to justify the reversal of the burden of proof. If the need to maintain an effective regulatory regime is relevant, it can be only in cases where the rationale for the presumption of innocence is attenuated, either because the penalty is minimal or the risk of wrongful conviction is low. In such cases, the need to maintain an effective regulatory regime would become a relevant factor in the proportionality inquiry. It could be said that it is 'necessary' to impose a reverse burden if the regulatory regime would be unworkable in the absence of the reverse burden.

Several other features often found in regulatory regimes support the argument that it is necessary to reverse the burden of proof. First, people operating within a regulatory framework commonly do so voluntarily and with knowledge of the regulations with which they are expected to comply. This was regarded as an important factor in *R v Davies*,[72] where the Court of Appeal considered whether an employer should bear the burden of proving that all practicable steps were taken to ensure a safe workplace. Tuckey LJ, delivering the reasons for the Court, stated:[73]

> The reversal of the burden of proof takes into account the fact that duty-holders are persons who have chosen to engage in work or commercial activity (probably for gain) and are in charge of it. They are not therefore unengaged or disinterested members of the public, and in choosing to operate in a regulated sphere of activity they must be taken to have accepted the regulatory controls that go with it.

Lord Hope paraphrased and approved this reasoning in *Chargot Limited*, describing it as the most important reason for holding that the reverse burden was not disproportionate.[74]

[71] Dennis (see n 27 above) 916.
[72] [2003] ICR 586 (CA). This passage is very similar to a passage in *R v The Wholesale Travel Group Inc* [1991] 3 SCR 154, 229 (Cory J).
[73] Ibid [25].
[74] [2009] 1 WLR 1 (HL) [29].

Similarly, in *Johnstone*,[75] the House of Lords considered whether a reverse burden could be justified in an offence of trademark infringement. Lord Nicholls considered it relevant that: 'Those who trade in brand products are aware of the need to deal with reputable suppliers and keep records and of the risks they take if they do not.'[76] This factor, together with the practical difficulties the prosecution would have in proving the trader knew the use of the trademark was an infringement, were regarded as 'compelling reasons' for reversing the burden of proof.[77]

The tenor of the 'voluntary involvement' argument is that it is not onerous to expect a person operating within a regulatory environment to comply with the regulations. This argument is sometimes coupled with a related argument that those who take part in regulated spheres can reasonably be expected to keep proof of their compliance with the regulations. Hence, in the decision of the South African Constitutional Court in *S v Coetzee*,[78] O'Regan J stated that, in a regime which imposed the burden of proof on the defendant, his or her regulatory obligations include an obligation to be able to prove compliance. O'Regan J stated that when a reverse burden is used: 'the accused must not only act with diligence to avoid the commission of offences, but he or she must have proof that such action was taken. If such proof is not kept, then it may not be possible to establish the necessary defence.'[79] RA Duff has adopted the same argument to justify reverse burdens.[80] He argues that when a person is obliged by a regulatory regime to prove compliance, the inability to tender such proof is itself evidence that the defendant has not complied. So, for example, if a machine was proven to be unsafe, and the defendant was unable to show what steps had been taken to ensure the machine was safe, it could be taken to be proved beyond reasonable doubt that such steps were not taken.[81]

Taken to its extreme, this argument could result in persons being convicted of a serious regulatory offence when, in truth, their only offence was the failure to keep proper records. Nevertheless, provided that the rationale for the presumption of innocence is attenuated, the voluntary participation in a regulated sphere, together with the obligation to keep records, might be relevant to showing that it was necessary to reverse the burden of proof. These factors would be relevant in the sense that considerations of 'balance' are included within the 'necessity' test. The need for the effective operation of the regulatory regime, and the importance of the goals pursued by the regime, would be balanced against the degree of unfairness caused to the defendant. It is not unfair to expect a person who voluntarily takes part in a regulated sphere to comply with the regulations in that sphere and to keep evidence capable of demonstrating compliance. Consequently, the fact

[75] [2003] 1 WLR 1736 (HL).
[76] Ibid [52].
[77] Ibid.
[78] 1997 (3) SA 527 (CC) [195] (O'Regan J).
[79] Ibid [195].
[80] RA Duff 'Strict Liability, Legal Presumptions, and the Presumption of Innocence' in AP Simester (ed) *Appraising Strict Liability* (OUP, Oxford 2005) 125, 138.
[81] Ibid 139.

that an offence takes place within a regulatory framework can have relevance in some cases to the allocation of the burden of proof.

D. Knowledge and Ease of Proof

The difficulty which the prosecution might face in the absence of a reverse burden or a presumption is said to be a relevant factor in the determination of the compatibility of a reverse burden with Article 6(2).[82] Practical difficulties for the prosecution in proving a crime cannot independently demonstrate that a reverse burden is acceptable. There are difficulties associated with the proof of nearly all crimes. If the presumption of innocence is to have any meaning the prosecution must be required, in the ordinary case, to clear such hurdles.[83] In respect of some matters, however, the prosecution would be faced with insurmountable hurdles in satisfying a burden of proof, while the defendant, if innocent, would be expected to satisfy a reverse burden more easily. In a related sense, it has been suggested that a reverse burden is more likely to be justifiable if it relates to a matter within the knowledge of the defendant.[84] Section one below will consider the argument that a reverse burden is more likely to be justified when proof is difficult for the prosecution, but comparatively easy for the defendant. Section two will consider the relevance of 'peculiar knowledge' within the possession of the defendant but not available to the prosecution.

1. Relative Ease of Proof

It has been suggested that it is permissible to reverse the burden of proof when it would be very difficult for the prosecution to satisfy the burden but conspicuously easy for the defendant to satisfy it.[85] Prior to the HRA, the relative ease with which each party could be expected to prove a matter was said to be relevant to the allocation of the burden of proof with respect to that matter. The House of Lords highlighted the relevance of this factor in a civil case, *Nimmo v Alexander Cowan & Sons Ltd*.[86] In that case, the House of Lords held by majority that an employer bore the burden of proving that all reasonably practicable steps had been taken to

[82] *Sheldrake v DPP; AG's Reference (No 4 of 2002)* [2005] 1 AC 264 (HL) [21] (Lord Bingham).

[83] V Tadros & S Tierney 'The Presumption of Innocence and the Human Rights Act' (2004) 67 *MLR* 402, 426.

[84] *R v DPP; ex p Kebilene* [2000] 2 AC 326 (HL) 386 (Lord Hope); *McIntosh v Lord Advocate* [2003] 1 AC 1078 (PC) [45] (Lord Hope); *L v DPP* [2003] QB 137 (QBD) [27] (Pill LJ); *International Transport Roth GmbH v Secretary of State for the Home Department* [2003] QB 728 (CA) [44] (Simon Brown LJ); *R v S* [2003] 1 Cr App R 35 (CA) [48] (Rose LJ, for the Court); *R v Johnstone* [2003] 1 WLR 1736 (HL) [50] (Lord Nicholls); *Sheldrake v DPP; AG's Reference (No 4 of 2002)* [2005] 1 AC 264 (HL) [41] (Lord Bingham).

[85] Ashworth (see n 49 above) 266–67.

[86] *Nimmo v Alexander Cowan & Sons Ltd* [1968] AC 107 (HL(Sc)).

ensure that a workplace was safe.[87] One reason given for allocating the burden of proof in this way was that the employer was in a better position than an employee, or a surviving relative of a deceased employee, to give evidence and to prove what steps were reasonably practicable.[88]

Lord Griffiths applied the same criteria in the context of a criminal case in *R v Hunt.*[89] Applying the decision of the majority in *Nimmo*, Lord Griffiths stated:[90]

> Their Lordships were in agreement that if the linguistic construction of the statute did not clearly indicate on whom the burden should lie the court should look to other considerations to determine the intention of Parliament, such as the mischief at which the Act was aimed and practical considerations affecting the burden of proof and, in particular, the ease or difficulty that the respective parties would encounter in discharging the burden. I regard this last consideration as one of great importance, for surely Parliament can never lightly be taken to have intended to impose an onerous duty on a defendant to prove his innocence in a criminal case, and a court should be very slow to draw any such inference from the language of a statute. When all the cases are analysed, those in which the courts have held that the burden lies on the defendant are cases in which the burden can be easily discharged.

It followed that the burden of proving the proportion of morphine in a bag of mixed powder rested on the prosecution. If the burden of proving the composition of the substance was placed on the defendant, he or she would have been 'faced with very real practical difficulties in discharging it' since the suspected substance was typically seized by the police and not returned.[91] Lord Griffiths emphasised that the burden should not be on the defendant when it would be difficult for him or her to discharge. A corollary to this is that, if a reverse burden would be easy for the defendant to discharge, it will be easier to justify.[92]

[87] Factories Act 1961, s 29(1).

[88] [1968] AC 107 (HL(Sc)) 122 (Lord Guest), 125–26 (Lord UpJohn), 132 (Lord Pearson). Lord Wilberforce (dissenting) argued that the relative ease of proof was a matter of policy rather than statutory construction: ibid 129. Lord Reid considered the relative ease of proof relevant, but argued that an employee could retain an expert witness to assist in proving what steps were reasonably practicable: ibid 115. Lord Reid noted that s 29(1) also created criminal liability and reasoned that the burden of proof in a civil case should be assigned on the same basis as in a criminal case: ibid. Lord Reid considered it would be inappropriate in a criminal case for the defendant to be convicted when the prosecution had not proved the failure to take all reasonably practicable steps, since this was one of the 'essential elements' of the offence: ibid.

[89] *R v Hunt* [1987] AC 352 (HL).

[90] Ibid 374. Lord Keith (at 363) and Lord Mackay (at 378) agreed with Lord Griffiths. Lord Ackner also noted that 'practical consequences of holding that the burden of proof rested on one party or the other' were relevant to the allocation of the burden: ibid 384. Lord Templeman, in a brief judgment, did not refer to the relative ease of proof: ibid 363–65.

[91] Ibid 377. One might add that the average defendant does not have easy access to facilities for proving the composition of chemical substances.

[92] *Cf* P Roberts 'The Presumption of Innocence Brought Home? Kebilene Deconstructed' (2002) 118 *LQR* 41, 66: 'The essential point to grasp is that ease of proof is, of itself, no reason whatsoever to depart from Woolmington by requiring a defendant to prove innocence. Ease of proof is relevant only in the negative sense, that an otherwise justifiable reverse onus provision becomes insupportable if the defendant's probative burden would in practice be too great.'

Under the HRA, the English courts have continued to suggest that a reverse burden will be easier to justify if the defendant could be expected to discharge the burden with relative ease. In *Lambert*,[93] Lord Clyde suggested that a factor supporting the requirement for the defendant to prove an absence of knowledge concerning the drugs he was carrying was that 'proof may be relatively easy for him'.[94] In *AG's Reference (No 1 of 2004)*,[95] the Court of Appeal, purporting to lay down definitive advice for lower courts, stated: 'The easier it is for the accused to discharge the burden the more likely it is that the reverse burden is justified.'[96] The House of Lords did not fully endorse the Court of Appeal's advice when it addressed the reverse burden problem again in *Sheldrake*.[97] However, with respect to ease of proof, Lord Bingham stated that 'the opportunity given to the defendant to rebut the presumption' would be relevant when considering compatibility with Article 6(2). If 'opportunity' is taken to include not only the formal right to present evidence, but also the practicalities of rebutting the presumption, it could be taken to include the consideration of ease of proof. In *DPP v Wright*,[98] the High Court stated that reverse burdens within the "the narrow exception described in *R v Edwards* . . . must be limited to matters which are straightforward for a defendant to prove."[99]

The relative ease of proof on the part of the defendant was critical to the Court of Appeal decision in *R v Clarke*.[100] In that case, the defendant had been charged with providing immigration services without the requisite qualifications, contrary to section 91 of the Immigration and Asylum Act 1999. A range of circumstances that would qualify a person to provide immigration services was set out in s 84. The Act did not specify whether the prosecution or defendant bore the persuasive burden with respect to the issue of qualifications and the Court of Appeal therefore applied the principles laid down in *R v Edwards* relating to the implied allocation of the persuasive burden. The Court of Appeal emphasised the large number of possible qualifying conditions in section 84 and stated:[101]

> [W]e agree that a legal burden on a defendant in these circumstances does not impose an onerous obligation. He (or she) will be well aware of the route whereby the criteria of the Act is satisfied and will have ready access to information or evidence to establish this qualification . . . If the burden was evidential, not legal, it would be sufficient for a defendant merely to raise the possibility of qualification by reference to employment by a lawyer in a foreign country thereby requiring the [prosecution] to undertake a costly investigation in circumstances where if the authority was genuine, it would be a simple matter for the defendant to prove it. Far from being simple for the prosecution to disprove qualification, it would be exceedingly complex.

93 [2002] 2 AC 545 (HL).
94 Ibid.
95 *AG's Reference (No 1 of 2004)* [2004] 1 WLR 2111 (CA).
96 Ibid [113].
97 [2005] 1 AC 264 (HL).
98 *DPP v Wright* [2009] EWHC 105 (Admin).
99 Ibid [54].
100 *R v Clarke* [2008] EWCA Crim 651.
101 Ibid [28].

Taking into account the ease with which a defendant would be expected to discharge the burden, by contrast with the difficulty likely to be faced by the prosecution, the Court of Appeal held the persuasive burden rested on the defendant.

It makes sense that a reverse burden will be easier to justify if an innocent defendant could be expected to discharge the burden with relative ease. In such cases, the risk of wrongful conviction is greatly reduced and accordingly one part of the rationale for the presumption of innocence is attenuated. One case has suggested that: 'How difficult it would be for the prosecution to establish the facts is also indicative of whether a reverse legal burden is justified.'[102] Similarly, in *Sheldrake*,[103] Lord Bingham stated that the courts should have regard to 'the difficulty which a prosecutor may face in the absence of a presumption'.[104] However, it is important to remember that it is the ease of proof for the defendant that shows that the rationale for the presumption of innocence is attenuated, rather than the difficulties of proof for the prosecution.[105] In general, the difficulties of proof for the prosecution are part and parcel of the obligation on the state to demonstrate the guilt of the defendant before it may impose conviction and punishment. Only if proof of a matter is conspicuously easy for a defendant, so that the rationale for the presumption of innocence is attenuated, will the difficulties of proof for the prosecution become relevant. In such case, difficulties for the prosecution might be said to demonstrate that there is a legitimate objective in reversing the burden of proof, or that the reversal of the burden of proof is 'necessary'.

One of the common situations in which ease of proof for the defendant is said to justify a reverse burden is the proof of possession of a licence. There is a long line of English cases in support of the principle that the defendant must prove possession of a licence to take part in a regulated activity or possess a regulated item.[106] In *Guyll v Bright*,[107] the court went so far as to say that unless the contrary intention appeared in the statute, the defendant would always be taken to bear the burden of proving a licence. The extent to which the risk of wrongful conviction is reduced when the defendant is required merely to prove a licence was emphasised by the Canadian Supreme Court in *R v Schwartz*.[108] McIntyre J, writing for the majority, held that a requirement to prove a licence does not infringe the presumption of innocence because production of the licence will be conclusive

[102] *AG's Reference (No 1 of 2004)* [2004] 1 WLR 2111 (CA) [52].

[103] [2005] 1 AC 264 (HL).

[104] Ibid [21] (Lord Bingham).

[105] Dennis (see n 27 above) 916; Ashworth (see n 49 above) 266–67.

[106] *The Apothecaries' Company v Bentley* (1824) 1 C & P 538; *R v Scott* (1921) 86 JP 69; *Patel v Willis* [1951] 2 KB 78 (CA) 81–82; *John v Humphreys* [1955] 1 WLR 325 (QBD) 327 (Lord Goddard CJ), *cf* 328 (Ormerod J); *R v Spurge* [1961] 2 QB 205 (CCA) 213; *R v Ewens* [1967] 1 QB 322 (CCA) 329–30; *Robertson v Bannister* [1973] RTR 109, 112; *Williams v Russell* (1933) 149 LT 190, 191 (Talbot J); *Winkle v Wiltshire* [1951] 1 KB 684 (KBD); *Philcox v Carberry* [1960] *Crim LR* 563; *Leathley v Drummond* [1972] RTR 293; *Baker v Sweet* [1966] *Crim LR* 51; *Gatland v MPC* [1968] 2 QB 279 (QBD) 286 (Parker CJ); *R v Oliver* [1944] KB 68 (CCA); *R v Edwards* [1975] QB 27 (CA) 39–40 (Lawton LJ, for the Court). *Cf R v Putland and Sorrell* [1946] 1 All ER 85 (CCA) 87 (Humphreys J, for the Court).

[107] *Guyll v Bright* [1987] RTR 104 (QBD).

[108] *R v Schwartz* [1988] 2 SCR 443.

and there is no risk the defendant will be convicted despite a reasonable doubt.[109] One might add that if the defendant is able to produce a licence, he or she would not be prosecuted in the first place. In the post-HRA case, *DPP v Barker*,[110] it was held that the burden of proving possession of a valid driving licence was on the defendant. Collins J stated that: 'It is a burden which is easily discharged because all he has to do is to produce the licence which has been issued to him.'[111] The need for the defendant to prove possession of a licence will therefore in most cases involve a very low risk of wrongful conviction.[112]

It does not follow from this, however, that the burden of proof should always be on the defendant to prove possession of a licence. The rationale of promoting the rule of law continues to operate, even in licence cases. Something is amiss in the relationship between state and citizen when the authorities can detain a person in the pursuit of a regulated activity, and require that person to produce a licence upon pain of conviction.[113] In order to be a justified departure from the presumption of innocence, it must be shown why a reverse burden is 'necessary'.[114] In former times, the best or only evidence of whether a person had a licence might have been the licence document itself and the defendant was the only person capable of presenting evidence. However, in modern times, a register of licences is virtually always kept, usually in a computerised format that is easily searchable to ascertain whether a named person is included on the register. It will be permissible for the person responsible for operating the register to give evidence that the defendant is not included in the register.[115] Such evidence would normally be convincing and, combined with the failure of the defendant to produce a licence, it would be conclusive.[116] Hence, it will not normally be 'necessary' to require the defendant to prove possession of a licence, since the prosecution can prove the absence of a licence with relative ease. As there is no compelling reason to depart

[109] Ibid 486.

[110] *DPP v Barker* (2004) 168 JP 617 (QBD).

[111] Ibid [11].

[112] There would be a residual risk in cases where the defendant was issued with a licence but had lost the documents. An important issue in such a case would be whether the licensing regime required a person to possess a licence or simply to have had a licence issued.

[113] This misgiving was articulated by Ormerod J in *John v Humphreys* [1955] 1 WLR 325 (QBD) 328: 'I agree [that the burden is on the defendant], although I come to the decision with some reluctance, as it seems to me an extraordinary position that if a police officer sees somebody driving in the street he can cause him to be summoned and put him to proof that he has a licence . . .'.

[114] See Ch 5.

[115] Under the Criminal Justice Act 2003, proof of the absence of an entry in a business record does not raise a hearsay problem. This is because the definition of 'statement' under s 115(3) requires that the 'matter stated' must be made with the purpose of causing another person to believe the matter or to cause another person or a machine to act on the basis that the matter is as stated. The absence of a record in a licence register will not usually have either of these purposes: Cross & Tapper 653. As under the old law, it is probably necessary that a person familiar with the custody and compilation of the register give the evidence: see *R v Patel* (1981) 73 Cr App R 117 (CA) 120; *R v Shone* (1982) 76 Cr App R 72 (CA) 75; *R v Muir* (1983) Cr App R 153 (CA) 156. In civil cases, there is explicit provision for proof of a negative from business records: Civil Evidence Act 1995, s 9(3).

[116] See A Zuckerman 'The Third Exception to the Woolmington Rule' (1976) 92 *LQR* 402, 423–24; A Zuckerman 'No Third Exception to the Woolmington Rule' (1987) 103 *LQR* 170, 175.

from the ordinary rule that the prosecution must prove guilt, the burden of proof with respect to possession of a licence ought to remain on the prosecution.[117]

2. 'Peculiar Knowledge'

Even before the HRA, the fact that a matter was likely to be within the knowledge of the defendant, but was unknown to the prosecution, had been well traversed in cases concerning the allocation of the burden of proof. The idea that the defendant should bear the burden of proof with respect to matters that are 'peculiarly within his or her own knowledge' may be traced to the early nineteenth century decision in *R v Turner*.[118] In that case, the defendant had been convicted before justices of possessing 'sixteen pheasants and five hares' even though he was not qualified or authorised to kill game. On a writ of certiorari before the King's Bench, it was argued that the justices had not recorded any evidence that the defendant lacked the necessary qualifications and that the conviction should therefore be quashed. Holroyd J held that the burden of proving the qualifications was on the defendant because that matter was 'peculiarly within the knowledge of the party himself, whereas the prosecutor has probably, no means whatever of proving a disqualification.'[119] Bayley J agreed stating that:[120]

> I have always understood it to be a general rule, that if a negative averment be made by one party, which is peculiarly within the knowledge of the other, the other party within whose knowledge it lies, and who asserts the affirmative is to prove it, and not he who avers the negative.

The rule explained by Bayley J appeared to depend upon the concurrence of peculiar knowledge with a negative averment, but the precise nature of the rule was left unclear.[121]

Four years later, in *R v Burdett*,[122] there was an attempt to clarify the rule laid down in *Turner*. Holroyd J stated: 'It is established as a general rule of evidence, that in every case the *onus probandi* lies on the person who wishes to support his case by a particular fact, which lies more peculiarly within his own knowledge, or of which he is supposed to be cognizant.'[123] However, Holroyd J immediately went on to clarify that this rule was 'not allowed to supply the want of necessary

[117] P Mirfield 'The Legacy of Hunt' [1988] *Crim LR* 19, 21; G Williams 'The Logic of "Exceptions"' (1988) 47 *CLJ* 261, 275; P Roberts 'Taking the Burden of Proof Seriously' [1995] *Crim LR* 783, 787 fn 18; R Cross *The Golden Thread of the English Criminal Law: The Burden of Proof* (CUP, Cambridge 1976) 15; *R v Schwartz* [1988] 2 SCR 443, 479 (Dickson CJC, dissenting).

[118] *R v Turner* (1816) 5 M & S 206.

[119] Ibid 213.

[120] Ibid 211–12.

[121] Lord Ellenborough CJ referred to the fact that proof of qualifications was 'easy on the one side, but almost impossible on the other': ibid 121. See also *Elkin v Janson* (1845) 13 M & W 655, 662 (Alderson B); *Doe d Bridger v Whitehead* (1838) 8 Ad & E 571, 575 (Lord Denman CJ).

[122] *R v Burdett* (1820) 4 B & Ald 95.

[123] Ibid 139–40.

proof, whether direct or presumptive, against a defendant of the crime with which he is charged'.[124] Instead, the rule was:

> to be applied in considering the weight of the evidence against him, whether direct or presumptive, when it is unopposed, unrebutted, or not weakened by contrary evidence, which it would be in the defendant's power to produce, if the fact directly or presumptively were not true.

James Thayer suggested, in his article highlighting the distinction between the evidential and persuasive burden, that the effect of the rule laid down in *Turner*, and clarified in *Burdett*, was that a defendant should bear an evidential burden on matters peculiarly within his own knowledge, but that the persuasive burden would remain with the prosecution.[125] Nevertheless, the rule laid down in *Turner* was applied in numerous cases so that a defendant bore the persuasive burden of proving necessary qualifications.[126]

The supposed rule relating to 'peculiar knowledge' was decisively rejected in *R v Spurge*.[127] In that case, the Court of Criminal Appeal laid down that: 'There is no rule that where the facts are peculiarly within the knowledge of the accused, the burden of establishing any defence based on these facts shifts to the accused.'[128] Salmon J noted that the facts relating to a defence of provocation or self-defence on a charge of murder may be known only to the defendant, since very often only the defendant and the victim were present at the time of the killing, yet the persuasive burden with respect to these matters still rested with the prosecution.[129] In *R v Edwards*,[130] Lawton LJ reaffirmed that: 'There is not, and never has been, a general rule of law that the mere fact that a matter lies peculiarly within the knowledge of the defendant is sufficient to cast the onus on him.'[131] Lawton LJ also pointed to the absurd consequences that would follow from such a rule, specifically, that 'anyone charged with doing an unlawful act with a specific intent would find himself having to prove his innocence because if there ever was a

124 Ibid.

125 J Thayer 'The Burden of Proof' (1890) 4 *Harvard Law Review* 45, 51. See also Cross & Tapper 153.

126 *The Apothecaries' Co v Bentley* (1824) 1 C & P 538; *R v Scott* (1921) 86 JP 69; *Williams v Russell* (1933) 149 LT 190; *R v Oliver* [1944] KB 68 (CCA); *John v Humphreys* [1955] 1 WLR 325 (QBD). Out of these cases, only *John v Humphreys* relied upon 'peculiar knowledge'. The others rested upon proof of a negative averment. The 'supposed' rule was also put into statutory form in s 106 of the Indian Evidence Act: 'When any fact is especially within the knowledge of any person, the burden of proving that fact is upon him.' This and similar provisions have been interpreted so as not to impose the persuasive burden on the defendant: *Attygale v R* [1936] AC 338 (PC); *Seneviratne v R* [1936] 3 All ER 36 (PC); *Ng v R* [1958] AC 173 (PC).

127 *R v Spurge* [1961] 2 QB 205 (CCA).

128 Ibid 212–13 (Salmon J).

129 Ibid 212. See also a much earlier decision denying a 'peculiar knowledge' rule: *Abrath v North Eastern Ry* (1883) 11 QBD 440, 457–58 (Bowen LJ). Despite the rejection of the rule in *Spurge*, a later case held that the possession by one party of 'peculiar knowledge' was relevant when interpreting a statute to determine who bore the burden of proof: *R v Ewens* [1967] 1 QB 322 (CCA) 329 (Melford Stevenson J).

130 *R v Edwards* [1975] QB 27 (CA).

131 Ibid 35.

matter which could be said to be peculiarly within a person's knowledge it is the state of his own mind.'[132]

The introduction of the HRA breathed new life into the argument that the knowledge of the defendant was a relevant factor in the allocation of the burden of proof. The factor has been raised in four out of the five decisions on reverse burdens before the House of Lords. In *Kebilene*,[133] Lord Hope listed three questions that should be asked when determining the compatibility of a reverse burden of proof. The second of these questions was: '[D]oes it relate to something which is likely to be difficult for him to prove, or does it relate to something which is likely to be within his knowledge or (I would add) to which he has ready access?'[134] In *Lambert*,[135] Lord Clyde considered it relevant that 'the question whether the accused was ignorant or had no reason to suspect that what he possessed was a controlled drug is a matter very much within his own knowledge.'[136] In *Johnstone*,[137] Lord Nicholls placed emphasis on 'the extent to which the burden on the accused relates to facts which, if they exist, are readily provable by him as matters within his own knowledge or to which he has ready access.'[138] Finally, in *Sheldrake*,[139] Lord Bingham justified a reverse burden with respect to the likelihood of driving on the ground that it was:[140]

> a matter so closely conditioned by his own knowledge and state of mind at the material time as to make it much more appropriate for him to prove on the balance of probabilities that he would not have been likely to drive than for the prosecutor to prove, beyond reasonable doubt, that he would.

The lower courts have also been quick to point out when a reverse burden relates to matters within the knowledge of the defendant. Hence, reverse burdens with respect to the reason for possession of a knife in a public place,[141] the steps taken to prevent illegal immigrants from stowing aboard trucks,[142] and the measures in place to ensure health and safety at a workplace have all been upheld,[143] in part, on the ground that the burden relates to a matter within the knowledge of the defendant. The somewhat archaic phrase 'peculiar knowledge' has even been revived in one case. In *R v S*,[144] the Court of Appeal held that it was acceptable to

[132] Ibid 35.
[133] [2000] 2 AC 326 (HL).
[134] Ibid 386.
[135] [2002] 2 AC 545 (HL).
[136] Ibid [153]. However, Lord Clyde went on to state, *obiter*, that the reverse burden could not be justified: ibid [156].
[137] [2003] 1 WLR 1736 (HL).
[138] Ibid [50].
[139] [2005] 1 AC 264 (HL).
[140] Ibid [41].
[141] *L v DPP* [2003] QB 137 (QBD) [27] (Pill LJ).
[142] *International Transport Roth GmbH v Secretary of State for the Home Department* [2003] QB 728 (CA) [44] (Simon Brown LJ).
[143] *R v Davies* [2003] ICR 586 (CA) [22] (Tuckey LJ). See also *R v Chargot Limited* [2009] 1 WLR 1 (HL) [29] (Lord Hope) approving *Davies*.
[144] [2003] 1 Cr App R 35 (CA).

require the defendant to prove he or she did not realise the offending use of a trademark was an infringement, because that matter was 'liable to be peculiarly within the knowledge of the accused'.[145]

The major fallacy in the 'peculiar knowledge' doctrine is the conflation of knowledge and ease of proof. The tendency to run these two ideas together is all too evident in the cases. For example, as part of its advice to lower courts, the Court of Appeal in *AG's Reference (No 1 of 2004)*[146] stated: 'The easier it is for the accused to discharge the burden the more likely it is that the reverse burden is justified. This will be the case where the facts are within the defendant's own knowledge.'[147] In *R v Davies*,[148] the Court of Appeal stated: 'The facts relied upon in support of the defence should not be difficult to prove because they will be within the knowledge of the defendant.'[149] There is, in one sense, a correlation between ease of proof and means of knowledge. A defendant who does not have knowledge of a matter, or access to relevant evidence, will in all cases be unable to prove that matter. However, the converse proposition does not hold. The fact that a matter is within the knowledge of the defendant does not make that matter easy for the defendant to prove.[150]

For instance, any issue of *mens rea* is liable to be within the knowledge of the defendant, but not within the knowledge of the prosecution. It does not follow that the defendant will easily be able to prove his mental state at the relevant time. The most important evidence will usually come from the defendant, but his or her evidence may well be discounted by the fact-finder on the ground that the desire to avoid conviction provides an obvious motive to lie.[151] It should also be stressed that the ease of producing evidence will not always be the same as ease of proof.[152] For example, in cases where the defendant is required to prove due diligence in a regulated sphere (such as health and safety) the defendant may well be in the best position to know what steps he or she took. The defendant may even be in a position to prove that those steps were taken because he or she has access to the documentary evidence. However, this evidence is still contestable because the question of whether procedures were duly diligent depends on the fact-finder's evaluation of what was reasonable in the circumstances. Even with knowledge of what was done, and access to the documents, the defendant is in no better position than the prosecution when it comes to convincing the fact-finder of what was reasonable.

This section has demonstrated a long history of reasoning to the effect that the defendant should prove matters within his or her exclusive knowledge because otherwise the prosecution would be unable to obtain convictions. This reasoning

[145] Ibid [48]. See also *Coetzee v Government of the Republic of South Africa; Matiso v Commanding Officer of Port Elizabeth Prison* 1995 (4) SA 631 (CC) [14] (Kriegler J).
[146] [2004] 1 WLR 2111 (CA).
[147] Ibid [52] (Lord Woolf CJ, for the Court).
[148] [2003] ICR 586 (CA).
[149] Ibid [28].
[150] Cross & Tapper 153; Tadros & Tierney (see n 83 above) 426–27; Duff (see n 80 above) 138 fn 58.
[151] Roberts (see n 117 above) 786–87.
[152] Dennis (see n 27 above) 919–20.

reflects a concern that the defendant will be able to submit no case to answer or rely on the gaps in the prosecution case whenever he or she has access to knowledge but the prosecution does not. However, as Thayer observed as long ago as the late nineteenth century, this problem can be satisfactorily resolved by imposing an evidential burden on the defendant.[153] By this means, the knowledge previously possessed only by the defendant is brought within the possession of the prosecution and the court so that it may be subjected to cross-examination or expert evaluation. Imposition of an evidential burden is sufficient to draw out the defendant's evidence and to prevent the unjustified submission of no case to answer. The possession of exclusive or 'peculiar' knowledge therefore does not necessitate the allocation of the persuasive burden to the defendant. The distinction must be drawn between means of knowledge and access to information on the one hand and ease of proof on the other. When it comes to allocation of the persuasive burden, it is only the ease of proof that has potential significance.

E. Importance of Matters Proved by Prosecution

In Chapter Three it was argued that the presumption of innocence requires that the prosecution prove all matters necessary for conviction. Hence, there is an interference with the presumption of innocence whenever there is a reverse burden regardless of how minor the matter the defendant is required to prove. It might nevertheless be argued that a reverse burden is a less significant limitation of the presumption if the prosecution has already proved some degree of wrongfulness, or has proved sufficient facts to make it highly probable that the defendant is guilty of the remaining aspects of the offence. In such cases, the risk of wrongful conviction might be lower so that the rationale for the presumption of innocence is attenuated. Section one below will consider cases where the prosecution has already proved some degree of wrongfulness. Included in this category are reverse burdens with respect to the defences of insanity and duress. Section two below will consider cases where the prosecution has proved enough facts to make it highly probable that the defendant is guilty.

1. Proof of Wrongfulness

In *R v Johnstone*,[154] Lord Nicholls stated that: 'The extent and nature of the factual matters required to be proved by the accused, and their importance relative to the

[153] Thayer (see n 125 above) 51. See also Dennis (see n 27 above) 915; Williams (see n 117 above) 268; JE Stannard 'A Presumption and Four Burdens' (2000) 51(4) *Northern Ireland Legal Quarterly* 560, 565, 576; G Williams 'The Evidential Burden: Some Common Misapprehensions' (1977) 127 *New Law Journal* 156, 156; BD Underwood 'The Thumb on the Scales of Justice: Burdens of Persuasion in Criminal Cases' (1977) 86 *Yale Law Journal* 1299, 1335–36.

[154] [2003] 1 WLR 1736 (HL).

matters required to be proved by the prosecution, have to be taken into account.'[155] This implies that if the prosecution has proved the most important matters, it might be legitimate to reverse the burden of proof with respect to more minor matters. In particular, it might suggest that if the prosecution has already proved some degree of wrongfulness, it will more likely be justifiable to impose the burden of proof on the defendant with respect to a defence. The English courts often put this in terms of whether the prosecution has proved the 'gravamen' or essential elements of the offence. For instance, Lord Woolf stated in *R v Lambert, Ali and Jordan* that: 'If the defendant is being required to prove an essential element of the offence this will be more difficult to justify. If, however, what the defendant is required to do is establish a special defence or exception this will be less objectionable.'[156]

It has already been shown in Chapter Three that concepts such as 'gravamen' or 'essential elements' are difficult to pin down.[157] For that reason, this section will use the word 'wrongfulness'. While the concept of wrongfulness is also controversial, it has the advantage in a linguistic sense of connoting non-innocence. If the prosecution has already proved some degree of wrongfulness, there is a reduced risk that an 'innocent' person will be convicted. Accordingly, it could be argued that the rationale for the presumption of innocence is attenuated. Even though there is a risk that a person entitled to a defence in law may be convicted, this might be thought a lesser evil than convicting a person who is not guilty of any wrongfulness. This might be said to be the case in relation to the defences of duress and insanity. These defences differ from other defences, such as self-defence, because they excuse rather than justify the wrongful behaviour. That is, a defendant who successfully pleads duress or insanity has not negated the wrongfulness of his or her conduct, but rather taken advantage of a rule of law that allows a 'concession to human frailty'.[158]

(a) Duress

The defence of duress becomes relevant only once the prosecution has proved that the defendant committed the acts and possessed the *mens rea* necessary to constitute the offence. At present, the prosecution is required to disprove duress beyond reasonable doubt once the defendant has satisfied an evidential burden.[159] However, in 1993, the Law Commission recommended that a defendant charged

[155] Ibid [50]. See also *R v DPP; ex p Kebilene* [2000] 2 AC 326 (HL) 386: 'What does the prosecution have to prove in order to transfer the onus to the defence?'

[156] *R v Lambert, Ali and Jordan* [2002] QB 1112 (CA) [16]. See also *AG of Hong Kong v Lee Kwong-kut* [1993] AC 951 (PC) 969–70 (Lord Woolf, for the Privy Council); *AG's Reference (No 1 of 2004)* [2004] 1 WLR 2111 (CA) [52] (Lord Woolf CJ, for the Court)

[157] See Ch 3.

[158] *R v Howe* [1987] AC 417 (HL) 432 (Lord Hailsham) (duress); A Stein 'Criminal Defences and the Burden of Proof' (1991) 28 Coexistence 133, 138 (insanity).

[159] *R v Gill* [1963] 1 WLR 841 (CCA) 846 (Edmund-Davies J); *DPP for Northern Ireland v Lynch* [1975] AC 653 (HL(NI)) 668 (Lord Morris); *R v Z* [2005] 2 AC 467 (HL) [20] (Lord Bingham).

with offences against the person should not be entitled to rely on duress unless he or she could prove the defence on the balance of probabilities.[160] Similarly, in 2006, the Law Commission recommended a change in the law so that duress would be permitted as a defence to murder and attempted murder.[161] However, the Law Commission recommended that the defendant should bear the burden of proving duress on the balance of probabilities.[162]

In 2006, the Law Commission reasoned that a reverse burden with respect to duress would not infringe the presumption of innocence as protected by Article 6(2). To begin with, the Law Commission considered it was not a 'foregone conclusion' that a reverse burden would constitute even a *prima facie* breach of the presumption of innocence. The Law Commission stated:[163]

> In our view, the presumption of innocence is much more plausibly found to exist in relation to a fully justificatory defence than in relation to an excusatory defence. Although in some cases of duress the circumstances come close to being justifications for killing, they cannot justify intentionally killing in the way that, for example, acting necessarily and proportionately in self-defence does.

Further, the Law Commission considered that, even if a reverse burden with respect to duress was a *prima facie* breach of the presumption of innocence, it would be proportionate.[164] One reason for this was that the prosecution was required to prove the definitional elements of the offence of murder, which always involved wrongfulness. The Law Commission stated: 'If the definitional elements themselves are satisfied, they reveal conduct on the part of D that amounts to the commission of the most serious of all wrongs. It will have been proved that D intended to kill or cause serious harm.'[165]

Since duress is an excuse, rather than a justification, it does not make otherwise wrongful conduct acceptable. The defence, if it is to be allowed, operates as a 'concession to human frailty'[166] for a defendant who has behaved wrongly but in circumstances where that is less culpable than otherwise. Reversing the burden of proof with respect to duress therefore does not create a risk of convicting a person who has not acted wrongfully. There is a risk that a person entitled to a defence in law, and therefore legally innocent, may be convicted. But there is a substantially reduced risk that a person who is morally innocent may be convicted. Therefore, the rationale of protecting the innocent is attenuated. Since one part of the rationale for the presumption is attenuated, it is appropriate to apply a proportionality test to determine whether the reverse burden of proof is 'necessary'.

[160] Law Commission *Legislating the Criminal Code: Offences Against the Person and General Principles (Law Com No 218)* (Cmnd 2370) (HMSO, London 1993) [33.1]–[33.16].

[161] Law Commission *Murder, Manslaughter and Infanticide (Law Com No 304)* (HC 30) (TSO, London 2006) pt 6. Under the current law, duress cannot be a defence to murder: *R v Howe* [1987] AC 417 (HL). It also cannot be a defence to attempted murder: *R v Gotts* [1992] AC 412 (HL).

[162] Law Com No 304 ibid [6.120].

[163] Ibid [6.122].

[164] Ibid [6.124]–[6.135].

[165] Ibid [6.129].

[166] See *R v Howe* [1987] AC 417 (HL) 432 (Lord Hailsham).

In considering whether it is 'necessary' to reverse the burden of proof, problems of proof will be vital. In 1993, the Law Commission argued that duress was a unique defence because 'it is more likely than any other defence to depend on assertions which are peculiarly difficult for the prosecution to investigate or subsequently to disprove.'[167] The reason for this was that the circumstances of duress usually occurred prior to and separate from the circumstances of the commission of the offence.[168] The Law Commission in 2006 cited similar reasons in favour of reversing the burden of proof when duress was alleged as a defence to murder.[169] The Commission went further to state that all the facts necessary for a defendant to prove a defence of duress would be 'within his or her own knowledge'.[170] The US Supreme Court has also held that a reverse burden with respect to duress would be justifiable.[171] In support of the rule, Justice Kennedy stated:[172]

> The claim of duress in most instances depends upon conduct that takes place before the criminal act; and, as the person who allegedly coerced the defendant is often unwilling to come forward and testify, the prosecution may be without practical means of disproving the defendant's allegations.

It is not clear that these problems of proof are any greater than in relation to other defences.[173] When the defendant pleads self-defence to homicide, in some cases the only people with knowledge of the events will be the deceased victim and the defendant. Similarly, when a defendant relies upon provocation as a partial defence to murder, the prosecution will not always have access to witnesses with knowledge of the events. Nevertheless, in both of these cases the persuasive burden is on the prosecution. At best, the problems of proof that may be faced by the prosecution show that there is a legitimate objective in reversing the burden of proof because otherwise there is a risk that defendants will invent false claims of duress that will be difficult or impossible for the prosecution to disprove. What must be considered is whether an evidential burden would suffice to resolve the problems faced by the prosecution.

An evidential burden would require the defendant to ensure that evidence was before the court sufficient to raise duress as an issue to go before the jury. The evidence before the court would need to be such as to satisfy all the requirements of duress before that defence need be left to the jury. It would not be sufficient for the

167 Law Com No 218 (see n 160 above) [33.6]. In *R v Z* [2005] 2 AC 467 (HL), Lord Bingham accepted that, at common law, the persuasive burden with respect to duress was on the prosecution, but also agreed with the Law Commission that 'the defence of duress is peculiarly difficult for the prosecution to investigate and disprove beyond reasonable doubt': ibid [20]. See also ibid [72] (Baroness Hale).

168 Law Com No 218 (see n 160 above) [33.7].

169 Law Com No 304 (see n 161 above) [6.104]–[6.108].

170 Ibid [6.131].

171 *Dixon v US*, 124 S Ct 2437 (2006).

172 Ibid 2449.

173 J Horder 'Occupying the Moral High Ground? The Law Commission on Duress' [1994] *Crim LR* 334, 336; A Ashworth 'Principles, Pragmatism and the Law Commission's Recommendations on Homicide Law Reform' [2007] *Crim LR* 333, 341–42.

defendant simply to allege duress in questions to prosecution witnesses or through counsel in argument. Further, it is probably correct that 'the more dreadful the circumstances of the [crime], the heavier the evidential burden of an accused advancing such a plea, and the stronger and more irresistible the duress needed before it could be regarded as affording any defence.'[174]

The potential for the allocation of the evidential burden to keep unmeritorious claims of duress from the jury is illustrated by the decision in *R v Bianco*.[175] In that case, the defendant alleged duress as a defence to a charge of drug smuggling on the ground that a drug dealer had said to him: 'We know where your family are, and we know how to get even.'[176] The Recorder declined to allow the defence of duress to go before the jury, on the ground that this threat was not sufficiently serious to constitute duress, and also that the defendant had a reasonable opportunity to avoid the coercer, or go to the police. The Court of Appeal held it was correct to withdraw the defence of duress from the jury. The Court of Appeal stated: 'There must at least be some evidence upon which a jury could properly conclude that the defence of duress had not been negatived.'[177] That is, the evidence before the court must relate to each aspect of the defence of duress. The difficulty of satisfying even an evidential burden with respect to duress suggests that it will be sufficient to prevent utterly unmeritorious cases from going before the jury.

In most cases, since the defence of duress will depend upon facts known only to the defendant, the defendant will need to testify in order to satisfy the evidential burden. The evidence previously known only to the defendant concerning the circumstances of the duress would then be revealed to the court and the jury and made subject to cross-examination. Once all the evidence is before the court the prosecution is in just as good a position as the defendant to satisfy the jury with regard to duress.

It is true that the evidential burden will not always require the defendant to testify since the evidential burden can be discharged by prosecution evidence. For instance, it would be possible for the defence of duress to be introduced through evidence of what the defendant said in interview.[178] If the defendant can satisfy the evidential burden without testifying, the prosecution would be deprived of the opportunity to undermine the defence in cross-examination. However, if the only evidence of duress were the assertions of the defendant in an interview, with no supporting evidence, the impact of the evidence would be substantially reduced.

[174] *R v Abbott* [1976] 3 All ER 140 (PC) 152 (Lords Wilberforce and Edmund-Davies, dissenting). See also D Ormerod *Smith and Hogan: Criminal Law* 11th edn (OUP, Oxford 2005) 299.

[175] *R v Bianco* [2001] EWCA Crim 2516.

[176] Ibid [9].

[177] Ibid [15].

[178] Law Com No 304 (see n 161 above) [6.108]. When the prosecution leads in evidence an interview that includes incriminating and exculpatory statements, the jury is to be allowed to hear the entire statement: *R v Donaldson* (1977) 64 Cr App R 59. Both the inculpatory and exculpatory parts of a mixed statement are admissible as evidence of their truth: *R v Duncan* (1981) 73 Cr App R 359 (CA) 365 (Lord Lane CJ); *R v Sharp* [1998] 1 WLR 7 (HL) 15 (Lord Havers); *R v Aziz* [1996] AC 41 (HL) 48–50 (Lord Steyn).

Further, it would be possible for the judge to direct the jury, in accordance with s 35 of the Criminal Justice and Public Order Act 1994 that adverse inferences could be drawn from the failure of the defendant to testify.[179]

Some further factors must also be borne in mind when considering whether a reversal of the burden of proof would be 'necessary'. Ease of proof is relevant to the extent that some matters are relatively easy for the defendant to prove. However, a defence of duress is not easy for the defendant to prove. The problems of proof that afflict the prosecution also apply to the defendant. For instance, the problem of obtaining co-operation from the alleged coercer will apply to the defendant as much as to the prosecution. Also, the defence depends upon evaluative determinations such as whether the defendant had a reasonable apprehension of harm, acted reasonably in the circumstances, and was deprived of any reasonable evasive action. It is no easier for the defendant to convince the fact-finder on these evaluative considerations than it would be for the prosecution. Hence, reversing the burden of proof creates a serious risk that a defendant will be convicted even though he or she was legally entitled to rely upon duress.

As stated above, the risk of wrongful conviction is less serious than normal because the defendant is, at least, guilty of wrongfulness. However, the second rationale for the presumption of innocence, the need to promote the rule of law, must be taken into account. If a defendant can be convicted due to a failure to satisfy the burden of proof, even though he or she was legally entitled to the defence of duress, the rule of law is undermined. The Law Commission has argued that reversal of the burden of proof is necessary on the defence of duress, especially in the case of murder, because Parliament will otherwise not allow any defence of duress at all.[180] However, this form of reasoning involves an inappropriate compromise. The rule of law requires that defendants be convicted in accordance with the merits of the case, and not on the basis of procedural mechanisms. If duress is to be allowed as a defence, the normal rule for criminal trials ought to be adhered to: the prosecution should bear the burden of proving guilt beyond reasonable doubt.

(b) Insanity

The defence of insanity in English law derives from the advice given by the House of Lords in the 1843 decision of *M'Naghten.*[181] In that case, Daniel M'Naghten was

[179] *R v Duncan* (1981) 73 Cr App R 359 (CA) 365 (Lord Lane CJ): '[W]here appropriate, as it usually will be, the judge may, and should, point out that the incriminating parts are likely to be true (otherwise why say them?), whereas the excuses do not have the same weight. Nor is there any reason why, again where appropriate, the judge should not comment in relation to the exculpatory remarks upon the election of the accused not to give evidence.' *R v Aziz* [1996] AC 41 (HL) 50 (Lord Steyn): '[A]s was emphasized in *Duncan* . . . a judge is entitled to comment adversely on the quality of the exculpatory parts of a mixed statement which has not been tested by cross-examination.'

[180] Law Com No 218 (see n 160 above) [33.2]–[33.3]. See also R Buxton 'The Convention and the English Law of Criminal Evidence' in Cambridge Centre for Public Law *The Human Rights Act and the Criminal and Regulatory Process* (Hart, Oxford 1999) 45, 53.

[181] *M'Naghten's Case* (1843) 10 C & F 200.

acquitted of murder on the ground of insanity after killing the secretary of Sir Robert Peel. The judges of the House of Lords were requested to clarify the basis of the defence of insanity, and the rules they laid down (known as the *M'Naghten Rules*) have remained authoritative ever since.[182] Lord Tindal CJ stated:[183]

> [T]he jurors ought to be told in all cases that every man is to be presumed to be sane, and to possess a sufficient degree of reason to be responsible for his crimes, until the contrary be proved to their satisfaction; and that to establish a defence on the ground of insanity, it must be clearly proved that, at the time of the committing of the act, the party accused was labouring under such a defect of reason, from disease of the mind, as not to know the nature and quality of the act he was doing; or, if he did know it, that he did not know he was doing what was wrong.

Two important points can be discerned from this quotation. First, the defence of insanity is available only when, because of a defect of reason caused by a disease of the mind: (a) the defendant did not know the nature and quality of his or her act; or (b) even if the defendant did know the nature and quality of the act, he or she did not know it was wrong. Second, since every man is presumed to be sane until the contrary is proven, the burden of proof with respect to insanity rests on the defendant.

The *M'Naghten* Rules were laid down at a time when the defendant bore the burden of proof with respect to all number of matters including the absence of malice on a charge of murder.[184] Further, no one at that time had drawn a distinction between the persuasive burden and the evidential burden so that the option of allowing the defendant to overcome the 'presumption of sanity' by presenting evidence capable of raising a doubt had not yet occurred to the courts.[185] The common law reversal of the persuasive burden with respect to insanity might therefore have been regarded as an 'historical anomaly' to be swept away when greater recognition was given to the principle that the prosecution must prove the guilt of the defendant

[182] Although answers to abstract questions posed to the House of Lords are not strictly binding, the *M'Naghten* Rules have long been treated as authoritative: *R v Stokes* (1848) 3 Car & Kir 185, 188 (Rolfe B); *R v Smith* (1910) 6 Cr App R 19; *R v Coelho* (1914) 30 TLR 535; *Bratty v AG for Northern Ireland* [1963] AC 386 (HL); *R v Sullivan* [1983] 2 All ER 673 (HL) 676 (Lord Diplock).

[183] (1843) 10 C & F 200, 210 (Lord Tindal CJ).

[184] See Ch 1, p 7.

[185] *R v Bonnor* [1957] VR 227, 260 (Sholl J). In 1895, the US Supreme Court held, in effect, that a defendant should bear the evidential burden with respect to insanity but not the persuasive burden: *Davis v US*, 160 US 469, 486–487 (1895) (Harlan J): 'In a certain sense it may be true that where the defence is insanity, and where the case made by the prosecution discloses nothing whatever in excuse or extenuation of the crime charged, the accused is bound to produce some evidence that will impair or weaken the force of the legal presumption in favor of sanity. But to hold that such presumption must absolutely control the jury until it is overthrown or impaired by evidence sufficient to establish the fact of insanity beyond all reasonable doubt or to the reasonable satisfaction of the jury, is in effect to require him to establish his innocence, by proving that he is not guilty of the crime charged.' Later, the US Supreme Court read *Davis* as stating a rule of interpretation applying to Federal statutes, so that there was no constitutional prohibition on reversing the burden of proof with respect to insanity: *Leland v Oregon*, 343 US 790 (1952). See also *Clark v Arizona*, 126 S Ct R 2709 (2006).

beyond reasonable doubt.[186] Nevertheless, in *Woolmington*,[187] the House of Lords affirmed the reversal of the burden of proof with respect to insanity. Viscount Sankey stated in relation to insanity that 'the onus is definitely and exceptionally placed upon the accused to establish such a defence . . .'[188] Insanity therefore remained as a common law exception to the 'golden thread' rule, even while the other exceptions were gradually abolished.[189]

In 1972, the Criminal Law Revision Committee recommended that all burdens on defendants should be evidential only, and specifically recommended that the persuasive burden in relation to insanity should rest on the prosecution.[190] This alteration in the law would have required statutory intervention that was never forthcoming. However, the introduction of the HRA, including the quasi-constitutional protection for the presumption of innocence in Article 6(2), offers a new opportunity for the English courts to consider the common law rule with regard to insanity. Under section 6 of the HRA, public authorities, including the courts, are prohibited from acting in a way that is incompatible with a Convention right. When the court is applying a common law rule concerning the burden of proof, it must consider whether the application of the rule would be consistent with its obligations under Article 6(2). The common law must develop in a way that is consistent with Convention rights.[191] Accordingly, the burden of proof with respect to insanity must be consistent with Article 6(2), and it would be open to the courts to find that the burden should rest on the prosecution.

This, of course, will be the case only if the reversal of the burden of proof with respect to insanity is inconsistent with Article 6(2).[192] Whenever the defendant bears the persuasive burden, there is a *prima facie* interference with the presumption of innocence because the defendant may be convicted in the absence of proof beyond reasonable doubt of one of the matters required for conviction.[193] The *prima facie* interference will not be justifiable unless the rationale for the presumption of innocence is attenuated.[194] Only if the rationale is attenuated is it necessary to consider whether the reversal of the burden of proof is a proportionate response to a legitimate objective. Therefore, the first matter to consider is whether the rationale for the presumption of innocence is attenuated in the case

[186] R Cross *The Golden Thread of the English Criminal Law: The Burden of Proof* (CUP, Cambridge 1976) 13. See also G Williams 'Offences and Defences' (1982) 2 *Legal Studies* 233, 235; CR Williams 'Placing the Burden of Proof' in Enid Campbell & Louis Waller (eds) *Well and Truly Tried: Essays on Evidence in Honour of Sir Richard Eggleston* (Law Book Company Sydney 1982) 284, 294–95.

[187] *Woolmington v DPP* [1935] AC 462 (HL).

[188] Ibid 475.

[189] See Ch 1, p 8.

[190] Criminal Law Revision Committee, *Eleventh Report, Evidence (General)* (Cmnd 4991) (HMSO London 1972) [140].

[191] AW Bradley & KD Ewing *Constitutional and Administrative Law* 13th edn (Pearson, Harlow 2003) 420. Cross & Tapper 152: 'It is worth noting that the impact of that Art[6(2)] extends beyond the construction of statutory provisions, into the area of crimes at common law . . .'.

[192] The Strasbourg Commission dismissed an allegation that the reversal of the burden of proof with respect to insanity was contrary to Art 6(2): *H v UK* (App No 15023/89) EComHR 4 April 1990.

[193] See Ch 3.

[194] See Ch 2.

of the insanity defence, so that the reversal of the burden of proof might, in principle, be justified.

Alex Stein has argued that the reversal of the burden of proof with respect to insanity is permissible because insanity is an excuse rather than a justification.[195] Insanity does not negate the wrongfulness of the defendant's conduct, but rather negates the capacity of the defendant to bear criminal responsibility. Stein states that insanity is available to an accused 'on the grounds of leniency, as a concession to human frailty, despite the fact that his act was damaging to the public interest protected by a criminal norm'.[196] Stein argues further that:[197]

> The principle of protecting the innocent should protect only those accused who have not been established to have infringed the public interest protected by the criminal law. Those who, having infringed such an interest, are asking to be excused ought not to be entitled to the similar degree of protection from the risks of error.

In accordance with this argument, the reversal of the burden of proof with respect to insanity would be a less serious breach of the presumption of innocence than other reverse burdens, because there is no risk that a person innocent of wrongful conduct will be convicted. Accordingly, the rationale for the presumption would be attenuated.

However, it is by no means clear that insanity operates only as an excuse.[198] As seen above, the insanity defence has two limbs: (a) proof that the defendant did not understand the nature and quality of the act; and (b) proof that the defendant did not understand that the act was wrong. In some cases where the defendant alleges insanity within the first limb, the defence may negate *mens rea*. In such cases, it is difficult to conclude that the insanity defence is acting as an excuse, since one of the key definitional elements of the offence is absent.[199] As a result of this, it has been suggested that when the defendant alleges insanity within the first limb the burden on the defendant should be evidential only, leaving the prosecution to prove *mens rea* beyond reasonable doubt.[200] On this suggestion, the defendant would bear the persuasive burden on the insanity defence only when the second limb is relied upon.

However, there are several reasons why this solution is not appropriate. First, insanity within the first limb does not always negate *mens rea*. In relation to crimes of intention or subjective recklessness, the inability to appreciate the nature and

195 A Stein 'Criminal Defences and the Burden of Proof' (1991) 28 *Coexistence* 133, 137.

196 Ibid 138.

197 Ibid 139. See also PH Robinson 'Criminal Law Defenses: A Systematic Analysis' (1982) 82 *Columbia Law Review* 199, 257–58: 'One might argue that it is particularly appropriate that the defendant carry the burden of persuasion on a defense which seeks exculpation while admitting the harm or evil of the offense.'

198 See generally RD Mackay *Mental Condition Defences in the Criminal Law* (OUP, Oxford 1995); Mackay, RD 'Craziness and Codification: Revising the Automatism and Insanity Defences' in IH Dennis (ed) *Criminal Law and Justice* (Sweet & Maxwell, London 1987) 109; Tadros, Victor 'Insanity and the Capacity for Criminal Responsibility' (2001) 5 *Edinburgh Law Review* 325.

199 See *R v Youssef* (1990) 50 A Crim R 1, 9 (Hunt J); O Dixon 'A Legacy of Hadfield, M'Naghten and Maclean (1957) 31 *Australian Law Journal* 255, 256.

200 G Williams *Criminal Law: The General Part* 2nd edn (Stevens, London 1961) 165. This solution is approved in Ormerod (see n 174 above) 267.

quality of an act will negate the requisite *mens rea*. However, in crimes subject to an objective standard, such as negligence, the insane delusions of the defendant will not affect *mens rea*.[201] Second, in some cases, the defendant may rely on both limbs of the insanity defence at the same time, or it may simply be unclear which limb is relied upon.[202] A differential standard based on the category of insanity attributed to the defendant would therefore be inconvenient and confusing.

Further, even in cases where the insanity defence has the capacity to negate *mens rea*, the issue of insanity must be kept distinct from the issue of *mens rea* as a definitional element of the offence. When the prosecution fails to prove *mens rea* as a definitional element, the defendant is entitled to an unqualified verdict of not guilty and will be released. By contrast, a defendant acquitted on the ground of insanity comes within the provisions of the Criminal Procedure (Insanity) Act 1964 and may be subjected to a range of orders including indefinite detention. The operation of this Act depends upon a differentiation between those who are guilty but insane, and those who are not guilty.

For this reason, when insanity is at issue in a criminal trial, the jury must be instructed to follow a two-stage process of reasoning.[203] In the first stage, the jury must consider whether the defendant committed the acts alleged with the requisite *mens rea*. At this point, the jury must presume that the defendant was sane and therefore capable of understanding the nature and quality of his or her acts. Only if this stage of the inquiry is satisfied will the jury need to consider whether the defendant was insane at the time of the offence. If satisfied that the defendant either was incapable of understanding the nature and quality of the acts or incapable of understanding that they were wrong, the verdict will be guilty but insane. Hence, even in cases where insanity negates *mens rea*, and is not strictly an excuse, it operates in the same way as an excuse. The defendant is relieved of criminal responsibility even though the prosecution has proved that his or her conduct was wrongful.

We might therefore conclude, notwithstanding complications concerning *mens rea*, that the rationale of protecting the innocent is attenuated in insanity cases. Even if this is accepted, it does not necessarily follow that it is consistent with the presumption of innocence to reverse the persuasive burden. If the rationale for the presumption is attenuated, it is still necessary to consider whether the departure from the normal rule is able to satisfy a 'necessity-focused' proportionality inquiry.

The principal justification given for the reversal of the burden of proof is that the defendant's mental state is a matter to which the prosecution does not have access, leading to problems of proof for the prosecution.[204] Under the proportionality

[201] T Jones 'Insanity, Automatism and the Burden of Proof on the Accused' (1995) 111 *LQR* 475, 485; C Wells 'Whither Insanity' [1983] *Crim LR* 787, 795. See also *Mullaney v Wilbur*, 421 US 684, 706 (1975) (Rehnquist J): 'the presence or nonexistence of legal insanity bears no necessary relationship to the existence of non-existence of the required mental elements of the crime.'

[202] *R v Antoine* [2001] 1 AC 340 (HL) 374 (Lord Hutton).

[203] Jones (see n 201 above) 486.

[204] *R v Chaulk* [1990] 3 SCR 1303, 1405 (McLachlin J). In that case, the Canadian Supreme Court held, by majority, that the reverse burden on insanity breached s 11(d) of the Charter, but that is was a justifiable limitation under s 1.

inquiry, it must be considered whether an evidential burden would be sufficient to overcome these problems. To satisfy an evidential burden, a defendant who alleges insanity at the time of the offence would need to introduce medical evidence.[205] This evidence would need to be based on an examination of the defendant by a medical expert and would then be subject to scrutiny by the prosecution. It is difficult to see how the defendant could satisfy the evidential burden without putting a full and frank analysis of his or her mental condition before the court and the jury. In that case, the prosecution would have access to the same evidence as the defendant. A problem may arise for the prosecution in disproving the allegations of the defendant beyond reasonable doubt. However, the prosecution is required to do this in relation to the defence of automatism,[206] which like insanity, relates to the mind of the defendant. If the prosecution is able to overcome the evidential problems in cases on automatism there is no reason to think it could not overcome those problems in cases of insanity.[207] Accordingly, as a matter of principle, the burden of proof ought to be placed on the prosecution in relation to the defence of insanity. There is much to be said for the English courts adopting this position at the earliest possible opportunity.

2. Connection Between Basic and Presumed Fact

It might be argued that if the prosecution has proved certain facts, leaving an inherently improbable defence to be proved by the defendant, there is a low risk of wrongful conviction. This argument can be put in the language of presumptions. If the prosecution has proved a basic fact that makes it very likely that a presumed fact is also true, the presumption of the second fact is reasonable. The closer the connection between the basic and the presumed fact, the more likely it is that the presumed fact is true. As Kenneth Dawkins puts the argument:[208]

> [A] combination of a presumption of fact and a reverse onus clause might be defended on the ground that proof of the basic fact renders the existence of the presumed fact so probable that it is sensible to assume the presence of the presumed fact until D proves

[205] Section 1 of the Criminal Procedure (Insanity and Unfitness to Plead) Act 1991 prevents a jury from returning a verdict of not guilty by reason of insanity except on the testimony of two or more registered medical practitioners with expertise in mental disorder.

[206] *Bratty v AG for Northern Ireland* [1963] AC 386 (HL).

[207] The same argument applies in respect of the burden of proof for the partial defence of diminished responsibility. Section 2(2) of the Homicide Act 1957 places the persuasive burden on the defendant to establish this defence. This was held consistent with Art6(2) in *R v Lambert, Ali and Jordan* [2002] QB 1112 (CA). See also *Robinson v UK* (App No 20858/92) EComHR 5 May 1993. The Law Commission argued in 2004 that the reverse burden was acceptable: Law Commission *Partial Defences to Murder (Law Com No 290)* (Cmnd 6301) (HMSO, Norwich 2004) [5.90]. However, if the problems of proof for the prosecution can be resolved by an evidential burden, then the persuasive burden is not necessary and is therefore disproportionate.

[208] KE Dawkins 'Statutory Presumptions and Reverse Onus Clauses in the Criminal Law: In Search of Rationality' (1987) 3 *Canterbury Law Review* 214, 216. The need for a 'rational connection' has been especially important in the US cases: *Tot v US*, 319 US 463 (1943); *Leary v US*, 395 US 623 (1969); County Court of *Ulster County v Allen*, 442 US 140 (1979).

otherwise. On this view presumptions save the cost and time of proving the same relationship between similar facts in different cases and thereby provide for more uniform adjudication.

The connection between the basic and the presumed fact was emphasised in some early Canadian cases concerning the presumption of innocence protected by section 11(d) of the Canadian Charter of Rights and Freedoms. In *R v Oakes*,[209] the Supreme Court of Canada considered a reverse burden in a drug trafficking offence. Upon proof of possession of a prohibited drug, it was to be presumed that the defendant was guilty of trafficking unless he or she proved otherwise. Dickson CJ considered that the reverse burden of proof could not be regarded as compatible with section 11(d) unless there was 'a rational connection between the basic fact of possession and the presumed fact of possession for the purpose of trafficking.'[210] Dickson CJ considered that 'it would be irrational to infer that a person had an intent to traffic on the basis of his or her possession of a very small quantity of narcotics'.[211] In Dickson CJ's view, the absence of a rational connection between the basic and presumed fact meant that the reverse burden could not satisfy the proportionality test and was therefore incompatible with section 11(d).[212]

In *Sheldrake*,[213] counsel for the defendant submitted that a presumption could be justified only if 'the facts presumed flow inexorably from the facts proved or if there was a rational connection between the fact proved and the fact presumed'.[214] Lord Bingham considered this argument and stated:[215]

> I am not sure that these propositions find much support in the Strasbourg jurisprudence, although sometimes the fact presumed would flow all but inexorably from the fact proved . . . and the closer the connection between the fact proved and the fact presumed the more reasonable the presumption would usually be. Conversely, the more far-fetched a presumption is, the more suspect it is likely to be. But it cannot be necessary that the facts presumed flow inexorably from the facts proved, since in such an event there would scarcely be a need for any presumption, and rarely, if ever, would a statutory presumption lack a rational connection with a fact proved.

The effect of this statement is that the presumed fact need not 'flow inexorably' from the basic fact, but the connection between the basic and presumed fact will be relevant to whether the presumption and an accompanying reverse burden is proportionate.

It would be possible for the presumed fact to be so closely related to the basic fact that it is inherently improbable that the basic fact exists without the presumed

[209] *R v Oakes* [1986] 1 SCR 103.
[210] Ibid 141.
[211] Ibid 142.
[212] See also *R v Downey* [1992] 2 SCR 10, 41 (McLachlin J, dissenting); *R v Laba* [1994] 3 SCR 965, 1008 (Sopinka J). See also, in South Africa, *S v Bhulwana*; *S v Gwadiso* 1996 (1) SA 388 (CC) [24] (O'Regan J); *S v Julies* 1996 (4) SA 313 (CC) [3] (Kriegler J).
[213] [2005] 1 AC 264 (HL).
[214] Ibid [43].
[215] Ibid.

fact. Hence, if the defendant is given the opportunity to disprove the presumed fact, there is a low risk of wrongful conviction because of the very high likelihood the presumed fact exists. This reasoning may explain why Parliament saw fit to require a defendant to prove, on a charge of drug possession, that he or she neither knew, nor suspected, nor had reason to suspect that an item possessed was a controlled drug.[216] There would be very few cases in which a person is in possession of a controlled drug but does not understand the nature of the item in his or her possession. Once the prosecution has proved possession, it is very likely the defendant is guilty of knowingly possessing the drug, so that the risk of convicting an innocent person is low.

It does not follow from this, however, that the persuasive burden ought to be placed on the defendant with respect to such a defence. The persuasive burden should be reversed only when that is 'necessary'. As Lord Steyn observed in *R v Lambert*,[217] where a defendant is found in possession of controlled drugs, the prosecution will not normally encounter difficulties in proving that the defendant knew the nature of the item in his or her possession.[218] When the defence is inherently improbable because the prosecution has already proved facts that make it very likely the defendant is guilty, it will not normally be necessary to reverse the burden of proof. The inherent improbability of the defence is itself a matter which the jury can take into account when assessing the evidence. As Barbara Underwood states:[219]

> The unusual character of a claim should ordinarily affect the factfinder's evaluation of the evidence. The factfinder is quite properly skeptical of a story that seems to him improbable in the light of his common-sense knowledge of ordinary human events. If, having discounted the defendant's claim for its improbability, he nevertheless finds the case a close one, it would be redundant to use a burden-of-proof rule that directs him to discount the claim still further for its improbability. Under such a rule, the defendant with an unusual claim is doubly damned for it.

The fact of a very close connection between the facts proved and the guilt of the defendant cannot, on its own, justify the reversal of persuasive burden. It is necessary to establish further that the prosecution is beset by difficulties of proof that cannot be ameliorated through the use of an evidential burden.

F. Conclusion

This chapter has analysed each of the factors relevant to the allocation of the burden of proof. It has identified three situations in which the rationale of protecting

216 Misuse of Drugs Act 1971, s 28(2).
217 [2002] 2 AC 545 (HL).
218 Ibid [39].
219 Underwood (see n 153 above) 1337.

the innocent is attenuated and in which a reversal of the burden of proof might therefore be permissible. The first is where the penalty for the offence is non-custodial. The second is where the defendant could prove his or her innocence with relative ease. The third is where the prosecution has proved sufficient facts to establish that the conduct of the defendant is wrongful. Other factors such as the seriousness of the offence, the existence of a regulatory regime and the possession of 'peculiar knowledge' do not point to the existence of a reduced risk to the innocent. In those cases where the rationale of protecting the innocent is attenuated, a necessity-focused proportionality analysis should be undertaken by the court to determine if a reverse burden would be consistent with Article 6(2). Only if an evidential burden will not suffice to resolve the problems of proof faced by the prosecution should the burden of proof be reversed.

Conclusion

THIS BOOK HAS argued for an approach to the presumption of innocence that emphasises the values underlying the presumption, rather than the 'balance' between the interests of the community and the rights of the individual. The rule placing the burden of proof on the prosecution and requiring proof beyond reasonable doubt is not a mere accident in the history of the common law. It is a rule that serves the vital and mutually-reinforcing values of protecting the innocent and promoting the rule of law. When there is a departure from this rule, so that the defendant in a criminal case is required to carry the persuasive burden of proof, there is an increased risk that an innocent person will be convicted. Further, the rule of law is undermined if conviction and punishment are imposed in the absence of the unequivocal demonstration before a court that the defendant is guilty. The proper recognition of these values leads to the conclusion that the interest of the individual in avoiding wrongful conviction outweighs the interest of the community in obtaining more convictions.

When considering cases under Article 6(2), English courts must begin from the position that every persuasive burden on a defendant constitutes a *prima facie* interference with the presumption of innocence. This is because a reverse persuasive burden allows conviction in the absence of proof beyond reasonable doubt that the defendant falls within the scope of the criminal prohibition. Following this, the court must ask whether the reverse burden is imposed in circumstances where the rationale of protecting the innocent is not really called into play, or is called into play only in an attenuated sense. This may be the case if there is a low risk of wrongful conviction or if the consequences of conviction are minimal. Outside of these situations, the courts should find that any reversal of the persuasive burden is incompatible with Article 6(2). Accordingly, using the interpretive power in section 3 of the HRA, the court should read the persuasive burden as an evidential burden.

Even when the rationale of protecting the innocent is attenuated, it does not follow that all reverse persuasive burdens will be compatible with Article 6(2). This is because the rationale of promoting the rule of law continues to operate. In such cases, the courts should use a proportionality analysis to determine whether the reverse burden is permissible. The proportionality analysis must focus upon whether it is 'necessary' to employ a persuasive burden, rather than an evidential burden. Considerations of 'balance' between the community interest in obtaining convictions and the residual interest of the defendant in avoiding wrongful conviction may be taken into account as part of the 'necessity' test. Further, the court should factor in the need to promote the rule of law by ensuring the demonstration of guilt. Only in those cases where a reverse persuasive burden is 'necessary' will it be compatible with Article 6(2). Few cases will fall into this category because, for the most part, an evidential burden is sufficient to overcome any problems of proof faced by the prosecution.

The approach to the presumption of innocence defended in this book is at odds with the approach taken by the Strasbourg Court. That court continually holds that the presumption of innocence is subject to 'reasonable limits' and, in general, permits criminal courts to impose the burden of proof on defendants. At a time when the English courts are developing the principles to apply under the HRA, it is important to re-affirm the values associated with the rule placing the persuasive burden in criminal trials on the prosecution and requiring proof beyond reasonable doubt. This rule should not be regarded as a concession to defendants that can be overlooked whenever the community interest demands it. Rather, it should be treated as a rule that is integral to the justification for the imposition of punishment. Departure from the rule ought to be permitted only in limited circumstances. By moving away from exclusive reliance upon a proportionality analysis to determine the compatibility of reverse burdens with Article 6(2), the English courts would be taking an important step in affirming and defending the right to be presumed innocent.

Less than a decade after the entry into force of the HRA, the principles currently applied by the English courts to determine the compatibility of reverse burdens with Article 6(2) should not be regarded as immutable. Article 6(2) expresses the presumption of innocence in unqualified terms, so that a proportionality-based approach to Article 6(2) is contrary to its wording. The right to be presumed innocent is a vital feature of a fair criminal trial, and English courts have the capacity to protect this feature by taking a more robust, value-based approach to Article 6(2). In turn, through the exchange of ideas with the Strasbourg Court, a more robust approach by the English courts could lead to the greater protection of the presumption of innocence throughout Europe. If this shared understanding were to develop, it would become increasingly difficult for any state, including the United Kingdom, to depart from the presumption of innocence without attracting adverse comment. English courts must seize every opportunity to strengthen support for the rule that the prosecution must bear the burden of proving the guilt of the defendant in all criminal trials, and in respect of every aspect of the offence.

BIBLIOGRAPHY

Ackerman, B, 'The Conclusive Presumption Shuffle' (1977) 125 *University of Pennsylvania Law Review* 761

—— 'The Emergency Constitution' (2004) 113 *Yale Law Journal* 1029

Adams, F, 'Onus of Proof in Criminal Cases' in RS Clark (ed) *Essays on Criminal Law in New Zealand* (Sweet and Maxwell, Wellington 1971) 67

Alder, M, 'Law and Incommensurability: Introduction' (1998) 146 *University of Pennsylvania Law Review* 1169

—— 'Expressive Theories of Law: A Skeptical Overview' (2000) 148 *University of Pennsylvania Law Review* 1363

Alder, J, 'Incommensurable Values and Judicial Review: The Case of Local Government' [2001] *PL* 717

Aleinikoff, TA, 'Constitutional Law in the Age of Balancing' (1987) 96 *Yale Law Journal* 943

Alexander, L, 'Reconsidering the Relationship Among Voluntary Acts, Strict Liability and Negligence in Criminal Law' (1990) *Social Philosophy and Policy* 84

Alexy, R, 'Constitutional Rights, Balancing and Rationality' (2003) 16 *Ratio Juris* 131

—— 'On Balancing and Subsumption: A Structural Comparison' (2003) 16 *Ratio* Juris 433

Alexy, R and J Rivers (tr), *A Theory of Constitutional Rights* (OUP, Oxford 2002)

Allan, TRS, *Constitutional Justice: A Liberal Theory of the Rule of Law* (OUP, Oxford 2001)

—— 'Common Law Reason and the Limits of Judicial Deference' in D Dyzenhaus (ed) *The Unity of Public Law* (Hart Publishing, Oxford 2004)

—— 'Human Rights and Judicial Review: A Critique of "Due Deference"' (2006) 65 *CLJ* 671

Allen, C *Legal Duties and Other Essays in Jurisprudence* (Clarendon Press, Oxford 1931)

Allen, RJ, 'Mullaney v Wilbur: The Supreme Court and the Substantive Criminal Law—An Examination of the Limits of Legitimate Intervention' (1977) 55 *Texas Law Review* 269

—— 'The Restoration of *In re Winship*: A Comment on Burdens of Persuasion in Criminal Cases after *Patterson v New York*' (1977) 76 *Michigan Law Review* 30

—— 'More on Constitutional Process of Proof Problems in Criminal Cases' (1980) 94 *Harvard Law Review* 1795

—— 'Structuring Jury Decision-Making in Criminal Cases: A Unified Constitutional Approach to Evidentiary Devices' (1980) 94 *Harvard Law Review* 321

Allen, RJ and LA De Grazia, 'The Constitutional Requirement of Proof Beyond Reasonable Doubt in Criminal Cases: A Comment Upon Incipient Chaos in the Lower Courts' (1982) 20 *American Criminal Law Review* 1

Allison, JWF, 'Fuller's Analysis of Polycentric Disputes and the Limits of Adjudication' [1994] *CLJ* 367

—— *A Continental Distinction in the Common Law: A Historical and Comparative Perspective on English Public Law* (Clarendon Press, Oxford 1996)

Arai-Takahashi, Y, *The Margin of Appreciation Doctrine and the Principle of Proportionality in the Jurisprudence of the ECHR* (Intersentia, Antwerp 2002)

Bibliography

Arenella, P 'Convicting the Morally Blameless: Reassessing the Relationship Between Legal and Moral Accountability' (1992) *UCLA Law Review* 1511

Ashford, HA and DM Risinger, 'Presumptions, Assumptions and Due Process in Criminal Cases: A Theoretical Overview' (1969) 79 *Yale Law Journal* 165

Ashworth, A, 'Defining Criminal Offences without Harm' in P Smith (ed) *Criminal Law: Essays in Honour of JC Smith* (Butterworths, London 1987) 7

—— 'The Scope of Criminal Liability for Omissions' (1989) 105 *LQR* 424

—— 'Towards a Theory of Criminal Legislation' (1989) 1 *Criminal Law Forum* 41

—— 'Taking the Consequences' in S Shute, J Gardner and J Horder (eds) *Action and Value in Criminal Law* (OUP, Oxford 1993) 107

—— 'Victim Impact Statements and Sentencing [1993] *Crim LR* 498

—— *The Criminal Process: An Evaluative Study* 2nd edn (OUP, Oxford 1998)

—— 'The European Convention and Criminal Law' in Cambridge Centre for Public Law *The Human Rights Act and the Criminal and Regulatory Process* (Hart, Oxford 1999) 37

—— 'Article 6 and the Fairness of Trials' [1999] *Crim LR* 261

—— 'Is the Criminal Law a Lost Cause?' (2000) 116 *LQR* 225

—— 'Criminal Proceedings after the Human Rights Act: The First Year' [2001] *Crim LR* 855

—— *Human Rights, Serious Crime and Criminal Procedure* (Sweet and Maxwell, London 2002)

—— 'Social Control and "Anti-Social Behaviour": The Subversion of Human Rights?' (2004) 120 *LQR* 263

—— 'Case and Comment: Burden of Proof' [2005] *Crim LR* 215

—— 'Victims' Rights, Defendants' Rights and Criminal Procedure' in A Crawford and J Goodey (eds) *Integrating a Victim Perspective within Criminal Justice* (Ashgate, Dartmouth 2000) 185

—— *Principles of Criminal Law* 5th edn (OUP, Oxford 2006)

—— 'Case and Comment: R v G' [2006] *Crim LR* 930

—— 'Four Threats to the Presumption of Innocence' (2006) 10 *E and P* 241

—— 'Four Threats to the Presumption of Innocence' (2006) 123 *South African Law Journal* 63

—— 'Principles, Pragmatism and the Law Commission's Recommendations on Homicide Law Reform' [2007] *Crim LR* 333

—— 'Security, Terrorism and the Value of Human Rights' in L Lazarus and B Goold *Security and Human Rights* (Hart Publishing, Oxford 2007) 203

Ashworth, A and M Blake, 'The Presumption of Innocence in English Criminal Law' [1996] *Crim LR* 306

Ashworth, A and M Redmayne, *The Criminal Process* 3rd edn (OUP Oxford 2005)

Bakalis, C, 'Anti-Social Behaviour Orders—Criminal Penalties or Civil Injunctions' (2003) 62 *CLJ* 583

Baker, JH, 'Criminal Courts and Procedure at Common Law 1550-1800' in JS Cockburn (ed) *Crime in England 1550-1800* (Methuen, London 1977)

—— *An Introduction to English Legal History* 4th edn (Butterworths, London 2002)

Bassiouni, MC, 'Human Rights in the Context of Criminal Justice: Identifying International Procedural Protections and Equivalent Protections in National Constitutions' (1993) 3 *Duke Journal of Comparative and International Law* 235

Beatty, D, *The Ultimate Rule of Law* (OUP, Oxford 2004)

Bennett, A, *The Queen v Palmer: Verbatim Report of the Trial of William Palmer at the Central Criminal Court, Old Bailey, London, May 14, and following days, 1856* (J Allen, London 1856)

Bennion, F, 'Statutory Exceptions: A Third Knot in the Golden Thread' [1988] *Crim LR* 31
Bentham, J, *A Comment on the Commentaries* (Clarendon Press, Oxford 1928) (original 1776)
—— *An Introduction to the Principles of Morals and Legislation* (Methuen, London 1982) (original 1789)
Best, W, *A Treatise on Presumptions of Law and Fact: With the Theory and Rules of Presumptive or Circumstantial Proof in Criminal Cases* (S Sweet, London 1844)
—— *A Treatise on the Principles of Evidence and Practice as to Proofs in Courts of Common Law: With Elementary Rules for Conducting the Examination and Cross-Examination of Witnesses* (S Sweet, London 1849)
Beyleveld, D, 'Identifying, Exploring and Predicting Deterrence' (1979) 19 *British Journal of Criminology* 205
Birch, D, 'Hunting the Snark: The Elusive Statutory Exception' [1988] *Crim LR* 221
—— 'Burden of Proof: R v Lambert' [2001] *Crim LR* 806
Blackstone, W, *Commentaries on the Laws of England: Book the First* (Clarendon Press, Oxford 1765)
—— *Commentaries on the Laws of England: Book the Fourth* (Clarendon Press, Oxford 1769)
Blake, N, 'Importing Proportionality: Clarification or Confusion' [2002] *EHRLR* 19
Boucher, D and P Kelly (eds), *The Social Contract from Hobbes to Rawls* (Routledge, London 1994)
Bradley, AW and KD Ewing, *Constitutional and Administrative Law* 13th edn, (Pearson, Harlow 2003)
Braithwaite, J, *Crime, Shame and Reintegration* (CUP, Cambridge 1989)
Braithwaite, J and P Pettit, *Not Just Deserts: A Republican Theory of Criminal Justice* (Clarendon Press, Oxford 1990)
Bridge, N, 'Presumptions and Burdens' (1949) 12 *MLR* 273
Brown, G, 'Deeming Provisions and the Presumption of Innocence—Rebuttable Presumption vs Irrebuttable Presumption' (1997) 7 *Caribbean Law Review* 392
Buxton, R, 'The Convention and the English Law of Criminal Evidence' in Cambridge Centre for Public Law *The Human Rights Act and the Criminal and Regulatory Process* (Hart, Oxford 1999) 45
Campbell, K, 'Offence and Defence' in IH Dennis (ed) *Criminal Law and Justice* (Sweet and Maxwell London 1987) 73
Cascarelli, J, 'Presumption of Innocence and Natural Law: Machiavelli and Aquinas' (1996) 41 *American Journal of Jurisprudence* 229
Chapman, P, 'The Politics of Judging: Section 1 of the Charter of Rights and Freedoms' (1986) 24 *Osgoode Hall Law Journal* 867
Cheney, D *et al*, *Criminal Justice and the Human Rights Act 1998* 2nd edn (Jordan, Bristol 2001)
Chrimes, SB (ed), *De Laudibus Legum Anglie* (CUP, Cambridge 1942)
Christie, GC and AK Pye, 'Presumptions and Assumptions in the Criminal Law: Another View' (1970) *Duke Law Journal* 919
Christie, N, 'Conflicts as Property' (1977) 17 *British Journal of Criminology* 1
Clayton, R, 'Regaining a Sense of Proportion: The Human Rights Act and the Proportionality Principle' [2001] *EHRLR* 504
—— 'Judicial Deference and Democratic Dialogue: The Legitimacy of Judicial Intervention under the Human Rights Act 1998' [2004] *PL* 33

Clayton, R and H Tomlinson, *The Law of Human Rights* (OUP, Oxford 2000)
Cole, D, 'The Priority of Morality: The Emergency Constitution's Blind Spot' (2004) 113 *Yale Law Journal* 173
Collier, C, 'The Improper Use of Presumptions in Recent Criminal Law Adjudication' (1986) 38 *Stanford Law Review* 423
Cooke, R, *Turning Points of the Common Law* (Sweet and Maxwell, London 1997)
Cooper, DE, 'Hegel's Theory of Punishment' in ZA Pelczynski (ed) *Hegel's Political Philosophy: Problems and Perspectives* (CUP, Cambridge 1971)
Cooper, J and A Marshall-Williams, *Legislating for Human Rights: The Parliamentary Debates on the Human Rights Bill* (Hart, Oxford 2000)
Council of Europe *Collected Edition of the "Travaux Preparatoires" of the European Convention on Human Rights, Vols I–VIII* (Martinus Nijhoff, The Hague 1977)
Craig, P, 'Formal and Substantive Conceptions of the Rule of Law: An Analytical Framework' [1997] *PL* 467
—— *Administrative Law* 5th edn (Sweet and Maxwell, London 2003)
Craig, P and G de Búrca, *EU Law: Text, Cases and Materials* 3rd edn (OUP, Oxford 2003)
Criminal Law Revision Committee *Eleventh Report, Evidence (General)* (Cmnd 4991) (HMSO, London 1972)
Cross, R, *Evidence* (Butterworth and Co, London 1958)
—— *The Golden Thread of the English Criminal Law: The Burden of Proof* (CUP, Cambridge 1976)
Damaška, M, *Evidence Law Adrift* (Yale University Press, New Haven 1997)
Dawkins, KE, 'Statutory Presumptions and Reverse Onus Clauses in the Criminal Law: In Search of Rationality' (1987) 3 *Canterbury Law Review* 214
De Búrca, G, 'The Principle of Proportionality and its Application in EC Law' (1993) 13 *Yearbook of European Law* 105
De Haan, W, *The Politics of Redress: Crime, Punishment and Penal Abolition* (Unwin Hyman, London 1990)
Dean, M, 'Negative Averments and the Burden of Proof' [1966] *Crim LR* 594
Denning, A, 'Presumptions and Burdens' (1945) 61 *LQR* 379
Dennis, IH 'Reverse Onuses and the Presumption of Innocence: In Search of Principle' [2005] *Crim LR* 901
—— *The Law of Evidence* 3rd edn (Sweet and Maxwell, London 2007)
Dingwall, G 'Statutory Exceptions, Burdens of Proof and the Human Rights Act 1998' (2002) 65 *MLR* 450
Dixon, O, 'A Legacy of Hadfield, M'Naghten and Maclean (1957) 31 *Australian Law Journal* 255
Dlamini, CRM, 'Proof Beyond a Reasonable Doubt: An Analysis of Its Meaning and Ideological and Philosophical Underpinnings' (1998) 11 *South African Journal of Criminal Justice* 423
Doran, S 'Alternative Defences: the Invisible Burden on the Trial Judge' [1991] *Crim LR* 878
Dripps, D, 'The Constitutional Status of the Reasonable Doubt Rule' (1987) 75 *California Law Review* 1665
Duff, RA, 'Codifying Criminal Fault: Conceptual Problems and Presuppositions' in IH Dennis (ed) *Criminal Law and Justice* (Sweet and Maxwell, London 1987) 93
—— *Punishment, Communication and Community* (OUP, Oxford 2001)
—— 'Rule Violations and Wrongdoings' in S Shute and AP Simester (eds) *Criminal Law Theory: Doctrines of the General Part* (OUP, Oxford 2002) 47

—— 'Strict Liability, Legal Presumptions, and the Presumption of Innocence' in AP Simester (ed) *Appraising Strict Liability* (OUP, Oxford 2005) 125
Dworkin, RB, 'Easy Cases, Bad Law, and Burdens of Proof' (1972) 25 *Vanderbilt Law Review* 1151
Dworkin, R, *Takings Rights Seriously* (Duckworth, London 1977)
—— 'Principle, Policy and Procedure' in CFH Tapper *Crime, Proof and Punishment: Essays in Memory of Sir Rupert Cross* (Butterworths, London 1981) 193
—— 'Right as Trumps' in Jeremy Waldron (ed) *Theories of Rights* (OUP, Oxford 1984) 153
—— *A Matter of Principle* (Harvard University Press, Cambridge 1985)
—— *Is Democracy Possible Here?* (Princeton University Press, Princeton 2006)
—— *Justice In Robes* (Harvard University Press, Cambridge 2006)
Dyzenhaus, D, 'Form and Substance in the Rule of Law: A Democratic Justification for Judicial Review?' in C Forsyth (ed) *Judicial Review and the Constitution* (Hart, Oxford 2000) 141
—— *The Constitution of Law: Legality in a Time of Emergency* (CUP, Cambridge 2006)
Edwards, R, 'Reading Down Legislation under the Human Rights Act' (2000) 20 *Legal Studies* 353
—— 'Judicial Deference under the Human Rights Act' (2002) 65 *MLR* 859
Eggleston, R, *Evidence Proof and Probability* 2nd edn (Weidenfeld and Nicolson, London 1983)
Eissen, M-A, 'The Principle of Proportionality in the Case-Law of the European Court of Human Rights' in Ronald MacDonald, Franz Matscher and Herbert Petzold (eds), *The European System for the Protection of Human Rights* (Martinus Nijhoff, London 1993) 125
Ekins, R, 'Judicial Supremacy and the Rule of Law' (2003) 119 *LQR* 127
Emiliou, N, *The Principle of Proportionality in European Law: A Comparative Study* (Kluwer Law International, London 1996) 23-66, 134-39
Emmerson, B, A Ashworth and A MacDonald, *Human Rights and Criminal Justice* 2nd edn (Sweet and Maxwell, London 2007)
Ewing, KD and C Gearty, 'Rocky Foundations for Labour's New Rights' [1997] *EHRLR* 146
Fallon, RH, 'Individual Rights and the Powers of Governments' (1993) 27 *Georgia Law Review* 343
Fawcett, JES, *The Application of the European Convention on Human Rights* 2nd edn (Clarendon Press, Oxford 1987)
Feinberg, J, 'The Expressive Function of Punishment' (1965) 49 *Monist* 397
—— 'The Expressive Function of Punishment' in Joel Feinberg, *Doing and Deserving: Essays in the Theory of Responsibility* (Princeton University Press, Princeton 1970) 95
—— *The Moral Limits of the Criminal Law: Harm to Others* (OUP, Oxford 1984)
Feldman, D, 'Proportionality and the Human Rights Act 1998' in Evelyn Ellis (ed) *The Principle of Proportionality in the Laws of Europe* (Hart, Oxford 1999) 117
—— *Civil Liberties and Human Rights in England and Wales* 2nd edn (OUP, Oxford 2002)
Ferguson, PW, 'Proof of Innocence' (2004) 36 *Scots Law Times* 223
—— 'Reverse Burdens of Proof' (2004) 22 *Scots Law Times* 133
Finnis, J, *Natural Law and Natural Rights* (Clarendon Press, Oxford 1980)
—— 'A Bill of Rights for Britain? The Moral of Contemporary Jurisprudence' (1985) *Proceedings of the British Academy* 303
—— 'The Authority of Law in the Predicament of Contemporary Social Theory' (1985) 1 *Notre Dame Journal of Law, Ethics and Public Policy* 115

Fletcher, G, 'Two Kinds of Legal Rules: A Comparative Study of Burden-of-Persuasion Practices in Criminal Cases' (1968) 77 *Yale Law Journal* 880

—— 'The Nature of Justification' in S Shute, J Gardner and J Horder (eds) *Action and Value in Criminal Law* (Clarendon Press, Oxford 1993) 175

—— *Rethinking Criminal Law* (OUP, Oxford 2000)

Fordham, M and T de la Mare, 'Identifying the Principles of Proportionality' in Jeffrey Jowell and Jonathan Cooper (eds), *Understanding Human Rights Principles* (Hart Oxford 2001) 27

Foster, M, *A Report of Some Proceedings on the Commission of Oyer and Terminer and Gaol Delivery For the Trial of the Rebels in the Year 1746 in the County of Surry and Other Crown Cases To Which are Added Discourses Upon a Few Branches of the Crown Law* (Clarendon Press, Oxford 1762)

Fox, WF, 'The "Presumption of Innocence" as Constitutional Doctrine' (1979) 28 *Catholic University Law Review* 253

Fraher, R, 'The Theoretical Justification for the New Criminal Law of the High Middle Ages: "Rei Publicae Interest ne Crimina Remaneant Impunita"' (1984) *University of Illinois Law Review* 577

—— 'Conviction According to Conscience: The Medieval Jurists' Debate Concerning Judicial Discretion and the Law of Proof' (1989) 7 *Law and History Review* 23

Fuller, A and R Urich 'An Analysis of the Constitutionality of Statutory Presumptions that Lessen the Burden of the Prosecution' (1971) 25 *University of Miami Law Review* 420

Fuller, L, 'The Forms and Limits of Adjudication' (1978) 92 *Harvard Law Review* 353

Gardner, J, 'Criminal Law and the Uses of Theory: A Reply to Laing' (1994) 14 *OJLS* 217

—— 'Justifications and Reasons' in AP Simester and ATH Smith (eds) *Harm and Culpability* (Clarendon Press, Oxford 1996) 103

—— 'Punishment—in Proportion and in Perspective' in A Ashworth and M Wasik (eds) *Fundamentals of Sentencing Theory* (OUP, Oxford 1998) 31

—— 'Wrongs and Faults' in AP Simester (ed) *Appraising Strict Liability* (OUP, Oxford 2005) 51

—— *Offences and Defences: Selected Essays in the Philosophy of Criminal Law* (OUP, Oxford 2007)

Gardner, J and H Jung, 'Making Sense of Mens Rea: Antony Duff's Account' (1991) 11 *OJLS* 559

Gardner, J and S Shute, 'The Wrongness of Rape' in J Horder (ed) *Oxford Essays in Jurisprudence: Fourth Series* (OUP, Oxford 2000) 193

Gardner, S, 'The Importance of Majewski' (1994) 14 *OJLS* 279

Gaskins, RH, *Burdens of Proof in Modern Discourse* (Yale University Press, New Haven 1992)

Gearty, C, 'Reconciling Parliamentary Democracy and Human Rights' (2002) 118 *LQR* 248

—— *Principles of Human Rights Adjudication* (OUP, Oxford 2004)

Godbey, AH, 'The Place of the Code of Hammurabi' (1905) 15 *The Monist* 199

Goldwag, C, 'The Constitutionality of Affirmative Defences after Patterson v New York' (1978) 78 *Columbia Law Review* 655

Goold, B, L Lazarus and G Swiney, *Public Protection, Proportionality and the Search for Balance*, Ministry of Justice Research Series 10/07

Gray, RL, 'Note: Eliminating The (Absurd) Distinction Between *Malum in Se* and *Malum Prohibitum* Crimes' (1995) 73 *Washington University Law Quarterly* 1369

Green, N, 'Proportionality and the Supremacy of Parliament in the UK' in E Ellis (ed) *The Principle of Proportionality in the Laws of Europe* (Hart Publishing, Oxford 1999) 145

Green, SP, 'Six Senses of Strict Liability: A Plea for Formalism' in AP Simester (ed) *Appraising Strict Liability* (OUP, Oxford 2005) 1
—— 'Why It's a Crime to Tear the Tag off a Mattress: Overcriminalization and the Moral Content of Regulatory Offences' (1997) 46 *Emory Law Journal* 1533
Greenleaf, S *A Treatise on the Law of Evidence* 3rd edn (A Maxwell and Son, London 1846)
Greer, S, '"Balancing" and the European Court of Human Rights: A Contribution to the Habermas-Alexy Debate' (2004) 63 *CLJ* 412
—— 'Constitutionalizing Adjudication under the European Convention on Human Rights' (2003) 23 *OJLS* 405
Gross, O, 'Chaos and Rules: Should Responses to Violent Crises Always be Constitutional? (2003) 112 *Yale Law Journal* 1011
Habermas, J and W Regh (tr), *Between Facts and Norms* (Polity Press, Cambridge 1996)
Hall, J, 'Negligent Behavior Should be Excluded from Penal Liability' (1963) 63 *Columbia Law Review* 632
Hamer, D, 'Probabilistic Standards of Proof, Their Complements, and the Errors that are Expected to Flow from Them' (2004) 1 *University of New England Law Journal* 71
—— 'The Presumption of Innocence and Reverse Burdens: A Balancing Act' (2007) 66 *CLJ* 142
Hare, I, 'Placing the Onus Back on the Trial' (2000) 59 *CLJ* 1
Harris, D, M O'Boyle and C Warbrick, *Law of the European Convention on Human Rights* (Butterworths, London 1995)
Harris, DJ, 'The European Convention on Human Rights and English Criminal Law: Parts I and II' [1966] *Crim LR* 205, 266
Hart, HLA ,*Punishment and Responsibility* (OUP, Oxford 1968)
Hatchard, J, B Huber and R Vogler, *Comparative Criminal Procedure* (BIICL, London 1996)
Healy, P, 'Proof and Policy: No Golden Threads' [1987] *Crim LR* 355
Ho, HL, *A Philosophy of Evidence Law: Justice in the Search for Truth* (OUP, Oxford 2008)
Hodivala, J, 'Lost Innocence' (2004) 148(44) *Solicitors Journal* 1336
Hoffman, D and J Rowe, *Human Rights in the UK: A General Introduction to the Human Rights Act 1998* (Longman, Harlow 2003)
Hoffman, L, 'The Influence of the European Principle of Proportionality Upon UK Law' in E Ellis (ed) *The Principle of Proportionality in the Laws of Europe* (Hart Publishing, Oxford 1999) 107
Hogg, P, *Constitutional Law of Canada (Looseleaf)* 5th edn (Thomson Carswell, Toronto 2007)
Home Office, *Rebalancing the Criminal Justice System In Favour of the Law-Abiding Majority: Cutting Crime, Reducing Reoffending and Protecting the Public* (Home Office, London 2006)
—— *Rights Brought Home: The Human Rights Bill* (Cm 3782) (HMSO, London 1997)
Honderich, T, 'On Justifying Protective Punishment' (1982) 22 *British Journal of Criminology* 268
—— *Punishment: The Supposed Justifications Revisited* (Pluto Press, London 2006)
Honoré, AM, *Responsibility and Fault* (Hart Publishing, Oxford 1999)
Horder, J, 'Cognition, Emotion and Criminal Culpability' (1990) 106 *LQR* 469
—— 'Occupying the Moral High Ground? The Law Commission and Duress' [1994] *Crim LR* 334
—— 'Rethinking Non-Fatal Offences Against the Person' (1994) 14 *OJLS* 335
—— 'A Critique of the Correspondence Principle in Criminal Law' [1995] *Crim LR* 759

Horder, J, 'Intention in the Criminal Law: A Rejoinder' (1995) 58 *MLR* 678, 687
—— 'Two Histories and Four Hidden Principles of Mens Rea' (1997) 113 *LQR* 95
—— 'Crimes of Ulterior Intent' in AP Simester and ATH Smith (eds) *Harm and Culpability* (Clarendon Press, Oxford 1996) 153
—— 'Questioning the Correspondence Principle—A Reply' [1999] *Crim LR* 206
—— 'Strict Liability, Statutory Construction, and the Spirit of Liberty' (2002) 118 *LQR* 458
—— *Excusing Crime* (OUP, Oxford 2004)
—— 'Whose Values Should Determine When Liability is Strict' in AP Simester (ed) *Appraising Strict Liability* (OUP, Oxford 2005) 105
Howes, V, 'Reverse Burden of Proof: An Overview of Recent Development' (2004) 168 *Justice of the Peace* 227
Hunt, M, 'Sovereignty's Blight: Why Contemporary Public Law Needs the Concept of 'Due Deference" in Nicholas Bamforth and Peter Leyland (eds), *Public Law in a Multi-Layered Constitution* (Hart Publishing, Oxford 2003) 337
Husak, D, 'Varieties of Strict Liability' (1995) 8 *Canadian Journal of Law and Jurisprudence* 198
—— 'Limitations on Criminalization and the General Part of Criminal Law' in S Shute and AP Simester (eds) *Criminal Law Theory: Doctrines of the General Part* (OUP, Oxford 2002) 13
—— 'Strict Liability, Justice and Proportionality' in AP Simester (ed) *Appraising Strict Liability* (OUP, Oxford 2005) 81
Huxley, P, 'Reverse Proof Burdens in Criminal Proceedings' (2000) 9 *Nottingham Law Journal* 69
Jacobs, F, *The European Convention on Human Rights* (Clarendon Press, Oxford 1975)
—— 'The "Limitation Clauses" of the European Convention on Human Rights' in A de Mestral (ed), *The Limitation of Human Rights in Comparative Constitutional Law* (Les Edition Yvon Blais Inc, Cowansville 1986) 21
—— 'Recent Developments in the Principle of Proportionality in European Community Law' in E Ellis (ed) *The Principle of Proportionality in the Laws of Europe* (Hart Publishing, Oxford 1999) 1
Jeffries, JC and PB Stephan III, 'Defences, Presumptions and the Burden of Proof in Criminal Law' (1979) 88 *Yale Law Journal* 1325
Jones, T, 'Insanity, Automatism and the Burden of Proof on the Accused' (1995) 111 *LQR* 475
Jowell, J, 'Due Deference under the Human Rights Act' in J Jowell and J Cooper (eds) *Delivering Rights? How the Human Rights Act is Working and for Whom* (Hart Publishing, London 2003)
—— 'Judicial Deference and Human Rights: A Question of Competence' in Paul Craig and Richard Rawlings (eds) *Law and Administration in Europe: Essays in Honour of Carol Harlow* (OUP, Oxford 2003) 67
—— 'Judicial Deference: Servility, Civility or Institutional Capacity?' [2003] *PL* 592
Jowell, J and A Lester, 'Proportionality: Neither Novel nor Dangerous' in JJowell and D Oliver (eds) *New Directions in Judicial Review* (Stevens and Sons London 1988)
Judicial Studies Board, *Specimen Directions* (2008) available at www.jsboard.co.uk/criminal_law/cbb
Kafka, F and W and E Muir (trs), *The Trial* (Vintage, London 1999)
Kamm, F, 'Conflict of Rights: Typology, Methodology and Non-Consequentialism (2001) 7 *Legal Theory* 239

Kant, I and H Paton (tr) *Groundwork of the Metaphysic of Morals* (Hutchinson, London 1948) (original 1785)
Kant, I and J Ladd (tr), *The Metaphysical Elements of Justice* (Bobbs-Merrill, Indianapolis 1965) (original 1797)
Keane, A, *The Modern Law of Evidence* 6th edn (OUP, Oxford 2006)
Kleinig, J, *Punishment and Desert* (Martinus Nijhoff, The Hague 1973)
Klug, F, 'Judicial Deference under the Human Rights Act' [2003] EHRLR 125
Kolb, R, 'The Jurisprudence of the European Court of Human Rights on Detention and Fair Trial in Criminal Matters from 1992 to the End of 1998' (2000) 21 *Human Rights Law Journal* 348
Kumm, M, 'Political Liberalism and the Structure of Rights: On the Place and Limits of the Proportionality Requirement' in G Pavlakos (ed) *Law, Rights and Discourse: The Legal Philosophy of Robert* Alexy (Hart, Oxford 2007) 131
La Forest, G, 'The Balancing of Interests under the Charter' (1992) 2 *National Journal of Constitutional Law* 133
Lacey, N, 'A Clear Concept of Intention: Elusive or Illusory?' (1993) 56 *MLR* 621
Laing, JA, 'The Prospects of a Theory of Criminal Culpability: Mens Rea and Methodological Doubt' (1994) 14 *OJLS* 57
Landau, N 'Summary Conviction and the Development of the Penal Law' (2005) 23 *Law and History Review* 173
Langbein, JH, *Torture and the Law of Proof: Europe and England in the Ancien Regime* (University of Chicago Press, Chicago 1977)
—— 'Criminal Trial Before the Lawyers' (1978) 45 *University of Chicago Law Review* 263
—— *The Origins of Adversary Criminal Trial* (OUP, Oxford 2003)
Laudan, L, 'The Presumption of Innocence: Material or Probatory' (2005) 11 *Legal Theory* 333
—— *Truth, Error and Criminal Law: An Essay in Legal Epistemology* (CUP, Cambridge 2006)
Laufer, WS, 'The Rhetoric of Innocence' (1995) 70 *Washington Law Review* 329
Law Commission, *Legislating the Criminal Code: Offences Against the Person and General Principles (Law Com No 218)* (Cmnd 2370) (HMSO, London 1993)
—— *Murder, Manslaughter and Infanticide (Law Com No 304)* (HC 30) (TSO, London 2006)
—— *Partial Defences to Murder (Law Com No 290)* (Cmnd 6301) (HMSO, Norwich 2004)
Laws, J, 'Law and Democracy' [1995] *PL* 72
—— 'The Limitations of Human Rights' [1998] *PL* 254
Lazarus, L and B Goold (eds), *Security and Human Rights* (Hart, Oxford 2007)
Leigh, I, 'Taking Rights Proportionately: Judicial Review, the Human Rights Act and Strasbourg' [2002] *PL* 265
Leigh, L, *Strict and Vicarious Liability* (Sweet and Maxwell, London 1982)
Lester, A, 'Developing Constitutional Principles of Public Law' [2001] *PL* 684
Lewis, C, 'The Humanitarian Theory of Punishment' (1949) in L Walmsley (ed) *CS Lewis Essay Collection: Literature, Philosophy and Short Stories* (Harper Collins, London 2000) 290
Locke, J, *Two Treatises of Government* (CUP, Cambridge 1967) (original 1690)
—— *An Essay Concerning Human Understanding* (OUP, Oxford 1979) (original 1690)
LSE Jury Projec,t 'Juries and the Rules of Evidence' [1973] *Crim LR* 208
Luban, D, 'Eight Fallacies about Liberty and Security' in RA Wilson (ed) *Human Rights in the 'War on Terror'* (CUP, Cambridge 2005) 242

MacCallum, G, 'Legislative Intent' in Robert Summers (ed) *Essays in Legal Philosophy* (Blackwells, Oxford 1968) 237
MacDonald, R, 'The Margin of Appreciation' in R MacDonald, F Matscher and H Petzold (eds) *The European System for the Protection of Human Rights* (Martinus Nijhoff, London 1993) 83
MacDonald, S, 'The Nature of the Anti-Social Behaviour Order—R (McCann and Others) v Crown Court at Manchester' (2003) 66 *MLR* 630
Mackay, RD, 'Craziness and Codification: Revising the Automatism and Insanity Defences' in IH Dennis (ed) *Criminal Law and Justice* (Sweet and Maxwell, London 1987) 109
—— *Mental Condition Defences in the Criminal Law* (OUP, Oxford 1995)
MacNally, L, *The Rules of Evidence on Pleas of the Crown Illustrated from Printed and Manuscript Trials and Cases* (J Butterworth, London 1802)
MacPhail, ID, 'Human Rights, Burden of Proof, Retrospectivity and Precedent in the House of Lords' (2002) 61 *CLJ* 1
Malek, H *et al* (eds), *Phipson on Evidence* 16th edn (Sweet and Maxwell, London 2005)
Martinson, R, 'What Works? Questions and Answers about Prison Reform' (1974) *Public Interest* 22
Masterman, R, 'Section 2(1) of the Human Rights Act 1998: Binding Domestic Courts to Strasbourg?' [2004] *PL* 725
—— 'Aspiration or Foundation? The Status of the Strasbourg Jurisprudence and the "Convention Rights" in Domestic Law' in H Fenwick, G Phillipson and R Masterman (eds) *Judicial Reasoning under the UK Human Rights Act* (CUP, Cambridge 2007) 57
Mathiesen, T, *The Politics of Abolition: Essays in Political Action* (Martin Robertson, Oxford 1974)
May, AN, *The Bar and the Old Bailey, 1750-1850* (University of North Carolina Press, Chapel Hill 2003)
McBride, J, 'Proportionality and the European Convention on Human Rights' in Evelyn Ellis (ed) *The Principle of Proportionality in the Laws of Europe* (Oxford, Hart Publishing, 1999) 23
McHarg, A, 'Reconciling Human Rights and the Public Interest: Conceptual Problems and Doctrinal Uncertainty in the Jurisprudence of the European Court of Human Rights' (1999) 62 *MLR* 671
Mendes, E, 'The Crucible of the Charter: Judicial Principles v. Judicial Deference in the Context of Section 1' (2005) 27 *Supreme Court Law Review, 2nd Series* 47
Menninger, K, *The Crime of Punishment* (Viking Press, New York 1968)
Meyerson, D, 'Why Courts Should not Balance Rights against the Public Interest' (2007) 31 *Melbourne University Law Review* 873
Michaels, AC, 'Constitutional Innocence' (1999) 112 *Harvard Law Review* 828
—— 'Imposing Constitutional Limits on Strict Liability: Lessons from the American Experience' in AP Simester (ed) *Appraising Strict Liability* (OUP, Oxford 2005) 219
Mill, JS, *On Liberty* (Penguin, Harmondsworth 1974) (original 1859)
Mirfield, P, 'An Ungrateful Reply' [1988] *Crim LR* 233
—— 'The Legacy of Hunt' [1988] *Crim LR* 19
—— 'Silence, Innocence and Human Rights' in P Mirfield and R Smith (eds) *Essays for Colin Tapper* (LexisNexis, London 2003) 126
—— 'How Many Standards of Proof are There?' (2009) 125 *LQR* 31
Mitchell, B, 'In Defence of a Principle of Correspondence' [1999] *Crim LR* 195

Mommsen, T, P Krueger and A Watson (eds), *The Digest of Justinian, Vol IV* (University of Pennsylvania Press, Philadelphia 1985)
Moore, MS, 'The Moral Worth of Retribution' in F Schoeman (ed) *Responsibility, Character and the Emotions* (CUP, Cambridge 1987) 179
Morano, AA, 'A Reexamination of the Development of the Reasonable Doubt Rule' (1975) 55 *Boston University Law Review* 507
Morgan, EM, 'Presumptions' (1937) 12 *Washington Law Review* 255
Morris, H, 'Persons and Punishment' (1968) 52 *Monist* 475
—— 'A Paternalistic Theory of Punishment' (1981) 18 *American Philosophical Quarterly* 263
Morton, J and S Hutchinson, *The Presumption of Innocence* (Carswell, Toronto 1987)
Mulrine, T, 'Reasonable Doubt: How in the World is it Defined?' (1997) 12 *American University Journal of International Law and Policy* 195
Munday, R, 'Name Suppression: An Adjunct to the Presumption of Innocence and to Mitigation of Sentence' [1991] *Crim LR* 680 and 753
—— *Evidence* 4th edn (OUP, Oxford 2007)
Murphy, JG, *Retribution, Justice and Therapy* (Reidel, Dordrecht 1979)
—— 'Retributivism, Moral Education and the Liberal State' (1985) 4 *Crim Just Ethics* 3
Nesson, C, 'Rationality, Presumptions and Judical Comment: A Response to Professor Allen' (1980) 94 *Harvard Law Review* 1574
Newman, J, 'Beyond "Reasonable Doubt"' (1993) 68 *New York University Law Review* 979
Nozick, R, *Anarchy, State and Utopia* (Basil Blackwell, Oxford 1974)
Orchard, G 'The Golden Thread Somewhat Frayed' (1988) 6 *Otago Law Review* 615
Ormerod, D 'Case and Comment: *R v Director of Public Prosecutions, ex p Kebilene and others*' [2000] *Crim LR* 486
—— *Smith and Hogan Criminal Law* 11th edn (OUP, Oxford 2005)
Ovey, C and R White, *Jacobs and White: The European Convention on Human Rights* 4th edn (OUP, Oxford 2006)
Packer, HL, *The Limits of the Criminal Sanction* (Stanford University Press, Stanford 1969)
——'Mens Rea and the Supreme Court' [1962] *Supreme Court Review* 107
Padfield, N, 'The Burden of Proof Unresolved' (2005) 64 *CLJ* 17
Paizes, A, 'A Closer Look at the Presumption of Innocence in our Constitution: What is an Accused Presumed to be Innocent *of*?' (1998) 11 *South African Journal of Criminal Justice* 409
—— 'Chasing Shadows: Exploring the Meaning, Function and Incidence of the Onus of Proof in the South African Law' (1999) 116 *South African Law Journal* 531
Pannick, D, 'Principles of Interpretation of Convention Rights under the Human Rights Act and the Discretionary Area of Judgment' [1998] *PL* 545
Pannick, D and A Lester (eds), *Human Rights: Law and Practice* 2nd edn (Lexis Nexis, London 2004)
Peiris, GL, 'Continuing Departures from Woolmington: A South Asian Perspective' (1987) 7 *Legal Studies* 279
Pennington, K, 'Innocent Until Proven Guilty: The Origins of Legal Maxim' (2003) 63 *Jurist* 106
Phillipps, SM, *A Treatise on the Law of Evidence* 2nd edn (J Butterworth, London 1815)
Phipson, S, *The Law of Evidence* (Stevens and Haynes, London 1892)
Posner, R, *Not a Suicide Pact: The Constitution in a Time of National Emergency* (OUP, New York 2006)

Putnam, AA, *Ten Years a Police Court Judge* (Funk and Wagnells, New York 1884)
—— 'The Presumption of Innocence in the French and Anglo-American Legal Traditions' (2010) 58 *Amercian Journal of Comparative Law* (forthcoming)
Rankin, GC, 'Presumptions and Burdens' (1946) 62 *LQR* 135
Rawls, J, 'Two Concepts of Rules' (1955) 64 *Philosophical Review* 3
Raz, J, 'The Rule of Law and its Virtue' (1977) 93 *LQR* 195
—— *The Authority of Law: Essays on Law and Morality* (Oxford, Oxford University Press, 1979)
—— *The Morality of Freedom* (Clarendon Press, Oxford 1986)
—— 'Autonomy, Toleration and the Harm Principle' in Ruth Gavison (ed) *Issues in Contemporary Legal Philosophy: The Influence of HLA Hart* (Clarendon Press, Oxford 1987) 313
—— 'Intention in Interpretation' in Robert George (ed) *The Autonomy of Law* (Clarendon Press, Oxford 1996) 249
Redmayne, M, 'Rethinking the Privilege Against Self-Incrimination' (2007) 27 *OJLS* 209
Rivers, J, 'Proportionality and Variable Intensity of Review' (2006) 65 *CLJ* 174
—— 'Proportionality, Discretion and the Second Law of Balancing' in G Pavlakos (ed) *Law, Rights and Discourse: The Legal Philosophy of Robert* Alexy (Hart, Oxford 2007) 16
Roberts, P, 'Taking the Burden of Proof Seriously' [1995] *Crim LR* 783
—— 'On the Preconditions and Possibilities of Criminal Law Theory' (1998) 11 *South African Journal of Criminal Justice* 285
—— 'Drug Dealing and the Presumption of Innocence: The Human Rights Act (almost) Bites' (2002) 6 *E and P* 17
—— 'The Presumption of Innocence Brought Home? Kebilene Deconstructed' (2002) 118 *LQR* 41
—— 'Strict Liability and the Presumption of Innocence: An Exposé of Functionalist Assumptions' in AP Simester (ed) *Appraising Strict Liability* (OUP, Oxford 2005) 151
—— 'Criminal Procedure, the Presumption of Innocence and Judicial Reasoning under the Human Rights Act' in H Fenwick, G Phillipson and R Masterman (eds) *Judicial Reasoning under the UK Human Rights Act* (CUP, Cambridge 2007)
Roberts, P and A Zuckerman, *Criminal Evidence* (OUP, Oxford 2004)
Robinson, P, 'Criminal Law Defenses: A Systematic Analysis' (1982) 82 *Columbia Law Review* 199
—— 'The Modern General Part: Three Illusions' in S Shute and AP Simester (eds) *Criminal Law Theory: Doctrines of the General Part* (OUP, Oxford 2002) 75
—— 'Competing Conceptions of Modern Desert: Vengeful, Deontological and Empirical' (2008) 67 *CLJ* 145
Robinson, P and J Darley, 'Does Criminal Law Deter? A Behavioural Science Investigation' (2004) 24 *OJLS* 173
Rolfe, JC, *Ammianus Marcellinus, Vol 1* (Harvard University Press, Cambridge 1935)
Romilly, S, *Observations on the Criminal Law of England as it Relates to Capital Punishment and on the Mode in which it is Administered* (T Cadell and W Davies, London 1810)
Sales, P and B Hooper, 'Proportionality and the Form of Law' (2003) 119 *LQR* 426
Samuels, A, 'What Do the Prosecution have to Prove?' (2005) 169 *JPN* 834
Sassoon, J, *Ancient Laws and Modern Problems: The Balance between Justice and a Legal System* (Third Millenium, London 2001)
Schauer, F, 'Commensurability and its Constitutional Consequences' (1994) 45 *Hastings Law Journal* 785

Schwartz, L, 'Innocence–A Dialogue with Professor Sundby' (1989) 41 *Hastings Law Journal* 153

Schwarze, J, *European Administrative Law* (Sweet and Maxwell, London 1992)

Schwikkard, PJ, 'The Presumption of Innocence: What is it?' (1998) 11 *South African Journal of Criminal Justice* 396

—— *Presumption of Innocence* (Juta and Co, Kenwyn 1999)

Schwikkard, PJ and SE Van der Merwe, *Principles of Evidence* 2nd edn (Juta Law, Cape Town 2002)

Scottish Law Commission, *Report on Insanity and Diminished Responsibility* (The Stationery Office, Edinburgh 2004)

Shapiro, B, '"To a Moral Certainty": Theories of Knowledge and Anglo-American Juries 1600-1850' (1986) *Hastings Law Journal* 153

—— *Beyond Reasonable Doubt and Probable Cause: Historical Perspectives on the Anglo-American Law of Evidence* (University of California Press, Berkeley 1991)

Sheldrick, B 'Shifting Burdens and Required Inferences: The Constitutionality of Reverse Onus Clauses' (1986) 44 *University of Toronto Faculty of Law Review* 179

Sheppard, S, 'The Metamorphoses of Reasonable Doubt: How Changes in the Burden of Proof Have Weakened the Presumption of Innocence' (2003) 78 *Notre Dame Law Review* 1165

Shute, S, 'Knowledge and Belief in the Criminal Law' in Stephen Shute and AP Simester (eds) *Criminal Law Theory: Doctrines of the General Part* (OUP, Oxford 2002) 171

Simester, AP, 'Why Omissions are Special' (1995) 1 *Legal Theory* 311

—— 'Is Strict Liability Always Wrong?' in AP Simester (ed) *Appraising Strict Liability* (OUP, Oxford 2005) 21

Simester, AP and S Shute, 'On the General Part in Criminal Law' in Stephen Shute and AP Simester (eds) *Criminal Law Theory: Doctrines of the General Part* (OUP, Oxford 2002) 1

Simester, AP and A von Hirsch, 'Rethinking the Offense Principle' (2002) 8 *Legal Theory* 269

Simon, RJ, 'Judges' Translations of Burdens of Proof into Statements of Probability' [1969] *Trial Law Guide* 103

Simon, RJ, '"Beyond a Reasonable Doubt": An Experimental Attempt at Quantification (1970) 6 *Journal of Applied Behavioral Science* 203

Simon, RJ and L Mahan, 'Quantifying Burdens of Proof: A View from the Bench the Jury and the Classroom' (1971) 5 *Law and Society Review* 319

Simons, K, 'When is Strict Criminal Liability Just?' (1997) 87 *Journal of Criminal Law and Criminology* 1075

Singh, M, *German Administrative Law in Common Law Perspective* 2nd edn (Springer, London 2001)

Singh, R, 'The Place of the Human Rights Act in a Democratic Society' in J Jowell and J Cooper (eds) *Understanding Human Rights Principles* (Oxford, Hart 2001) 179

Smith, BP, 'Did the Presumption of Innocence Exist in Summary Proceedings?' (2005) 23 *Law and History Review* 191

—— 'The Presumption of Guilt and the English Law of Theft, 1750–1850' (2005) 23 *Law and History Review* 133

Smith, JC, 'The Presumption of Innocence' (1987) 38 *Northern Ireland Legal Quarterly* 223

Smith, P, 'Omission and Responsibility in Legal Theory' (2003) 9 *Legal Theory* 221

Solan, LM, 'Refocusing the Burden of Proof in Criminal Cases: Some Doubt About Reasonable Doubt' (1999) 78 *Texas Law Review* 105
Spencer, J, 'European Convention and the Rules of Criminal Procedure and Evidence in England' in Cambridge Centre for Public Law *The Human Rights Act and the Criminal and Regulatory Process* (Hart, Oxford 1999) 57
—— 'The Danger of Convicting the Innocent' (2004) 154 *New Law Journal* 1364
Spencer, J and A Pedain, 'Approaches to Strict and Constructive Liability in Continental Criminal Law' in AP Simester (ed) *Appraising Strict Liability* (OUP, Oxford 2005) 237
Stannard, JE, 'A Presumption and Four Burdens' (2000) 51 *Northern Ireland Legal Quarterly* 560
Starkie, T, *A Practical Treatise of the Law of Evidence and Digest of Proofs in Civil and Criminal Proceedings* (J and WT Clarke, London 1824)
Starmer, K, 'Positive Rights under the Convention' in J Jowell and JCooper (eds) *Understanding Human Rights Principles* (Oxford, Hart 2001) 139
Stavros, S, *The Guarantees for Accused Persons Under Article 6 of the European Convention on Human Rights: An Analysis of the Application of the Convention and a Comparison with Other Instruments* (Martinus Nijhoff, Dordrecht 1993)
Stein, A, 'After Hunt: The Burden of Proof, Risk of Non-Persuasion and Judicial Pragmatism' (1991) 54 *MLR* 570
—— 'Criminal Defences and the Burden of Proof' (1991) 28 *Coexistence* 133
—— 'From Blackstone to Woolmington: On the Development of a Legal Doctrine' (1993) 14 *Legal History* 14
—— *Foundations of Evidence Law* (OUP, Oxford 2005)
Stephen, JF, *A Digest of the Law of Evidence* (MacMillan and Co, London 1876)
—— *A History of the Criminal Law of England* (London, MacMillan 1883)
Stone, J, 'Burden of Proof and the Judicial Process: A Commentary on *Joseph Constantine Steamship, Ltd v Imperial Smelting Corporation, Ltd*' (1944) 60 *LQR* 262
Sullivan, GR, 'Strict Liability for Criminal Offences in England and Wales Following Incorporation into English Law of the European Convention on Human Rights' in AP Simester (ed) *Appraising Strict Liability* (OUP, Oxford 2005) 195
Summers, S, 'Presumption of Innocence' (2001) 1 *The Juridical Review* 37
Sundby, SE, 'The Reasonable Doubt Rule and the Meaning of Innocence' (1988) 40 *Hastings Law Journal* 457
Sunstein, C, 'Incommensurability and Valuation in Law' (1994) 92 *Michigan Law Review* 779
Tadros, V, 'Insanity and the Capacity for Criminal Responsibility' (2001) 5 *Edinburgh Law Review* 325
—— 'The Characters of Excuse' (2001) 21 *OJLS* 495
—— 'Recklessness and the Duty to Take Care' in S Shute and AP Simester (eds) *Criminal Law Theory: Doctrines of the General Part* (OUP, Oxford 2002) 227
—— *Criminal Responsibility* (Oxford, OUP 2005)
—— 'Rethinking the Presumption of Innocence' (2007) 1 *Criminal Law and Philosophy* 193
Tadros, V and S Tierney, 'The Presumption of Innocence and the Human Rights Act' (2004) 67 *MLR* 402
Tanovich, D, 'The Unravelling of the Golden Thread: The Supreme Court's Compromise of the Presumption of Innocence' (1993) 35 *Criminal Law Quarterly* 194
Tapper, C, *Cross and Tapper on Evidence* 11th edn (OUP, Oxford 2007)

Taylor, J *A Treatise on the Law of Evidence as Administered in England and Ireland with Illustrations from the American and Other Foreign Laws* (A Maxwell and Son, London 1848)
Ten, CL, *Crime, Guilt and Punishment: A Philosophical Introduction* (Clarendon Press, Oxford 1987)
Thayer, JB, 'The Burden of Proof' (1890) 4 *Harvard Law Review* 45
—— 'The Presumption of Innocence in Criminal Cases' (1896) 6 *Yale Law Journal* 185
—— *A Preliminary Treatise on Evidence at the Common Law* (Sweet and Maxwell, London 1898)
Thorne, SE, (ed) *Bracton on the Laws and Customs of England, Vol III* (Harvard University Press, Cambridge 1977)
Trechsel, S, *Human Rights in Criminal Proceedings* (OUP, Oxford 2005)
Tribe, LH and PO Gudridge, 'The Anti-Emergency Constitution' (2004) 113 *Yale Law Journal* 1801
Takis T, 'The Principle of Proportionality in Community Law: From the Rule of Law to Market Integration' (1996) 31 *The Irish Jurist* 83
—— 'Proportionality in Community Law: Searching for the Appropriate Standard of Scrutiny' in Evelyn Ellis (ed) *The Principle of Proportionality in the Laws of Europe* (Hart Publishing, Oxford 1999) 65
—— *The General Principles of EC Law* (OUP, Oxford 1999) chs 3-4
Turenne, S, 'The Compatibility of Criminal Liability with Freedom of Expression' [2007] *Crim LR* 866
Tushnet, M, 'Constitutional Limitation of Substantive Criminal Law: An Examination of the Meaning of *Mullaney v Wilbur*' (1975) 55 *Boston University Law Review* 775
Ullmann-Margalit, E, 'On Presumption' (1983) 80 *Journal of Philosophy* 143
Underwood, BD, 'The Thumb on the Scales of Justice: Burdens of Persuasion in Criminal Cases' (1977) 86 *Yale Law Journal* 1299
Usher, J *General Principles of EC Law* (Longman, New York 1998) 37-51
van Dijk, P *et al* (eds), *Theory and Practice of the European Convention on Human Rights* 4th edn (Intersentia, Oxford 2006)
van Gerven, W, 'The Effect of Proportionality on the Actions of Member States of the European Community: National Viewpoints from Continental Europe' in E Ellis (ed) *The Principle of Proportionality in the Laws of Europe* (Hart Publishing, Oxford 1999) 37
van Zyl Smit, D and A Ashworth, 'Disproportionate Sentences as Human Rights Violations' (2004) 67 *MLR* 541
Volokh, A, '*n* Guilty Men' (1997) 146 *University of Pennsylvania Law Review* 173
von Hirsch, A, 'Proportionality in the Philosophy of Punishment: From "Why Punish?" to "How Much?"' (1990) 1 *Criminal Law Forum* 259
—— 'Selective Incapacitation: Some Doubts' in A von Hirsch and A Ashworth (eds) *Principled Sentencing: Readings on Theory and Policy* (Hart Publishing, Oxford 1998) 119
—— *Censure and Sanctions* (Clarendon Press, Oxford 1993)
von Hirsch, A and A Ashworth, *Proportionate Sentencing: Exploring the Principles* (OUP, Oxford 2005)
von Hirsch, A *et al*, *Criminal Deterrence and Sentence Severity: An Analysis of Recent Research* (Hart, Oxford 1999)
Waldman, T, 'Origins of the Legal Doctrine of Reasonable Doubt' (1959) 20 *Journal of the History of Ideas* 299
Waldron, J, 'Security and Liberty: The Image of Balance' (2003) *11 Journal of Political Philosophy* 191

Walker, N, *Punishment Danger and Stigma* (Blackwell, Oxford 1980)
—— *Why Punish?* (OUP, Oxford 1991)
Wasik, M, 'Shifting the Burden of Strict Liability' [1982] *Crim LR* 567
Weiser, I, 'The Presumption of Innocence in section 11(d) of the Charter and Persuasive and Evidential Burdens' (1989) 31 *Criminal Law Quarterly* 318
Wells, C, 'Swatting the Subjectivist Bug' [1982] *Crim LR* 209
—— 'Whither Insanity' [1983] *Crim LR* 787
Wiley, J, 'The New Federal Defence: Not Guilty by Reason of Blamelessness' (1999) 85 *Virginia Law Review* 1021
Wilkins, J, *Of the Principles and Duties of Natural Religion* 8th edn (J Knapton, London, 1722) (original 1678)
Williams, CR, 'Placing the Burden of Proof' in Enid Campbell and Louis Waller (eds) *Well and Truly Tried: Essays on Evidence in Honour of Sir Richard Eggleston* (Law Book Company Sydney 1982) 284
Williams, G, 'The Definition of Crime' (1955) 8 *Current Legal Problems* 107
—— *Criminal Law: The General Part* 2nd edn (Stevens, London 1961)
—— *The Proof of Guilt: A Study of the English Criminal Trial* 3rd edn (Stevens, London 1963)
—— 'Evidential Burdens on the Defence' (1977) 127 *New Law Journal* 182
—— 'The Evidential Burden: Some Common Misapprehensions' (1977) 127 *New Law Journal* 156
—— 'Offences and Defences' (1982) 2 *Legal Studies* 233
—— 'The Logic of "Exceptions"' (1988) 47 *CLJ* 261
Wilson, V, 'Shifting Burdens in Criminal Law: A Burden on Due Process' (1981) 8 *Hastings Constitutional Law Quarterly* 731
Wood, D, 'Dangerous Offenders, and the Morality of Protective Sentencing' [1988] *Crim LR* 424
Wootton, B, *Crime and the Criminal Law* (Stevens, London 1963)
—— *Crime and the Criminal Law: Reflections of a Magistrate and Social Scientist* 2nd edn (Steven and Sons, London 1981)
Young, A, 'Judicial Sovereignty and the Human Rights Act 1998' (2002) 61 *CLJ* 53
Zander, M, 'The Criminal Standard of Proof—How Sure is Sure? (2000) 150 *New Law Journal* 1517
Zedner, L, *Criminal Justice* (OUP, Oxford 2004)
—— 'Securing Liberty in the Face of Terror' (2005) 32 *Journal of Law and Society* 507
—— 'Seeking Security by Eroding Rights: The Side-Stepping of Due Process' in L Lazarus and B Goold *Security and Human Rights* (Hart Publishing, Oxford 2007) 257
Zimring, FE and G Hawkins, *Incapacitation: Penal Confinement and the Restraint of Crime* (OUP, New York 1995)
Zuckerman, A, 'The Third Exception to the Woolmington Rule' (1976) 92 *LQR* 402
—— 'No Third Exception to the Woolmington Rule' (1987) 103 *LQR* 170

INDEX

Index

www.ingramcontent.com/pod-product-compliance
Ingram Content Group UK Ltd.
Pitfield, Milton Keynes, MK11 3LW, UK
UKHW020804290926
15470UKWH00003B/953